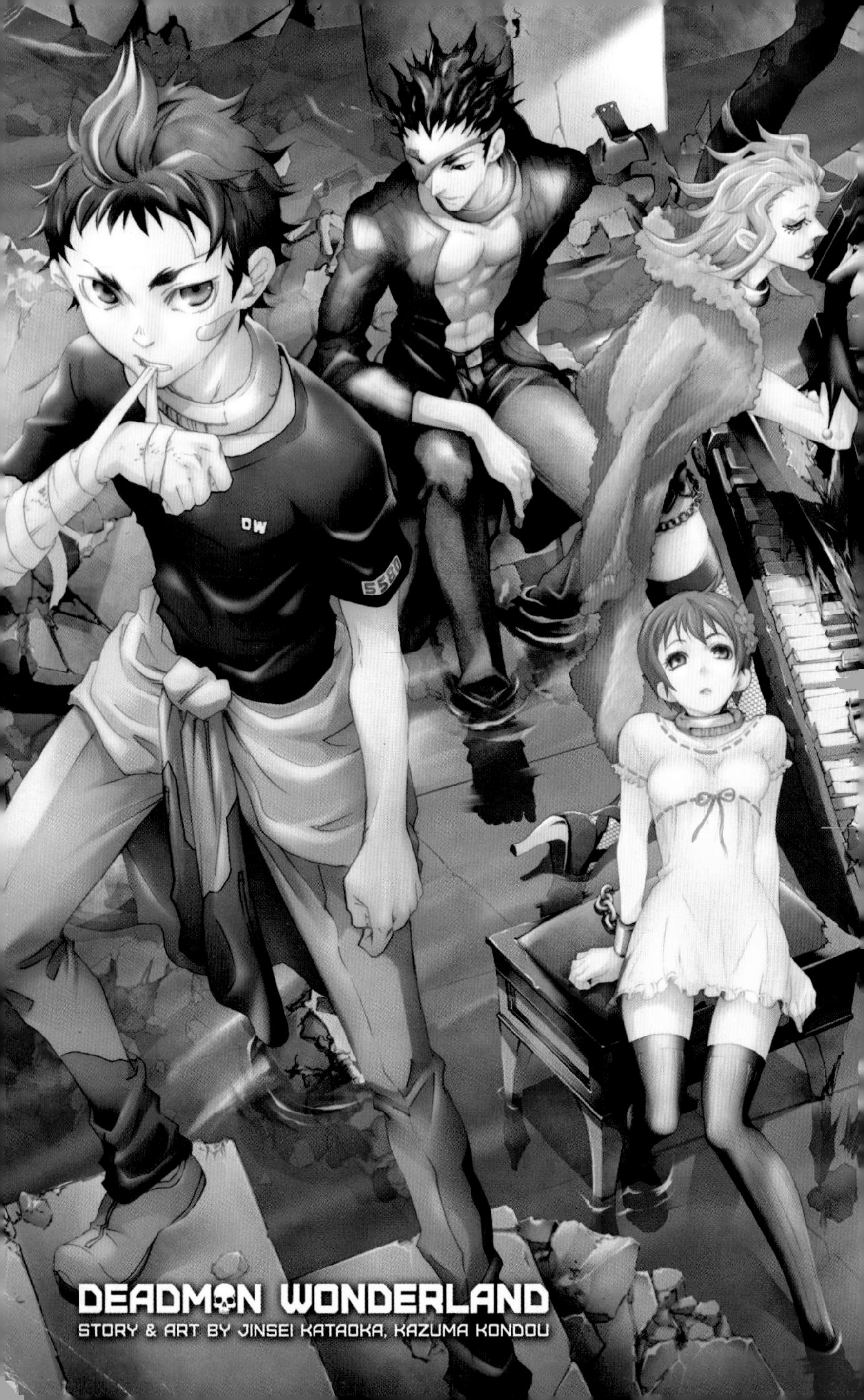
DW
DEADMAN WONDERLAND
STORY & ART BY JINSEI KATAOKA, KAZUMA KONDOU

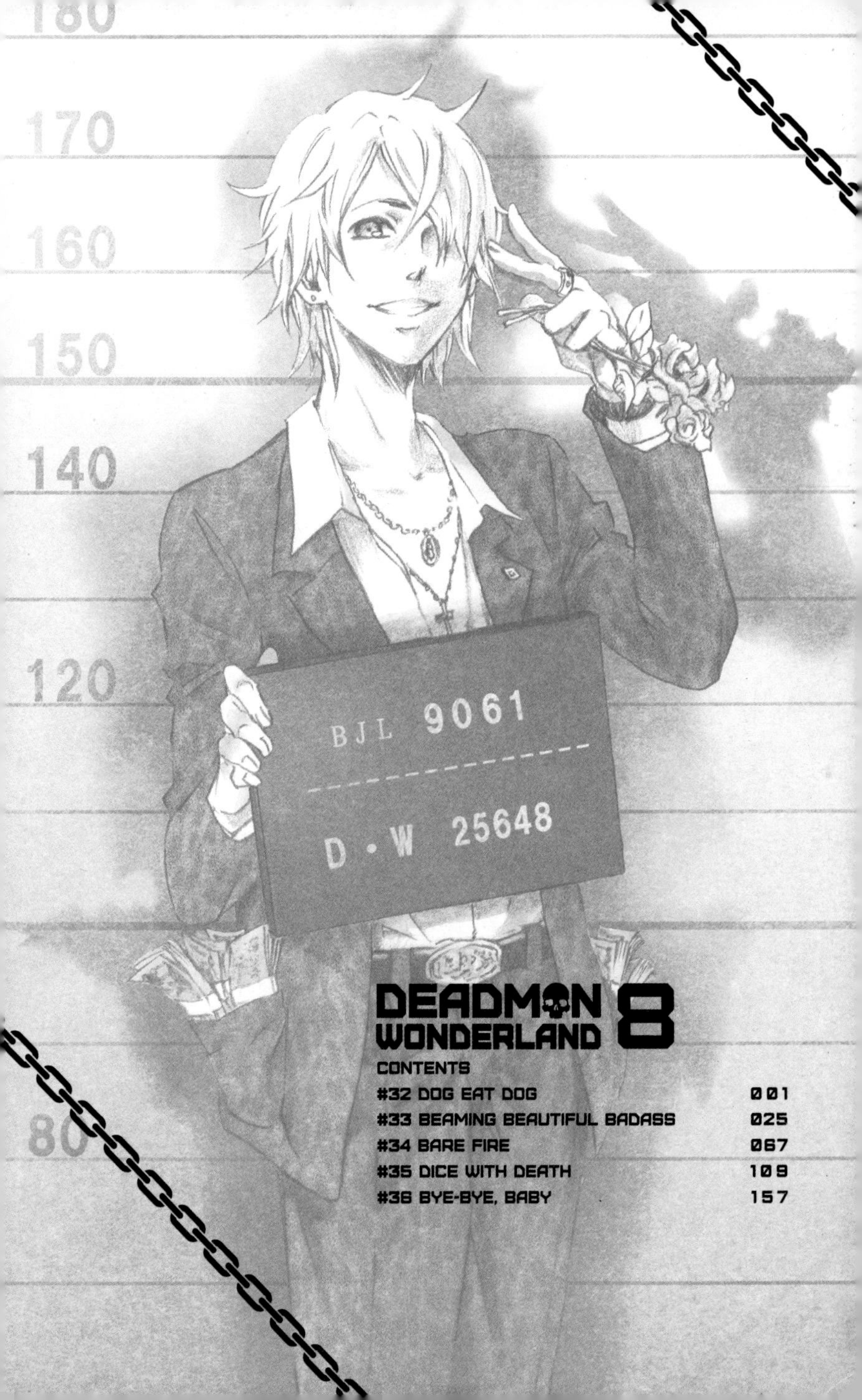
180
170
160
150
140
120
80
BJL 9061
D・W 25648

DEADMAN WONDERLAND 8

CONTENTS

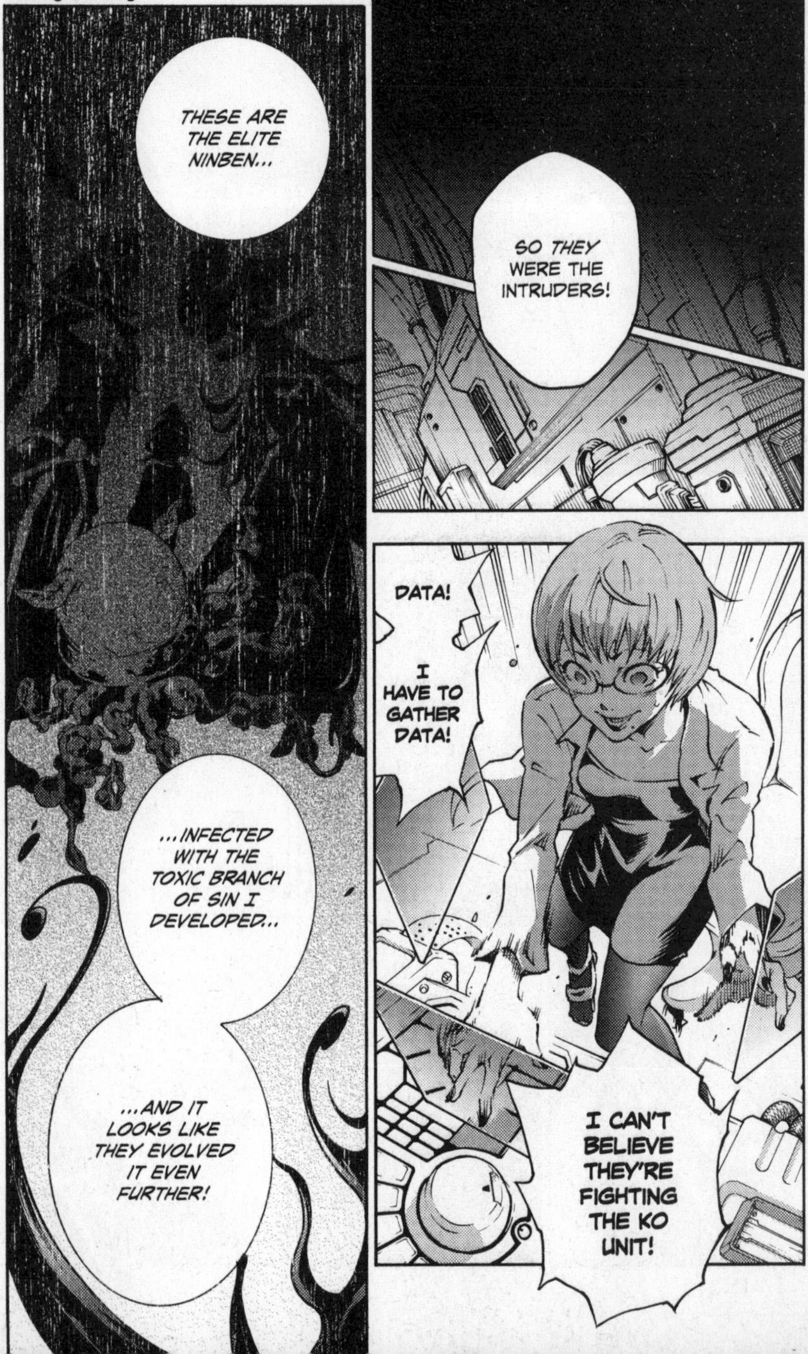
SO THEY WERE THE INTRUDERS!
DATA!
I HAVE TO GATHER DATA!
I CAN'T BELIEVE THEY'RE FIGHTING THE KO UNIT!
THESE ARE THE ELITE NINBEN...
...INFECTED WITH THE TOXIC BRANCH OF SIN I DEVELOPED...
...AND IT LOOKS LIKE THEY EVOLVED IT EVEN FURTHER!

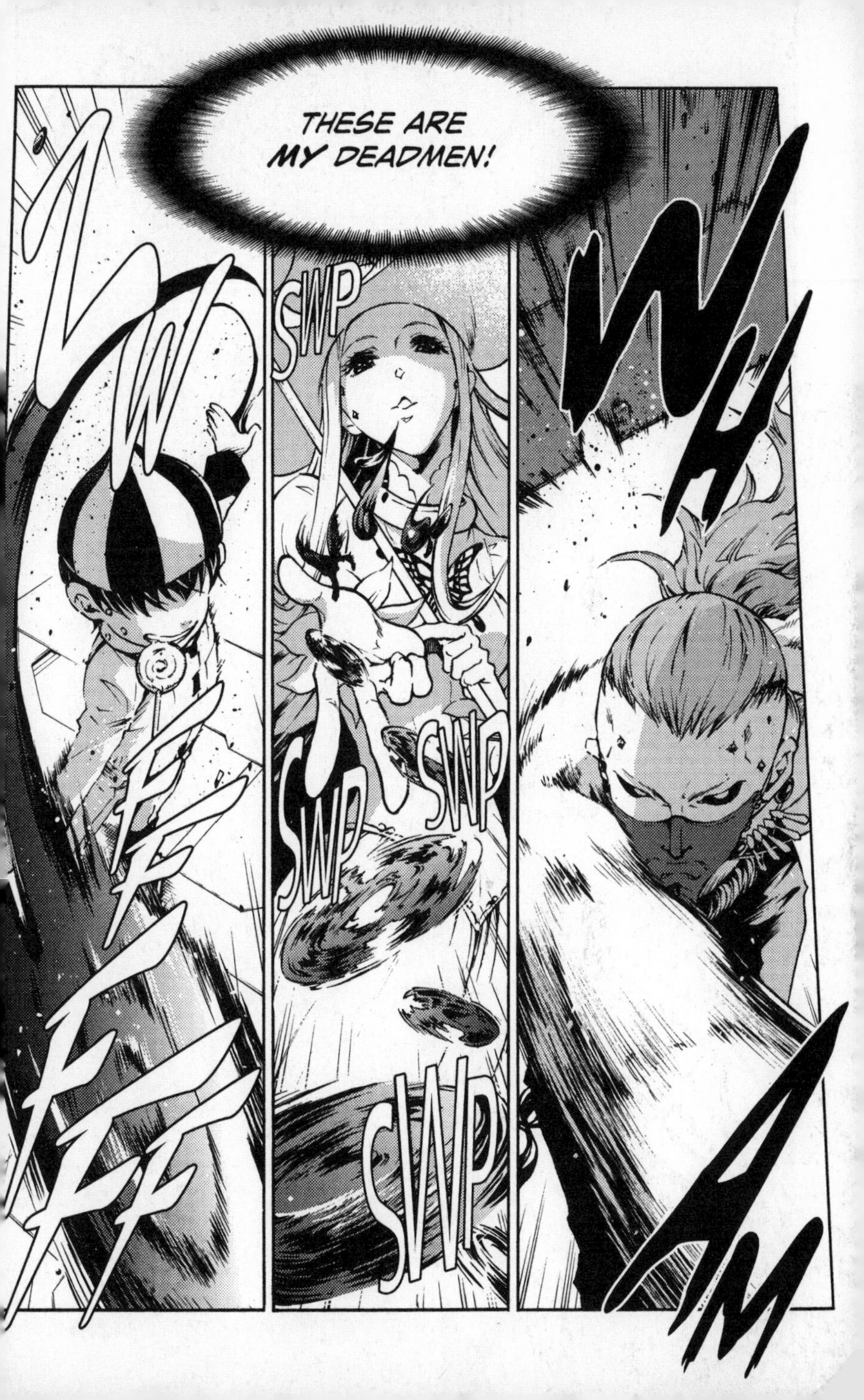
THESE ARE MY DEADMEN!
SWP
SWP
SWP
SWP

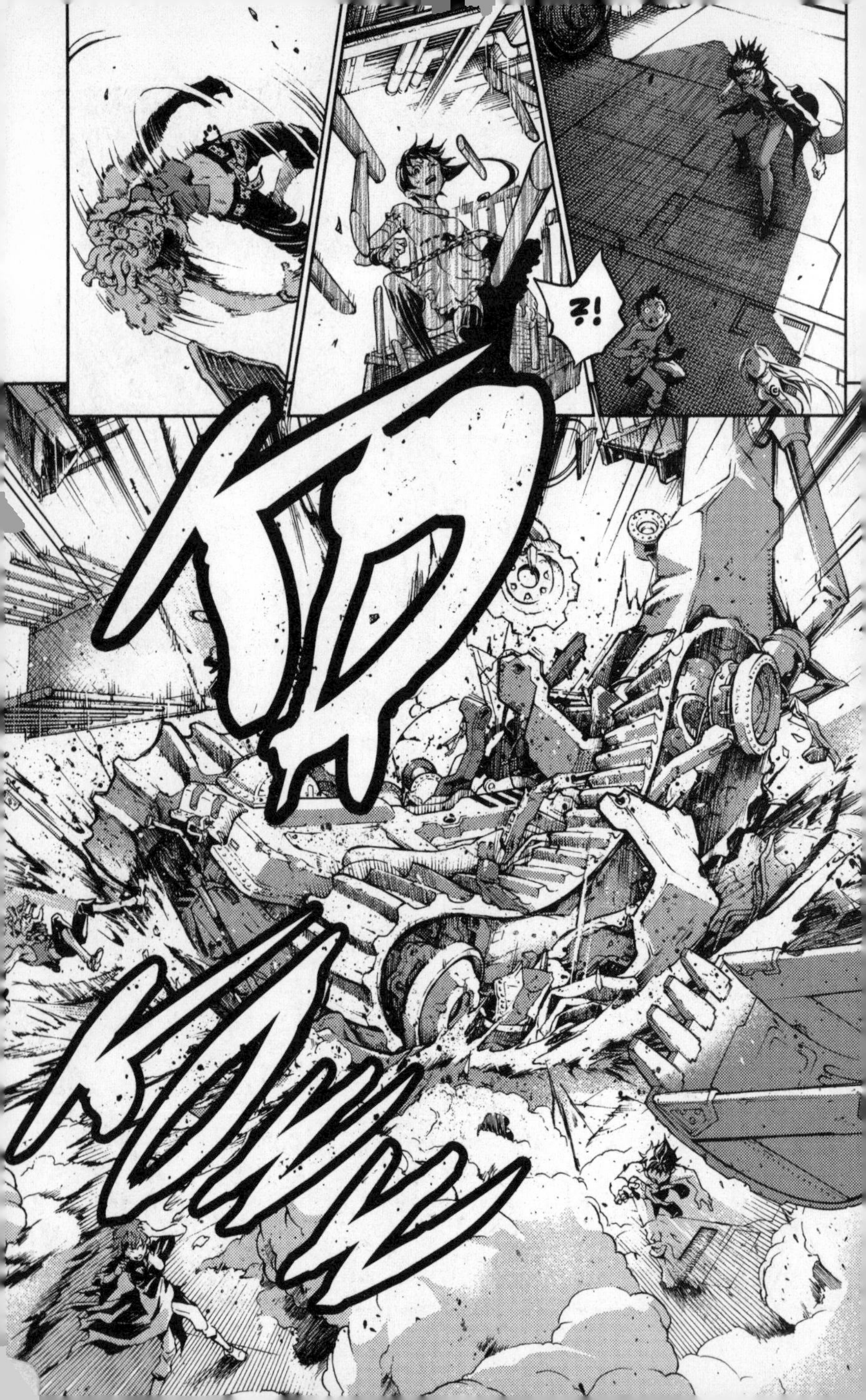
?!

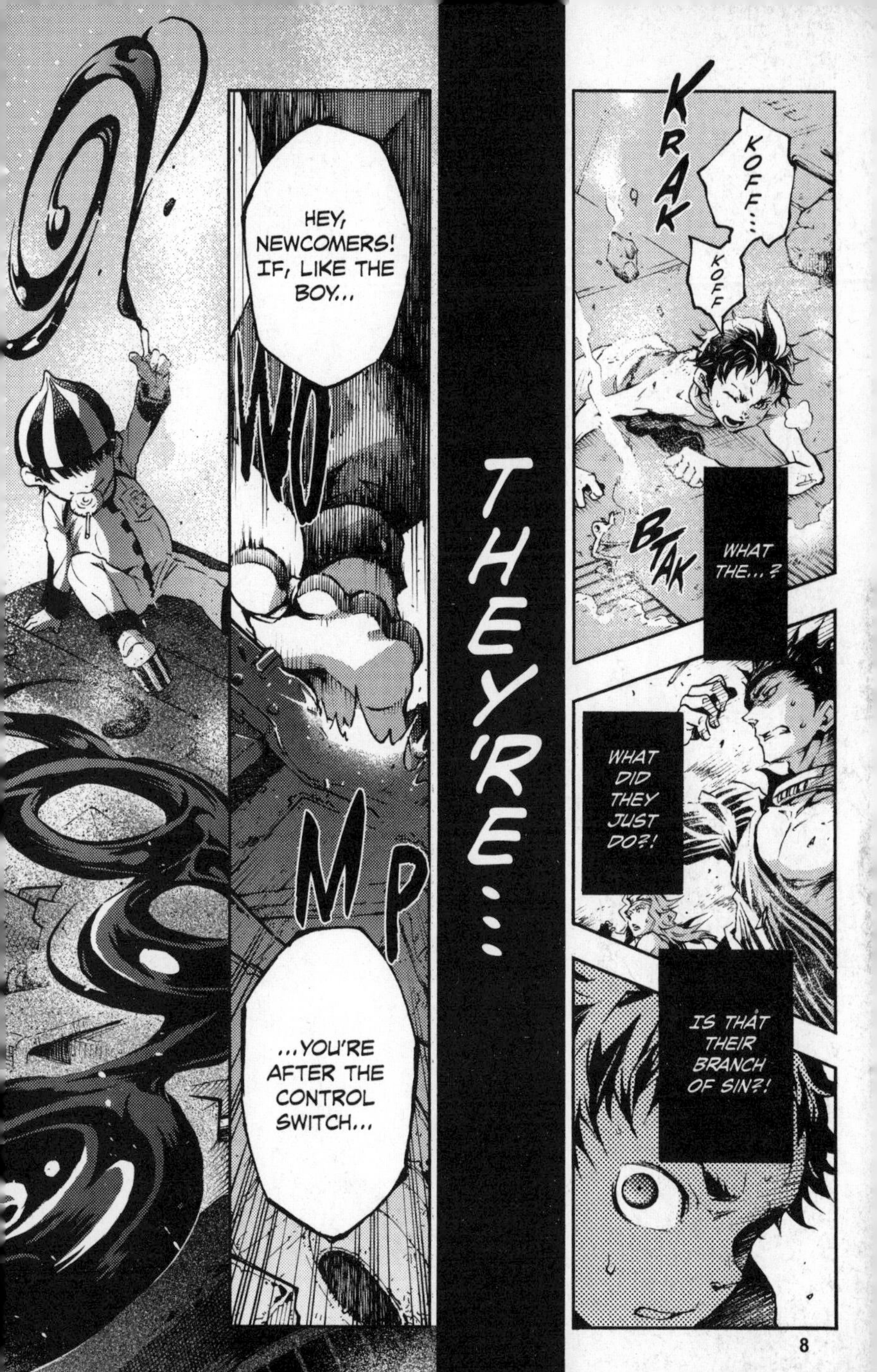
KRAK
KOFF...
KOFF
BTAK
WHAT THE...?
WHAT DID THEY JUST DO?!
IS THAT THEIR BRANCH OF SIN?!
THEY'RE...
HEY, NEWCOMERS! IF, LIKE THE BOY...
...YOU'RE AFTER THE CONTROL SWITCH...

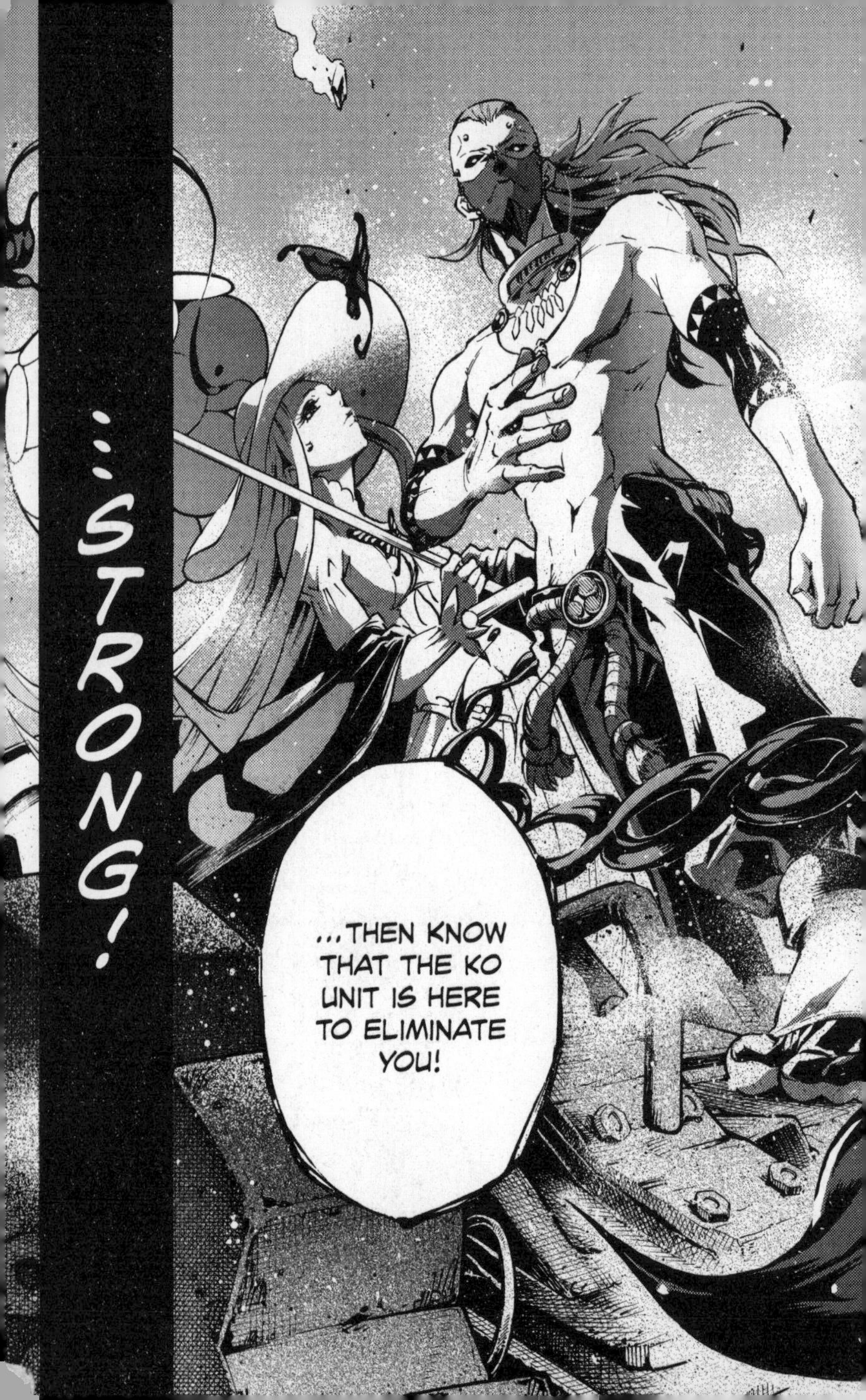

...STRONG!
...THEN KNOW THAT THE KO UNIT IS HERE TO ELIMINATE YOU!

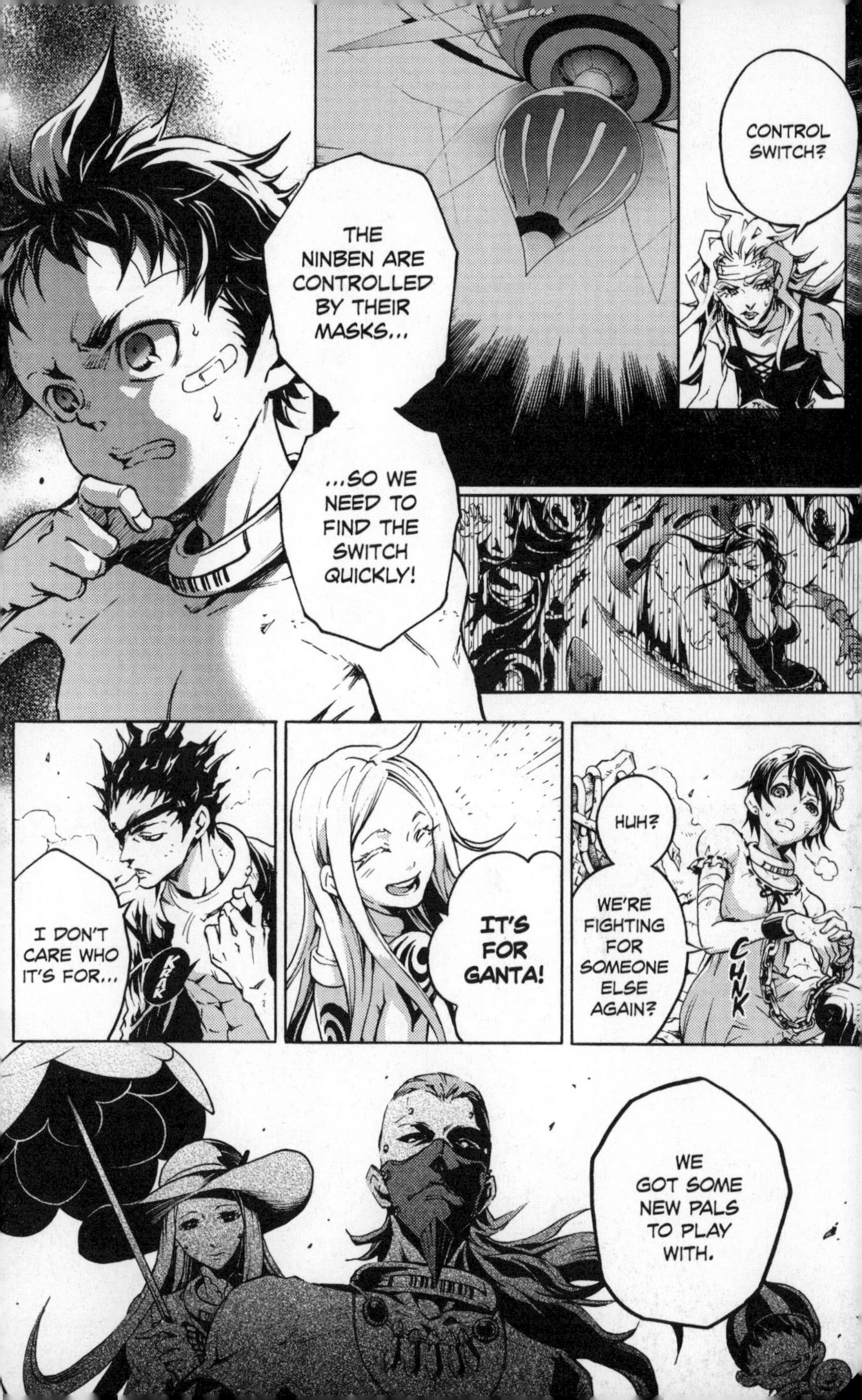
CONTROL SWITCH?
THE NINBEN ARE CONTROLLED BY THEIR MASKS...
...SO WE NEED TO FIND THE SWITCH QUICKLY!
HUH?
WE'RE FIGHTING FOR SOMEONE ELSE AGAIN?
CHNK
IT'S FOR GANTA!
I DON'T CARE WHO IT'S FOR...
KRAK
WE GOT SOME NEW PALS TO PLAY WITH.

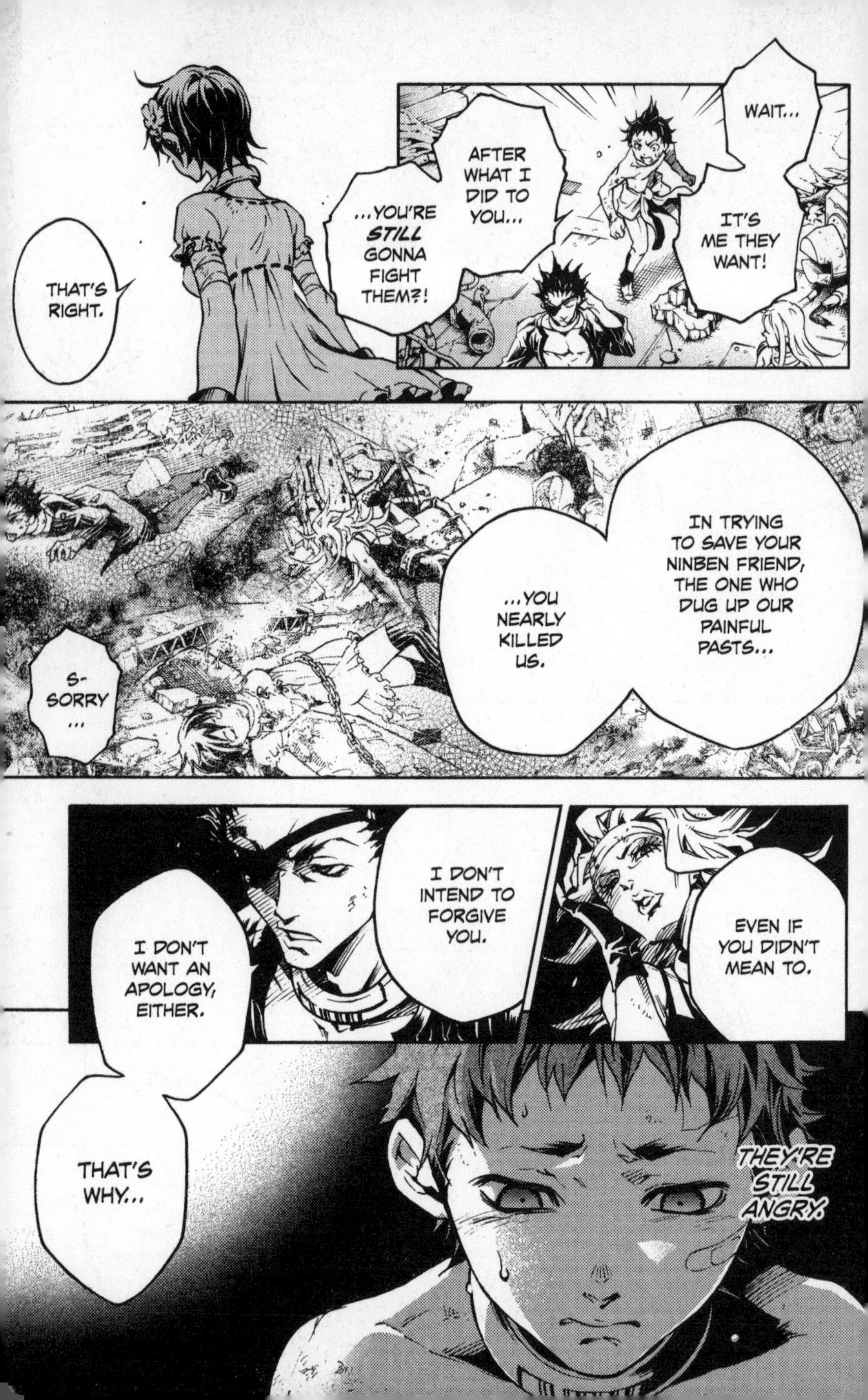
WAIT...
IT'S ME THEY WANT!
AFTER WHAT I DID TO YOU...
...YOU'RE STILL GONNA FIGHT THEM?!
THAT'S RIGHT.
IN TRYING TO SAVE YOUR NINBEN FRIEND, THE ONE WHO DUG UP OUR PAINFUL PASTS...
...YOU NEARLY KILLED US.
S-SORRY...
EVEN IF YOU DIDN'T MEAN TO.
I DON'T INTEND TO FORGIVE YOU.
I DON'T WANT AN APOLOGY, EITHER.
THEY'RE STILL ANGRY.
THAT'S WHY...

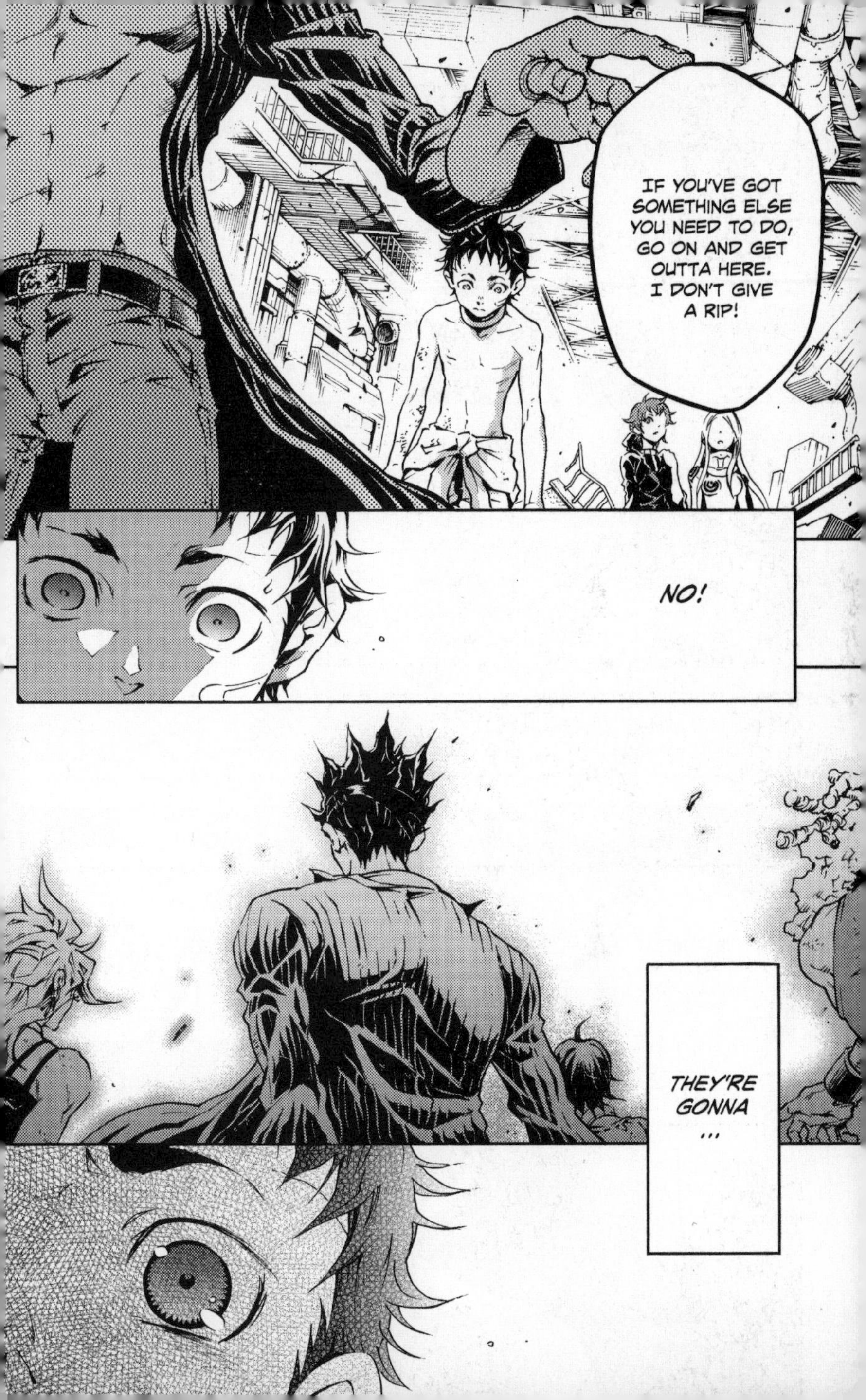
IF YOU'VE GOT SOMETHING ELSE YOU NEED TO DO, GO ON AND GET OUTTA HERE. I DON'T GIVE A RIP!
NO!
THEY'RE GONNA ...

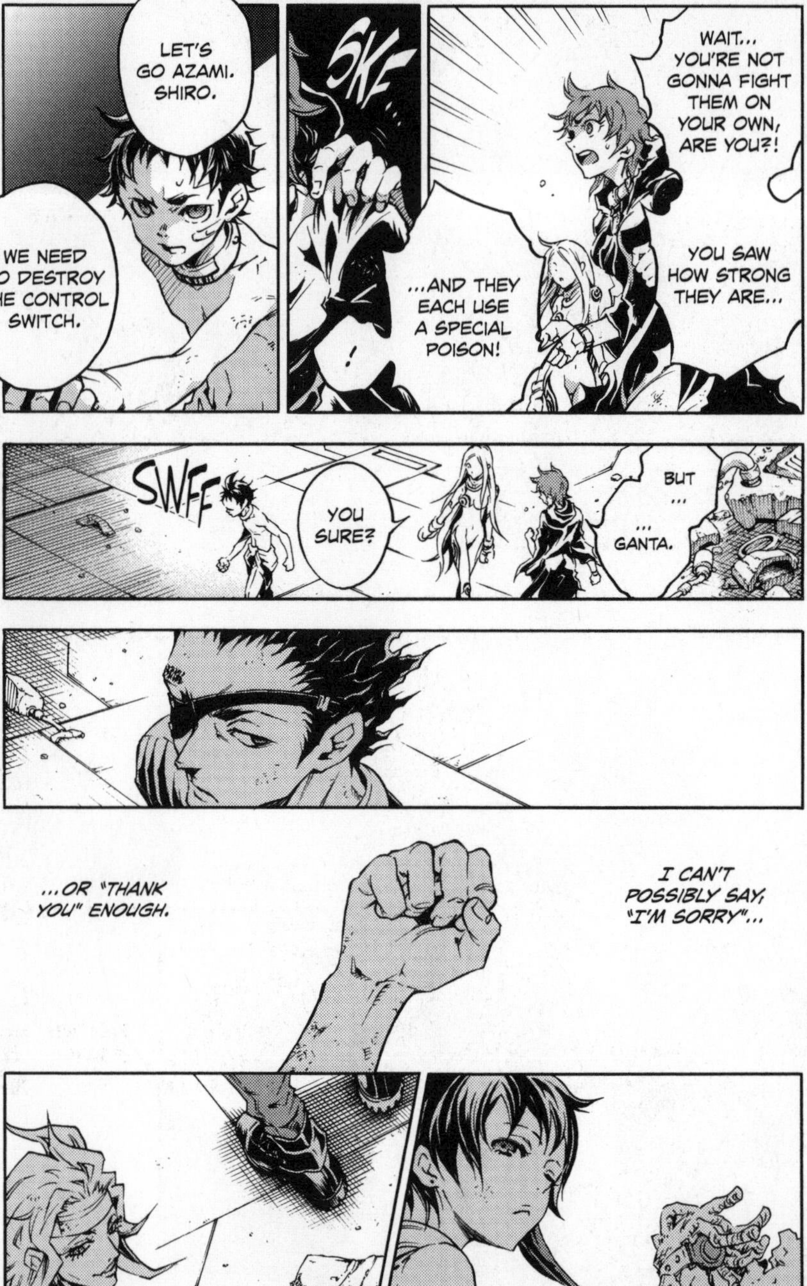
WAIT... YOU'RE NOT GONNA FIGHT THEM ON YOUR OWN, ARE YOU?!
YOU SAW HOW STRONG THEY ARE...
...AND THEY EACH USE A SPECIAL POISON!
SKF
!
LET'S GO AZAMI. SHIRO.
WE NEED TO DESTROY THE CONTROL SWITCH.
BUT ...
... GANTA.
YOU SURE?
SWFF
I CAN'T POSSIBLY SAY, "I'M SORRY"...
...OR "THANK YOU" ENOUGH.

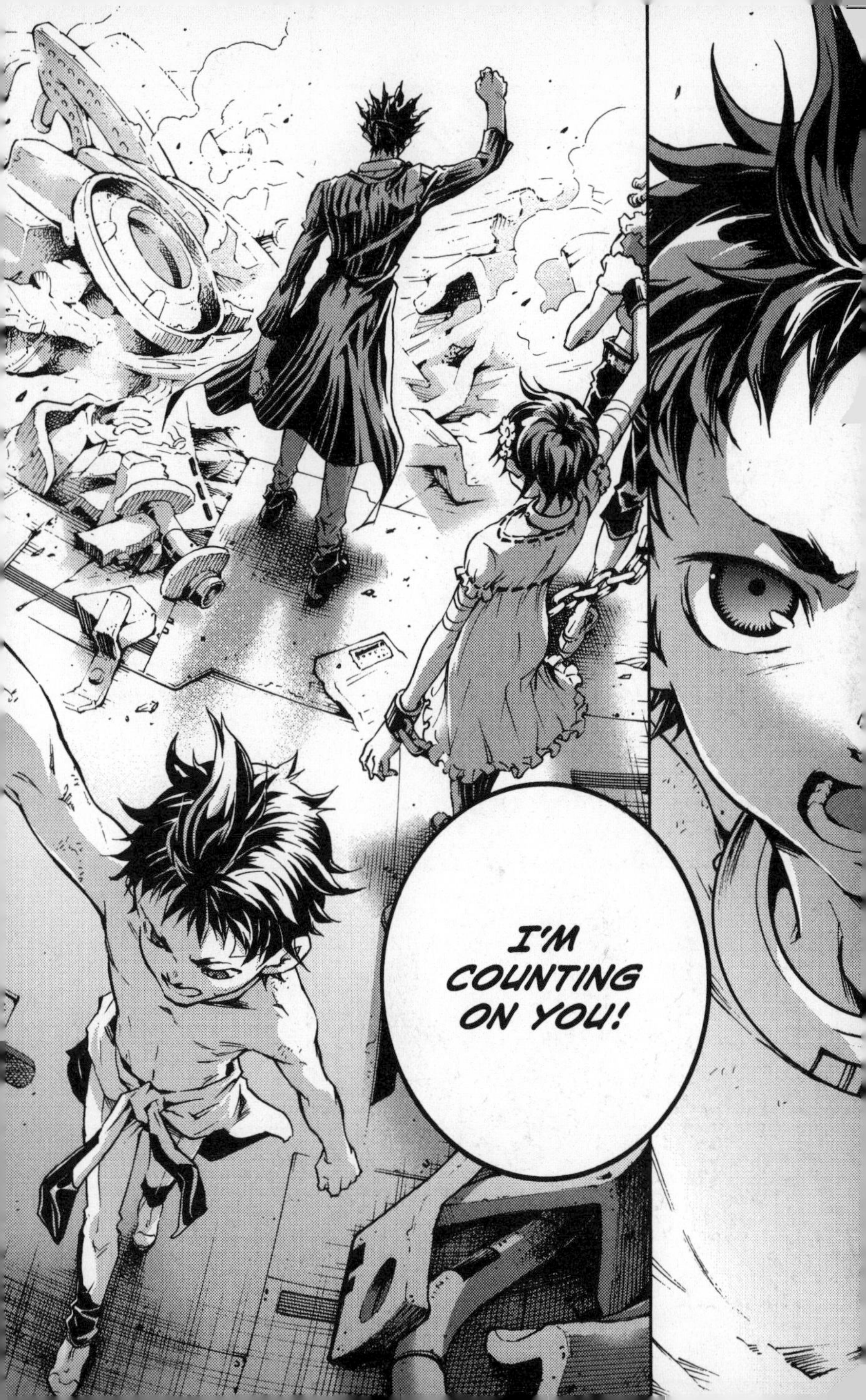
I'M COUNTING ON YOU!

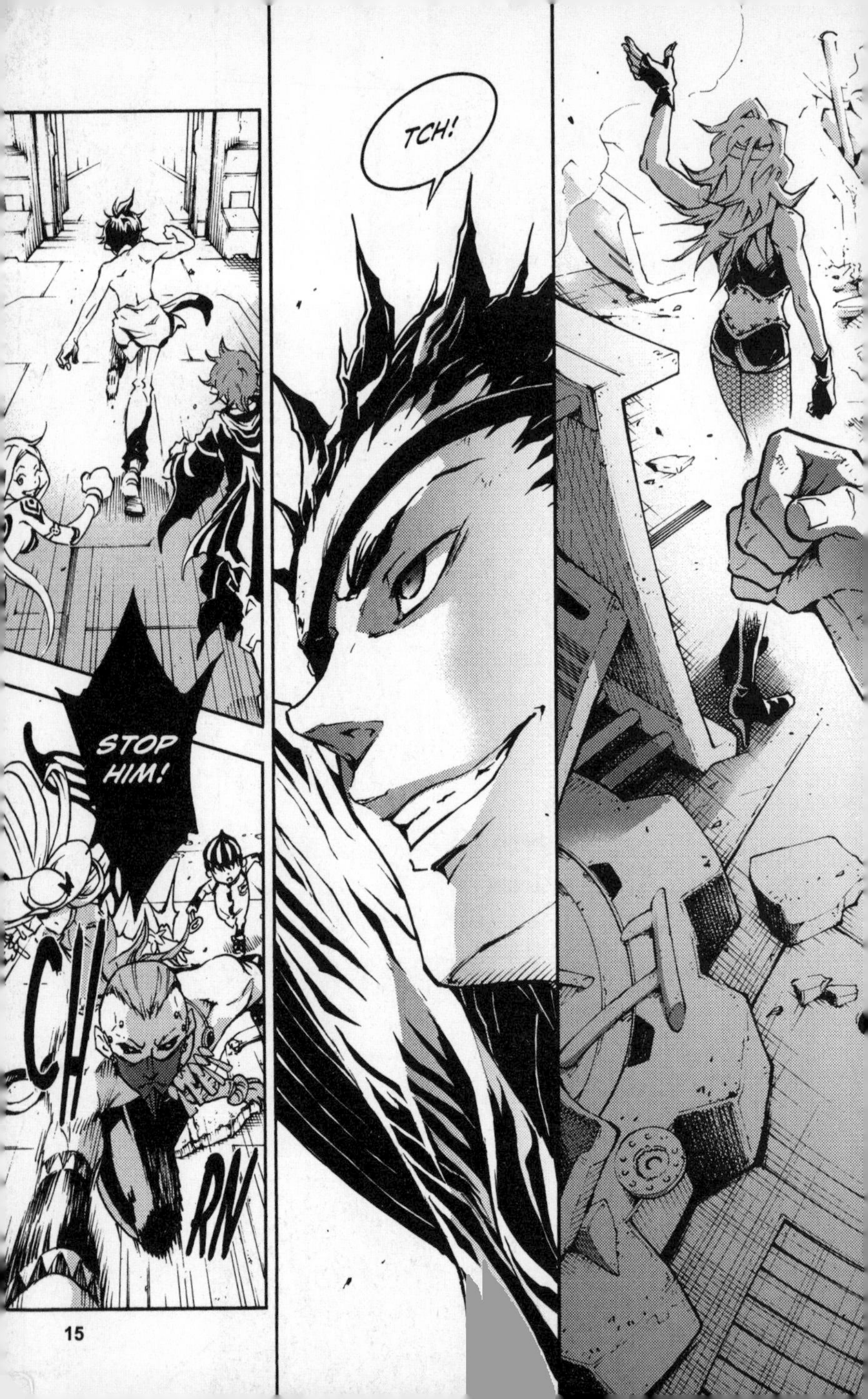
TCH!
STOP HIM!
CHRN

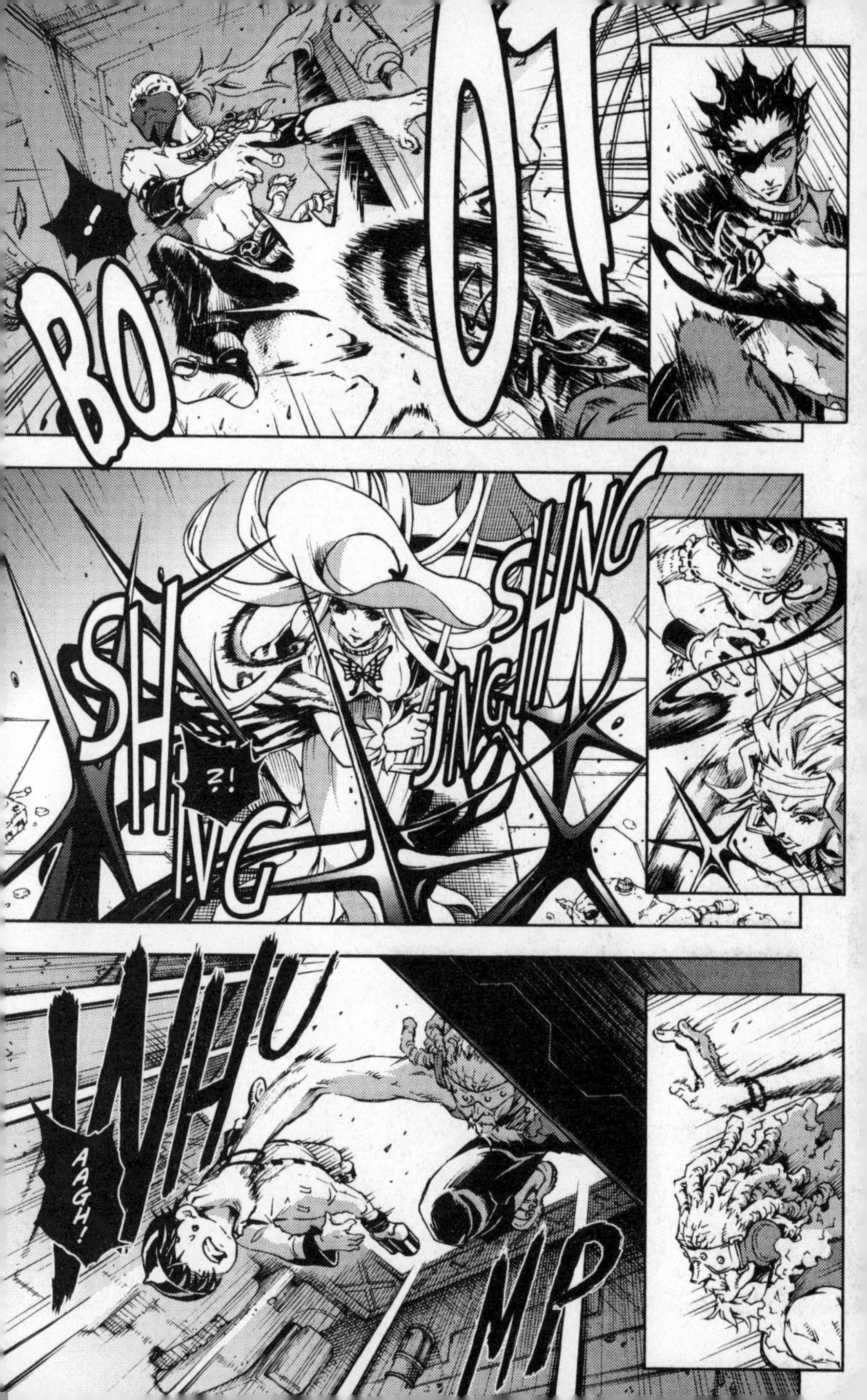
!
BOOM
?!
SHING
SHING
SHING
WHUMP
AAGH!

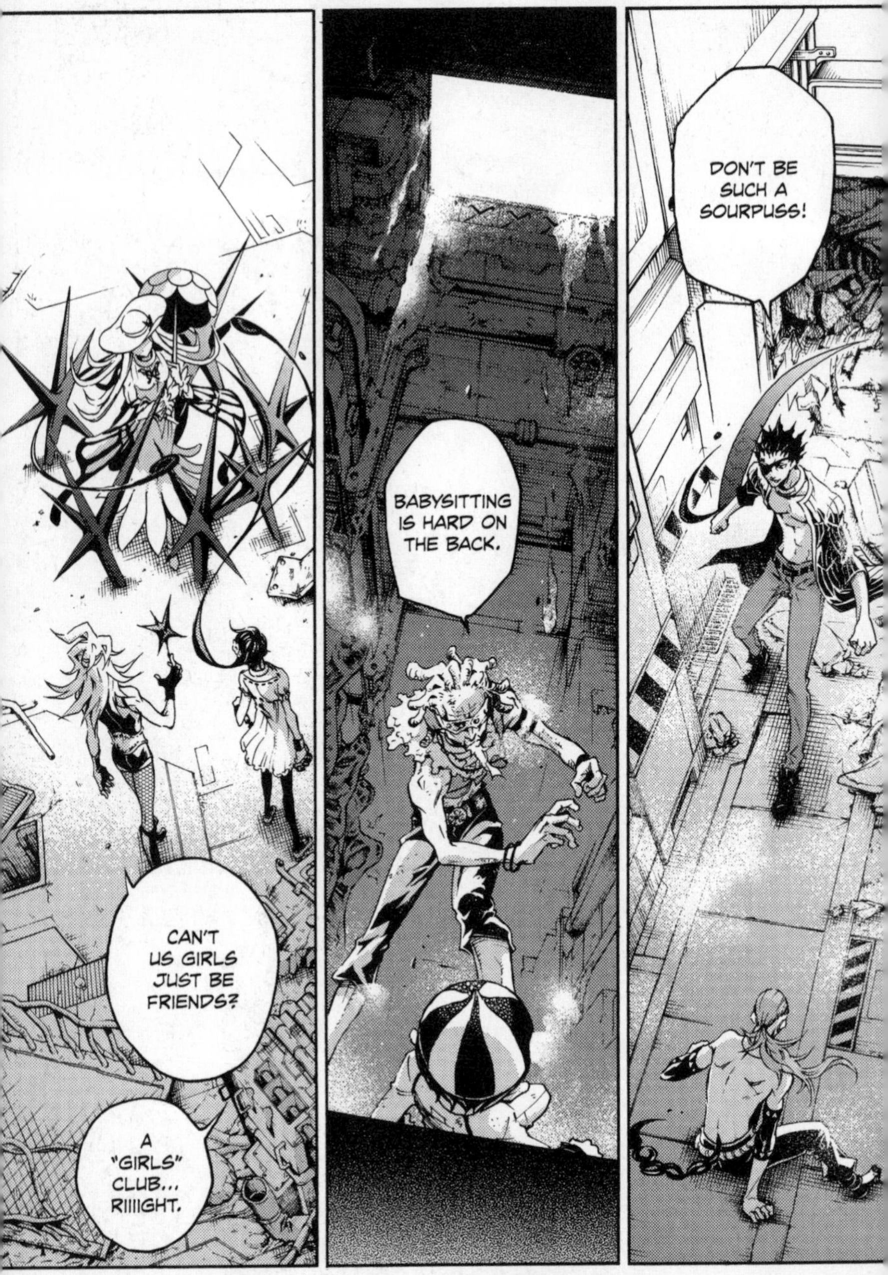
DON'T BE SUCH A SOURPUSS!
BABYSITTING IS HARD ON THE BACK.
CAN'T US GIRLS JUST BE FRIENDS?
A "GIRLS" CLUB... RIIIIGHT.

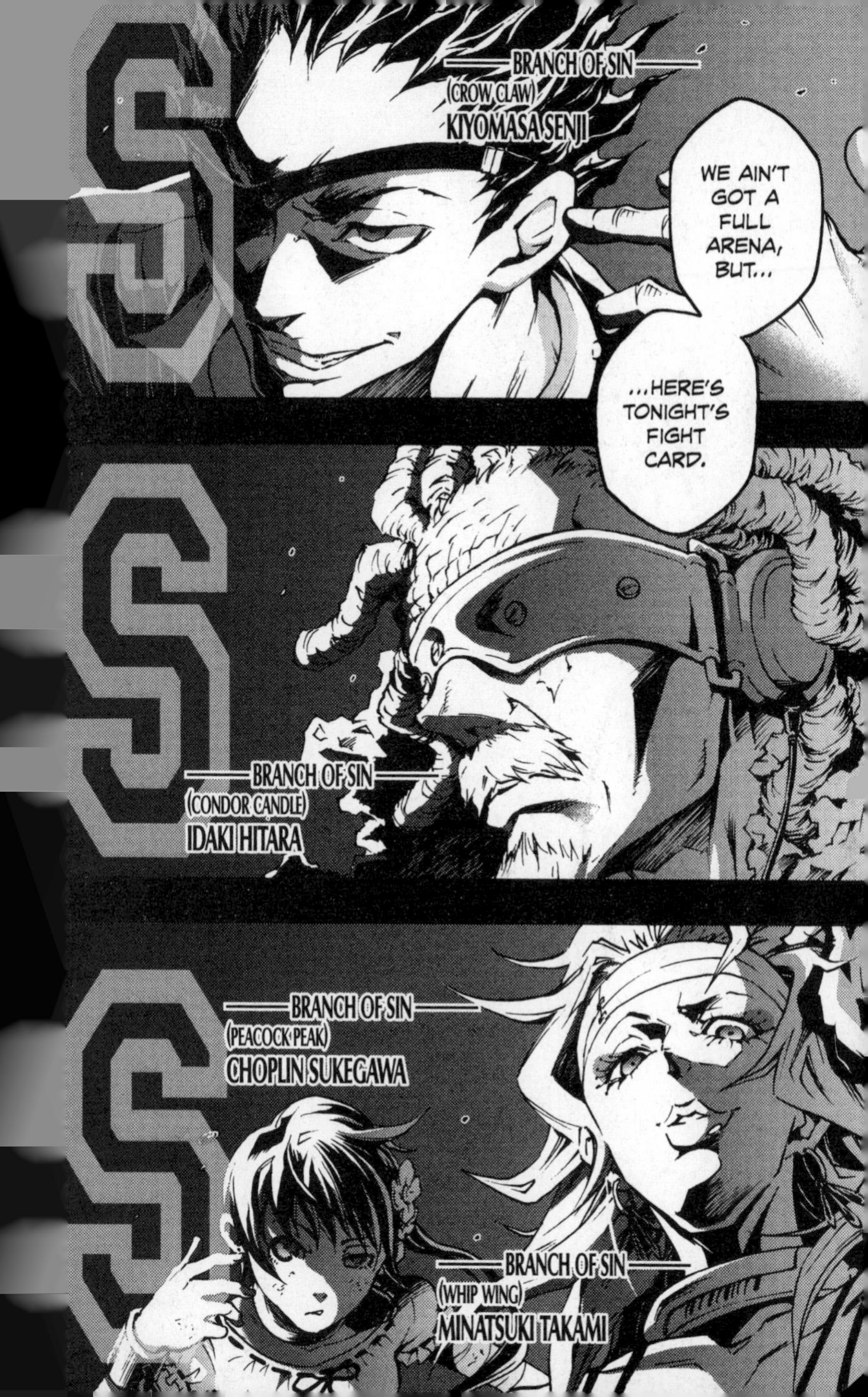
WE AIN'T GOT A FULL ARENA, BUT...
...HERE'S TONIGHT'S FIGHT CARD.
BRANCH OF SIN
(CROW CLAW)
KIYOMASA SENJI
BRANCH OF SIN
(CONDOR CANDLE)
IDAKI HITARA
BRANCH OF SIN
(PEACOCK PEAK)
CHOPLIN SUKEGAWA
BRANCH OF SIN
(WHIP WING)
MINATSUKI TAKAMI

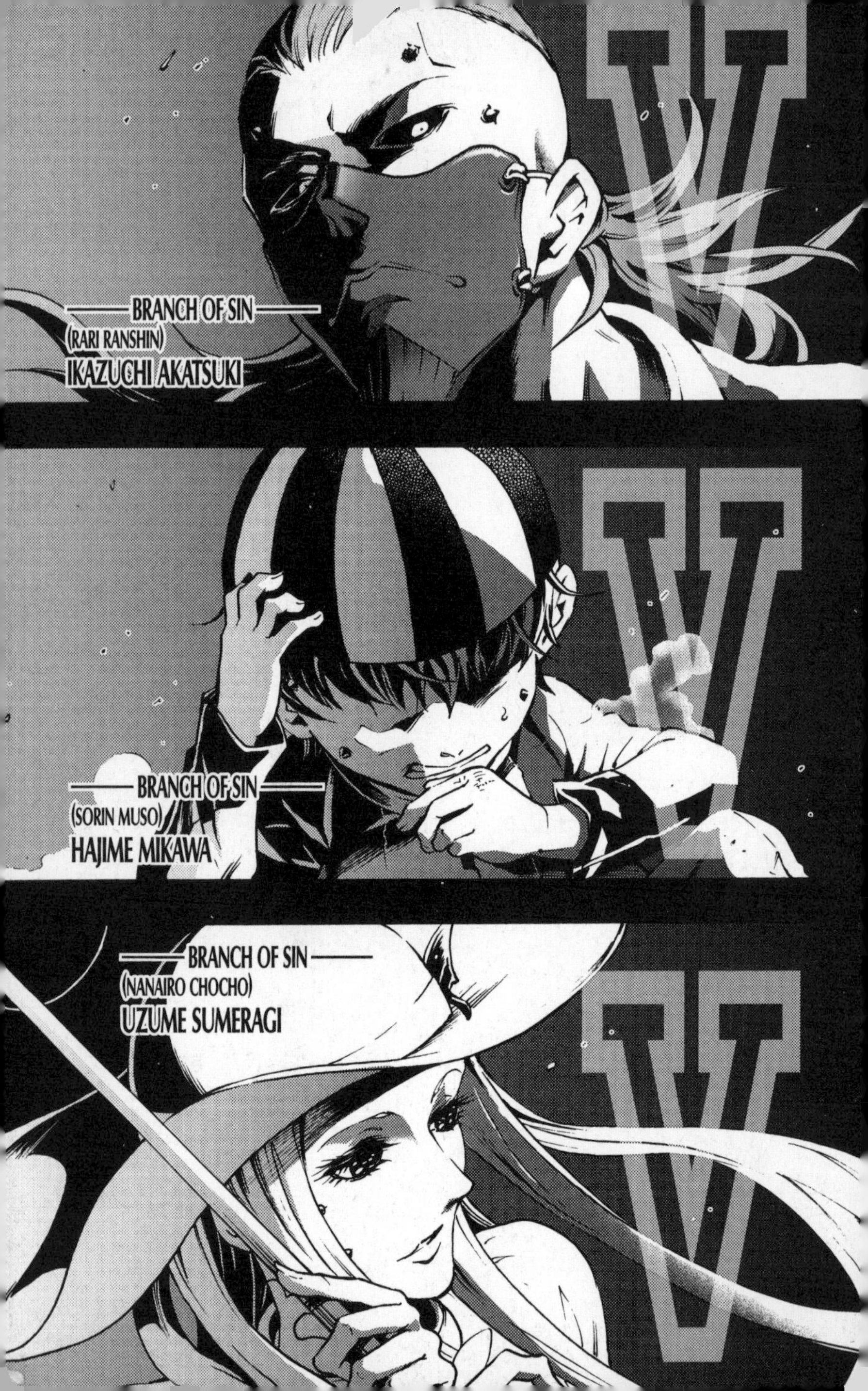
BRANCH OF SIN
(RARI RANSHIN)
IKAZUCHI AKATSUKI
BRANCH OF SIN
(SORIN MUSO)
HAJIME MIKAWA
BRANCH OF SIN
(NANAIRO CHOCHO)
UZUME SUMERAGI

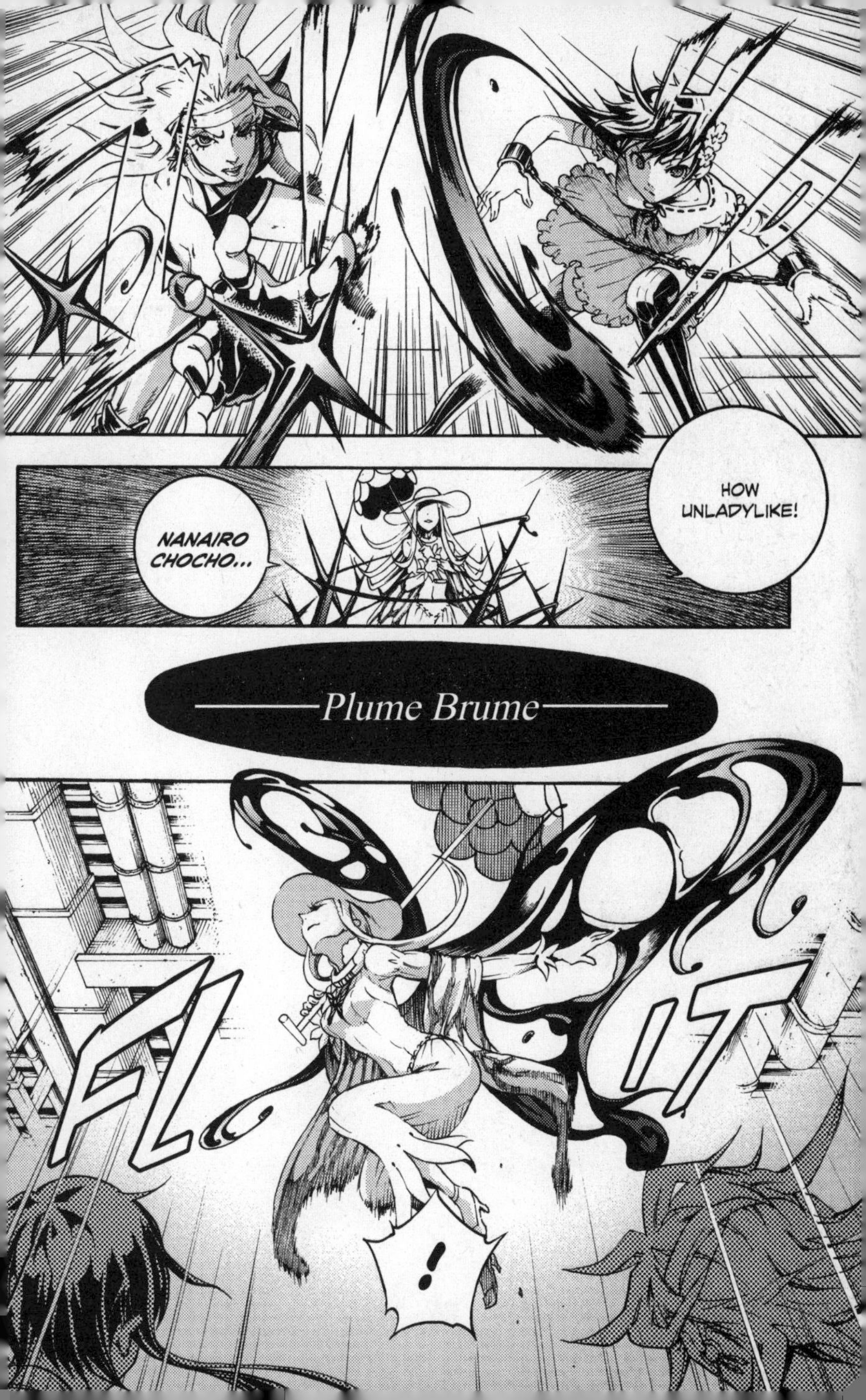
HOW UNLADYLIKE!
NANAIRO CHOCHO...
Plume Brume
FLIT
!

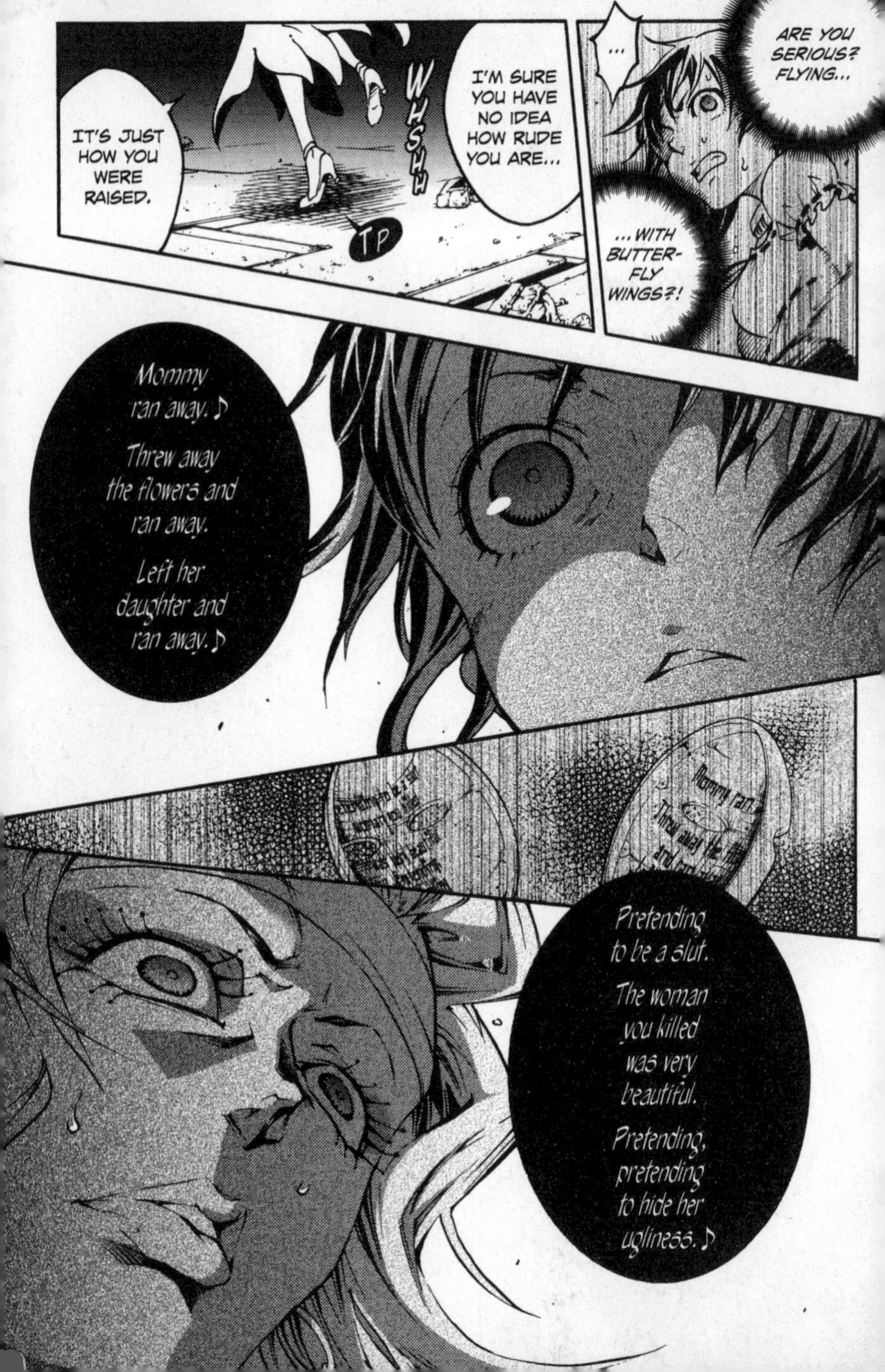
...
ARE YOU SERIOUS? FLYING...
...WITH BUTTER-FLY WINGS?!
I'M SURE YOU HAVE NO IDEA HOW RUDE YOU ARE...
WHSHH
TP
IT'S JUST HOW YOU WERE RAISED.
Mommy ran away.♪ Threw away the flowers and ran away. Left her daughter and ran away.♪
Pretending to be a slut. The woman you killed was very beautiful. Pretending, pretending to hide her ugliness.♪

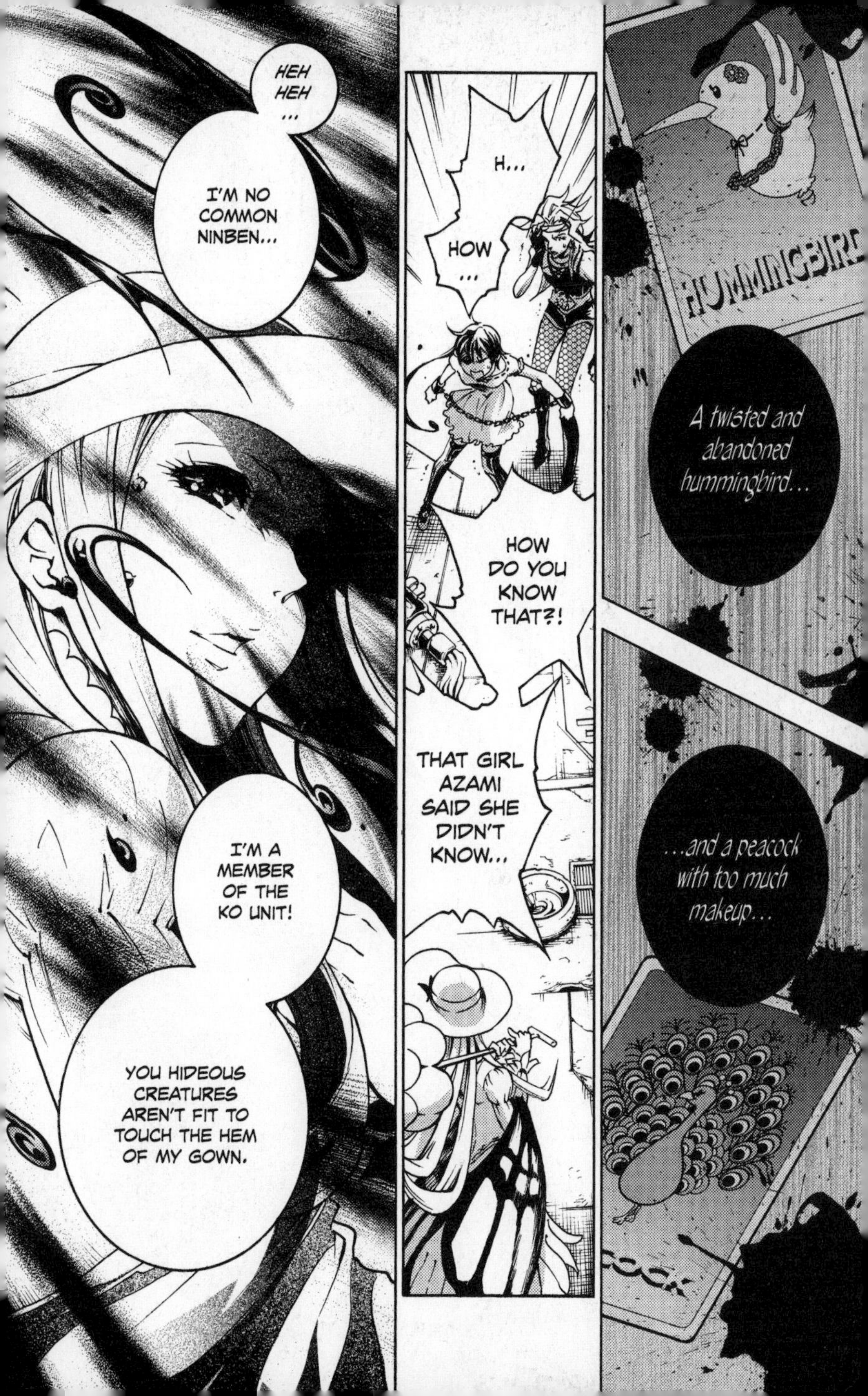
HUMMINGBIRD
A twisted and abandoned hummingbird...
...and a peacock with too much makeup...
H... HOW ...
HOW DO YOU KNOW THAT?!
THAT GIRL AZAMI SAID SHE DIDN'T KNOW...
HEH HEH ...
I'M NO COMMON NINBEN...
I'M A MEMBER OF THE KO UNIT!
YOU HIDEOUS CREATURES AREN'T FIT TO TOUCH THE HEM OF MY GOWN.

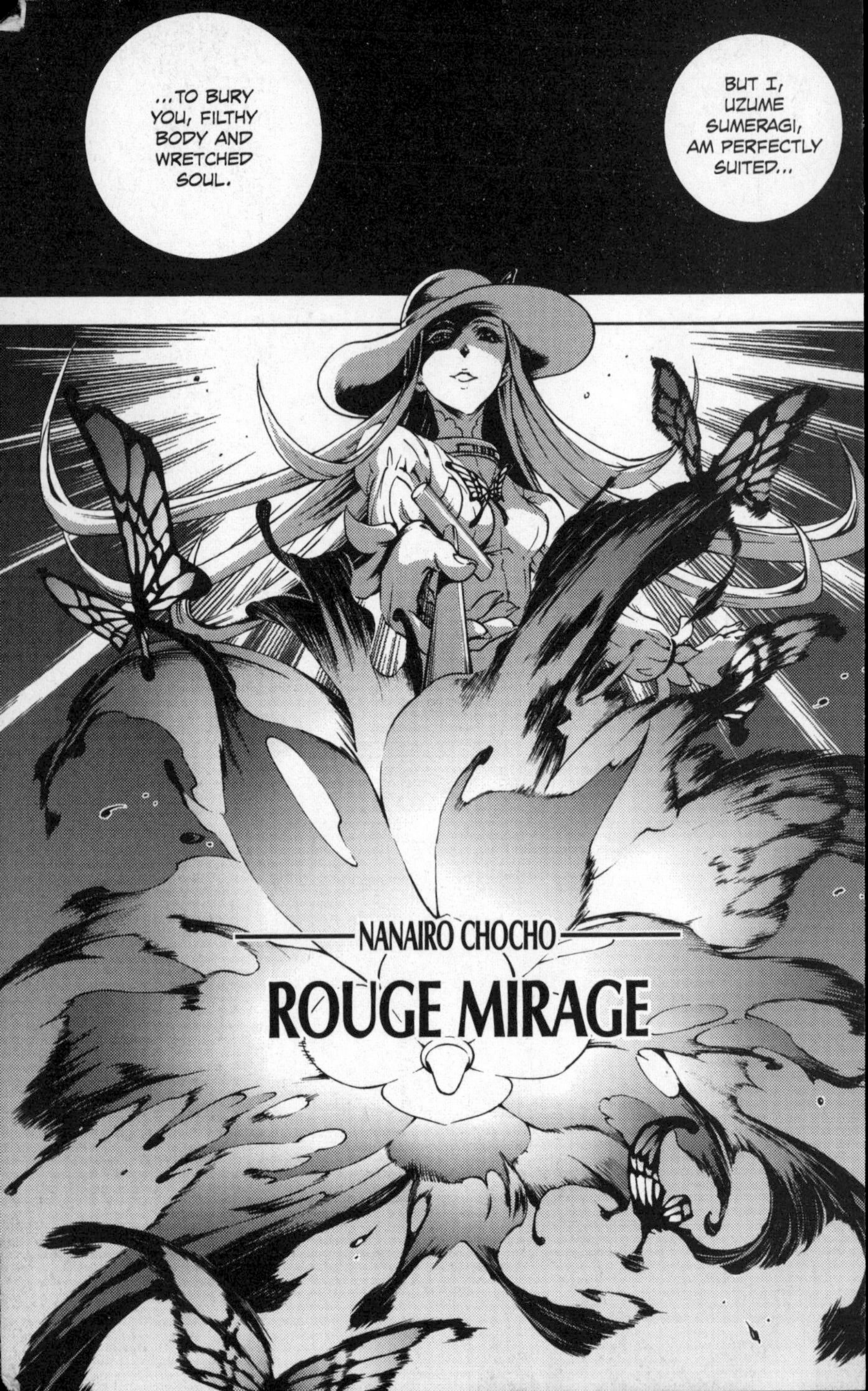
BUT I, UZUME SUMERAGI, AM PERFECTLY SUITED...
...TO BURY YOU, FILTHY BODY AND WRETCHED SOUL.
NANAIRO CHOCHO
ROUGE MIRAGE

DEADMAN WONDER LAND

DEADMAN WONDER LAND

DEADMAN WONDER LAND

DEADMAN WONDER LAND

DEADMAN WONDER LAND

DEADMAN WONDER LAND

DEADMAN WONDER LAND

DEADMAN WONDER LAND

DEADMAN WONDER LAND

DEADMAN WONDER LAND

DEADMAN WONDER LAND

DEADMAN WONDER LAND

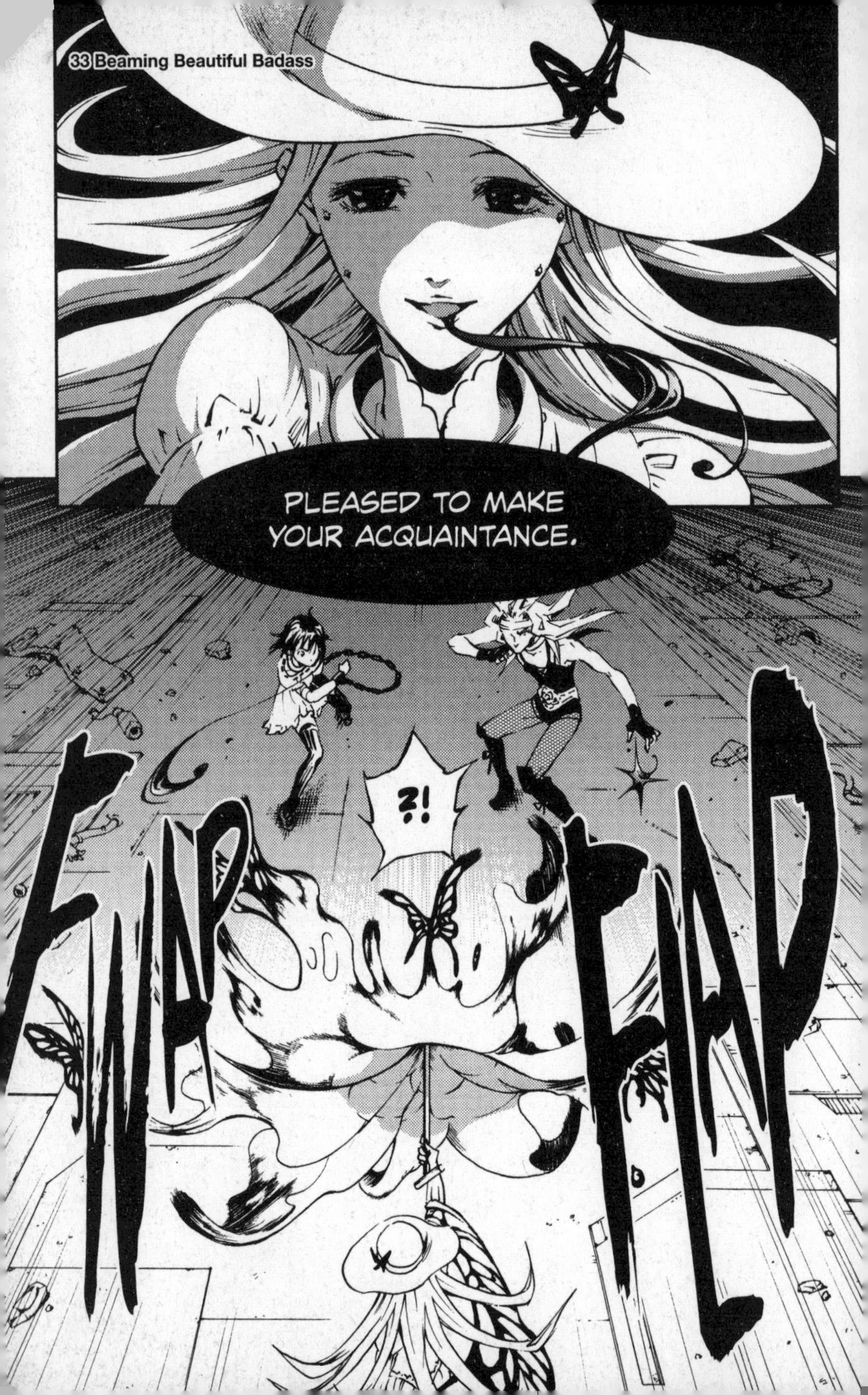
PLEASED TO MAKE YOUR ACQUAINTANCE.
?!

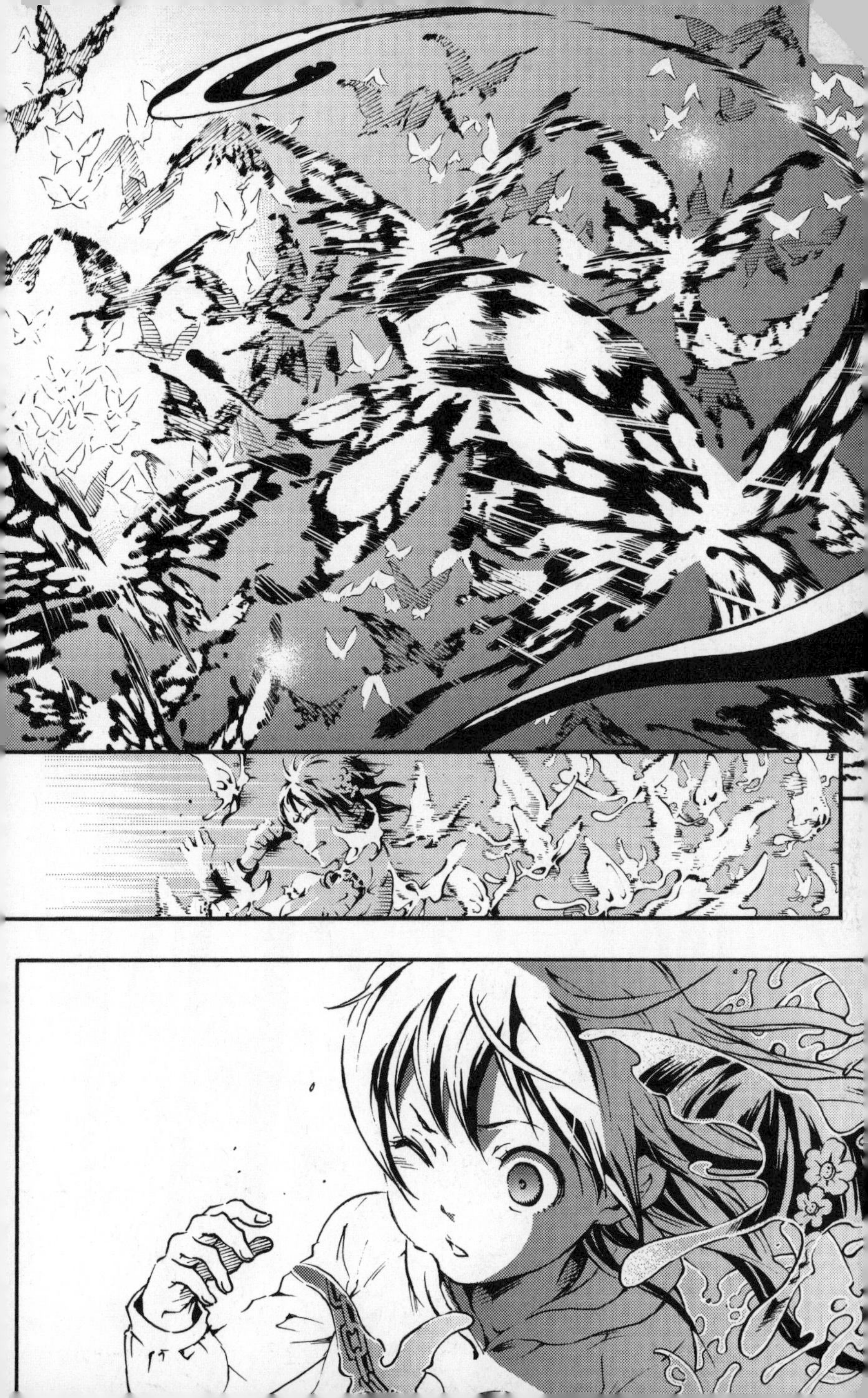

33 Beaming Beautiful Badass

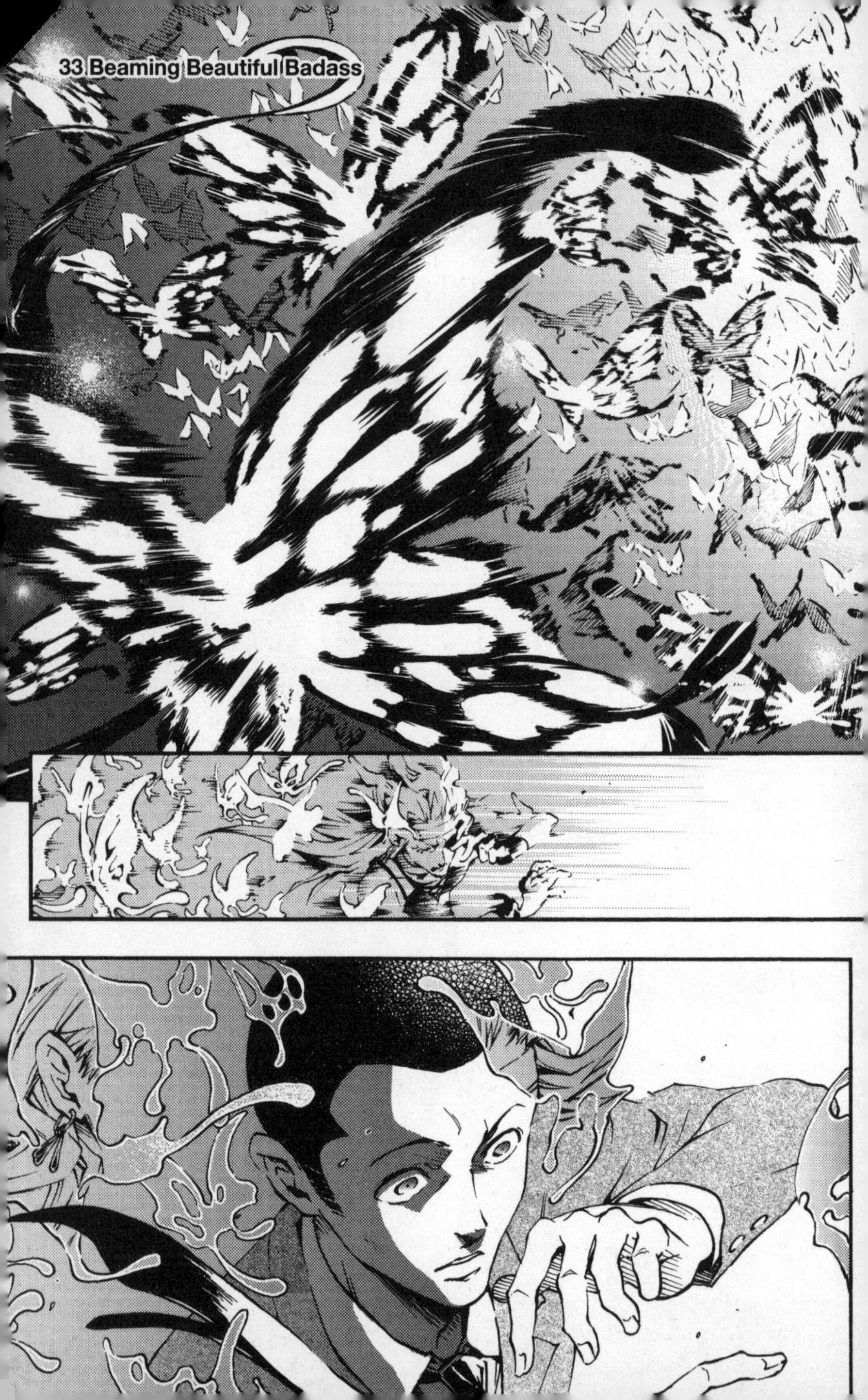

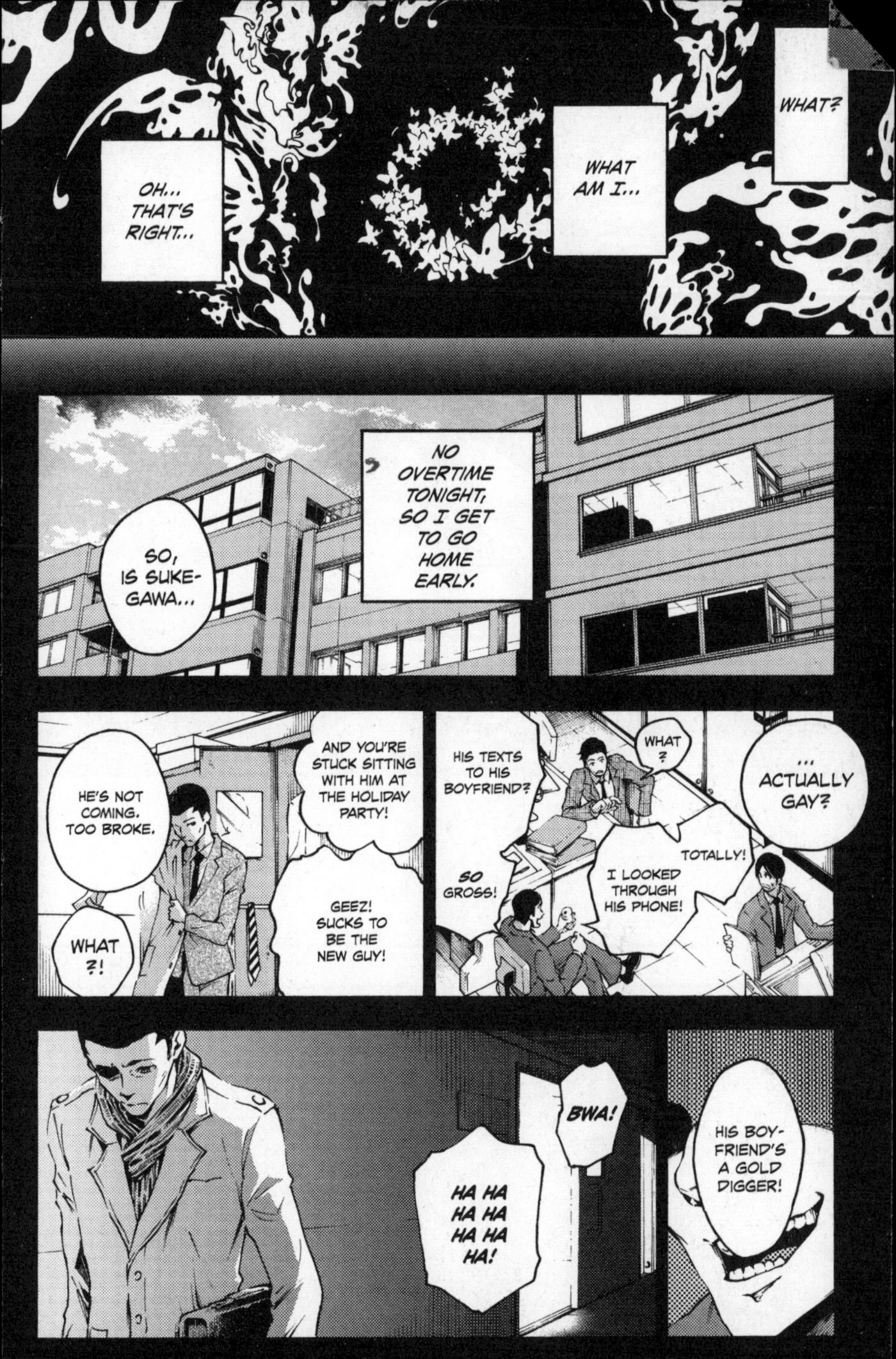
WHAT?
WHAT AM I...
OH... THAT'S RIGHT...
NO OVERTIME TONIGHT, SO I GET TO GO HOME EARLY.
SO, IS SUKE-GAWA...
... ACTUALLY GAY?
WHAT ?
HIS TEXTS TO HIS BOYFRIEND?
TOTALLY!
I LOOKED THROUGH HIS PHONE!
SO GROSS!
AND YOU'RE STUCK SITTING WITH HIM AT THE HOLIDAY PARTY!
HE'S NOT COMING. TOO BROKE.
GEEZ! SUCKS TO BE THE NEW GUY!
WHAT ?!
HIS BOY-FRIEND'S A GOLD DIGGER!
BWA!
HA HA HA HA HA HA HA!

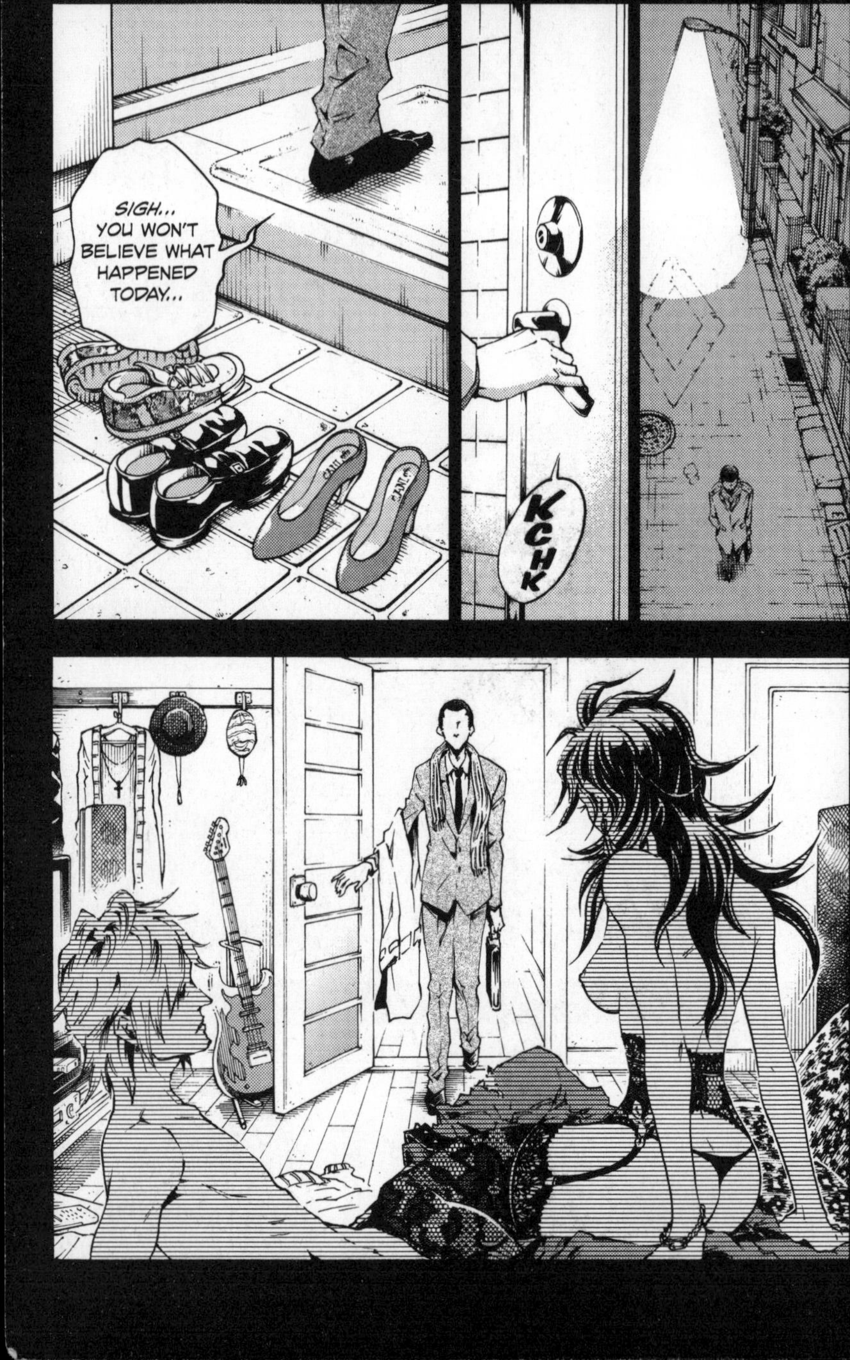
KCHK
SIGH... YOU WON'T BELIEVE WHAT HAPPENED TODAY...

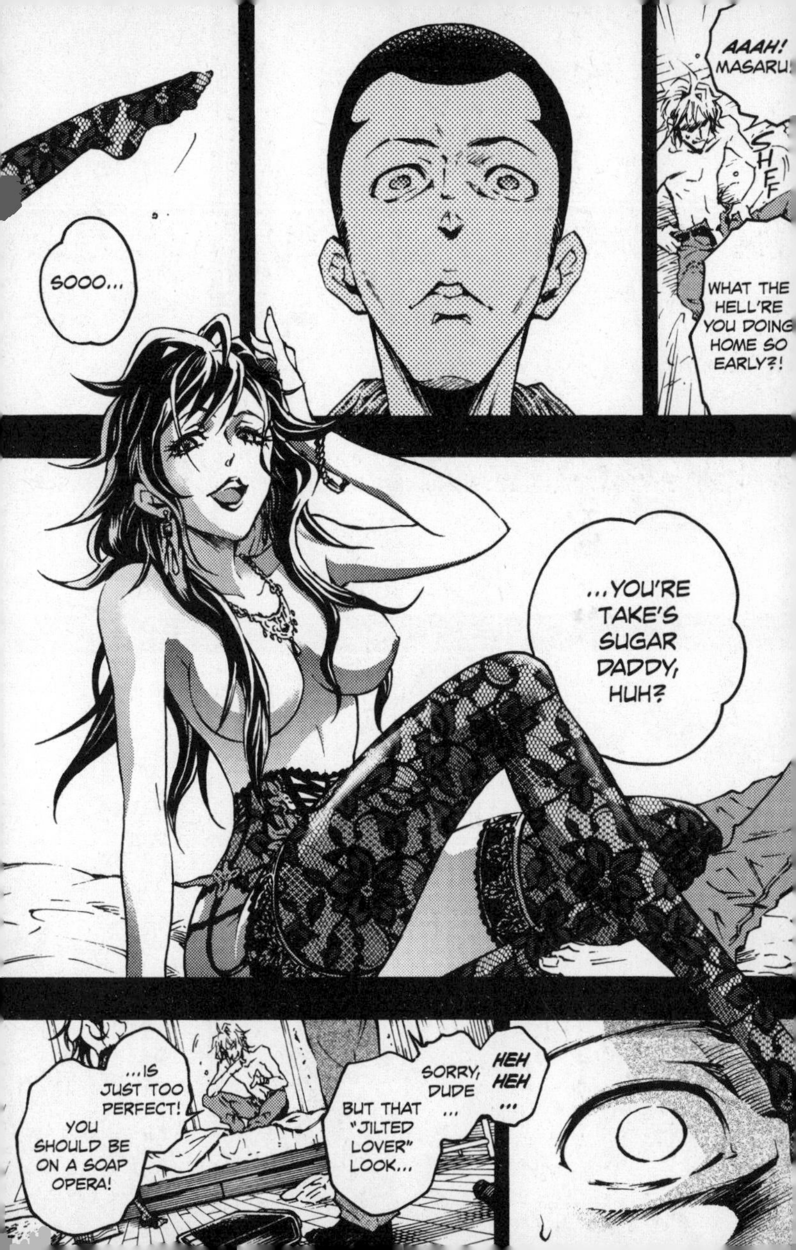
AAAH! MASARU!
SHFF
WHAT THE HELL'RE YOU DOING HOME SO EARLY?!
SOOO...
...YOU'RE TAKE'S SUGAR DADDY, HUH?
HEH HEH ...
SORRY, DUDE ...
BUT THAT "JILTED LOVER" LOOK...
...IS JUST TOO PERFECT!
YOU SHOULD BE ON A SOAP OPERA!

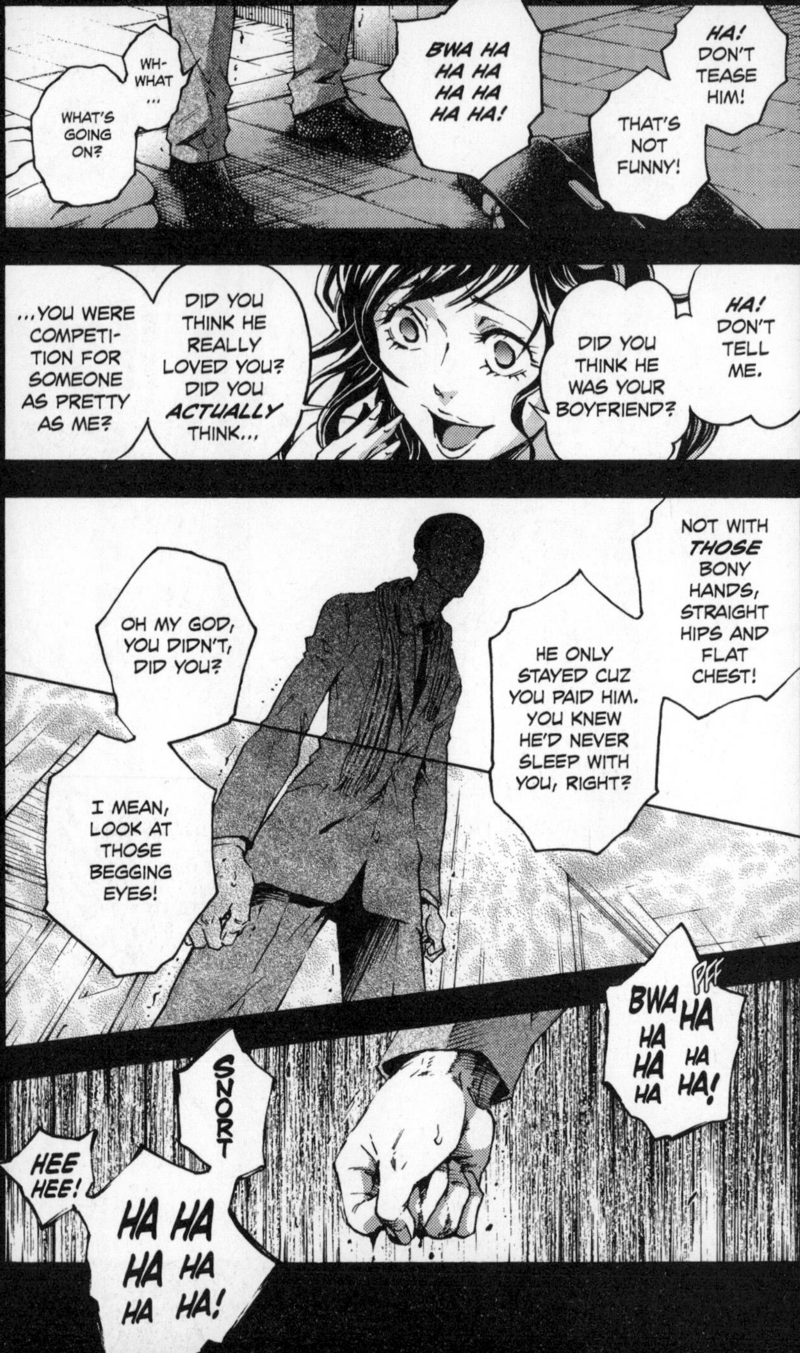
HA! DON'T TEASE HIM!
THAT'S NOT FUNNY!
BWA HA HA HA HA HA HA HA!
WH-WHAT ...
WHAT'S GOING ON?
HA! DON'T TELL ME.
DID YOU THINK HE WAS YOUR BOYFRIEND?
DID YOU THINK HE REALLY LOVED YOU? DID YOU ACTUALLY THINK...
...YOU WERE COMPETITION FOR SOMEONE AS PRETTY AS ME?
NOT WITH THOSE BONY HANDS, STRAIGHT HIPS AND FLAT CHEST!
HE ONLY STAYED CUZ YOU PAID HIM. YOU KNEW HE'D NEVER SLEEP WITH YOU, RIGHT?
OH MY GOD, YOU DIDN'T, DID YOU?
I MEAN, LOOK AT THOSE BEGGING EYES!
PFF
BWA HA HA HA HA HA HA HA!
SNORT
HEE HEE!
HA HA HA HA HA HA!

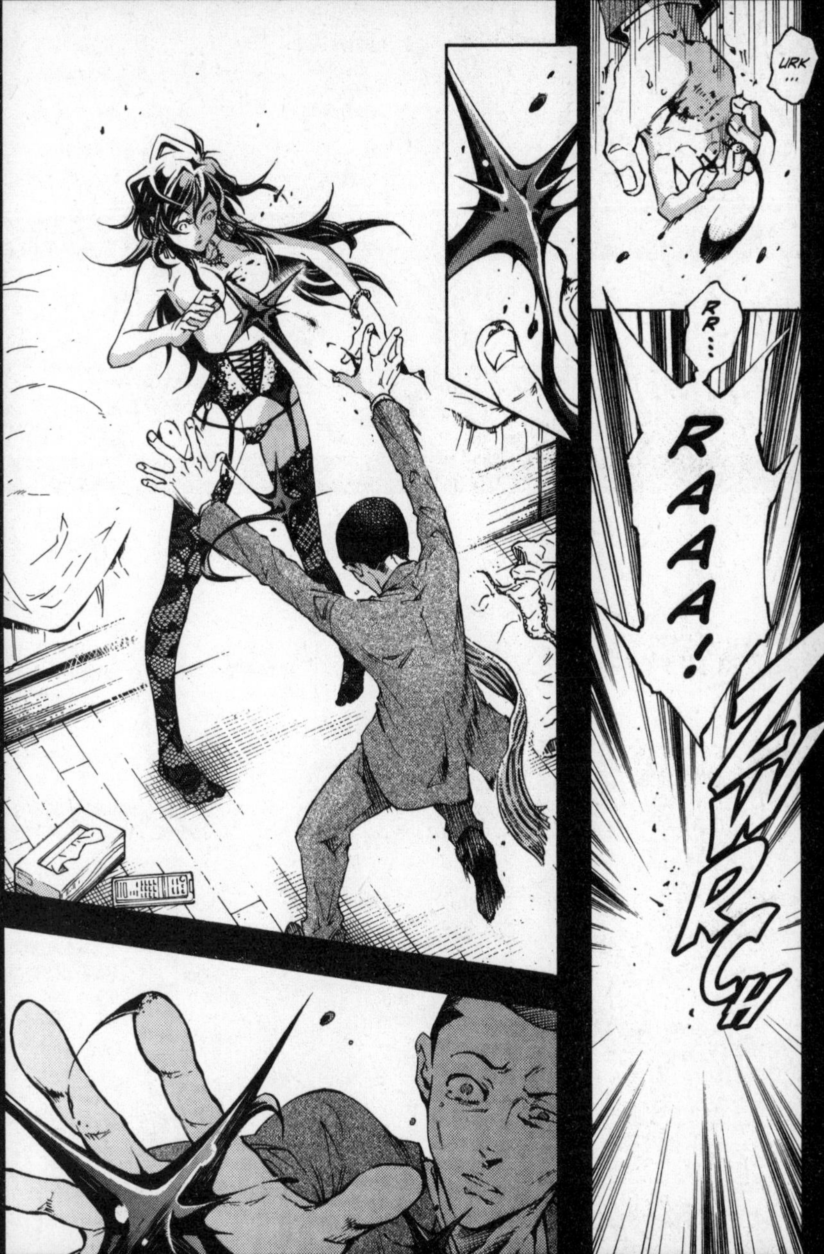
URK ...
RR...
RAAAA!
WWWRCH

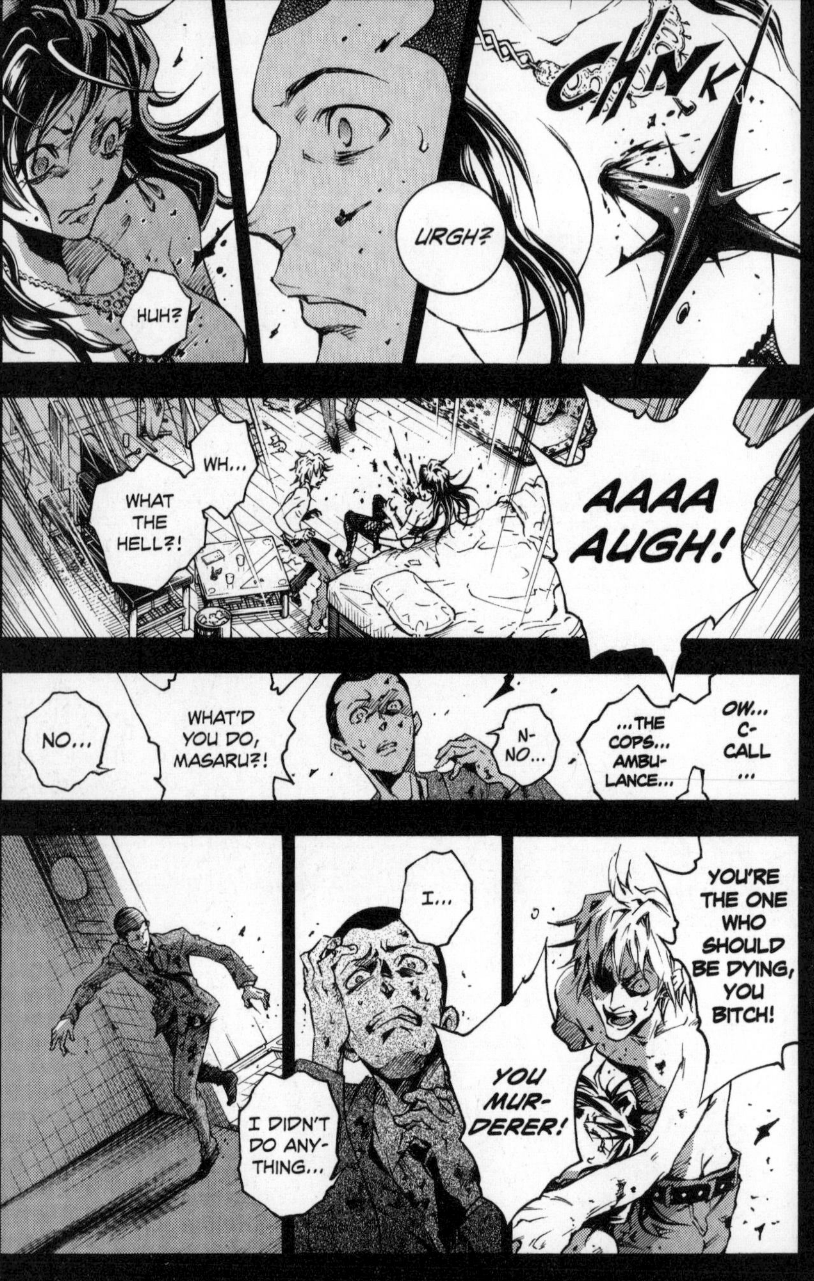
CHNK
URGH?
HUH?
AAAA AUGH!
WH...
WHAT THE HELL?!
OW... C- CALL ...
...THE COPS... AMBULANCE...
N- NO...
WHAT'D YOU DO, MASARU?!
NO...
YOU'RE THE ONE WHO SHOULD BE DYING, YOU BITCH!
YOU MURDERER!
I...
I DIDN'T DO ANYTHING...

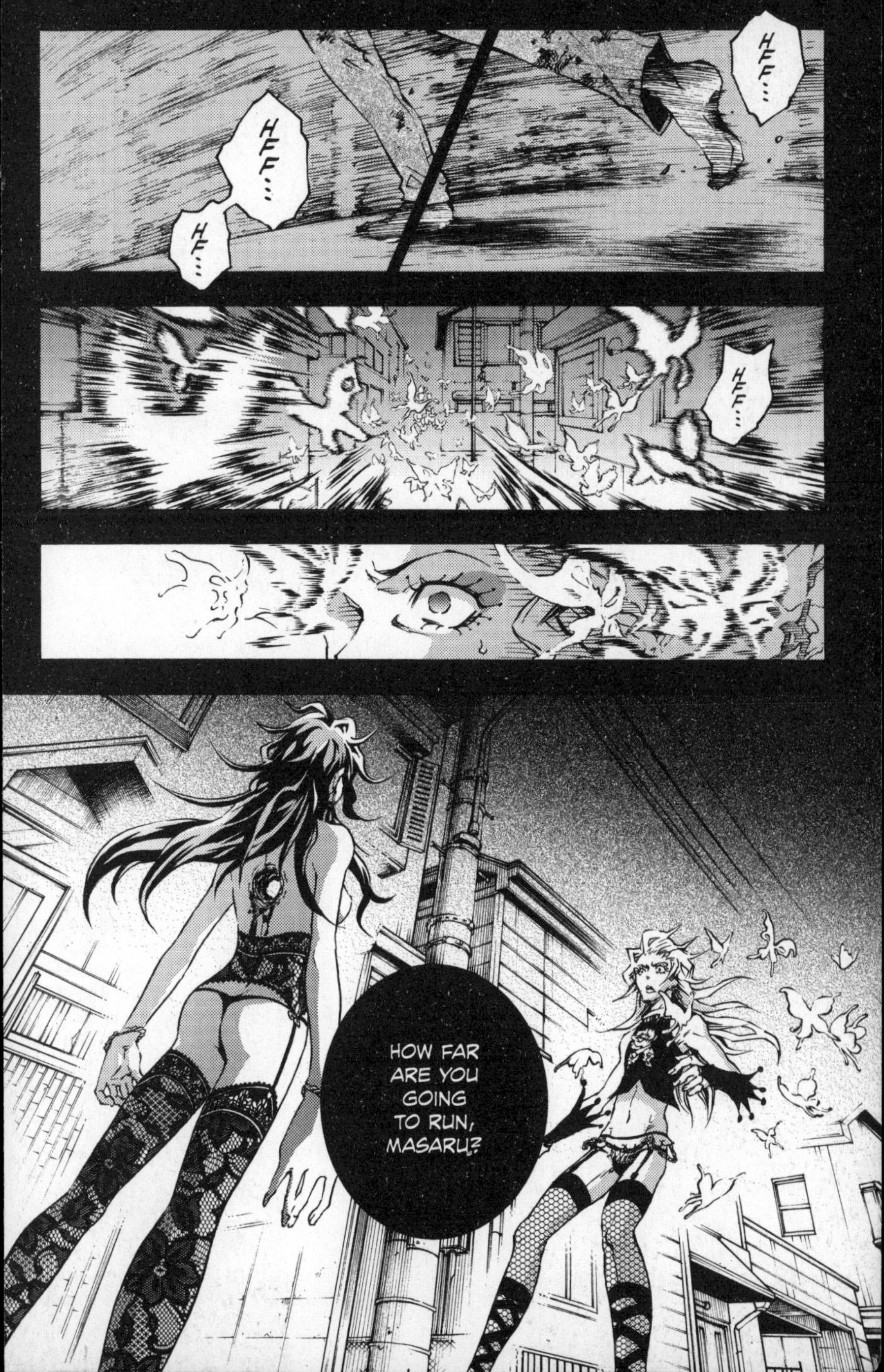
HFF...
HFF...
HF...
HFF...
HOW FAR ARE YOU GOING TO RUN, MASARU?

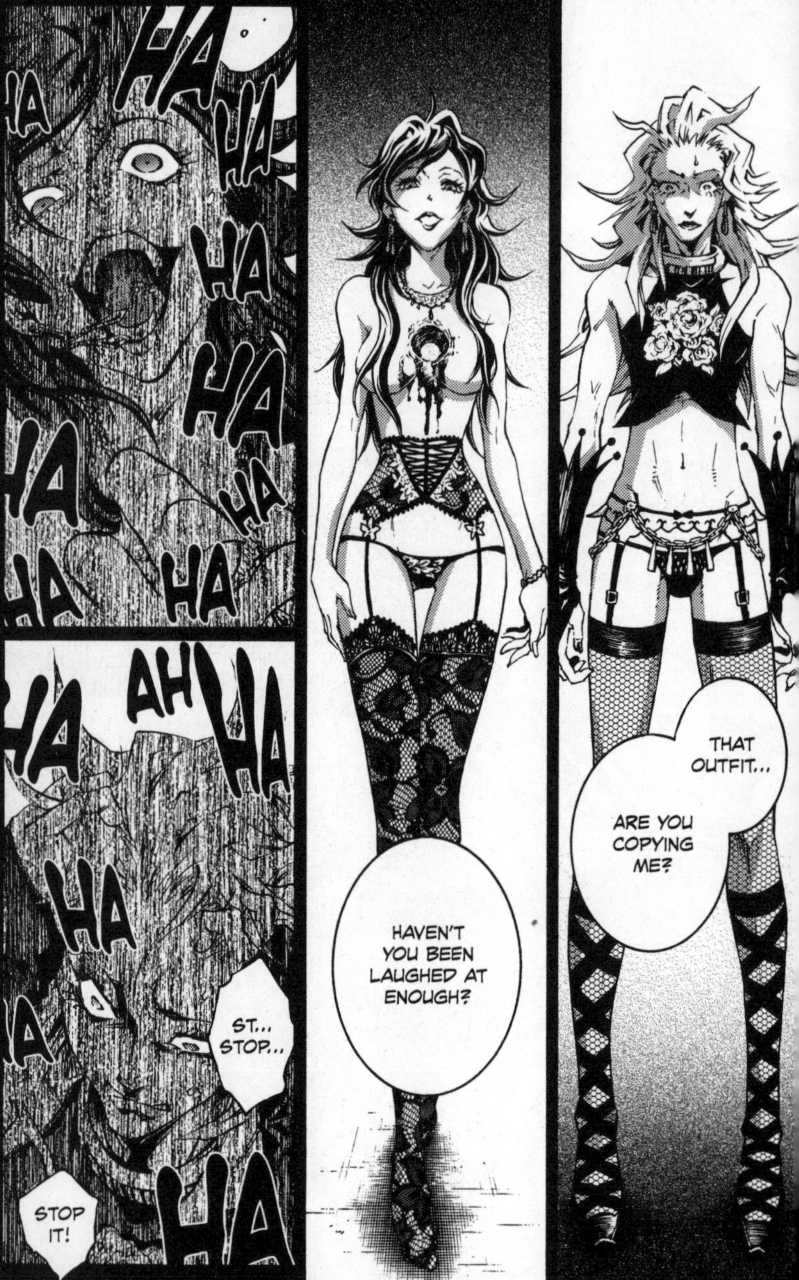
THAT OUTFIT...
ARE YOU COPYING ME?
HAVEN'T YOU BEEN LAUGHED AT ENOUGH?
HA HA HA HA HA HA HA HA HA HA HA
HA AH HA HA
HA
HA
ST... STOP...
HA
STOP IT!

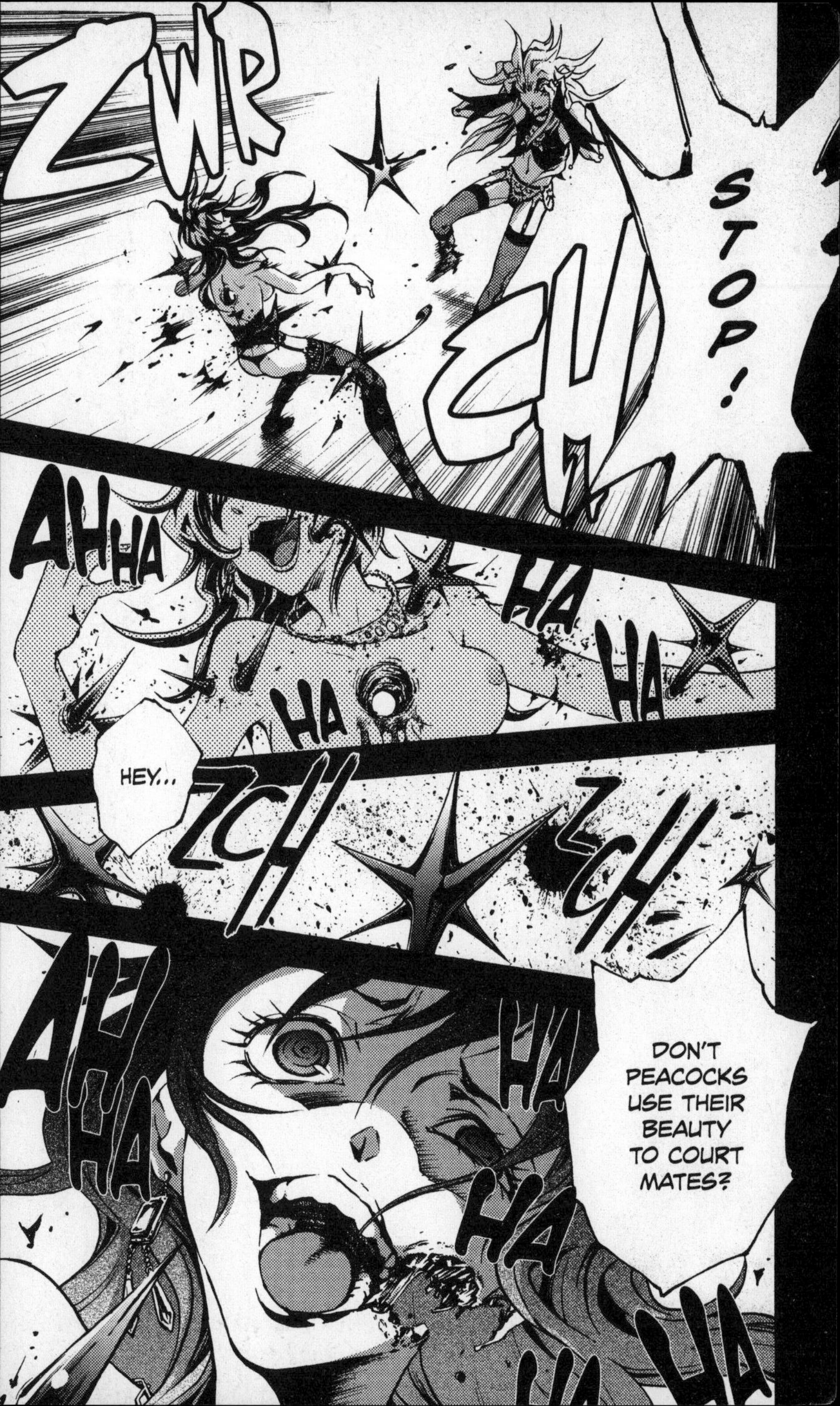
STOP!
CH
ZWIP
AHHA
HA
HA
HA
HEY...
ZCH
ZCH
DON'T PEACOCKS USE THEIR BEAUTY TO COURT MATES?
HA
HA
HA
AHAHAHA

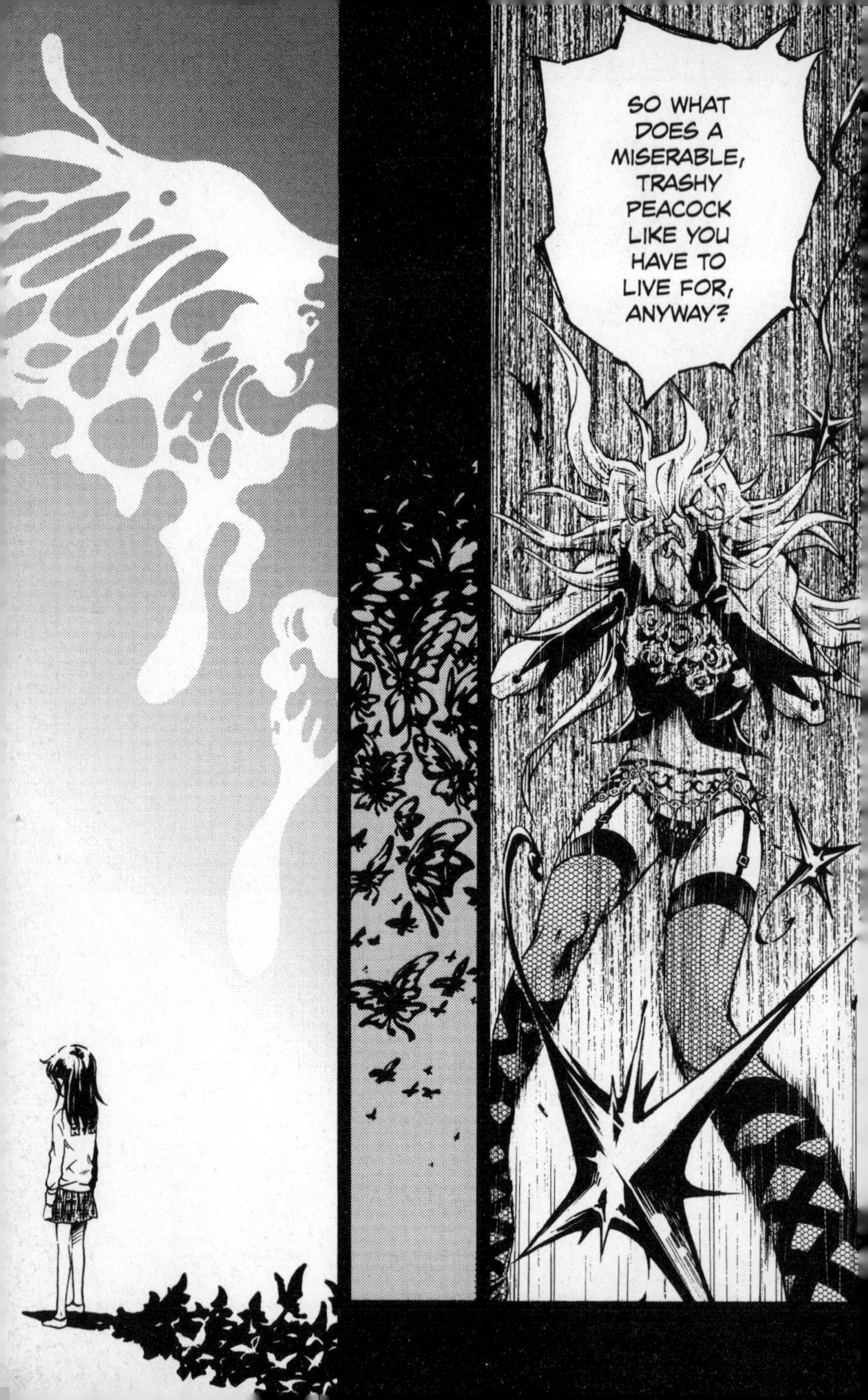
SO WHAT DOES A MISERABLE, TRASHY PEACOCK LIKE YOU HAVE TO LIVE FOR, ANYWAY?

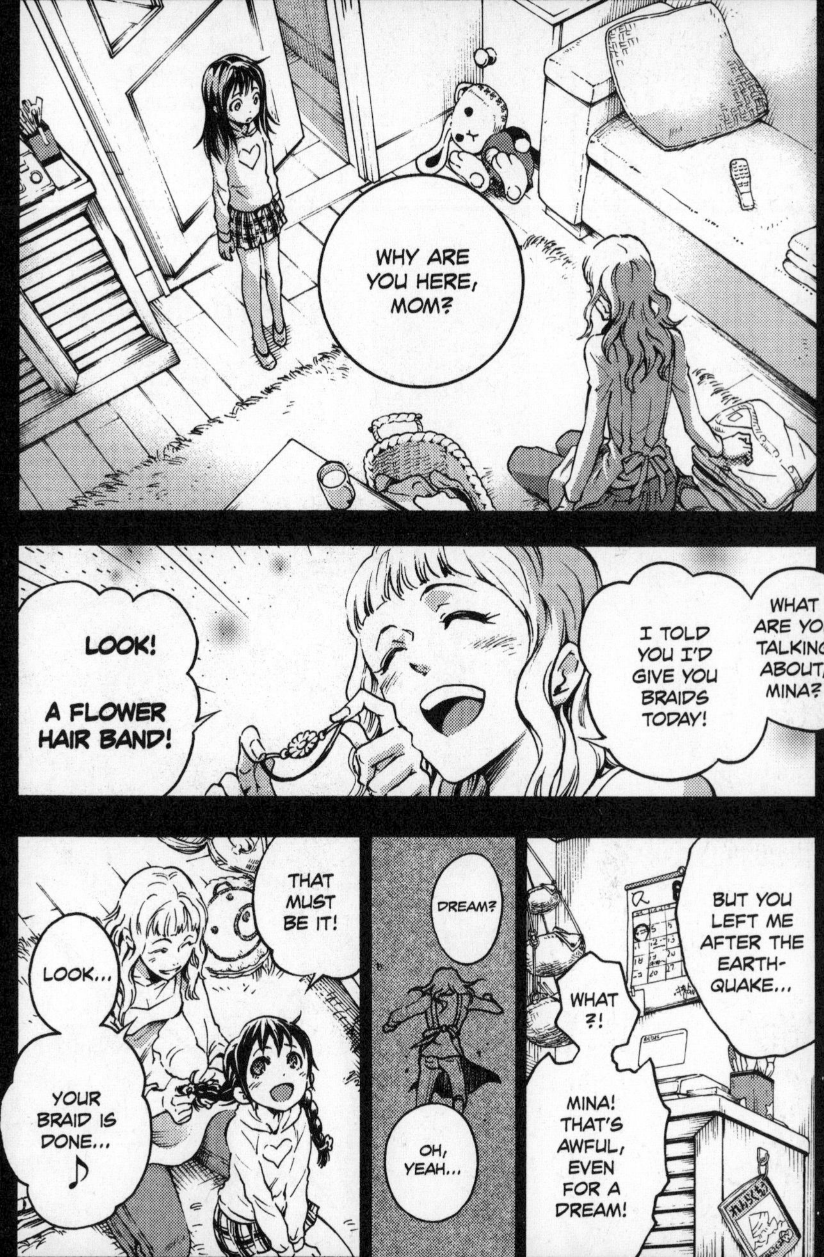
WHY ARE YOU HERE, MOM?
WHAT ARE YOU TALKING ABOUT, MINA?
I TOLD YOU I'D GIVE YOU BRAIDS TODAY!
LOOK!
A FLOWER HAIR BAND!
BUT YOU LEFT ME AFTER THE EARTH-QUAKE...
WHAT?!
MINA! THAT'S AWFUL, EVEN FOR A DREAM!
DREAM?
OH, YEAH...
THAT MUST BE IT!
LOOK...
YOUR BRAID IS DONE... ♪

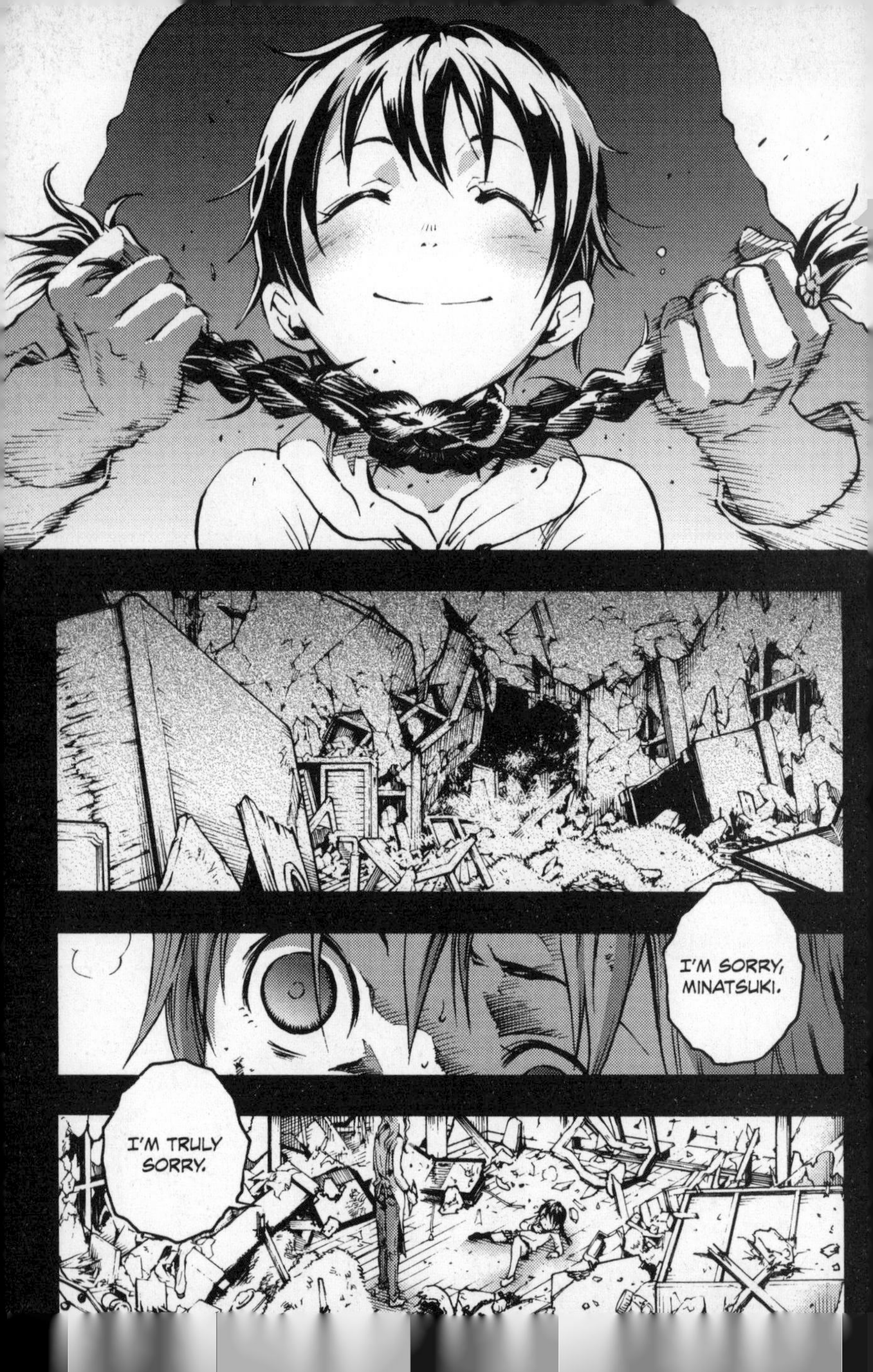
I'M SORRY, MINATSUKI.
I'M TRULY SORRY.

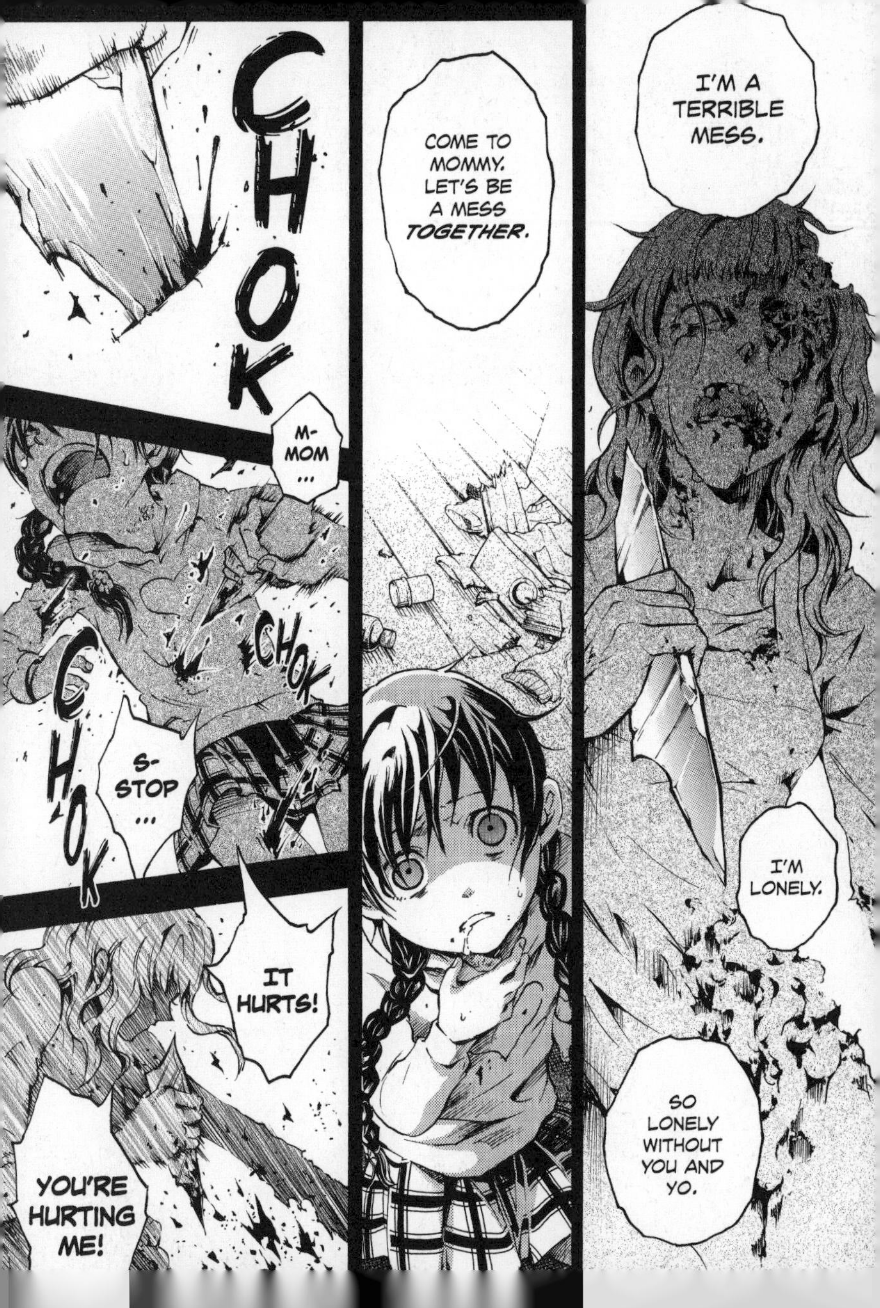
I'M A TERRIBLE MESS.
I'M LONELY.
SO LONELY WITHOUT YOU AND YO.
COME TO MOMMY. LET'S BE A MESS *TOGETHER*.
CHOK
M-MOM...
CHOK
CHOK
S-STOP...
IT HURTS!
YOU'RE HURTING ME!

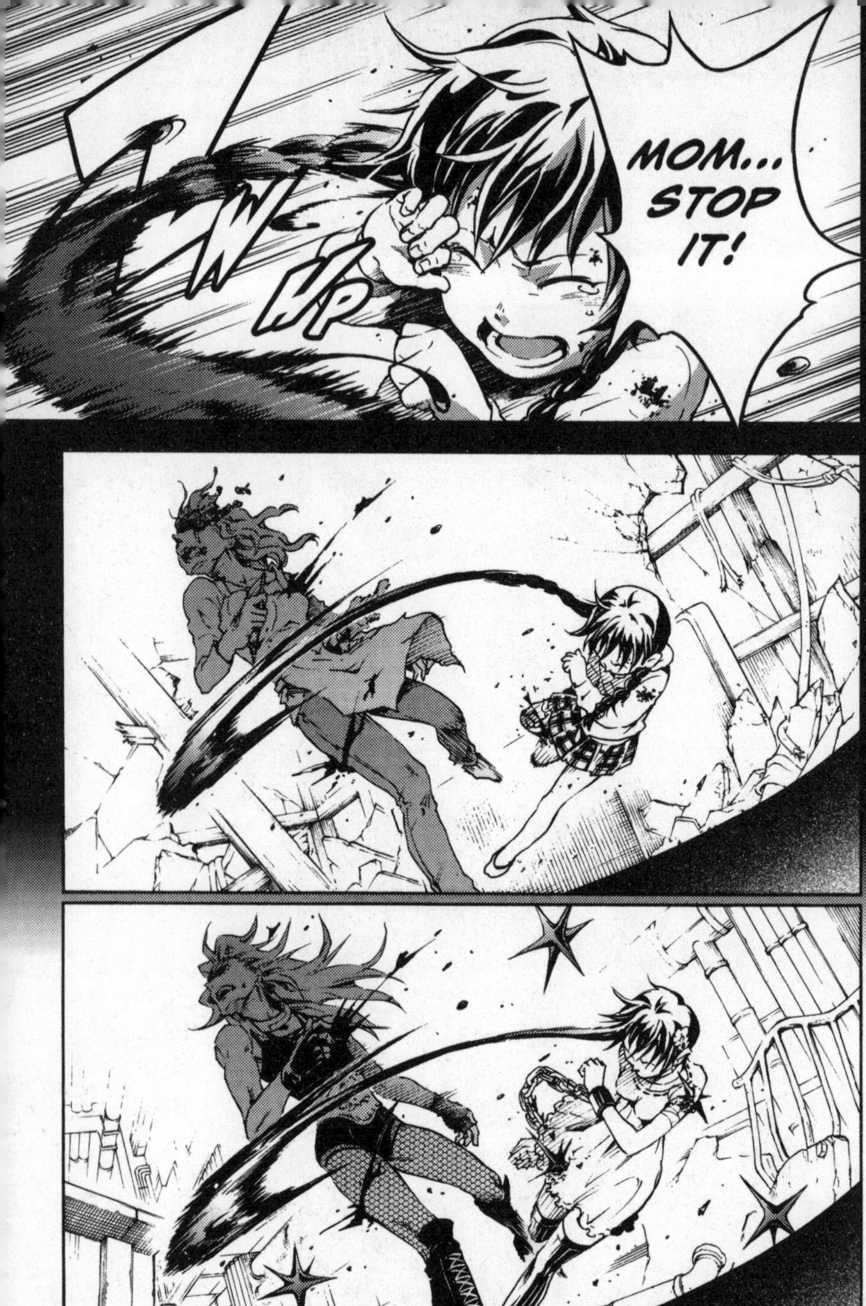
MOM... STOP IT!
WHIP

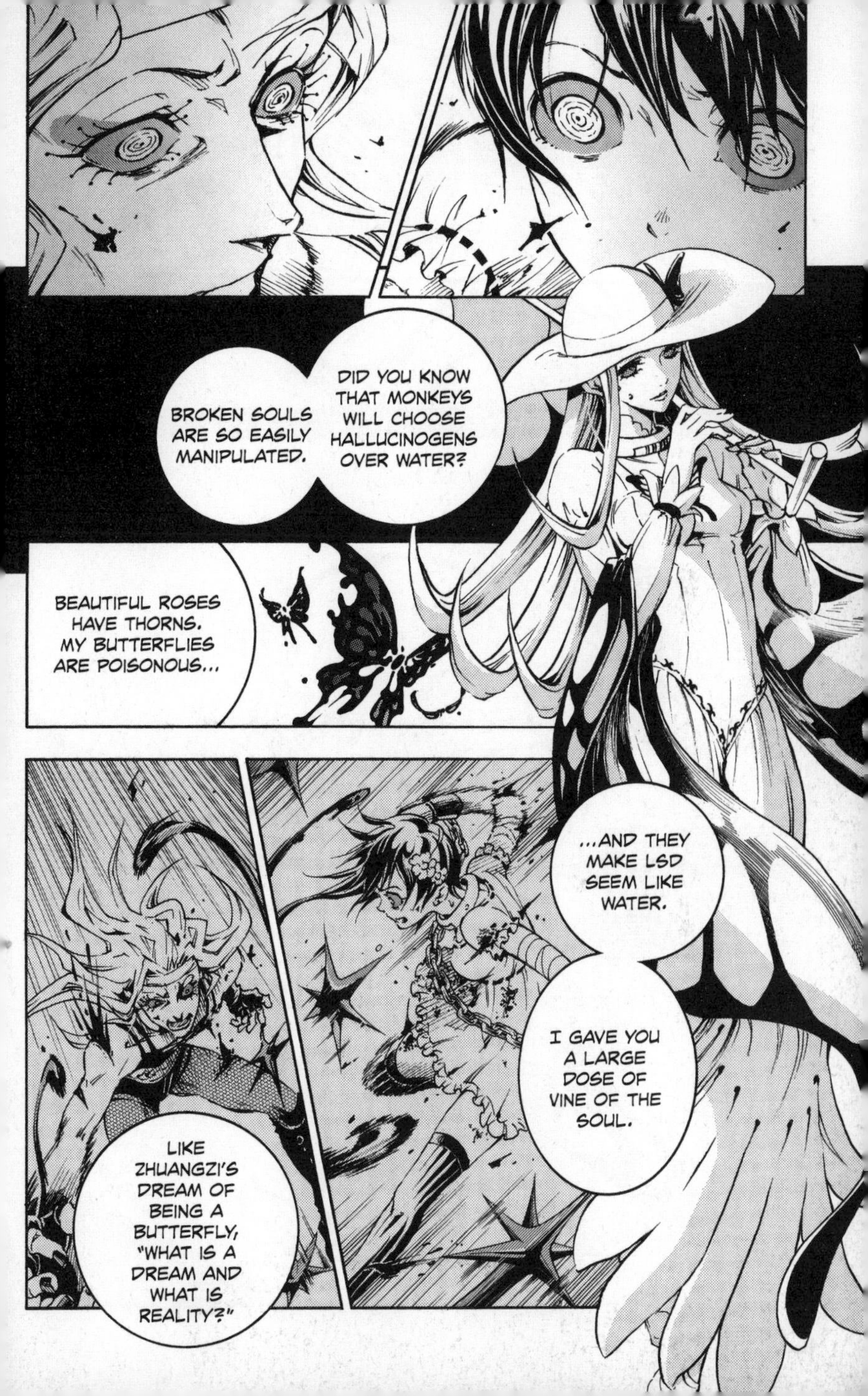
DID YOU KNOW THAT MONKEYS WILL CHOOSE HALLUCINOGENS OVER WATER?
BROKEN SOULS ARE SO EASILY MANIPULATED.
BEAUTIFUL ROSES HAVE THORNS. MY BUTTERFLIES ARE POISONOUS...
...AND THEY MAKE LSD SEEM LIKE WATER.
I GAVE YOU A LARGE DOSE OF VINE OF THE SOUL.
LIKE ZHUANGZI'S DREAM OF BEING A BUTTERFLY, "WHAT IS A DREAM AND WHAT IS REALITY?"

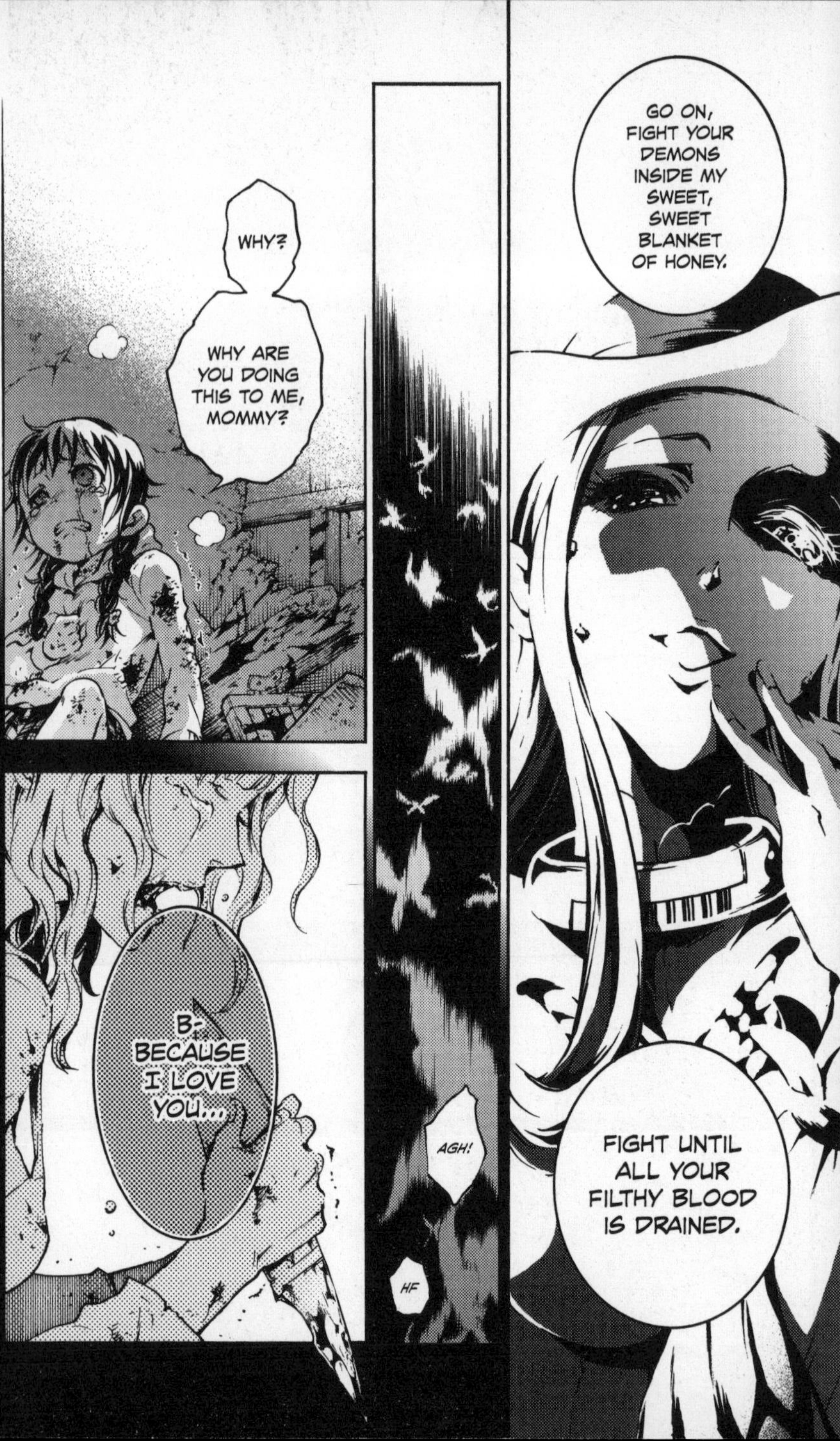
GO ON, FIGHT YOUR DEMONS INSIDE MY SWEET, SWEET BLANKET OF HONEY.
FIGHT UNTIL ALL YOUR FILTHY BLOOD IS DRAINED.
AGH!
HF
WHY?
WHY ARE YOU DOING THIS TO ME, MOMMY?
B-BECAUSE I LOVE YOU...

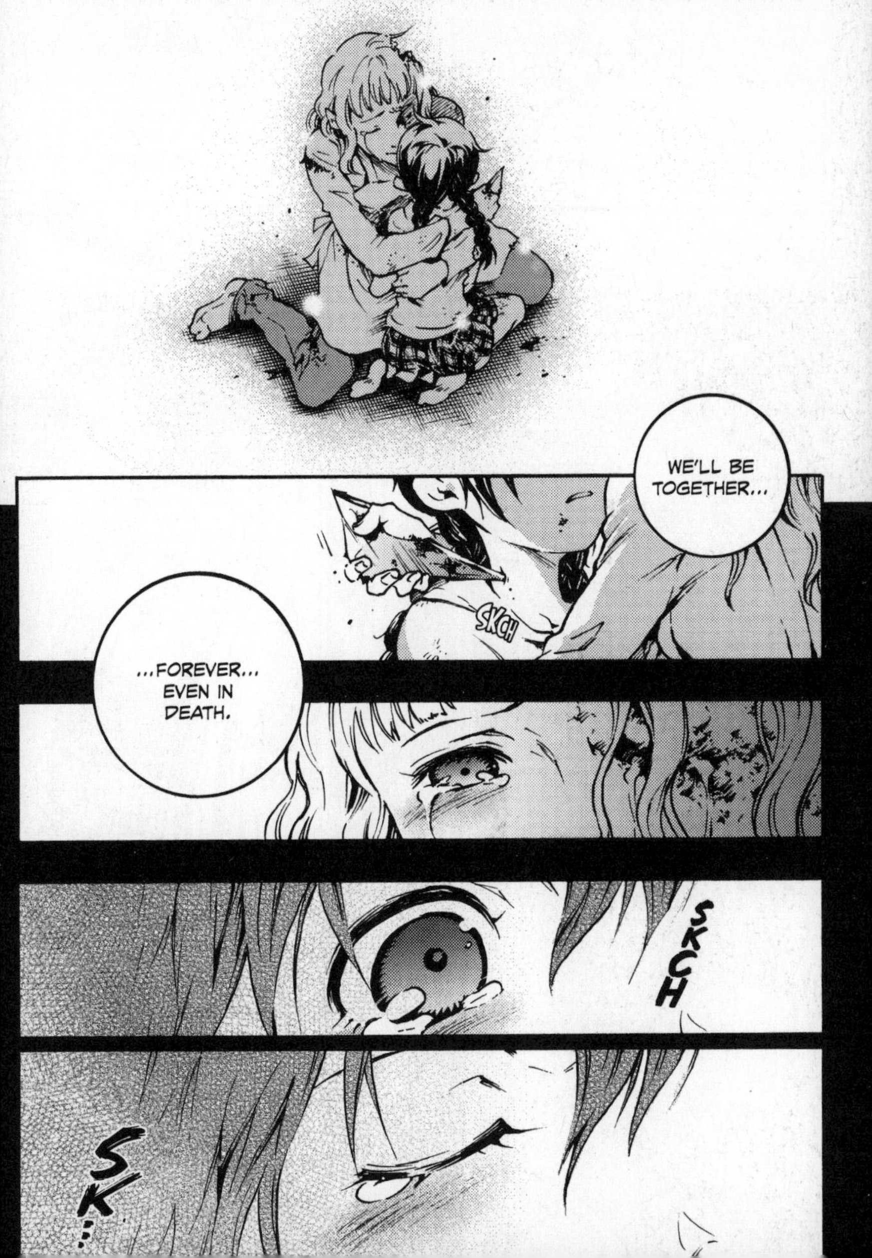
WE'LL BE TOGETHER...
SKCH
...FOREVER... EVEN IN DEATH.
SKCH
SK...

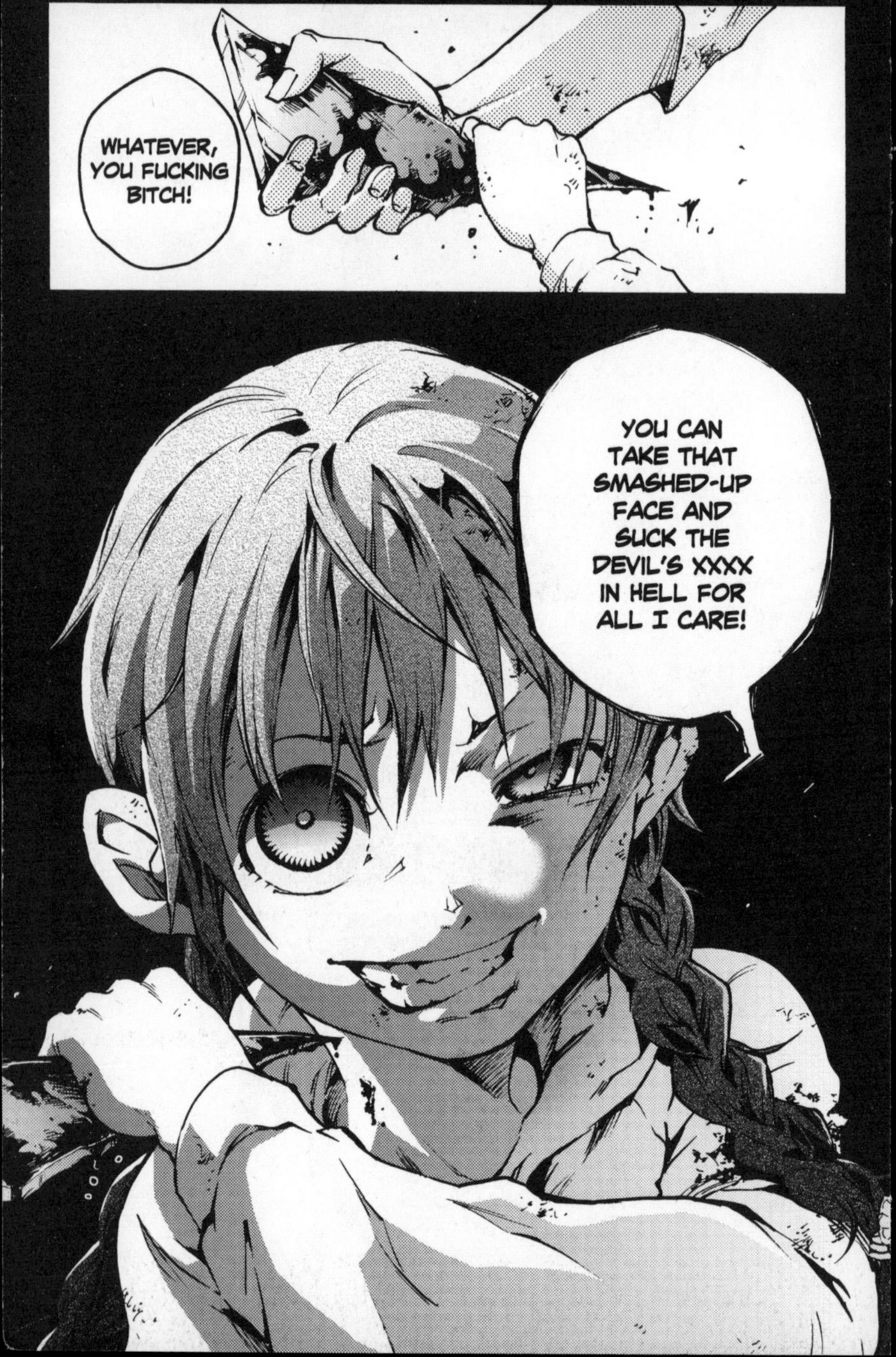
WHATEVER, YOU FUCKING BITCH!
YOU CAN TAKE THAT SMASHED-UP FACE AND SUCK THE DEVIL'S XXXX IN HELL FOR ALL I CARE!

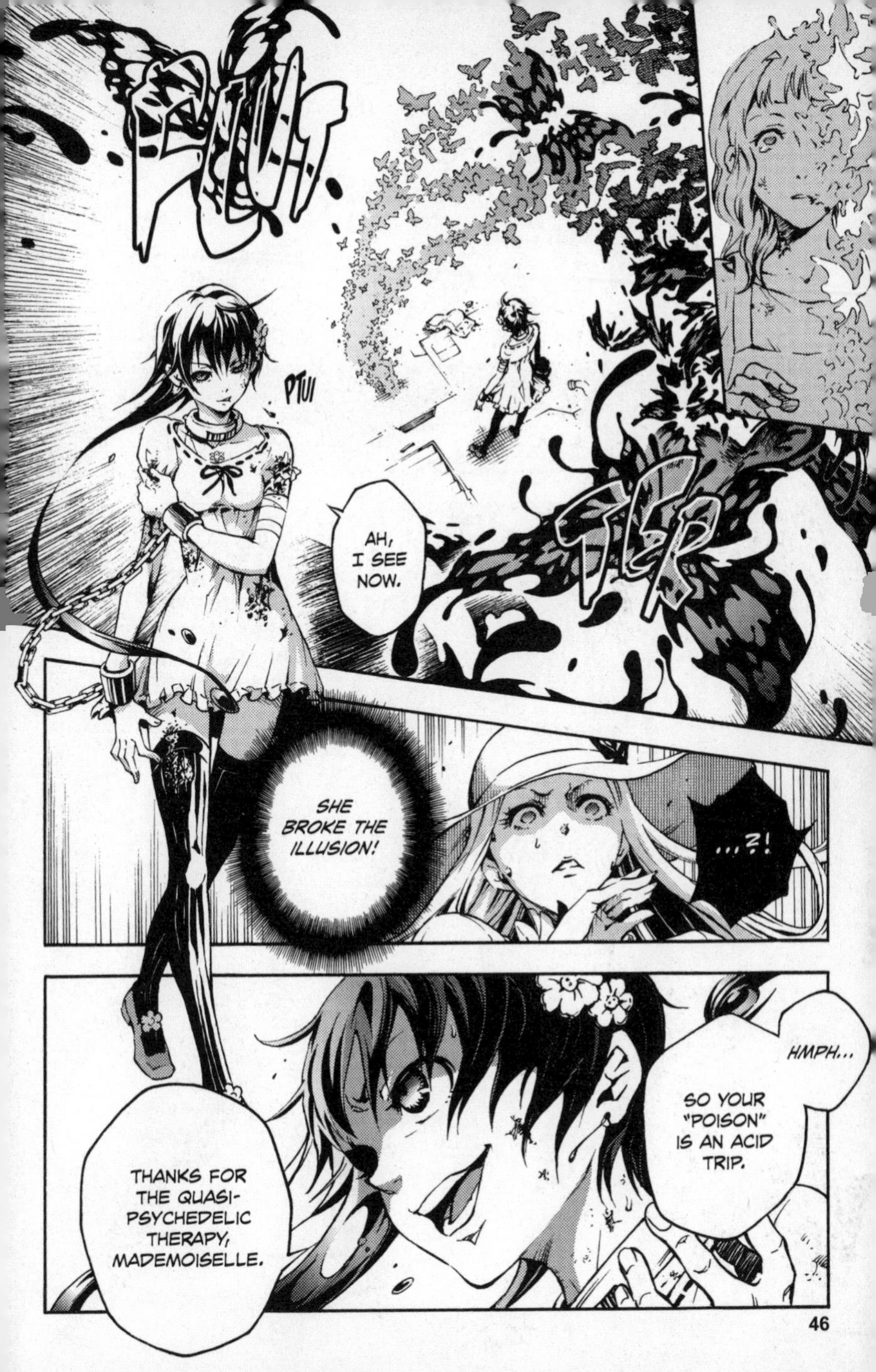
PTUI
AH, I SEE NOW.
...?!
SHE BROKE THE ILLUSION!
HMPH...
SO YOUR "POISON" IS AN ACID TRIP.
THANKS FOR THE QUASI-PSYCHEDELIC THERAPY, MADEMOISELLE.

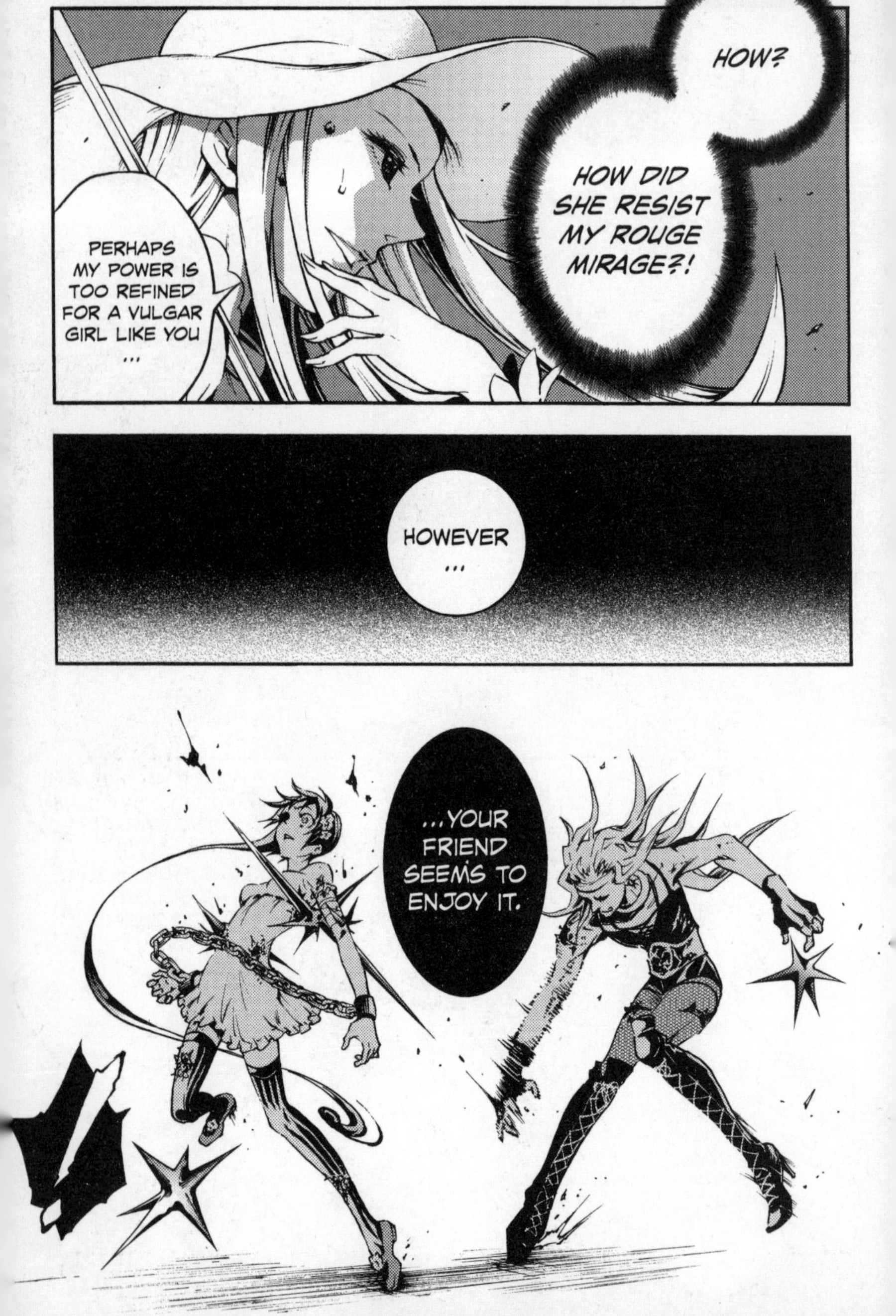
HOW?
HOW DID SHE RESIST MY ROUGE MIRAGE?!
PERHAPS MY POWER IS TOO REFINED FOR A VULGAR GIRL LIKE YOU ...
HOWEVER ...
...YOUR FRIEND SEEMS TO ENJOY IT.

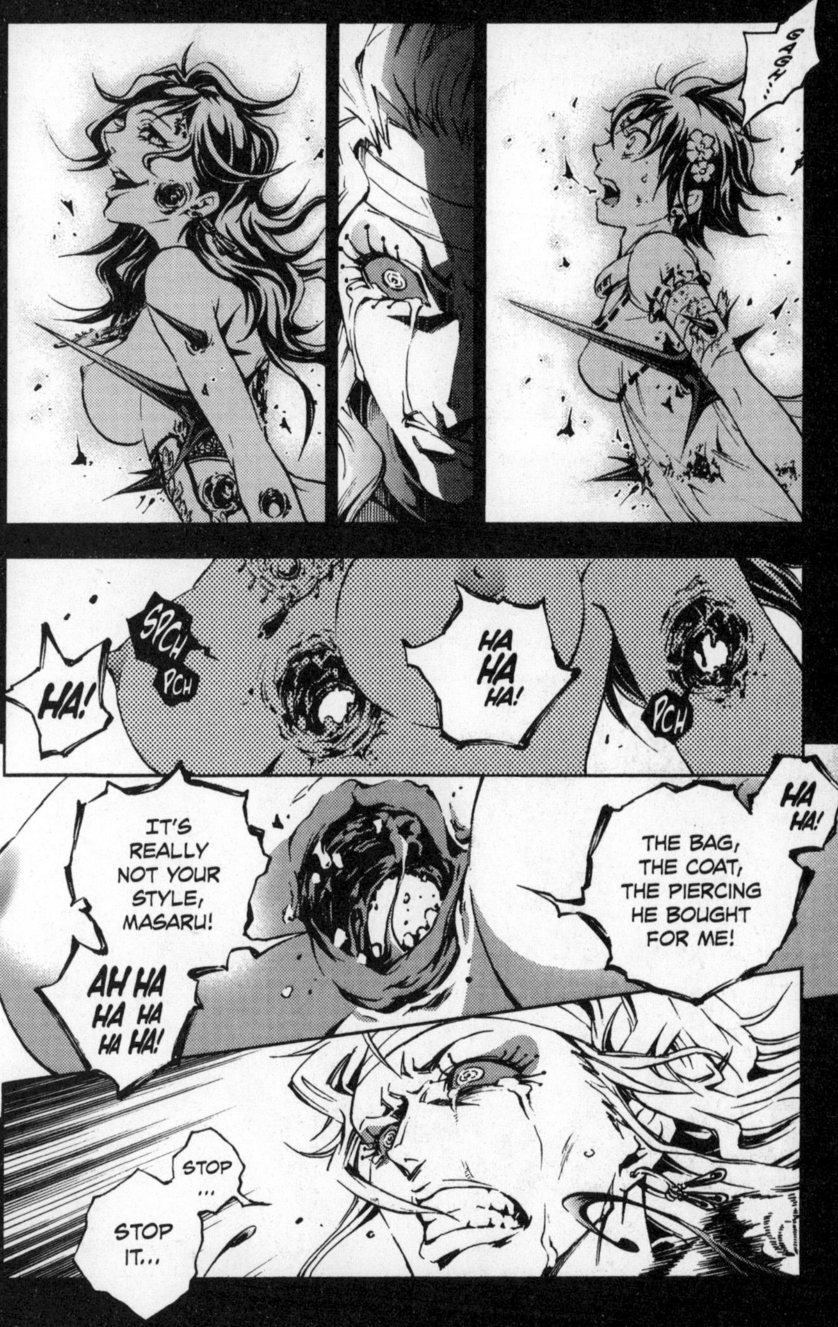
GAGH...
PCH
HA HA HA!
SPCH PCH
HA!
HA HA!
THE BAG, THE COAT, THE PIERCING HE BOUGHT FOR ME!
IT'S REALLY NOT YOUR STYLE, MASARU!
AH HA HA HA HA HA!
STOP ...
STOP IT...

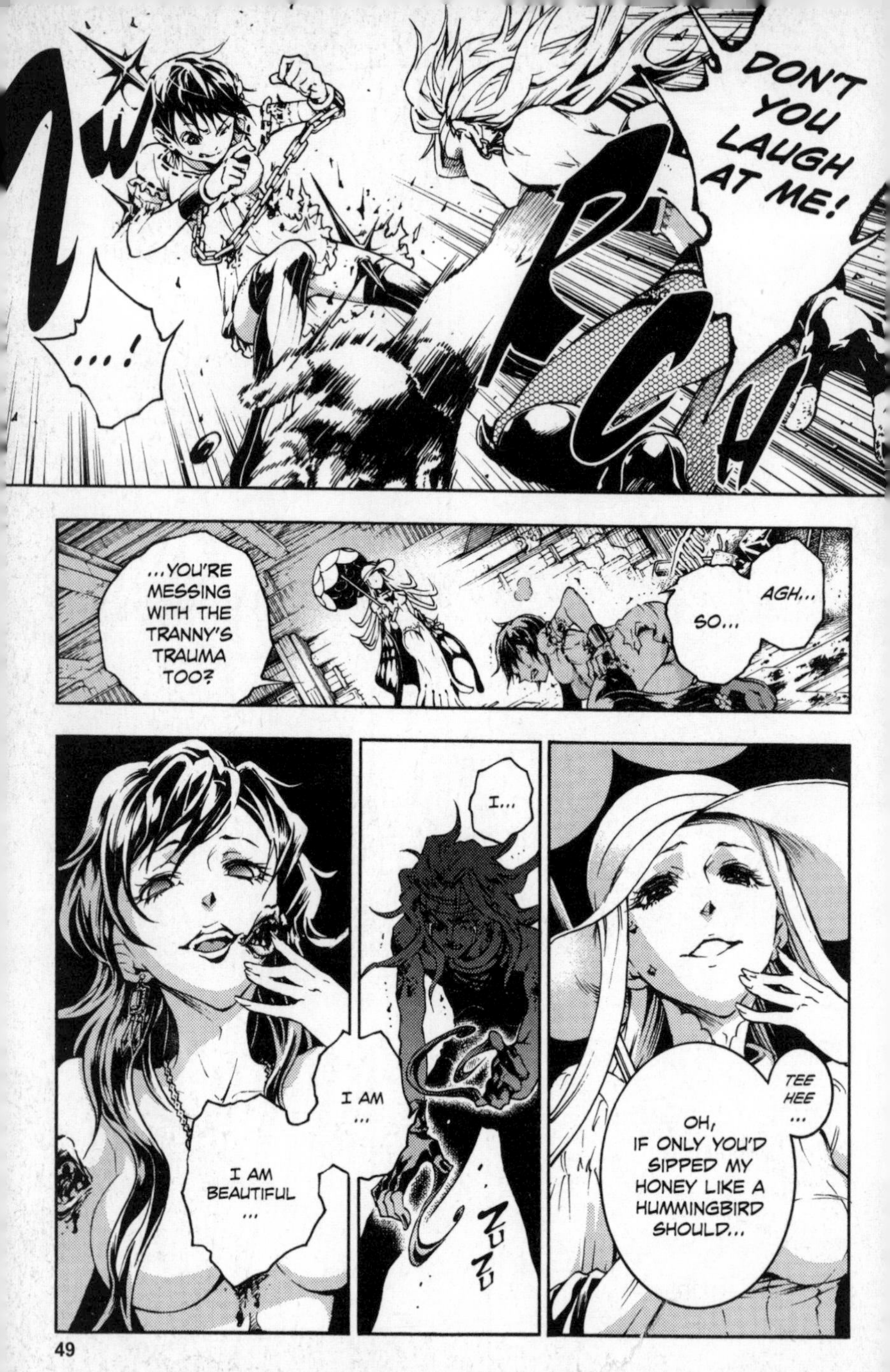
DON'T YOU LAUGH AT ME!
...!
AGH... SO...
...YOU'RE MESSING WITH THE TRANNY'S TRAUMA TOO?
TEE HEE ...
OH, IF ONLY YOU'D SIPPED MY HONEY LIKE A HUMMINGBIRD SHOULD...
I...
I AM ...
ZUZU
I AM BEAUTIFUL ...

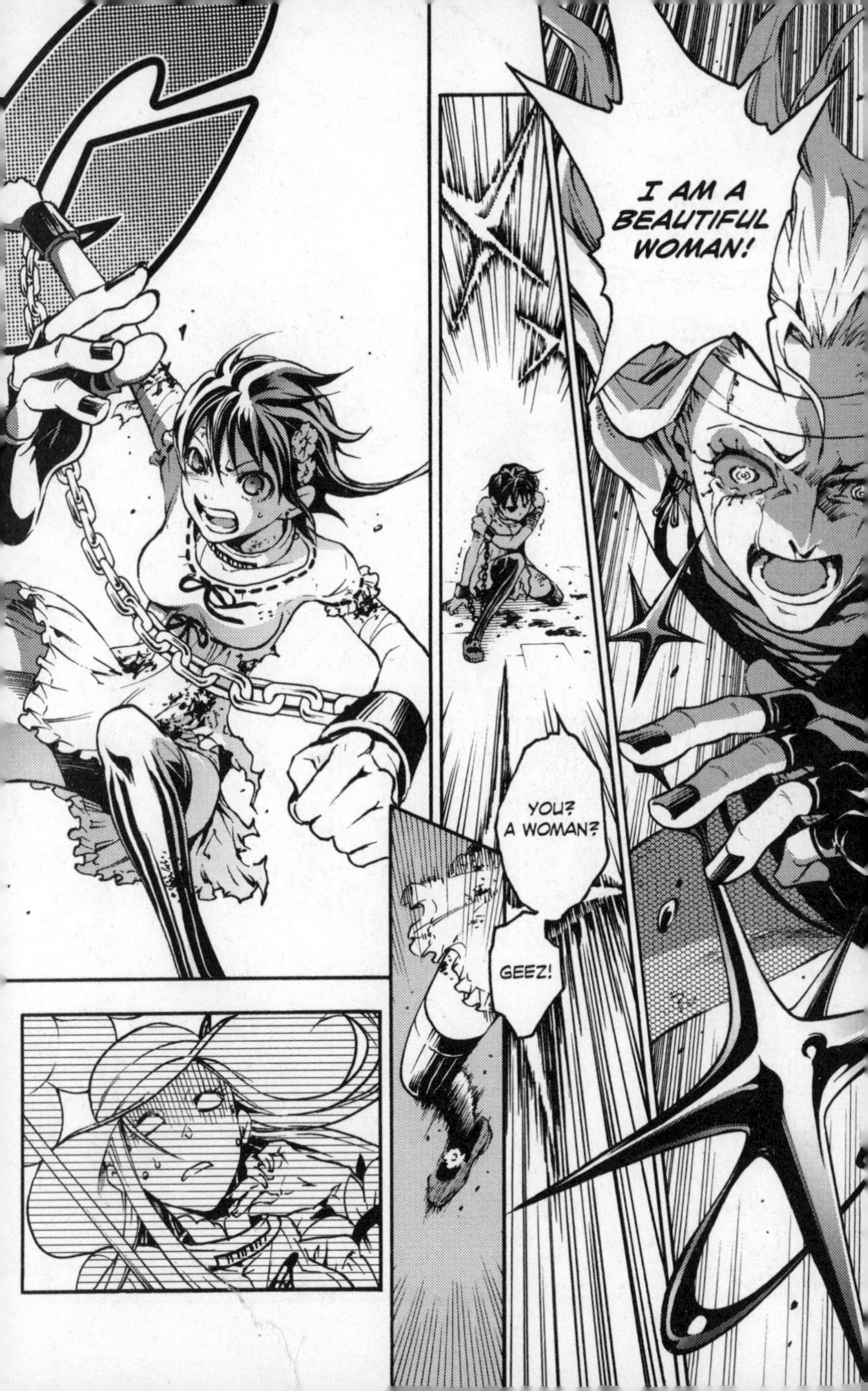
I AM A BEAUTIFUL WOMAN!
YOU? A WOMAN?
GEEZ!

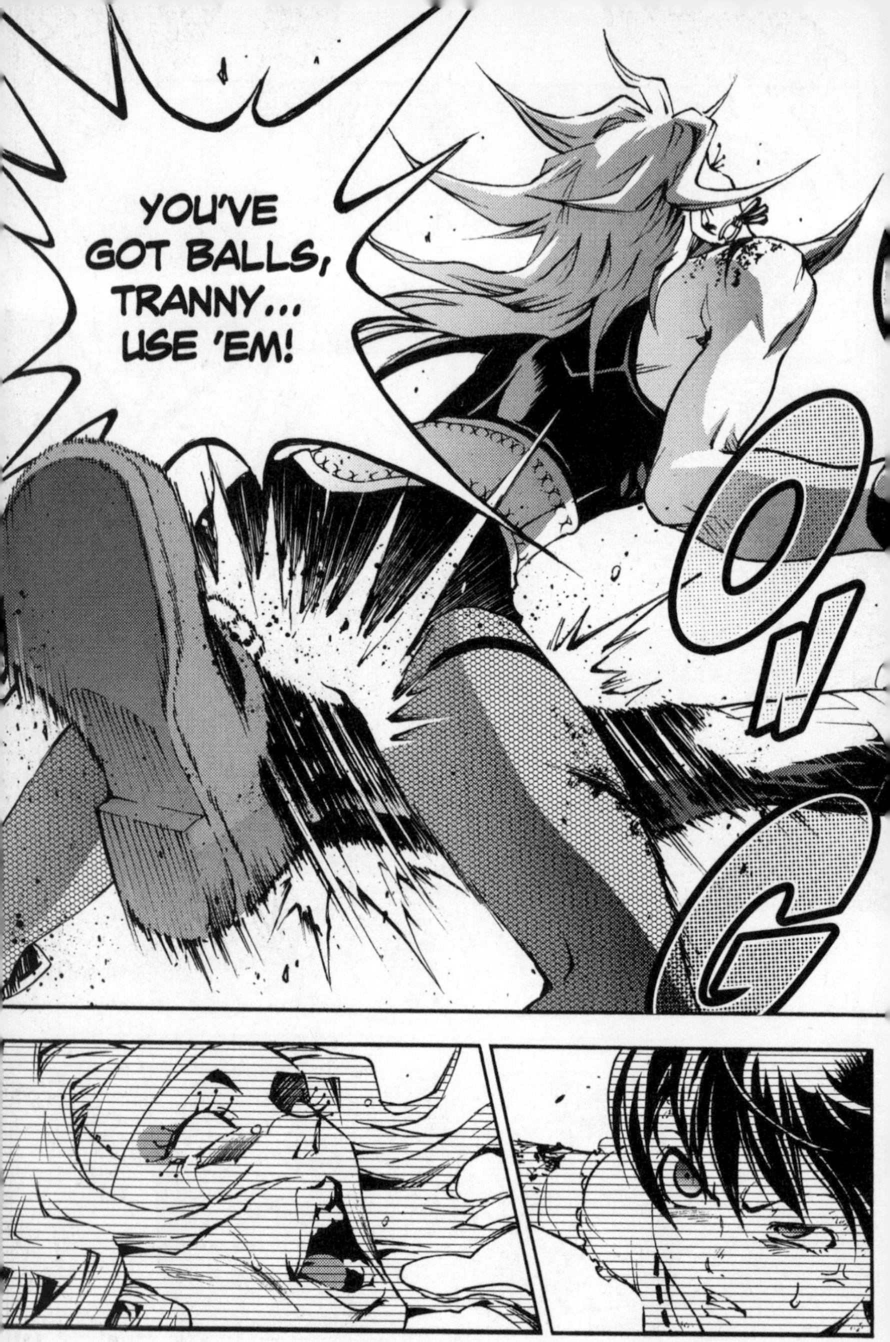
YOU'VE GOT BALLS, TRANNY... USE 'EM!

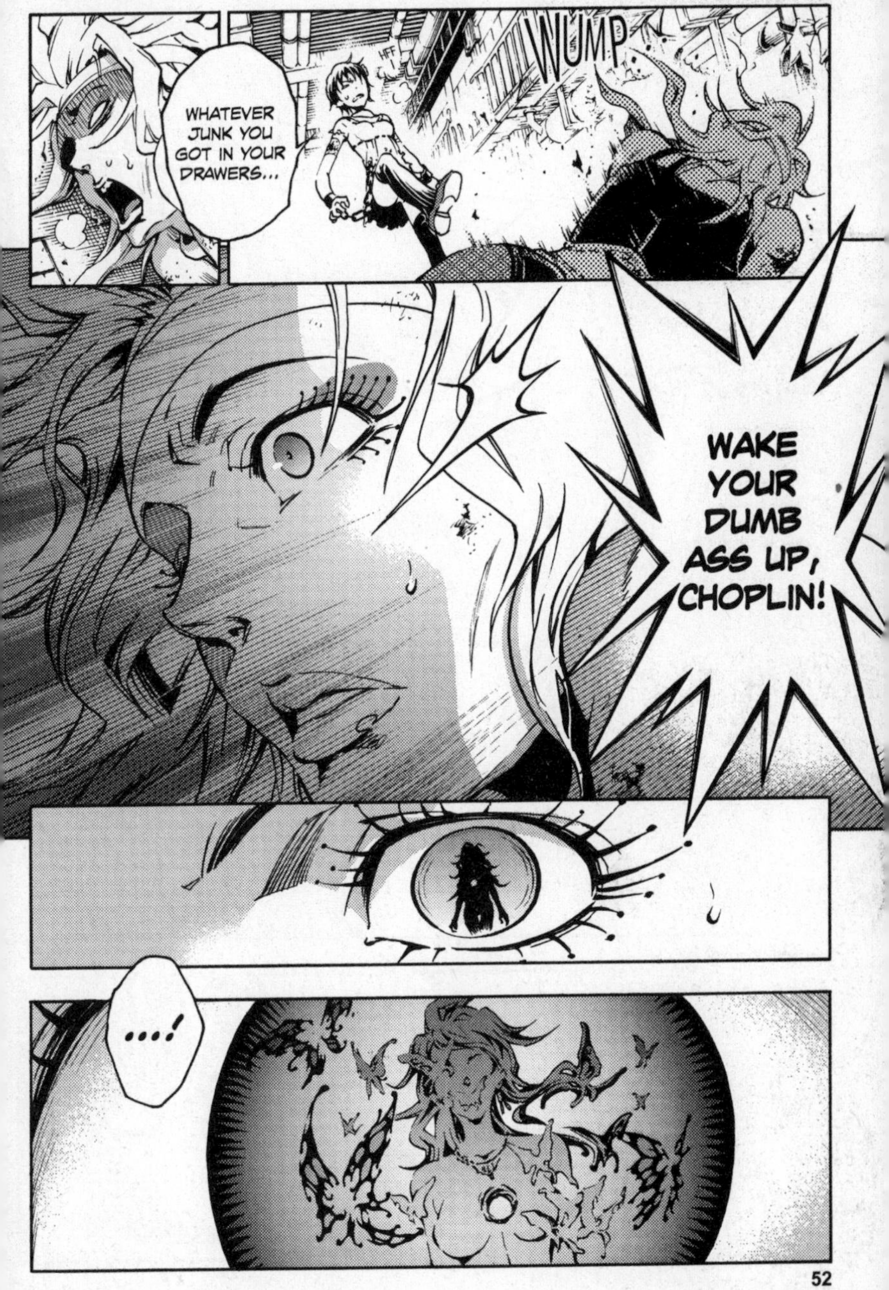
WUMP
HFF
WHATEVER JUNK YOU GOT IN YOUR DRAWERS...
WAKE YOUR DUMB ASS UP, CHOPLIN!
...!

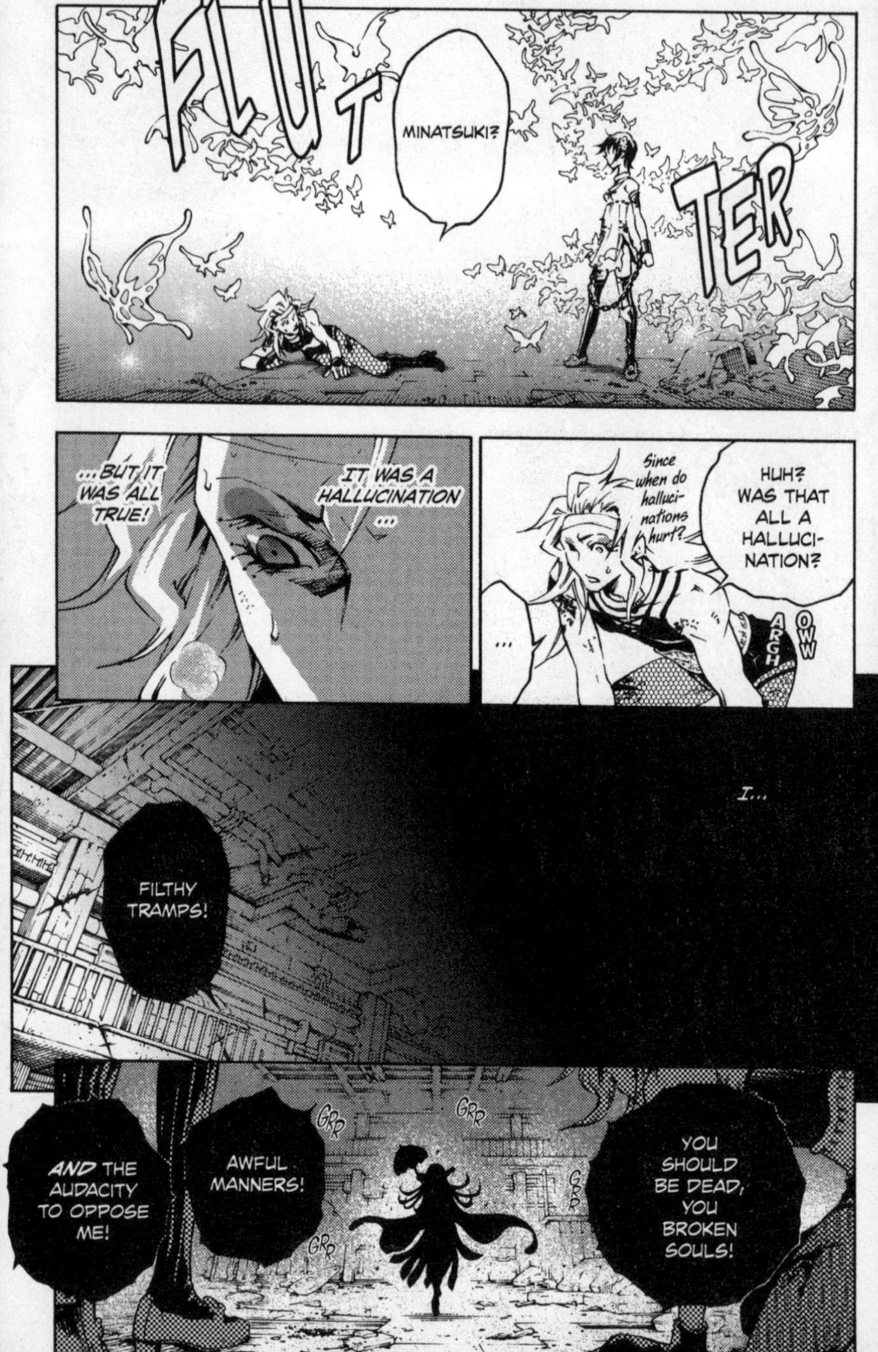
FLUTTER
MINATSUKI?
HUH? WAS THAT ALL A HALLUCINATION?
Since when do hallucinations hurt?
OWW
ARGH
...
IT WAS A HALLUCINATION...
...BUT IT WAS ALL TRUE!
I...
FILTHY TRAMPS!
YOU SHOULD BE DEAD, YOU BROKEN SOULS!
GRR
GRR
GRR
GRR
AWFUL MANNERS!
AND THE AUDACITY TO OPPOSE ME!

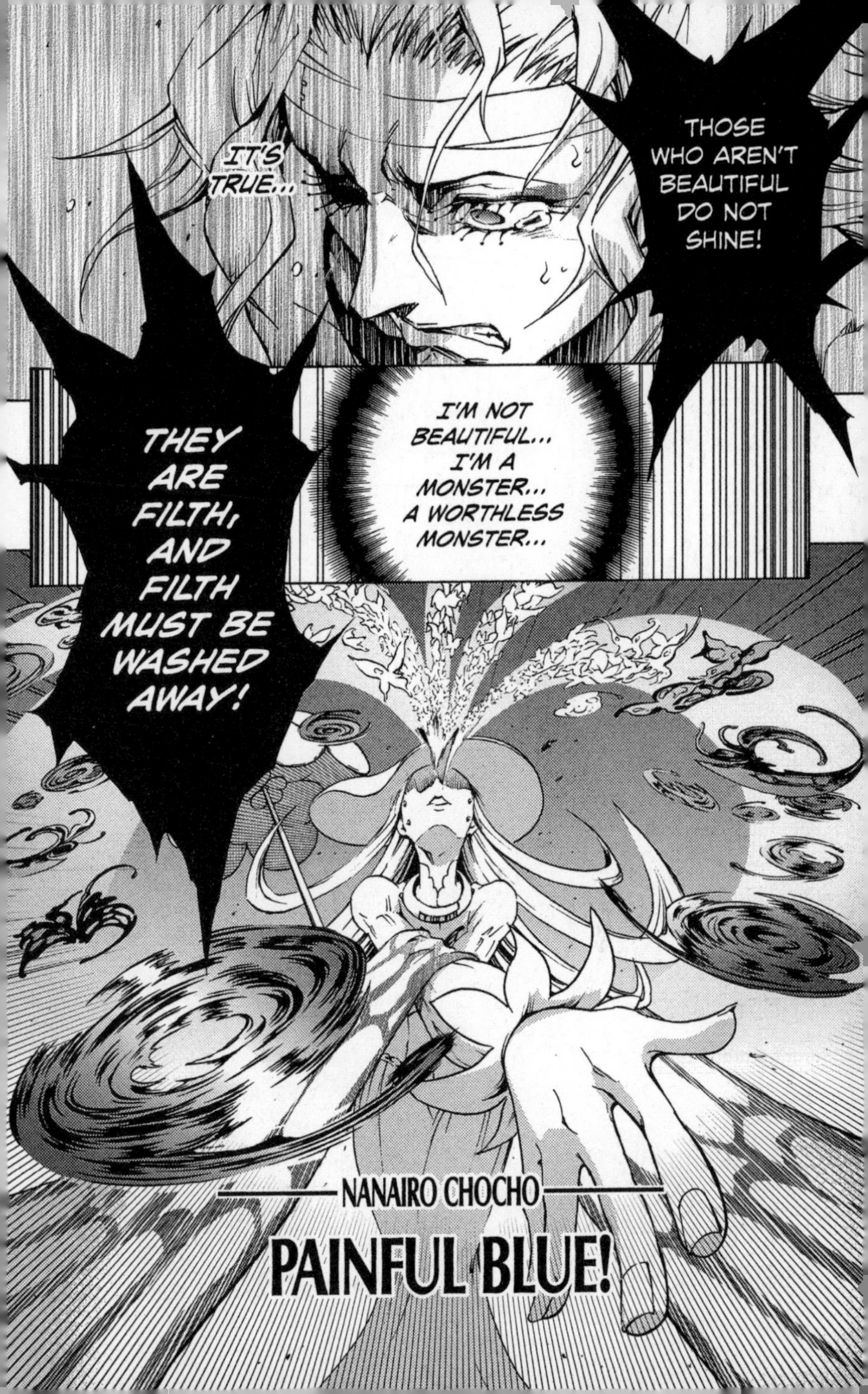
THOSE WHO AREN'T BEAUTIFUL DO NOT SHINE!
IT'S TRUE...
I'M NOT BEAUTIFUL... I'M A MONSTER... A WORTHLESS MONSTER...
THEY ARE FILTH, AND FILTH MUST BE WASHED AWAY!
NANAIRO CHOCHO
PAINFUL BLUE!

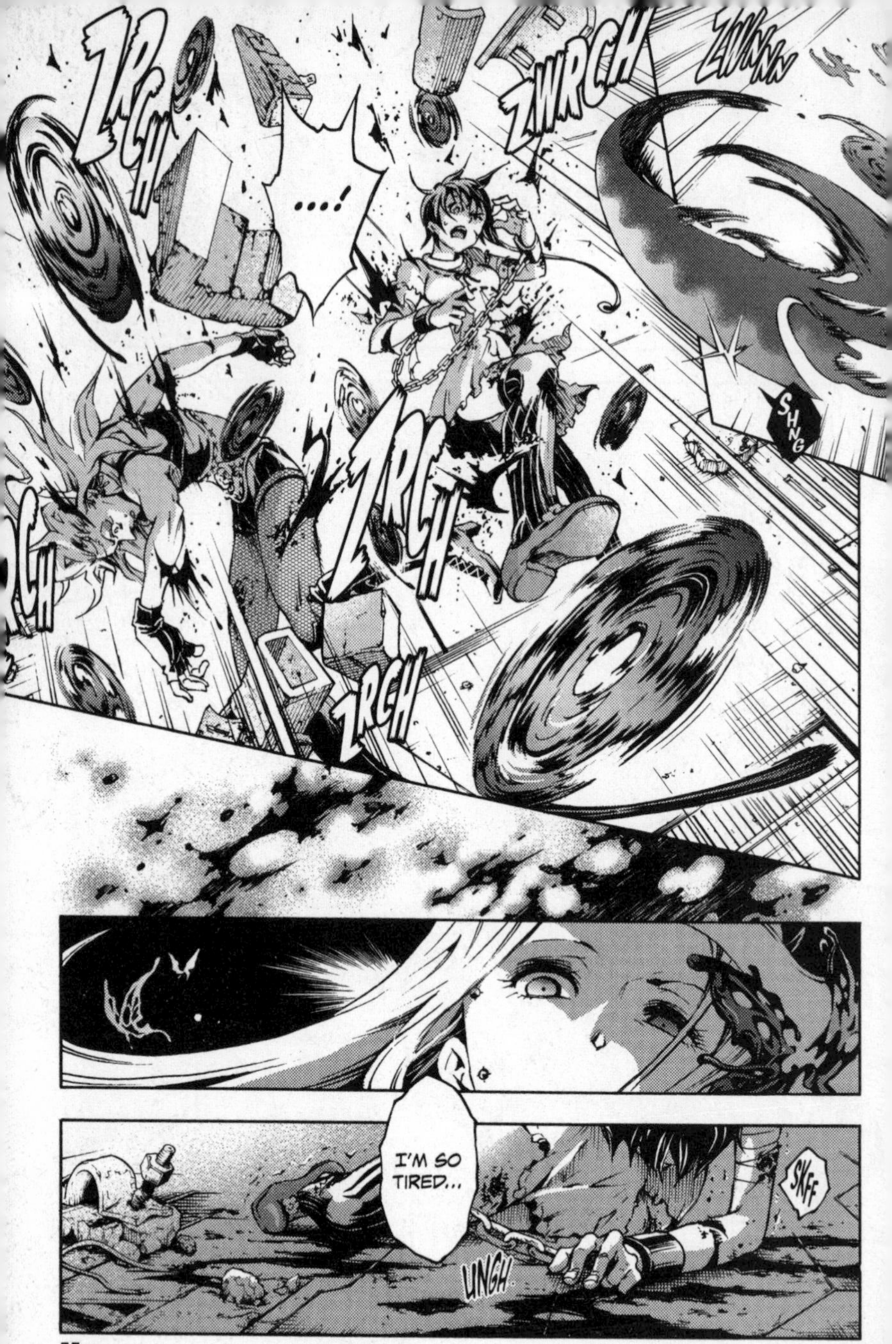
ZWNNN
ZWRCH
...!
ZRCH
SHNG
ZRCH
ZRCH
SKFF
I'M SO TIRED...
UNGH

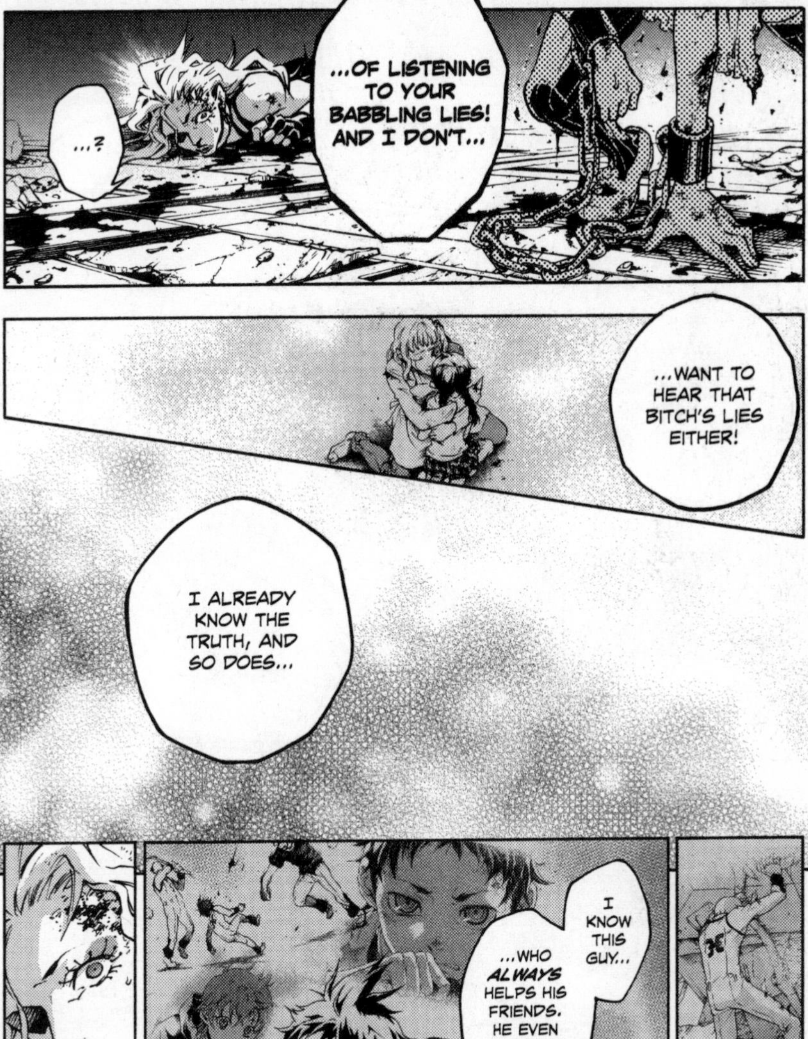
...OF LISTENING TO YOUR BABBLING LIES! AND I DON'T...
...?
...WANT TO HEAR THAT BITCH'S LIES EITHER!
I ALREADY KNOW THE TRUTH, AND SO DOES...
...MY STUPID BROTHER!
I KNOW THIS GUY...
...WHO *ALWAYS* HELPS HIS FRIENDS. HE EVEN HELPS HIS ENEMIES...
...IF THE CAUSE IS RIGHT.
HE NEVER QUITS, EVEN IF IT MEANS HE'S GONNA SUFFER.

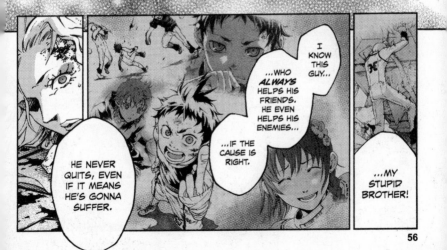

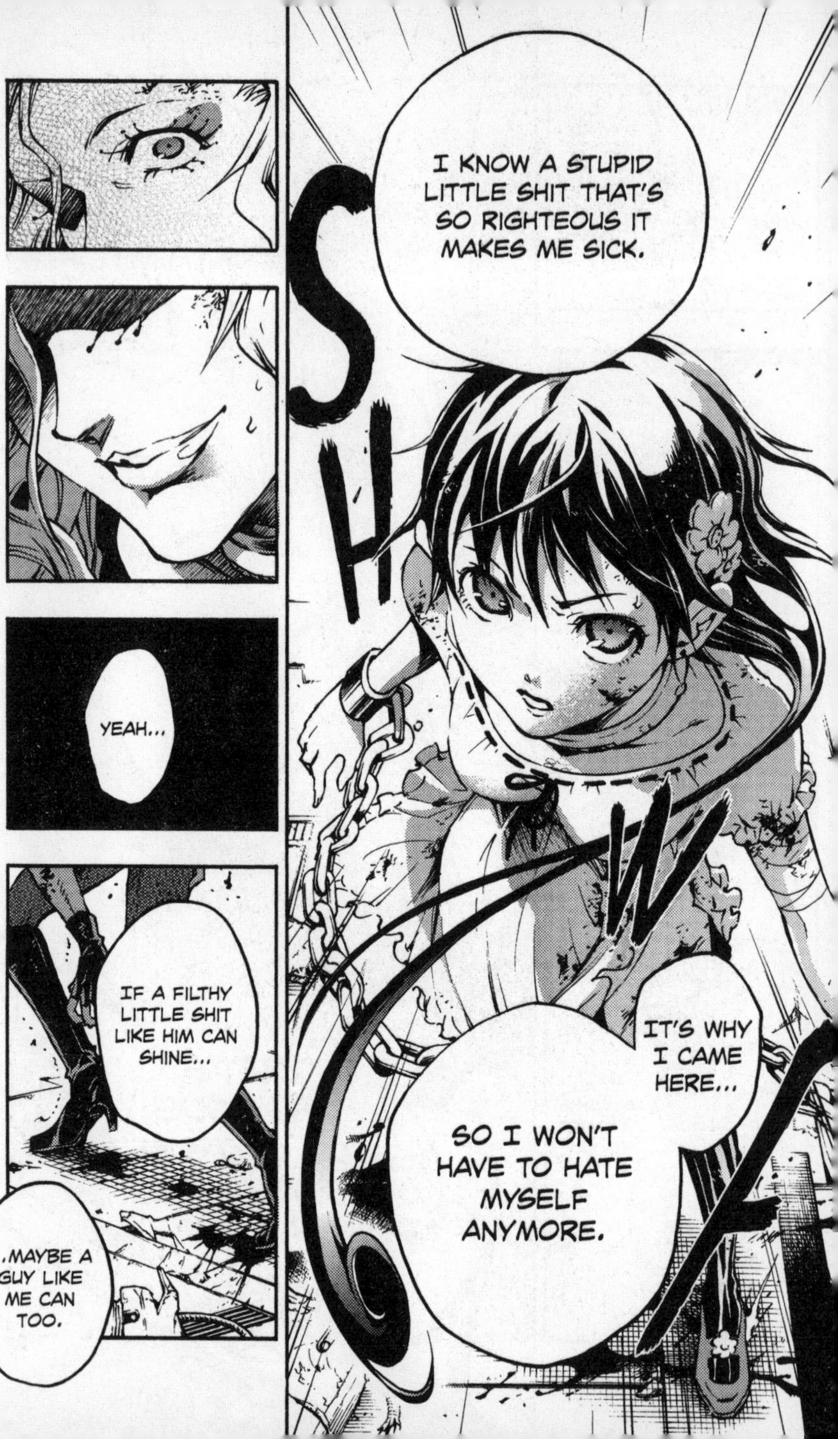
I KNOW A STUPID LITTLE SHIT THAT'S SO RIGHTEOUS IT MAKES ME SICK.
SHW
IT'S WHY I CAME HERE...
SO I WON'T HAVE TO HATE MYSELF ANYMORE.
YEAH...
IF A FILTHY LITTLE SHIT LIKE HIM CAN SHINE...
...MAYBE A GUY LIKE ME CAN TOO.

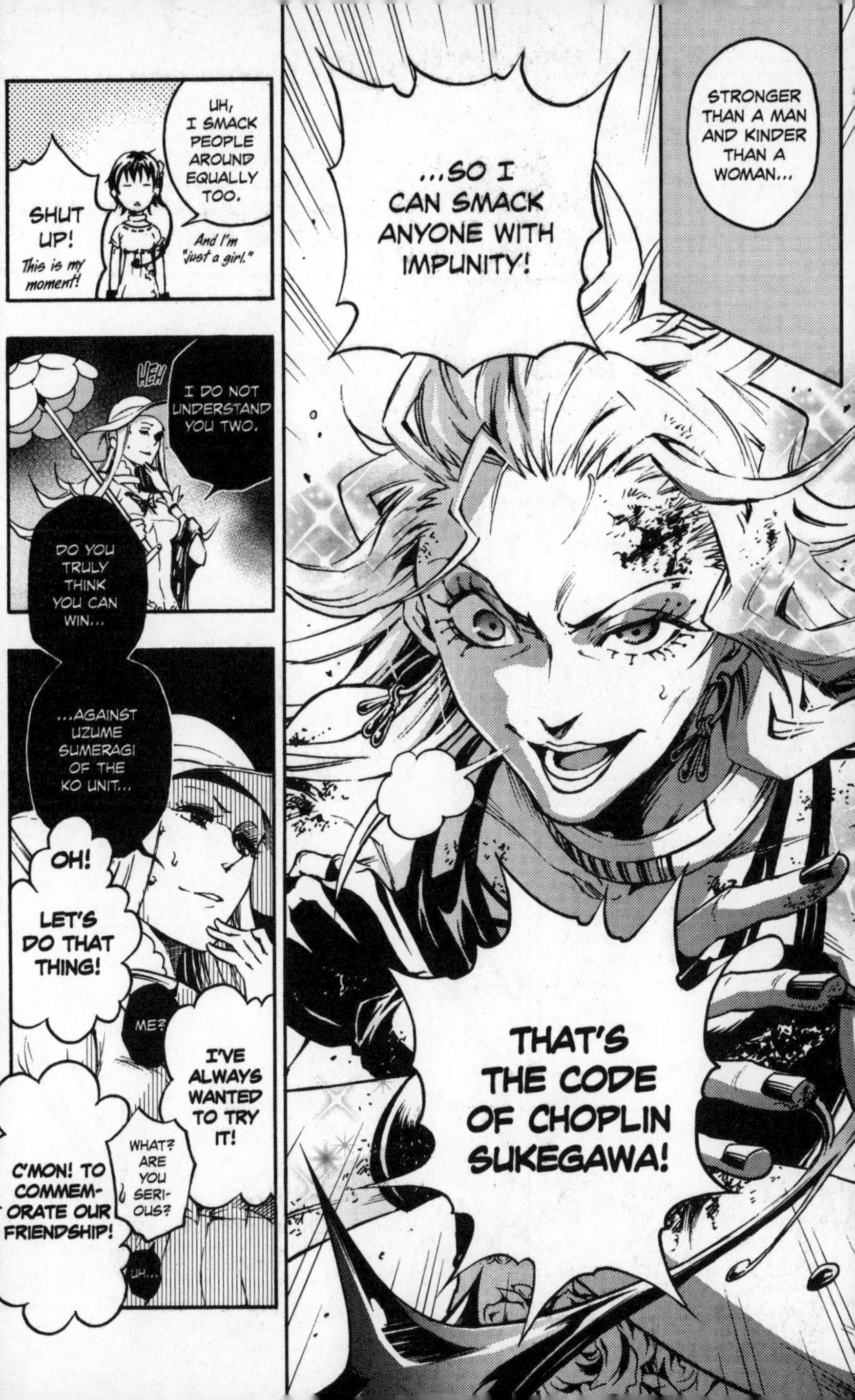
STRONGER THAN A MAN AND KINDER THAN A WOMAN...
...SO I CAN SMACK ANYONE WITH IMPUNITY!
THAT'S THE CODE OF CHOPLIN SUKEGAWA!
UH, I SMACK PEOPLE AROUND EQUALLY TOO.
And I'm "just a girl."
SHUT UP! This is my moment!
HEH
I DO NOT UNDERSTAND YOU TWO.
DO YOU TRULY THINK YOU CAN WIN...
...AGAINST UZUME SUMERAGI OF THE KO UNIT...
OH!
LET'S DO THAT THING!
I'VE ALWAYS WANTED TO TRY IT!
ME?
WHAT? ARE YOU SERIOUS?
C'MON! TO COMMEMORATE OUR FRIENDSHIP!
UH...

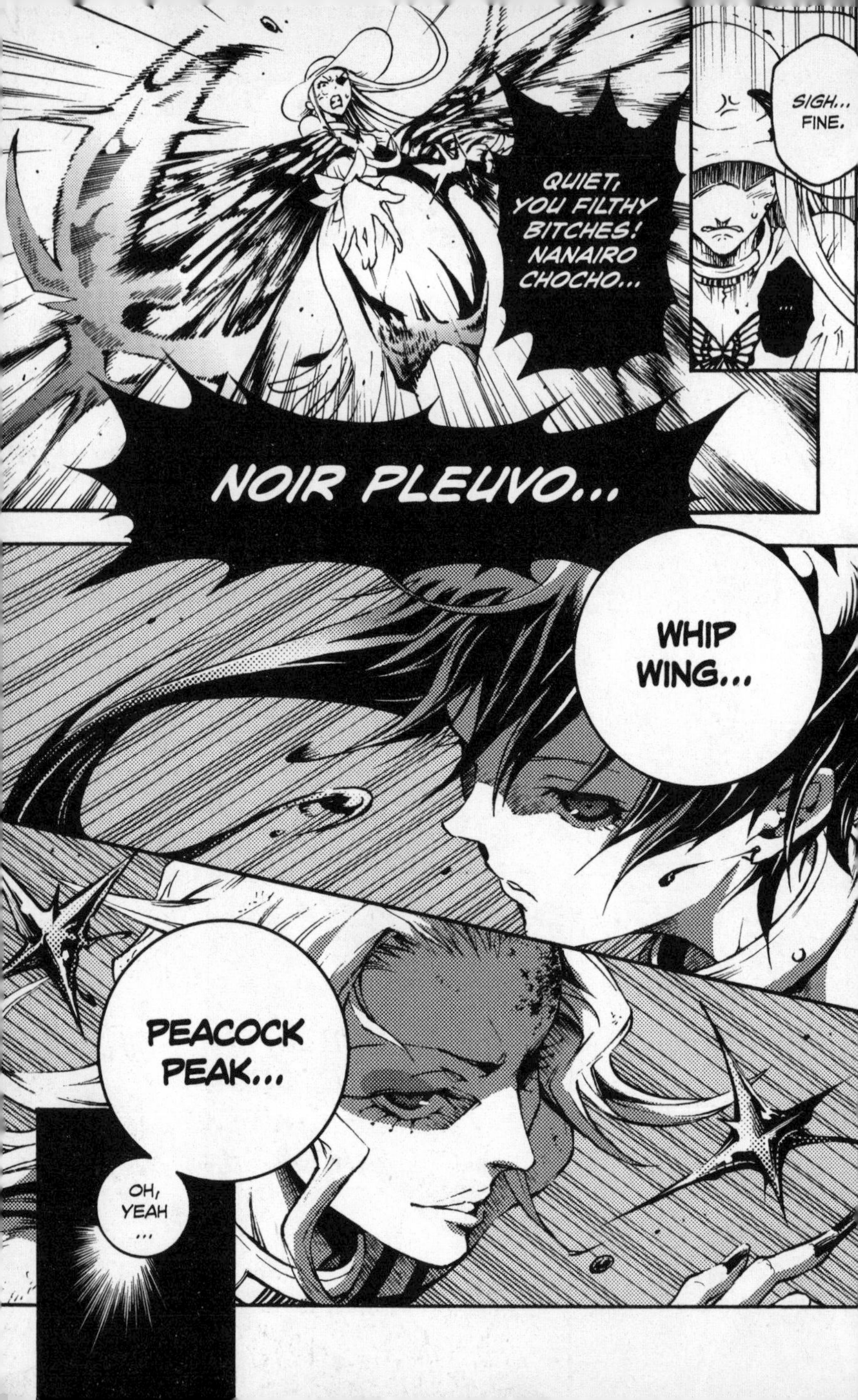
SIGH... FINE.
...
QUIET, YOU FILTHY BITCHES! NANAIRO CHOCHO...
NOIR PLEUVO...
WHIP WING...
PEACOCK PEAK...
OH, YEAH ...

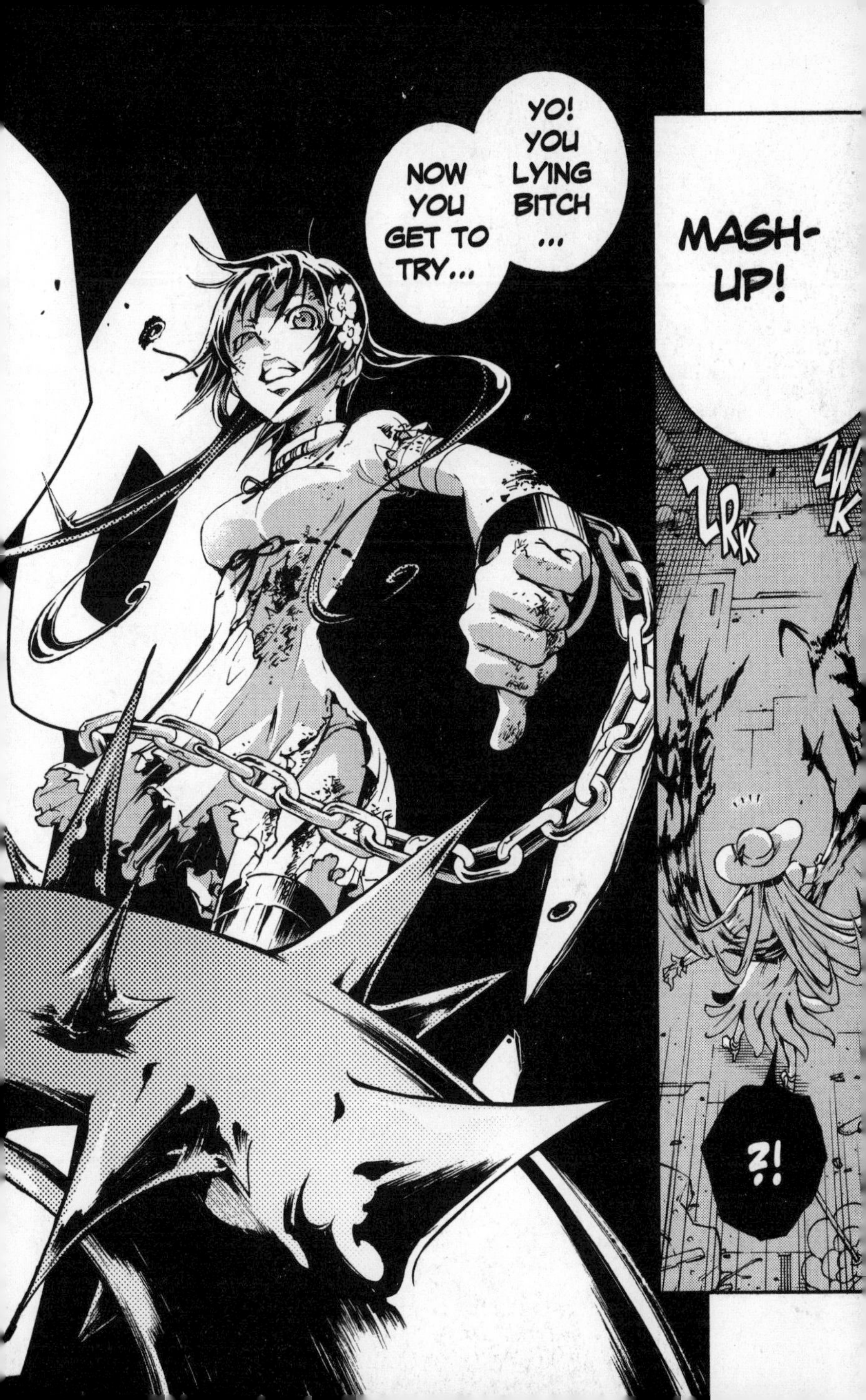
MASH-UP!
ZWK
ZRK
?!
YO! YOU LYING BITCH...
NOW YOU GET TO TRY...

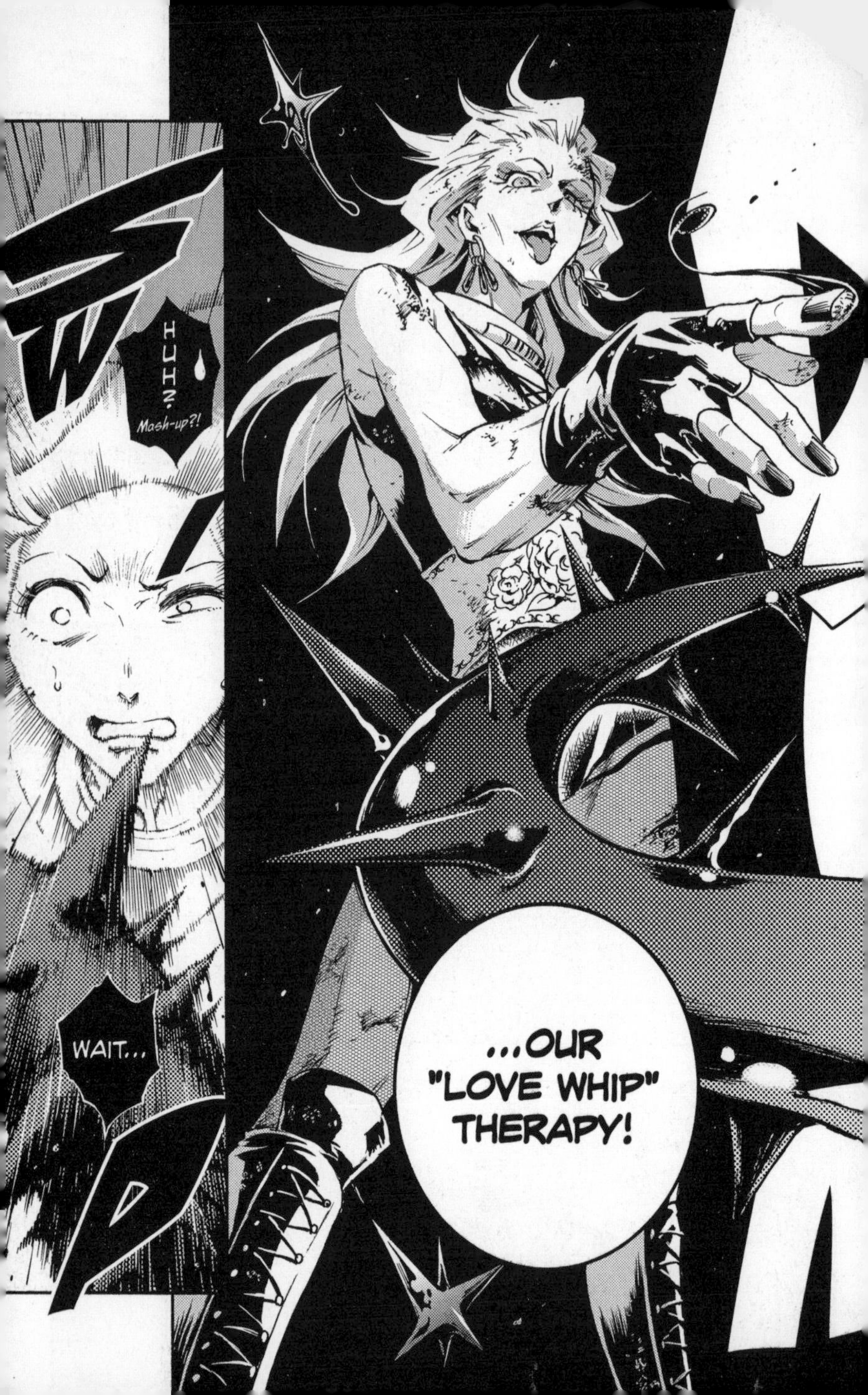
...OUR "LOVE WHIP" THERAPY!
HUH?
Mash-up?!
WAIT...

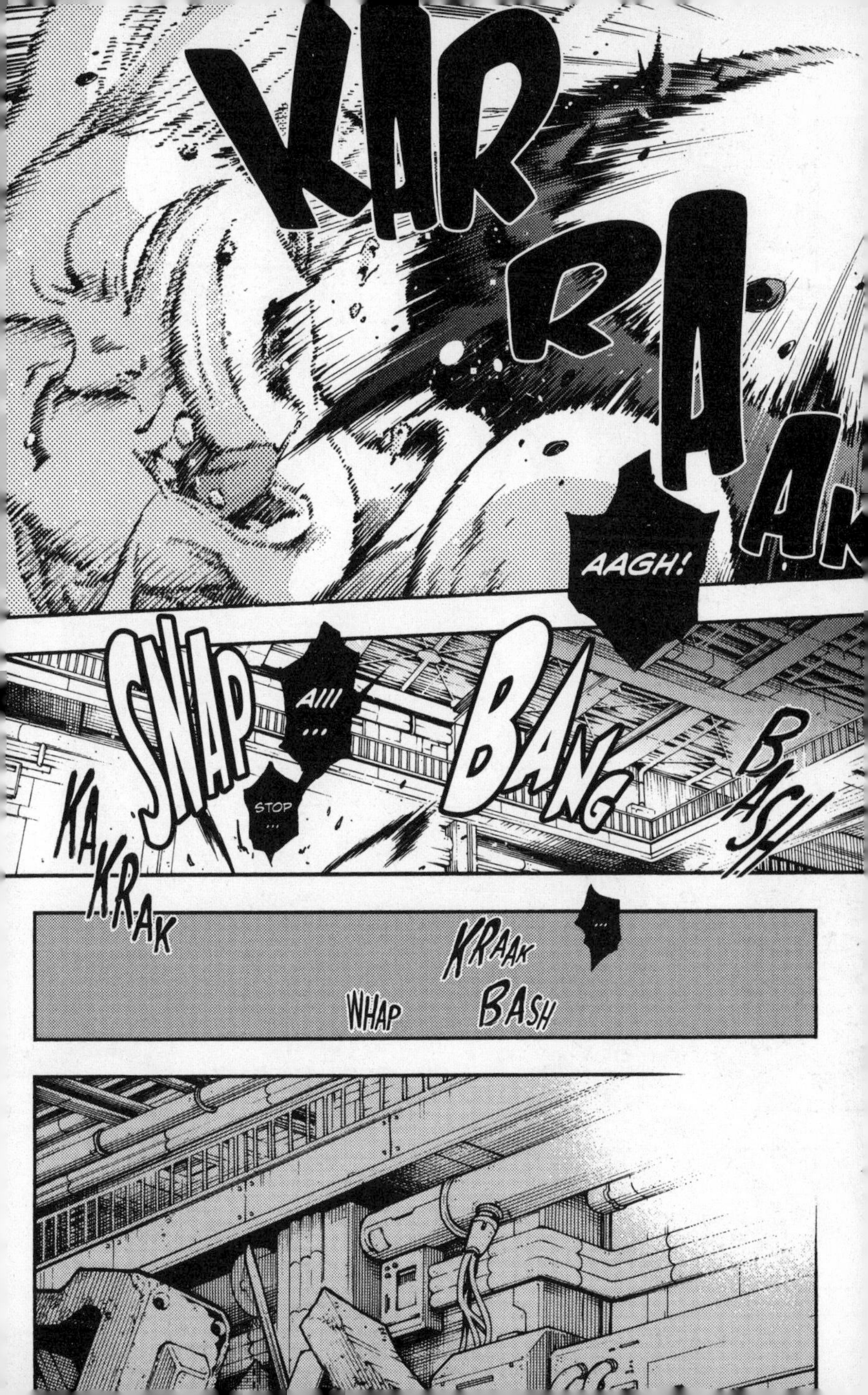
KARRAAAK
AAGH!
BASH
BANG
AIII...
STOP...
SNAP
KAKRAK
...
KRAAK
BASH
WHAP

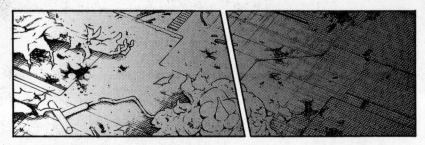

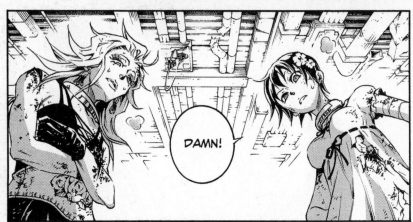

DAMN!

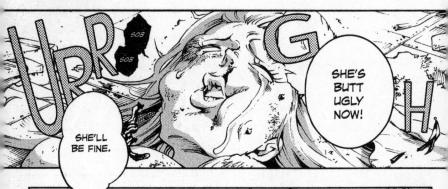

SOB
SOB

SHE'S BUTT UGLY NOW!

SHE'LL BE FINE.

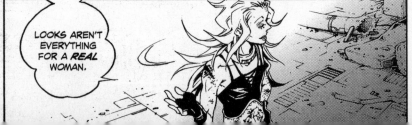

LOOKS AREN'T EVERYTHING FOR A *REAL* WOMAN.

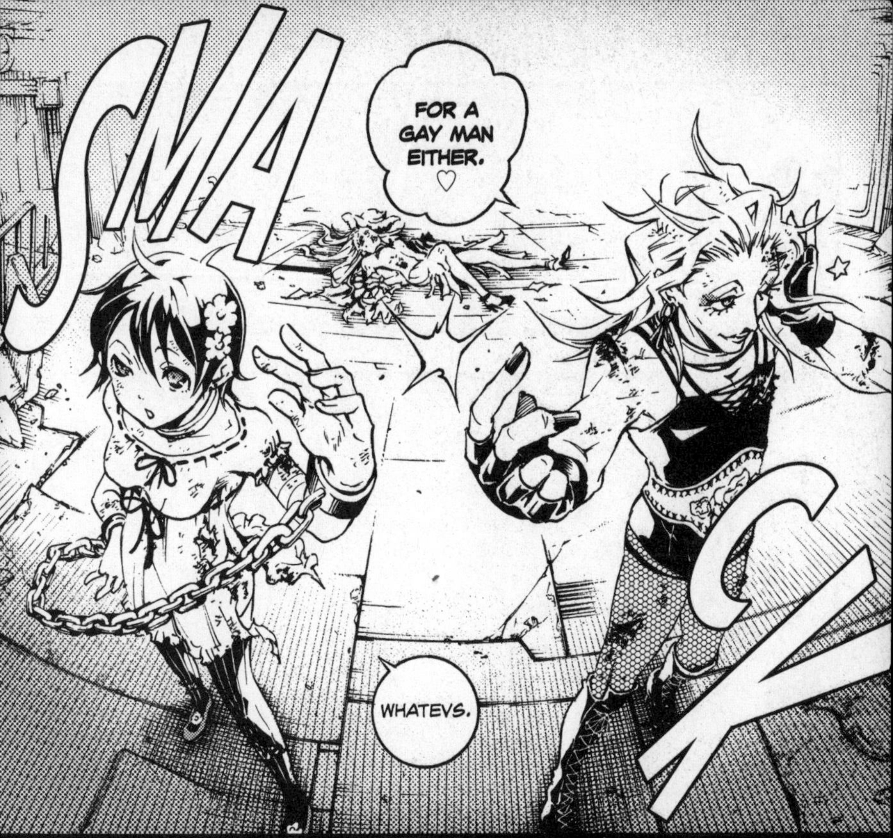
FOR A GAY MAN EITHER. ♡
SMACK
WHATEVS.

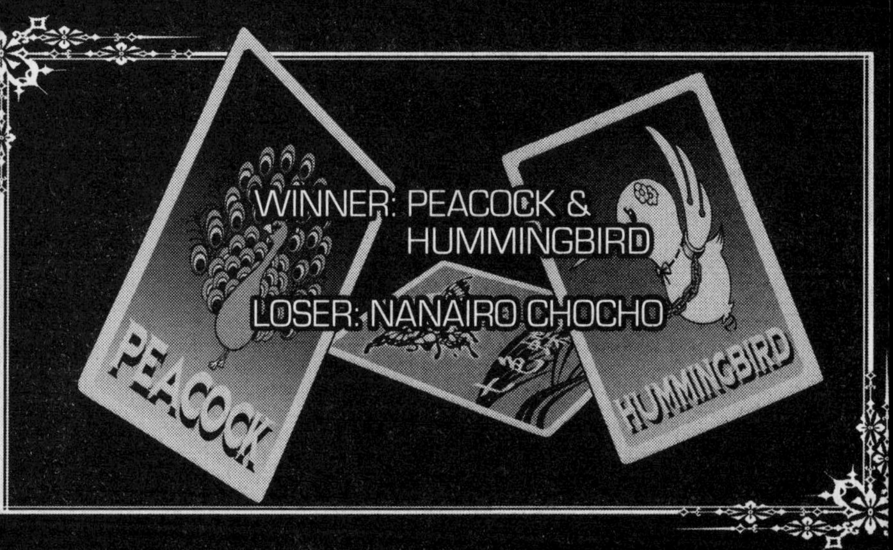
WINNER: PEACOCK & HUMMINGBIRD
LOSER: NANAIRO CHOCHO
PEACOCK
HUMMINGBIRD

DEADMAN WONDERLAND

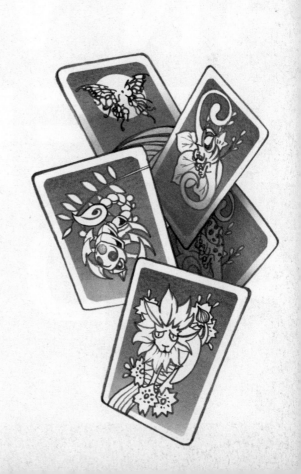

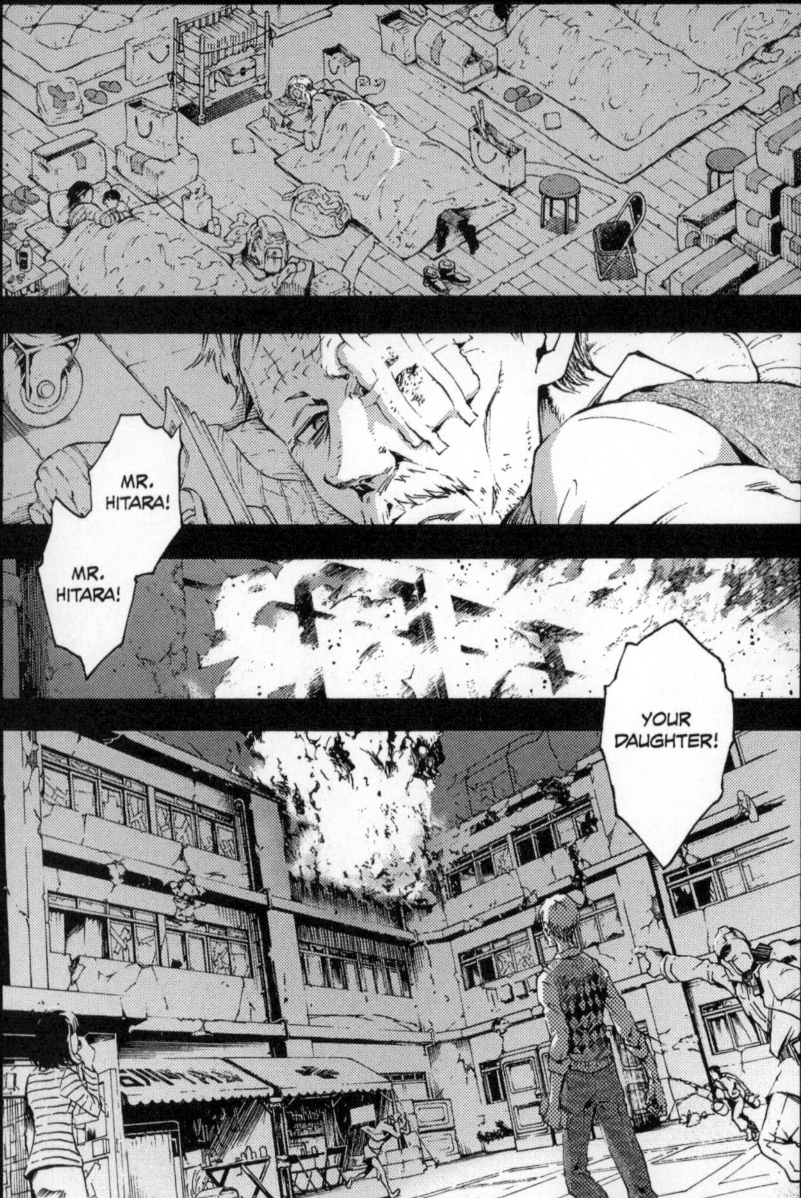
MR. HITARA!
MR. HITARA!
YOUR DAUGHTER!

YOUR PENANCE IS ETERNAL.

Your broken daughter
screams energetically
Cover your ears;
but you can still hear
Cover your eyes;
but she's still broken

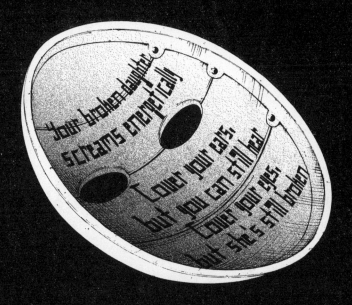

ENDLESS REPENTANCE YIELDS A LIFE WITH NO FORGIVENESS.

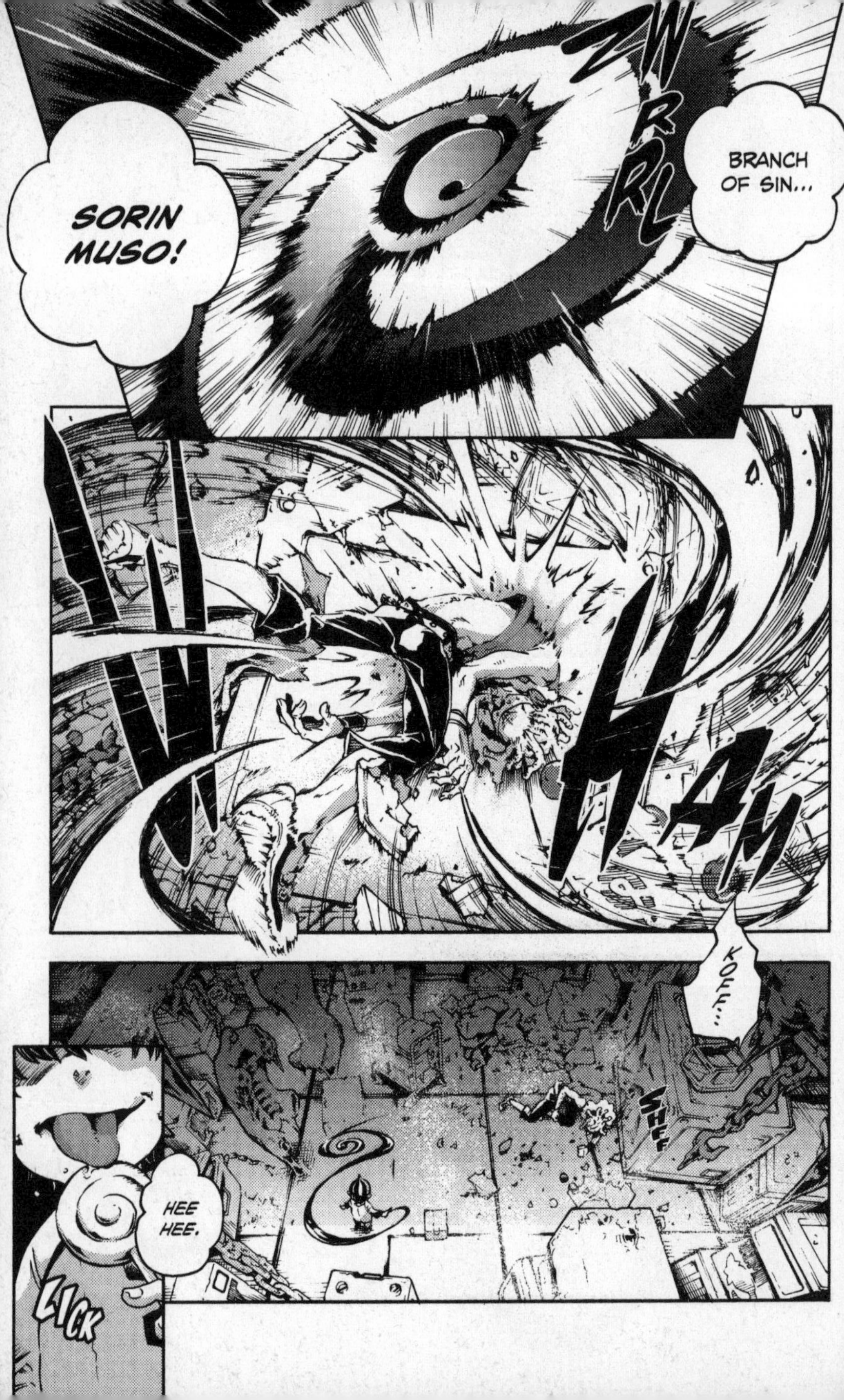
BRANCH OF SIN...
ZWRRL
SORIN MUSO!
WHAM
KOFF...
SHFF
HEE HEE.
LICK

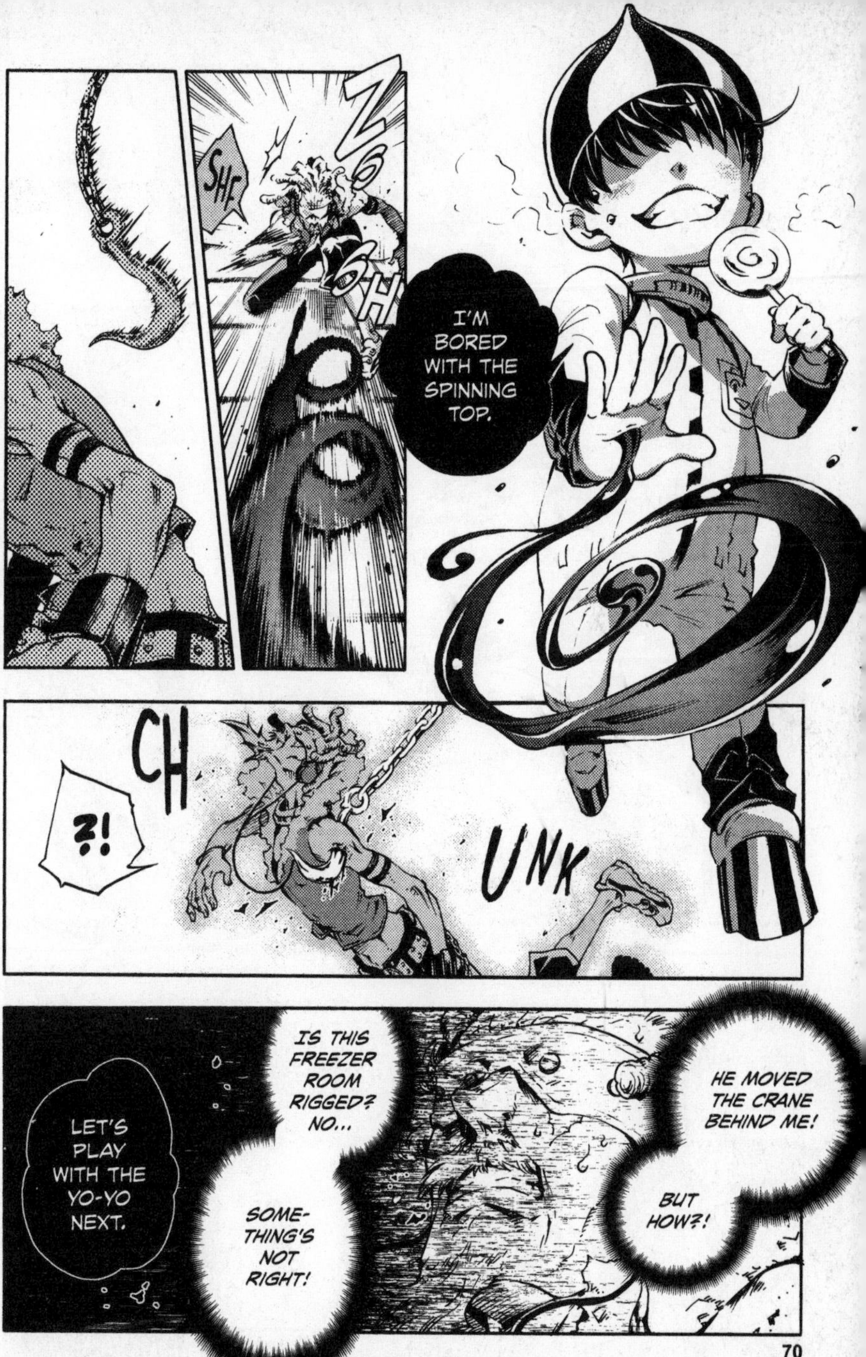
I'M BORED WITH THE SPINNING TOP.
SHF
ZOOSH
CHUNK
?!
HE MOVED THE CRANE BEHIND ME!
BUT HOW?!
IS THIS FREEZER ROOM RIGGED? NO...
SOME-THING'S NOT RIGHT!
LET'S PLAY WITH THE YO-YO NEXT.

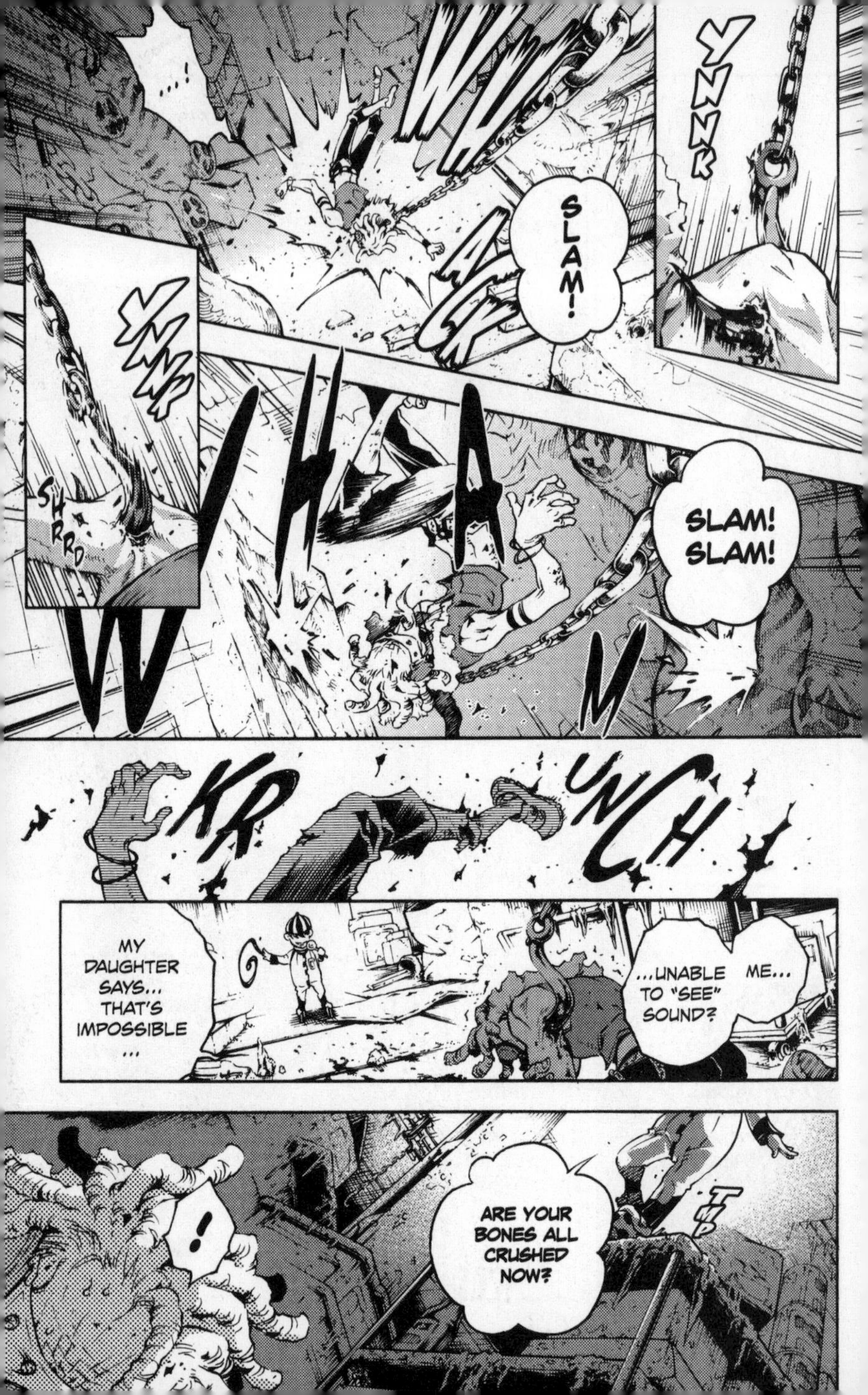
YNNNK
WHACK
SLAM!
...!
YNNNK
SHRRD
SLAM! SLAM!
WHAM
KRUNCH
ME...
...UNABLE TO "SEE" SOUND?
MY DAUGHTER SAYS... THAT'S IMPOSSIBLE...
TMP
ARE YOUR BONES ALL CRUSHED NOW?
!

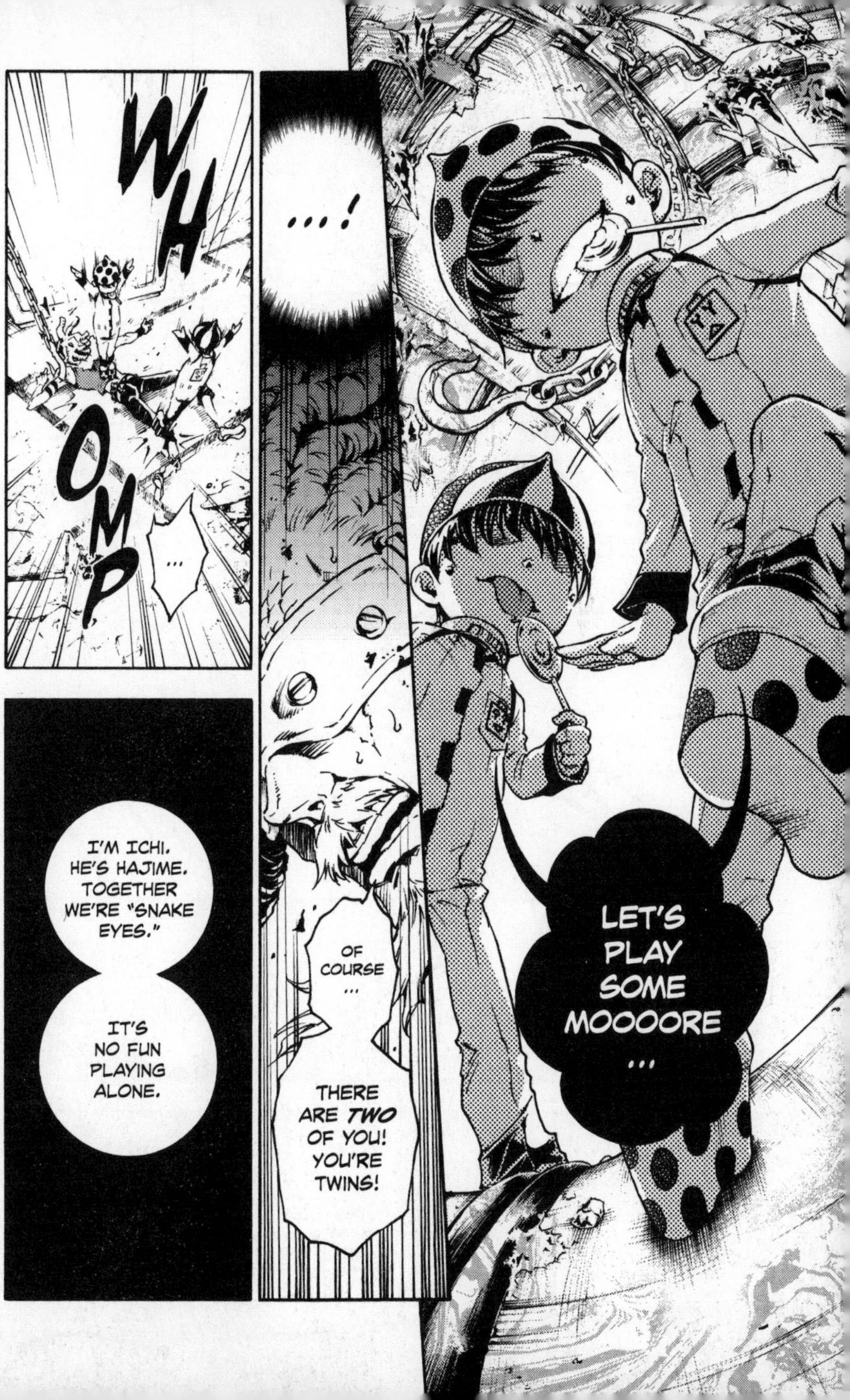
LET'S PLAY SOME MOOOORE ...
...!
OF COURSE ...
THERE ARE *TWO* OF YOU! YOU'RE TWINS!
WHOMP
...
I'M ICHI. HE'S HAJIME. TOGETHER WE'RE "SNAKE EYES."
IT'S NO FUN PLAYING ALONE.

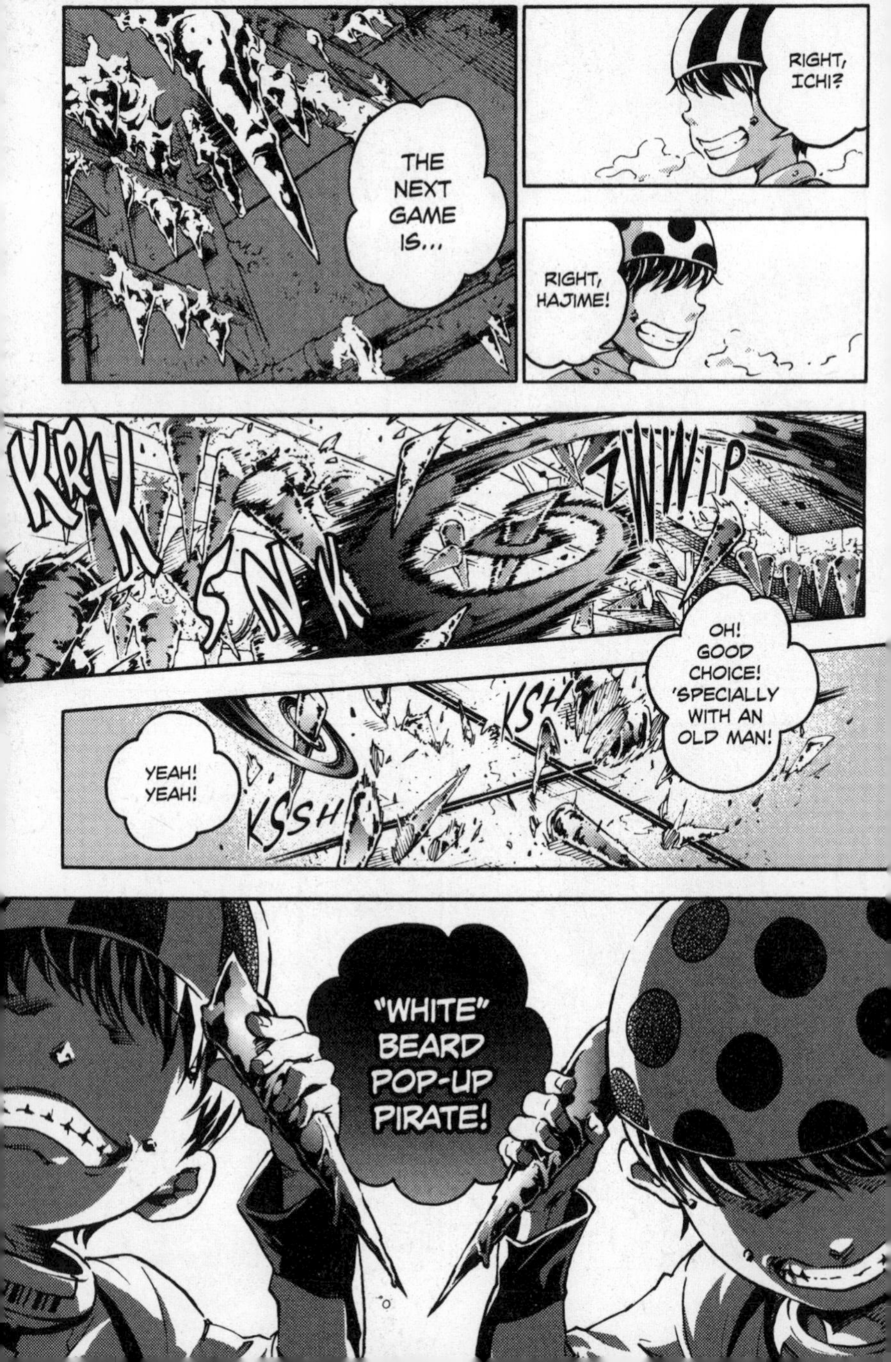
RIGHT, ICHI?
RIGHT, HAJIME!
THE NEXT GAME IS...
ZWWIP
KRK
SNK
OH! GOOD CHOICE! 'SPECIALLY WITH AN OLD MAN!
KSH
YEAH! YEAH!
KSSH
"WHITE" BEARD POP-UP PIRATE!

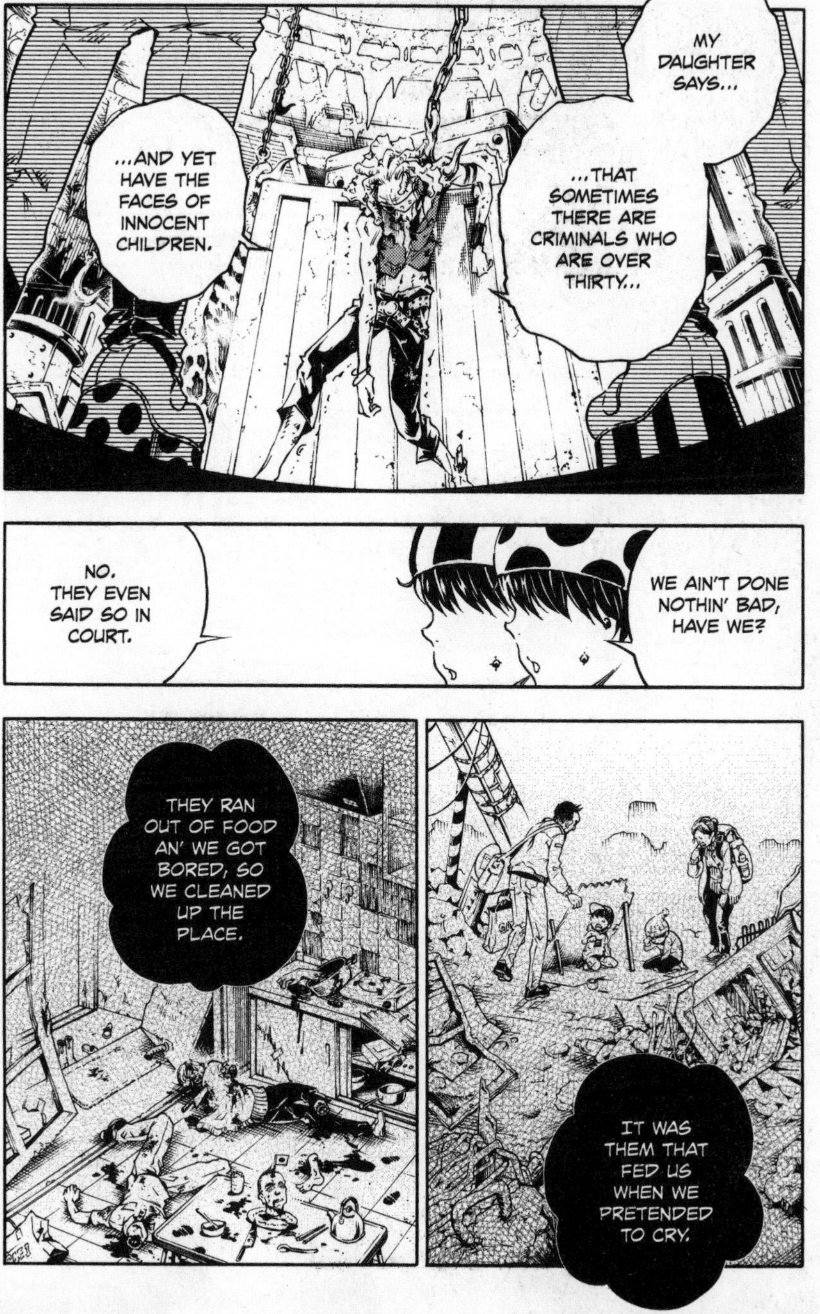
MY DAUGHTER SAYS...
...THAT SOMETIMES THERE ARE CRIMINALS WHO ARE OVER THIRTY...
...AND YET HAVE THE FACES OF INNOCENT CHILDREN.
WE AIN'T DONE NOTHIN' BAD, HAVE WE?
NO. THEY EVEN SAID SO IN COURT.
IT WAS THEM THAT FED US WHEN WE PRETENDED TO CRY.
THEY RAN OUT OF FOOD AN' WE GOT BORED, SO WE CLEANED UP THE PLACE.

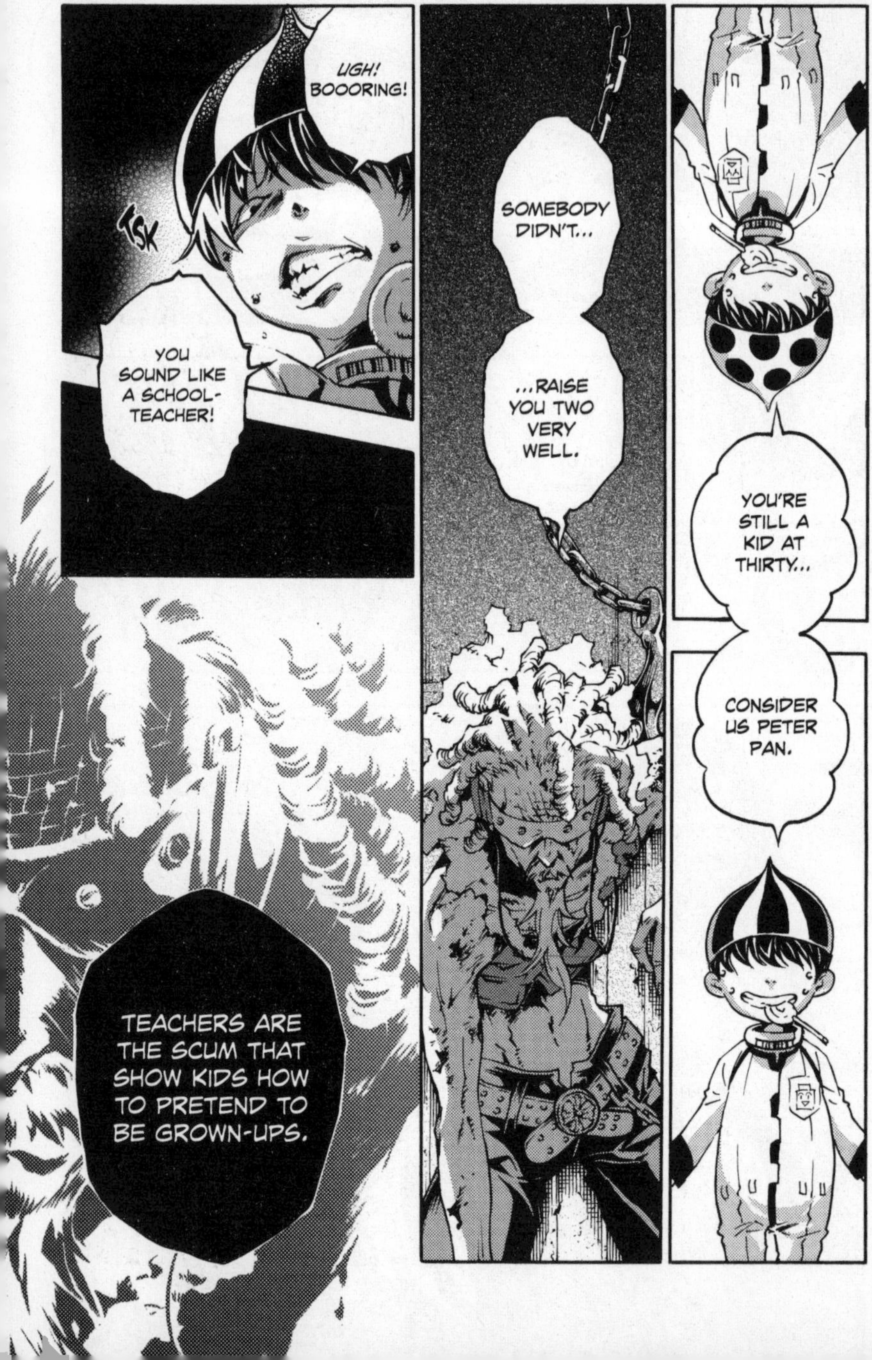
YOU'RE STILL A KID AT THIRTY...
CONSIDER US PETER PAN.
SOMEBODY DIDN'T...
...RAISE YOU TWO VERY WELL.
UGH! BOOORING!
TSK
YOU SOUND LIKE A SCHOOL-TEACHER!
TEACHERS ARE THE SCUM THAT SHOW KIDS HOW TO PRETEND TO BE GROWN-UPS.

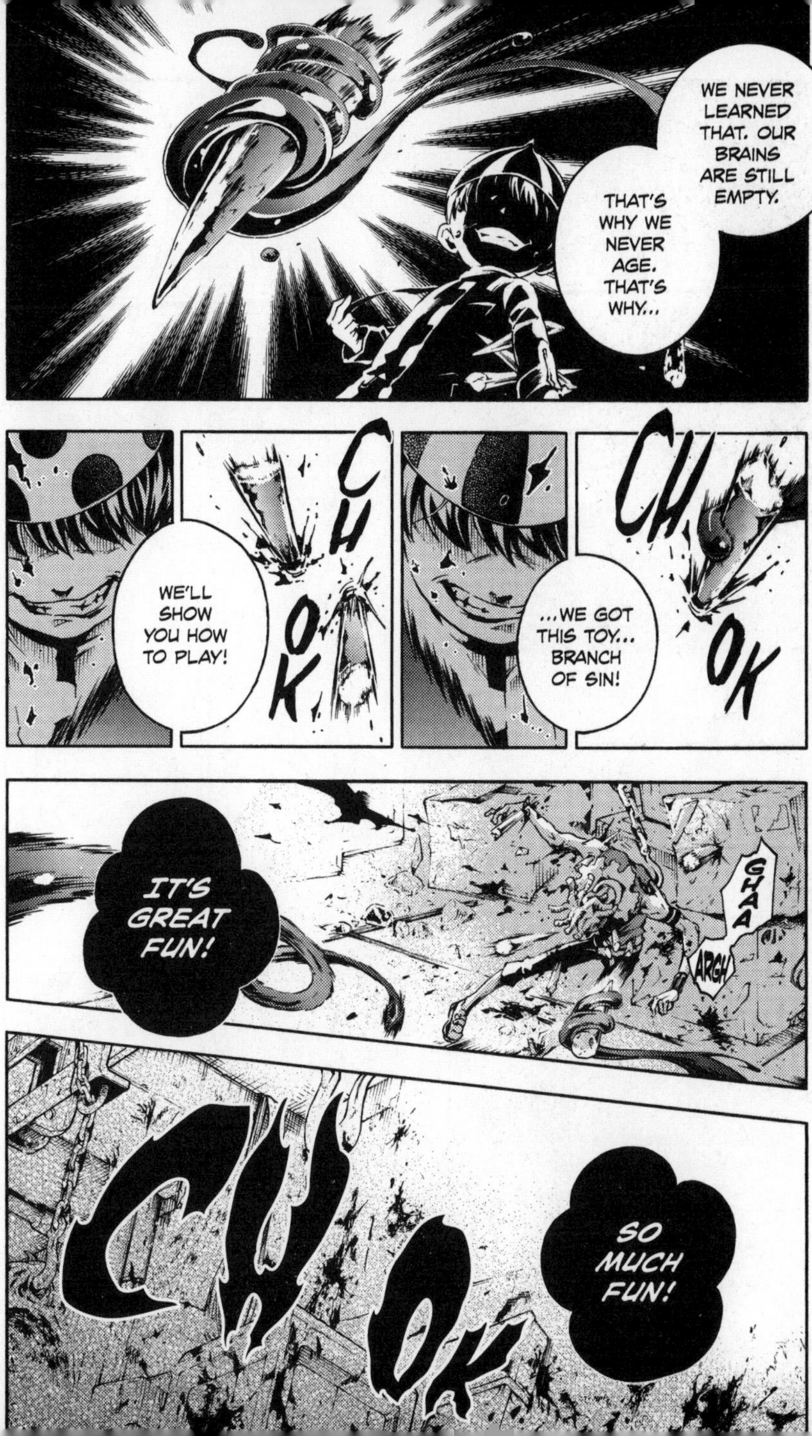
WE NEVER LEARNED THAT. OUR BRAINS ARE STILL EMPTY.
THAT'S WHY WE NEVER AGE. THAT'S WHY...
CHOK
...WE GOT THIS TOY... BRANCH OF SIN!
CHOK
WE'LL SHOW YOU HOW TO PLAY!
GHAA
ARGH
IT'S GREAT FUN!
SO MUCH FUN!
CHOK

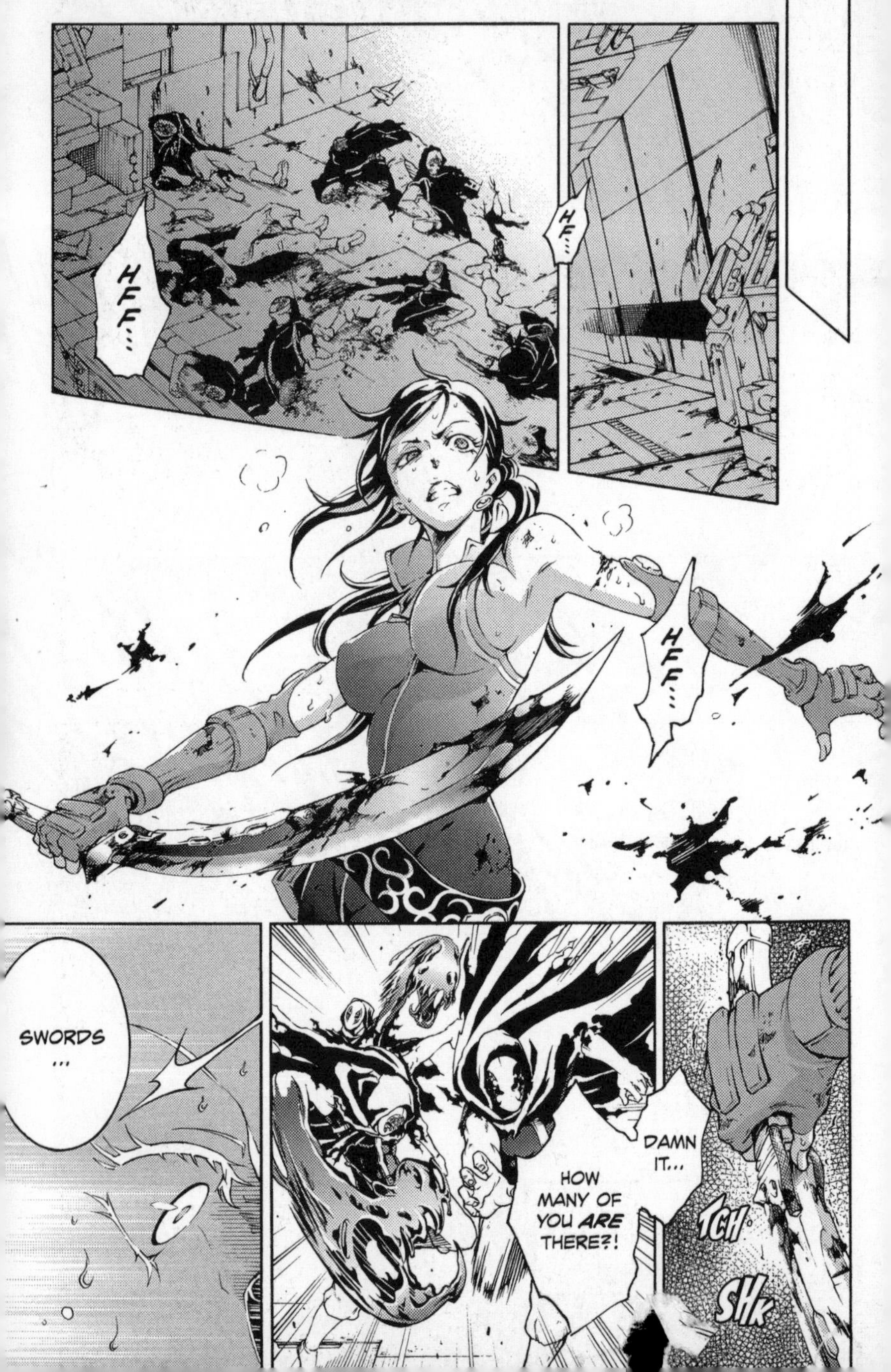
HF...
HFF...
HFF...
TCH
SHK
DAMN IT...
HOW MANY OF YOU *ARE* THERE?!
SWORDS ...

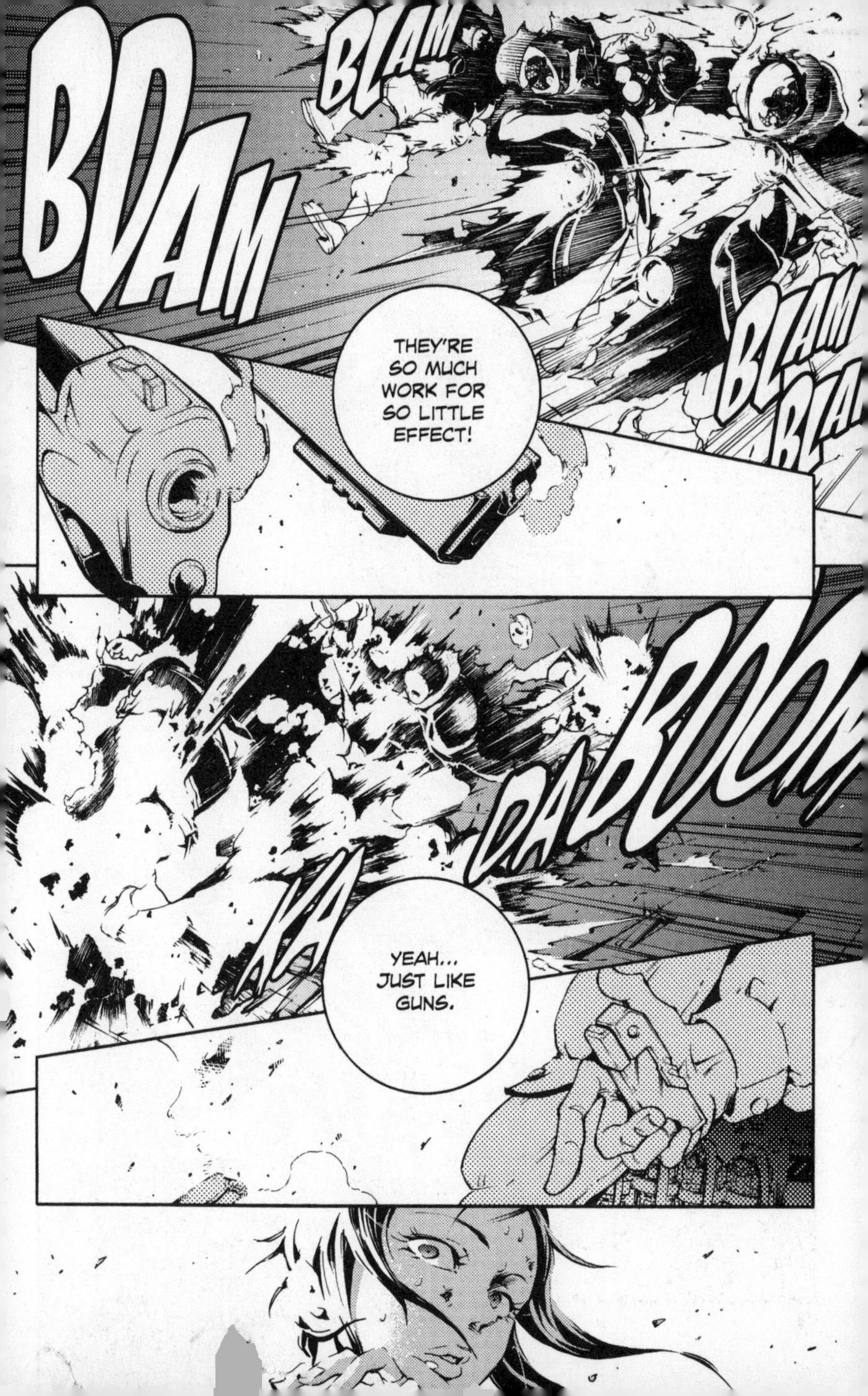
BLAM
BLAM
THEY'RE SO MUCH WORK FOR SO LITTLE EFFECT!
YEAH... JUST LIKE GUNS.

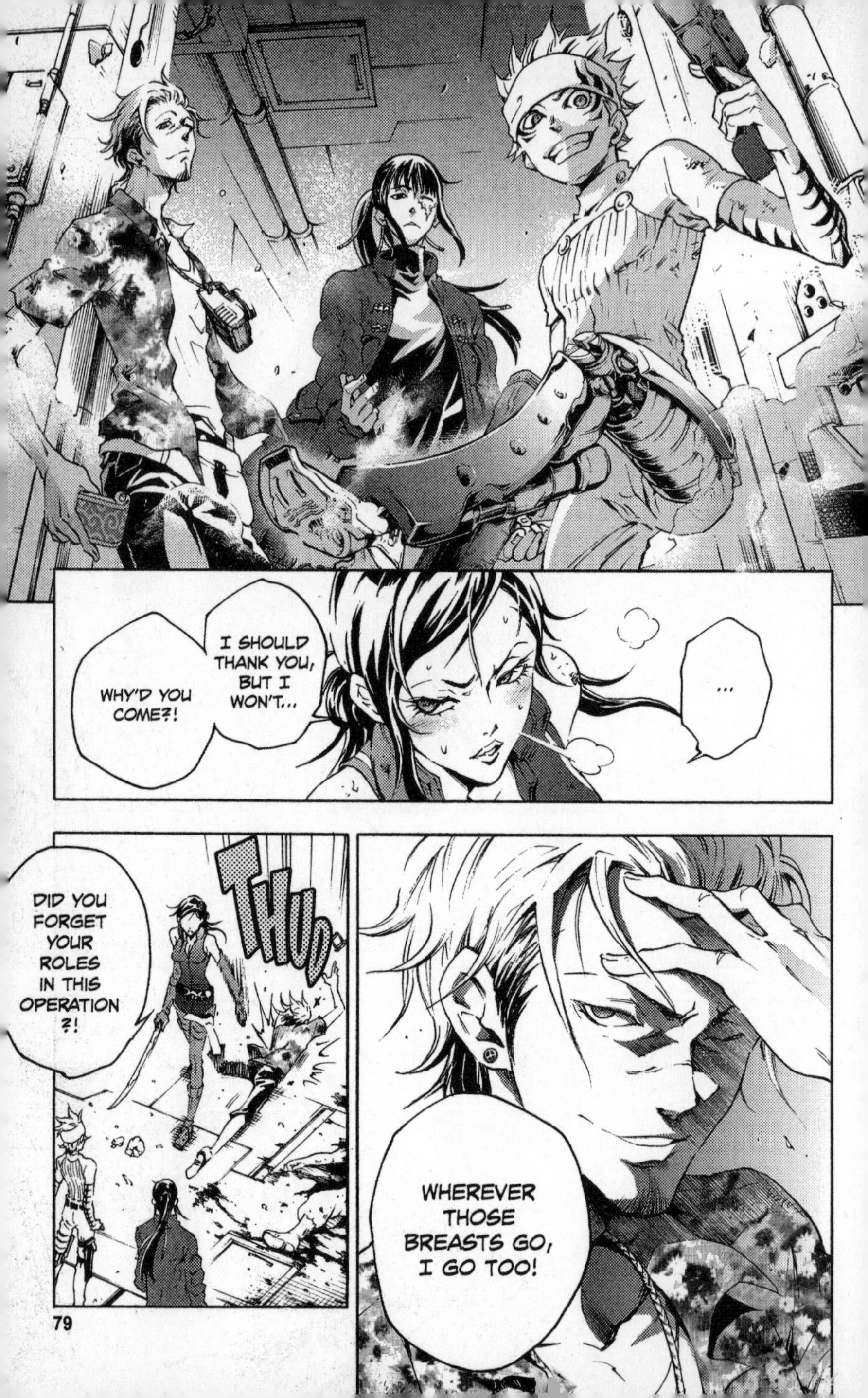
...
I SHOULD THANK YOU, BUT I WON'T...
WHY'D YOU COME?!
WHEREVER THOSE BREASTS GO, I GO TOO!
THUD
DID YOU FORGET YOUR ROLES IN THIS OPERATION?!

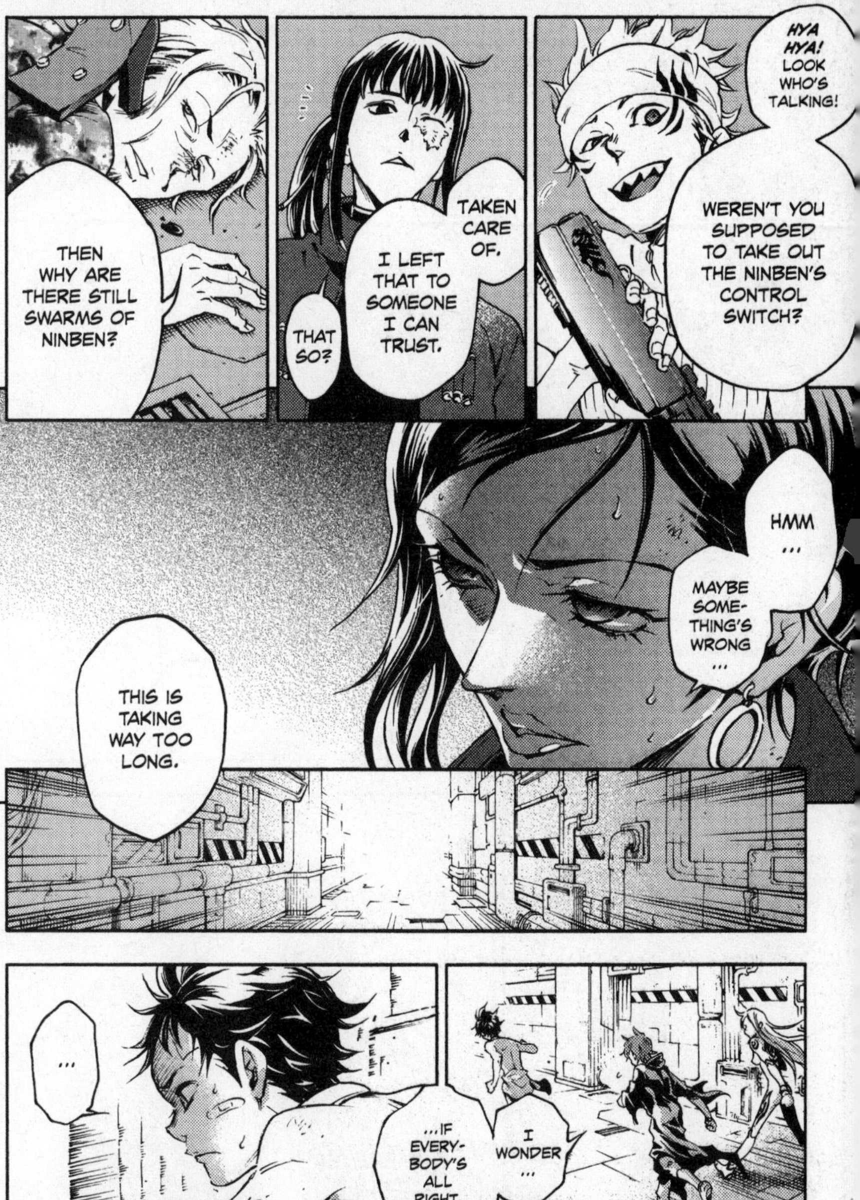
HYA HYA! LOOK WHO'S TALKING!
WEREN'T YOU SUPPOSED TO TAKE OUT THE NINBEN'S CONTROL SWITCH?
TAKEN CARE OF.
I LEFT THAT TO SOMEONE I CAN TRUST.
THAT SO?
THEN WHY ARE THERE STILL SWARMS OF NINBEN?
HMM ...
MAYBE SOME-THING'S WRONG ...
THIS IS TAKING WAY TOO LONG.
I WONDER ...
...IF EVERY-BODY'S ALL RIGHT.
...

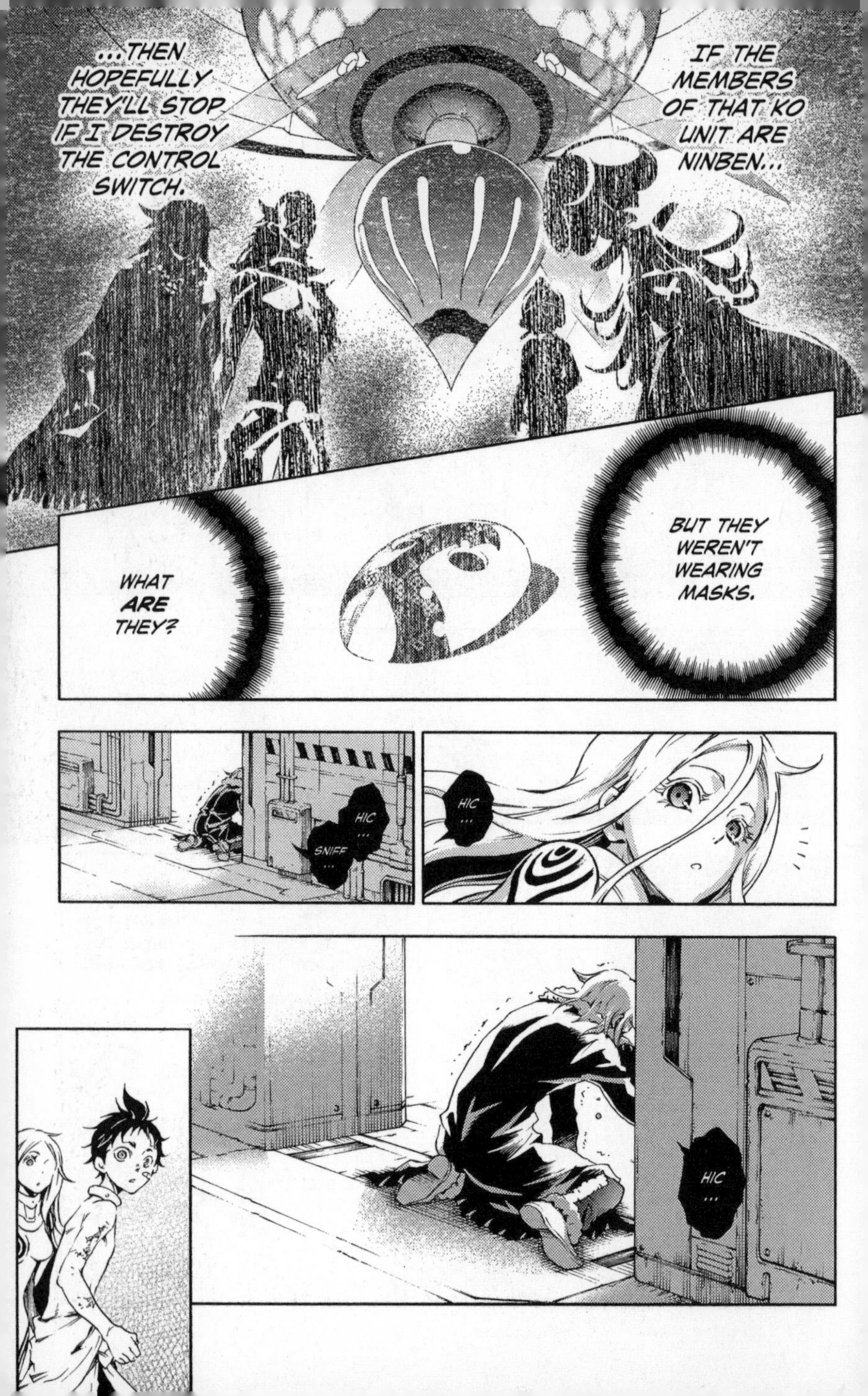
IF THE MEMBERS OF THAT KO UNIT ARE NINBEN...
...THEN HOPEFULLY THEY'LL STOP IF I DESTROY THE CONTROL SWITCH.
BUT THEY WEREN'T WEARING MASKS.
WHAT ARE THEY?
HIC ...
HIC ...
SNIFF ...
HIC ...

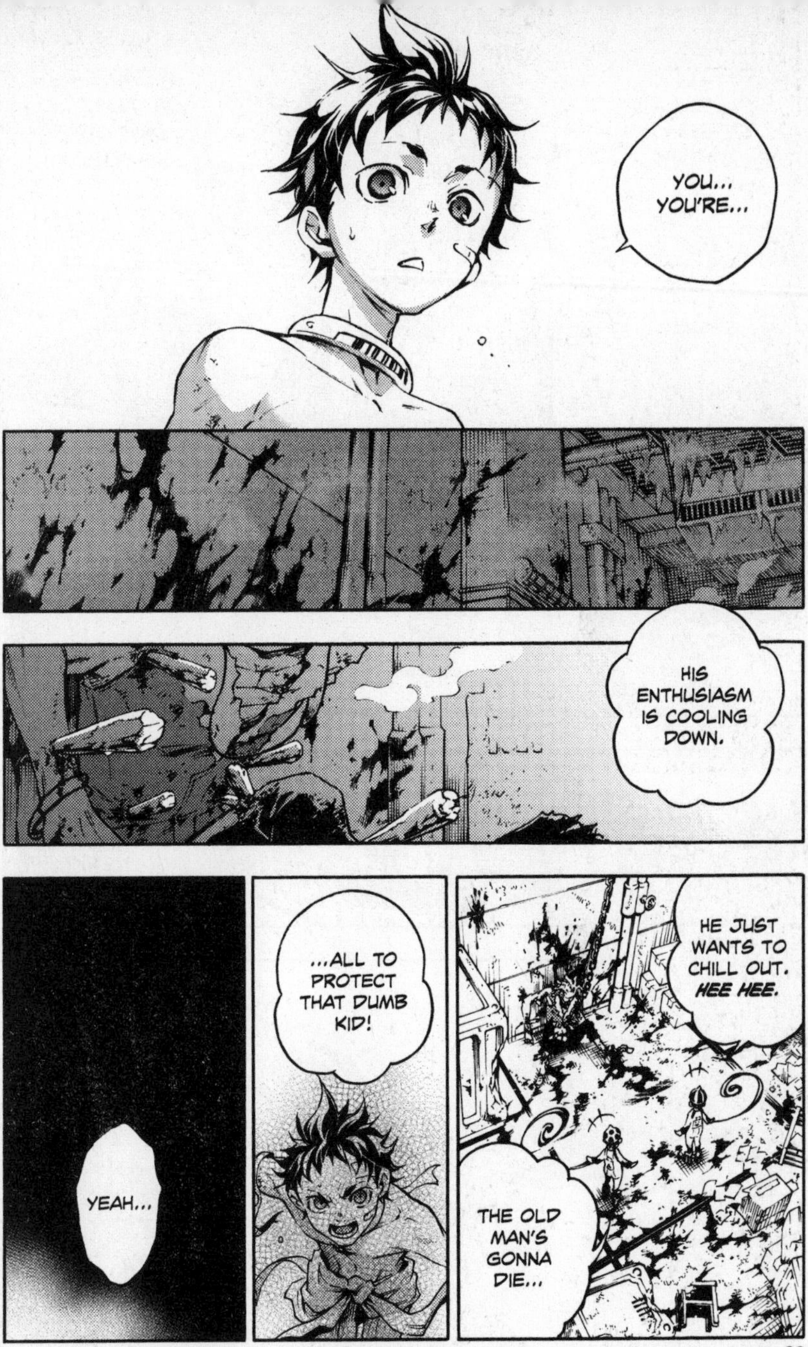
YOU... YOU'RE...
HIS ENTHUSIASM IS COOLING DOWN.
HE JUST WANTS TO CHILL OUT. *HEE HEE.*
THE OLD MAN'S GONNA DIE...
...ALL TO PROTECT THAT DUMB KID!
YEAH...

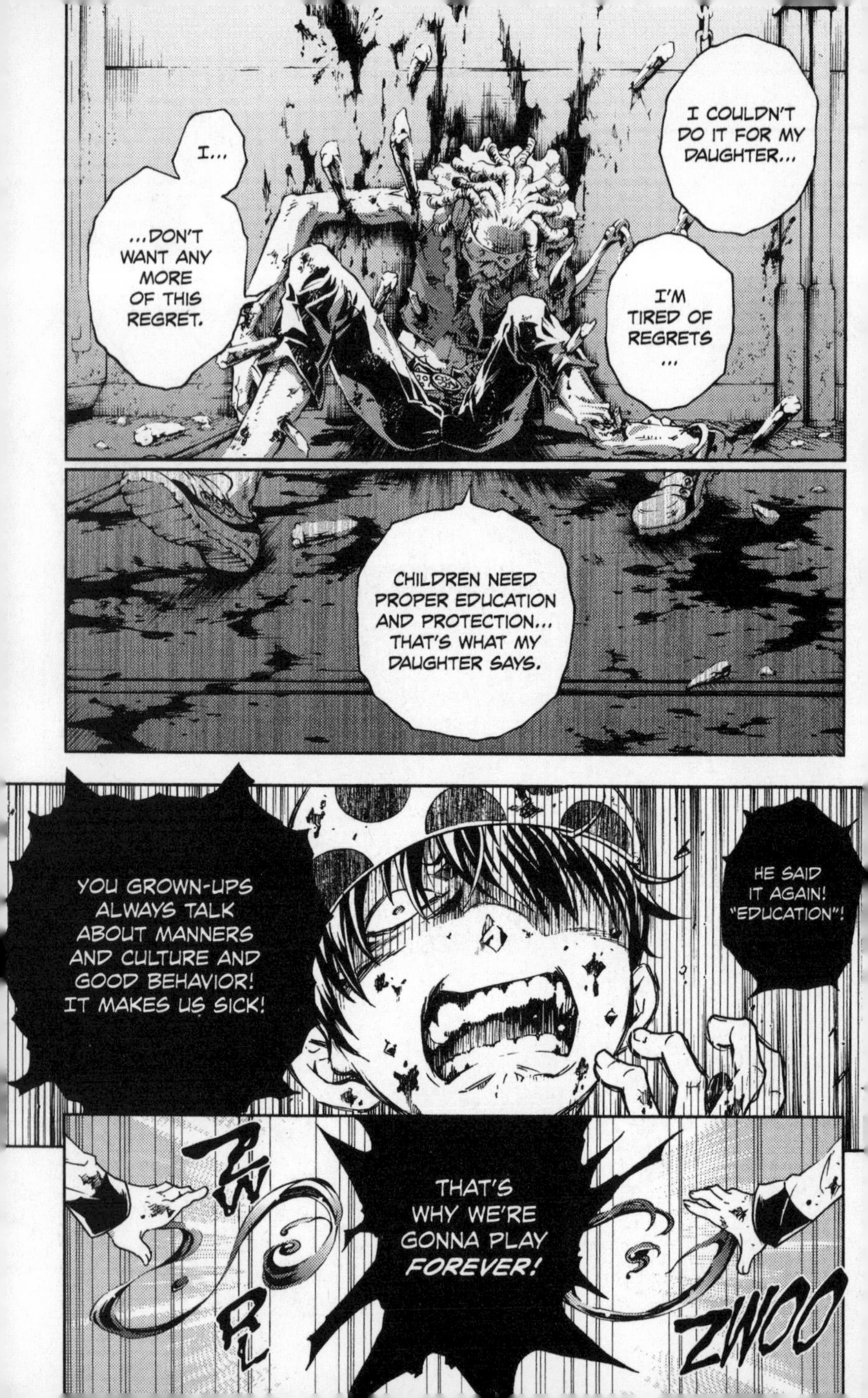
I COULDN'T DO IT FOR MY DAUGHTER...
I'M TIRED OF REGRETS ...
I...
...DON'T WANT ANY MORE OF THIS REGRET.
CHILDREN NEED PROPER EDUCATION AND PROTECTION... THAT'S WHAT MY DAUGHTER SAYS.
HE SAID IT AGAIN! "EDUCATION"!
YOU GROWN-UPS ALWAYS TALK ABOUT MANNERS AND CULTURE AND GOOD BEHAVIOR! IT MAKES US SICK!
ZWOO
THAT'S WHY WE'RE GONNA PLAY *FOREVER!*
ZWRL

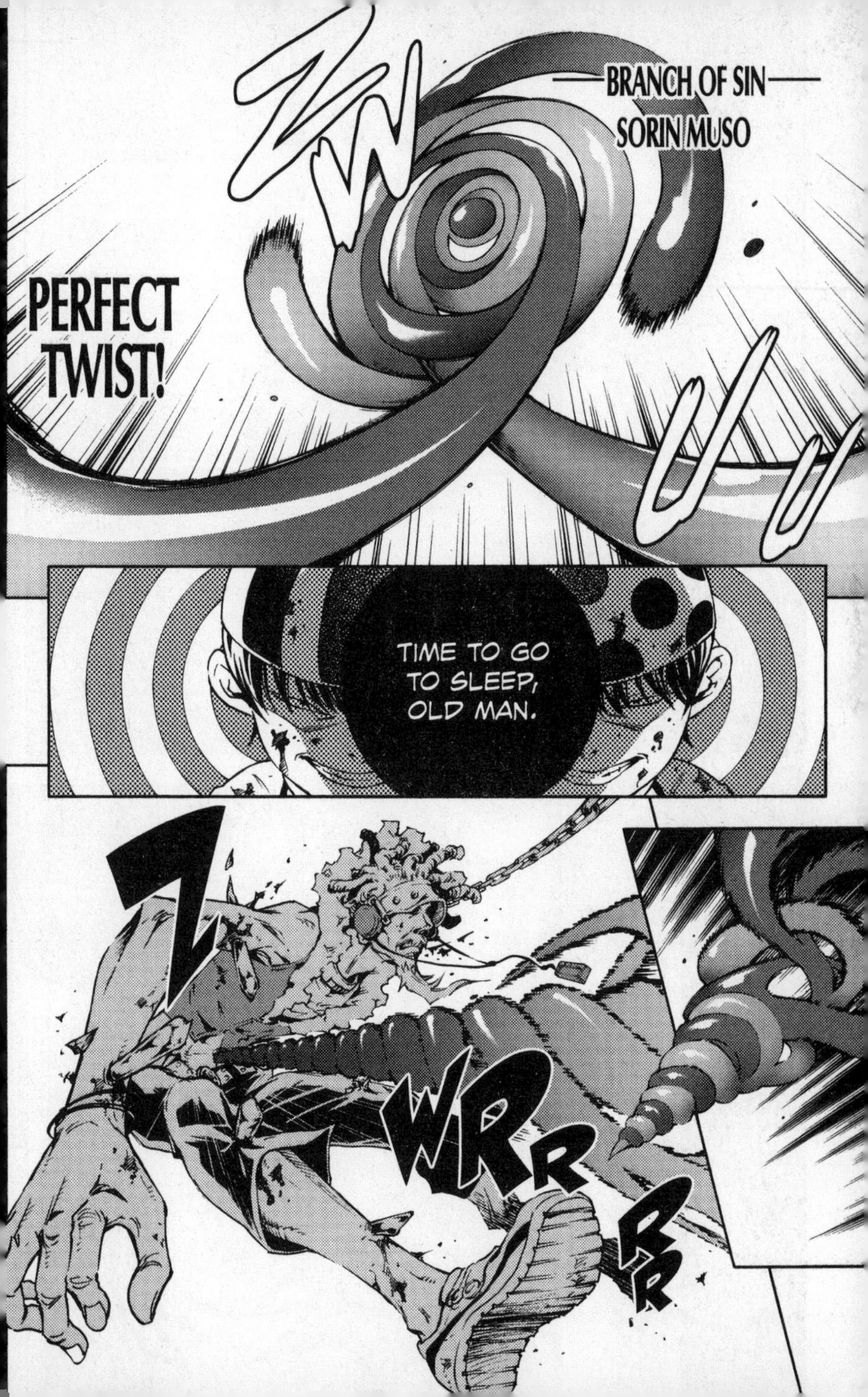
ZWW
—BRANCH OF SIN—
SORIN MUSO
PERFECT TWIST!
TIME TO GO TO SLEEP, OLD MAN.
Z
WRRRR

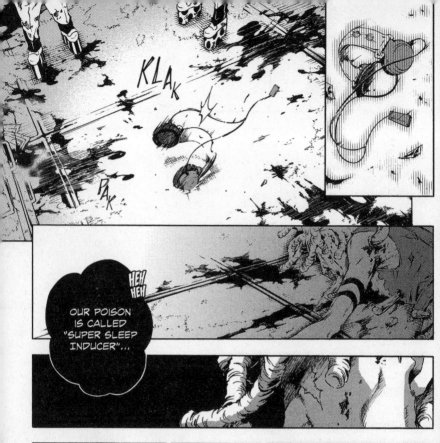

KLAK

PLAK

HEH HEH

OUR POISON IS CALLED "SUPER SLEEP INDUCER"...

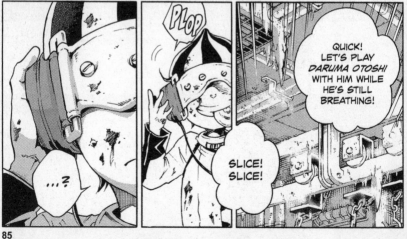

...Z

PLOP

QUICK! LET'S PLAY *DARUMA OTOSHI* WITH HIM WHILE HE'S STILL BREATHING!

SLICE! SLICE!

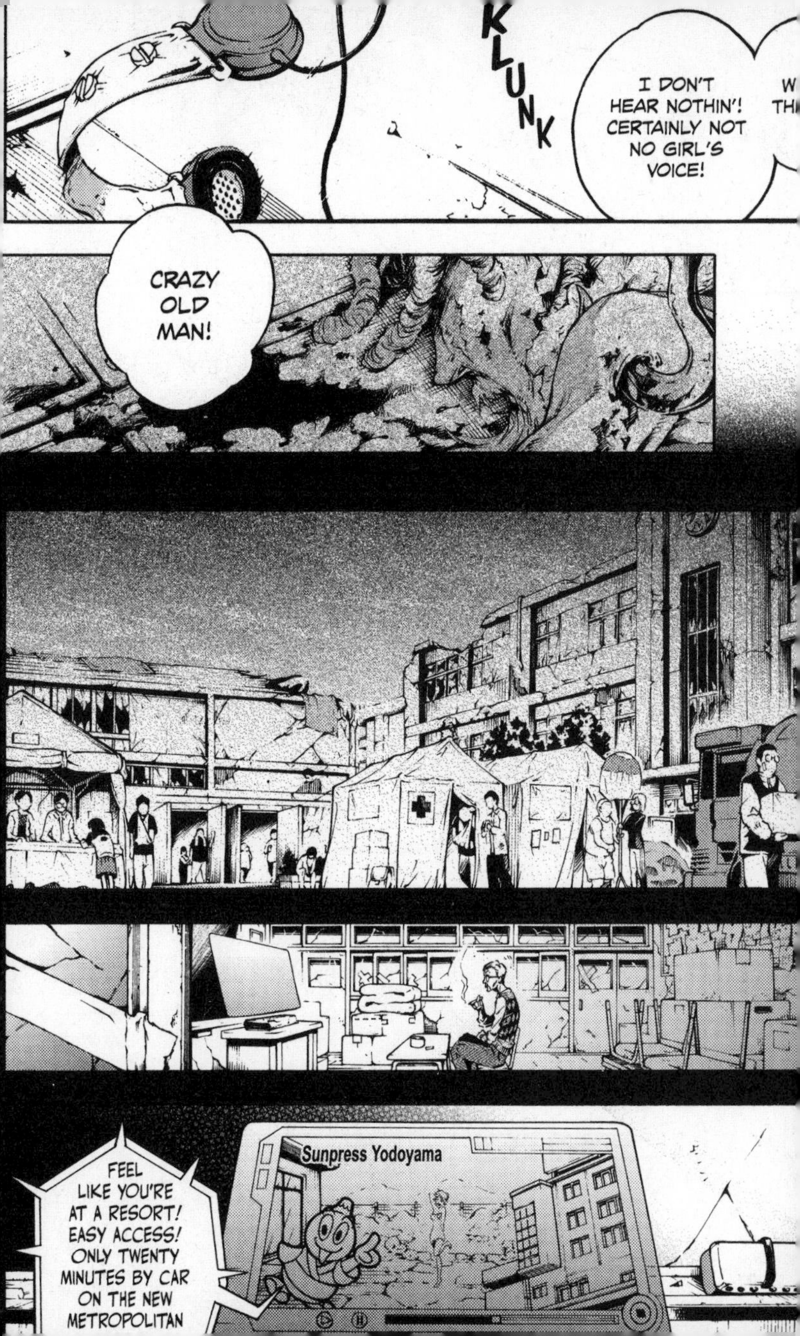
I DON'T HEAR NOTHIN'! CERTAINLY NOT NO GIRL'S VOICE!
KLUNK
CRAZY OLD MAN!
Sunpress Yodoyama
FEEL LIKE YOU'RE AT A RESORT! EASY ACCESS! ONLY TWENTY MINUTES BY CAR ON THE NEW METROPOLITAN

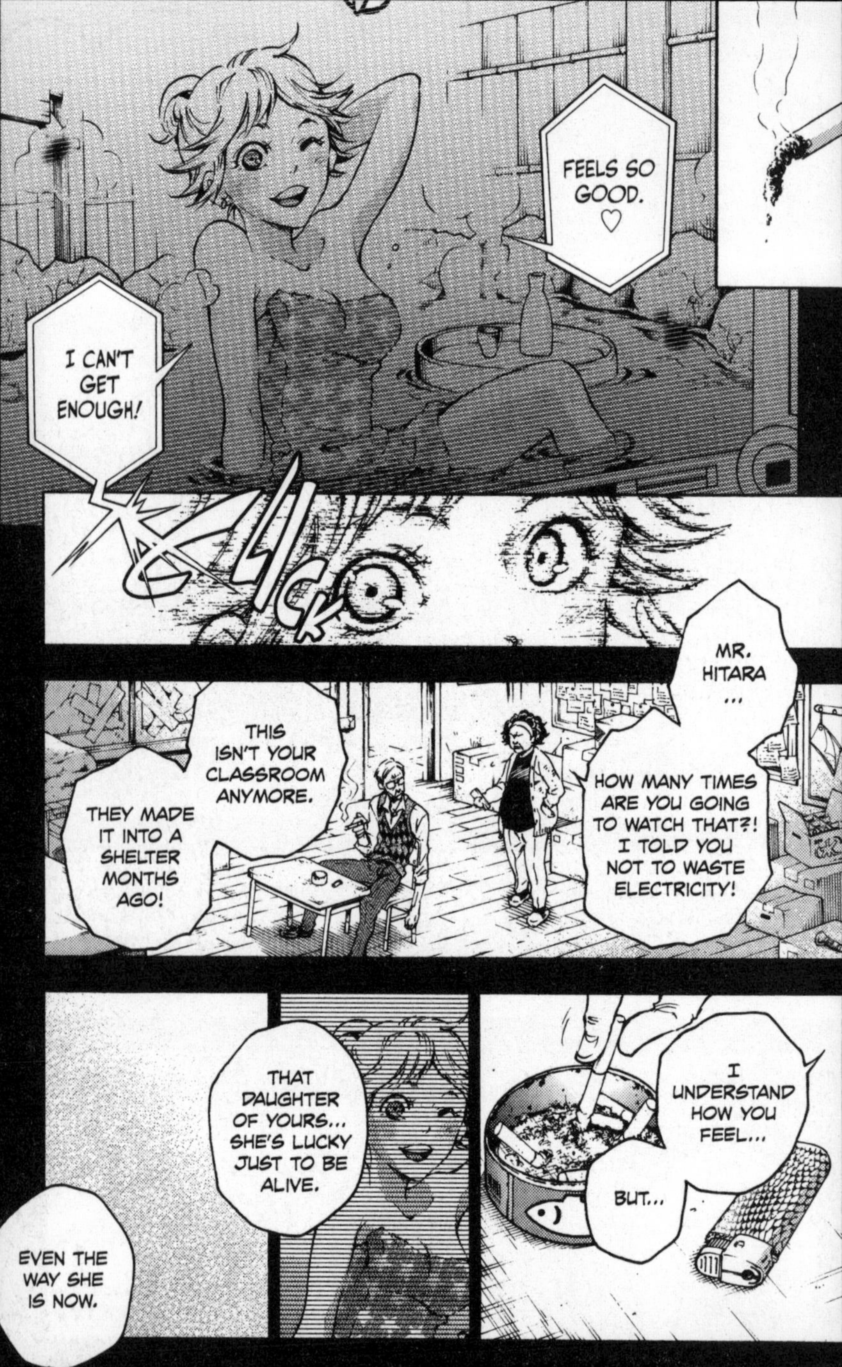
FEELS SO GOOD. ♡
I CAN'T GET ENOUGH!
CLICK
MR. HITARA...
HOW MANY TIMES ARE YOU GOING TO WATCH THAT?! I TOLD YOU NOT TO WASTE ELECTRICITY!
THIS ISN'T YOUR CLASSROOM ANYMORE.
THEY MADE IT INTO A SHELTER MONTHS AGO!
I UNDERSTAND HOW YOU FEEL...
BUT...
THAT DAUGHTER OF YOURS... SHE'S LUCKY JUST TO BE ALIVE.
EVEN THE WAY SHE IS NOW.

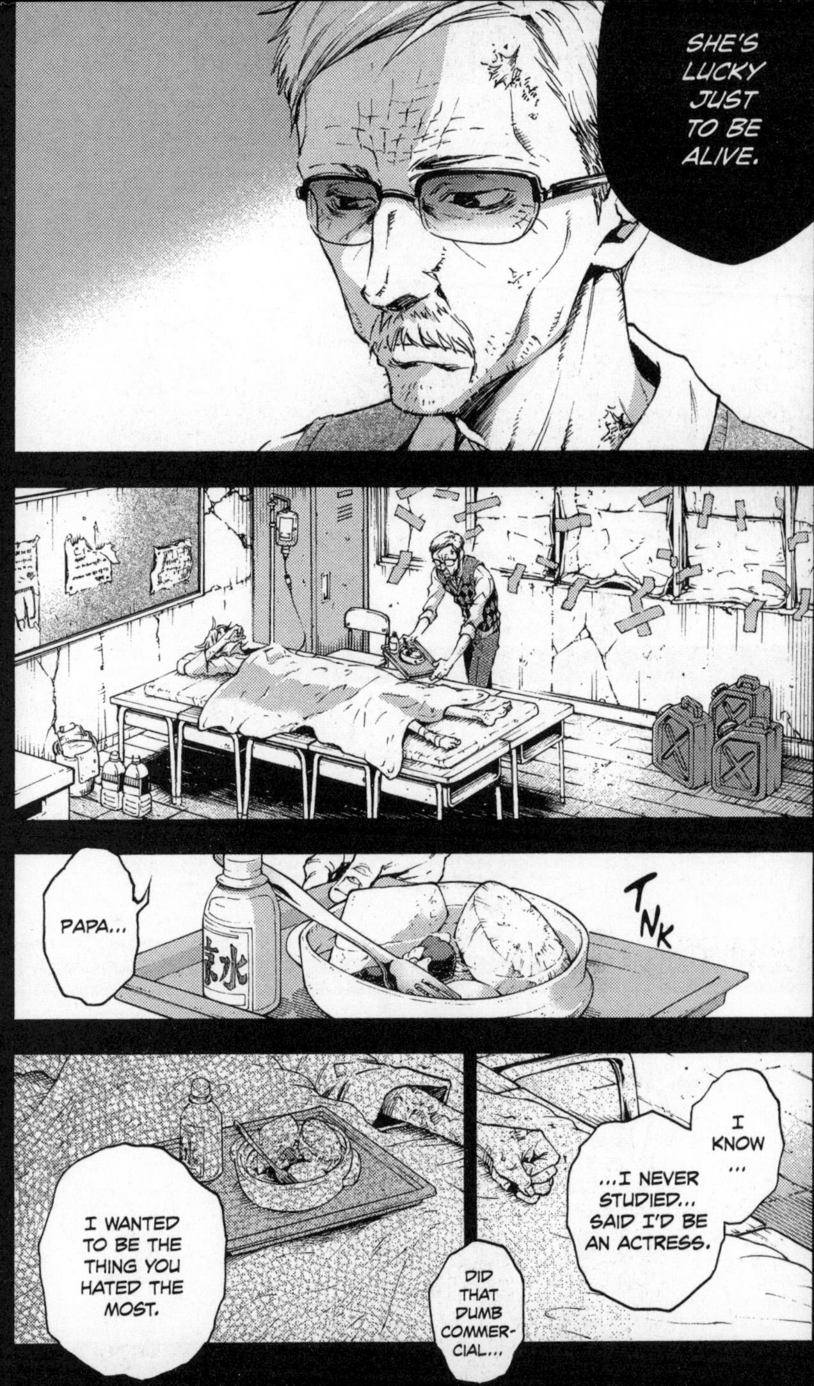
SHE'S LUCKY JUST TO BE ALIVE.
TNK
PAPA...
I KNOW...
...I NEVER STUDIED... SAID I'D BE AN ACTRESS.
DID THAT DUMB COMMER-CIAL...
I WANTED TO BE THE THING YOU HATED THE MOST.

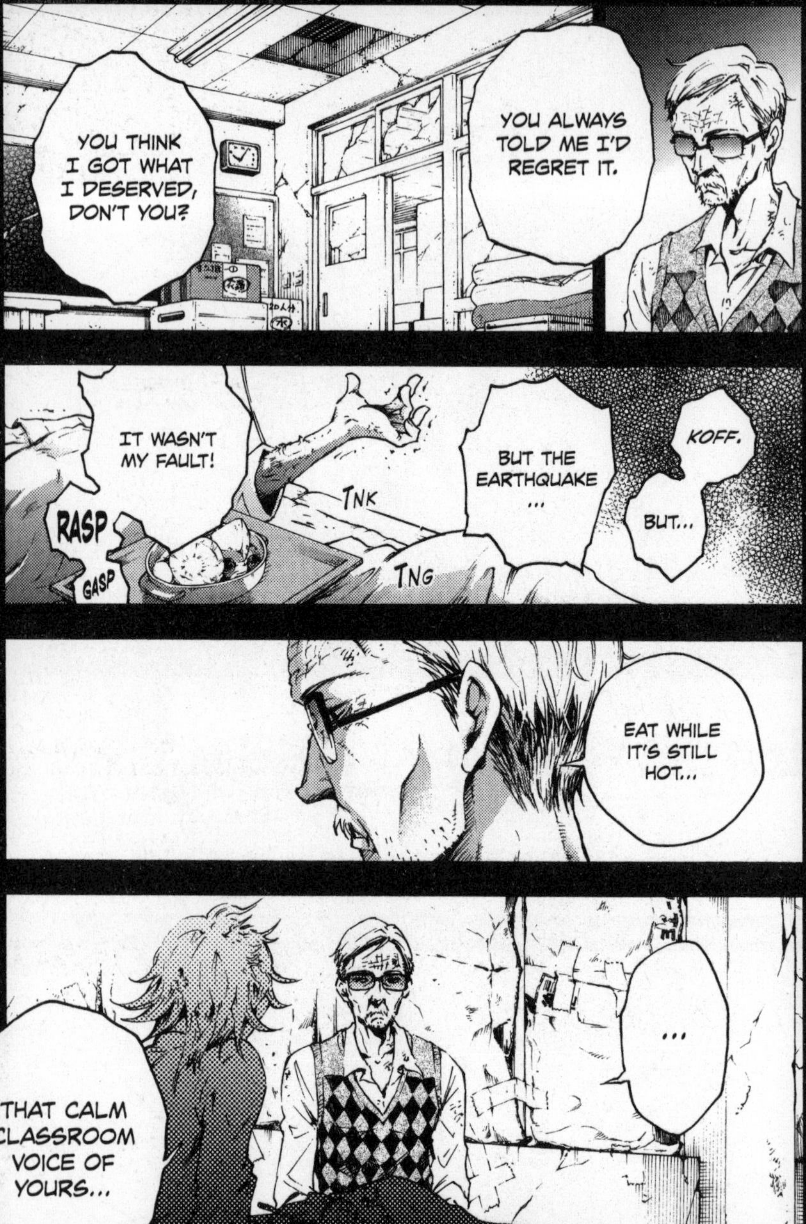
YOU ALWAYS TOLD ME I'D REGRET IT.
YOU THINK I GOT WHAT I DESERVED, DON'T YOU?
KOFF.
BUT...
BUT THE EARTHQUAKE ...
TNG
TNK
IT WASN'T MY FAULT!
RASP
GASP
EAT WHILE IT'S STILL HOT...
...
THAT CALM CLASSROOM VOICE OF YOURS...

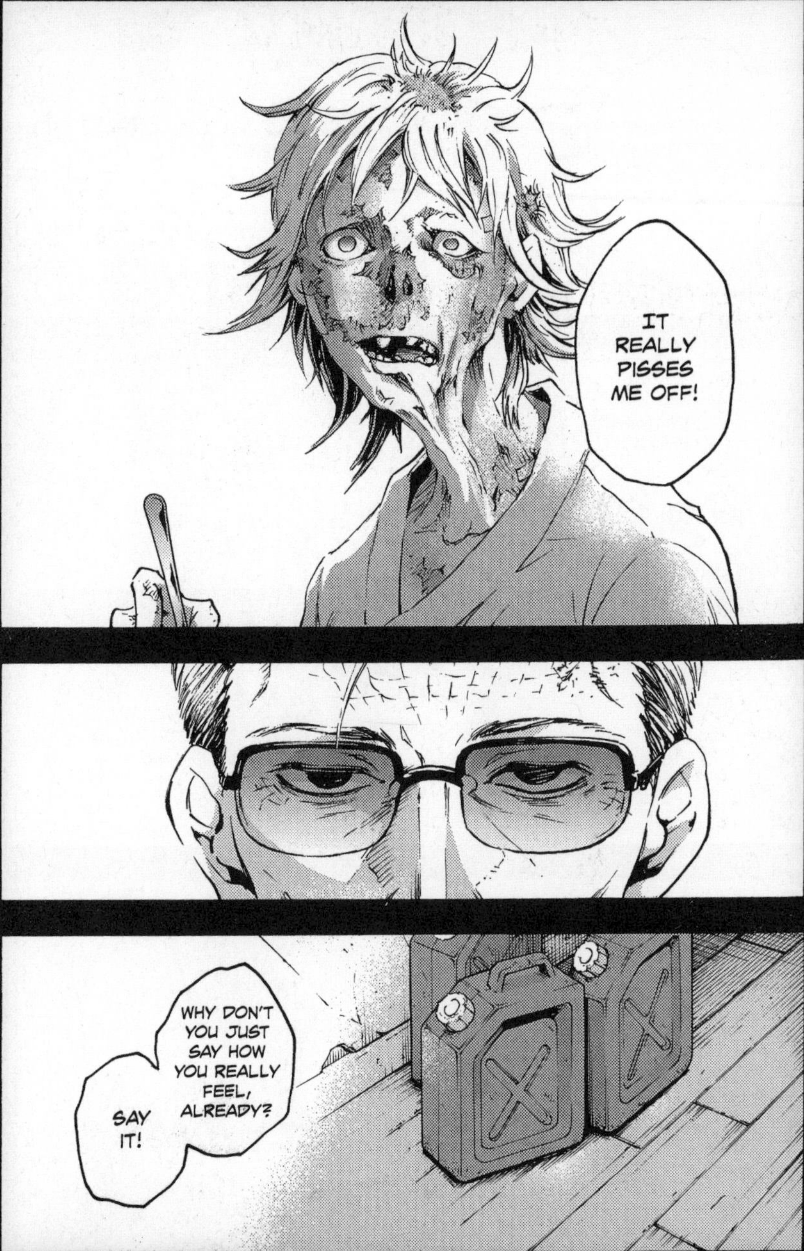
IT REALLY PISSES ME OFF!
WHY DON'T YOU JUST SAY HOW YOU REALLY FEEL, ALREADY?
SAY IT!

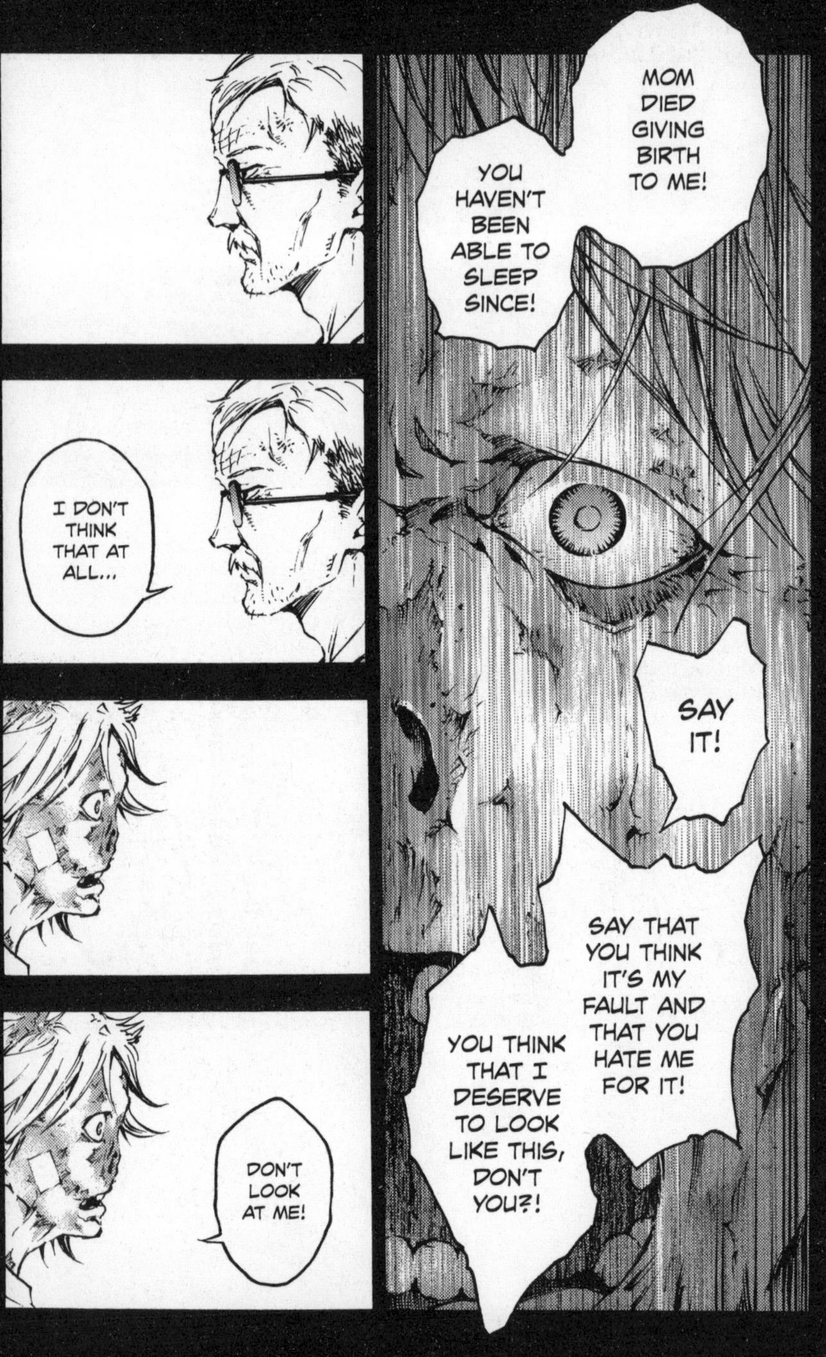
MOM DIED GIVING BIRTH TO ME!
YOU HAVEN'T BEEN ABLE TO SLEEP SINCE!
SAY IT!
SAY THAT YOU THINK IT'S MY FAULT AND THAT YOU HATE ME FOR IT!
YOU THINK THAT I DESERVE TO LOOK LIKE THIS, DON'T YOU?!
I DON'T THINK THAT AT ALL...
DON'T LOOK AT ME!

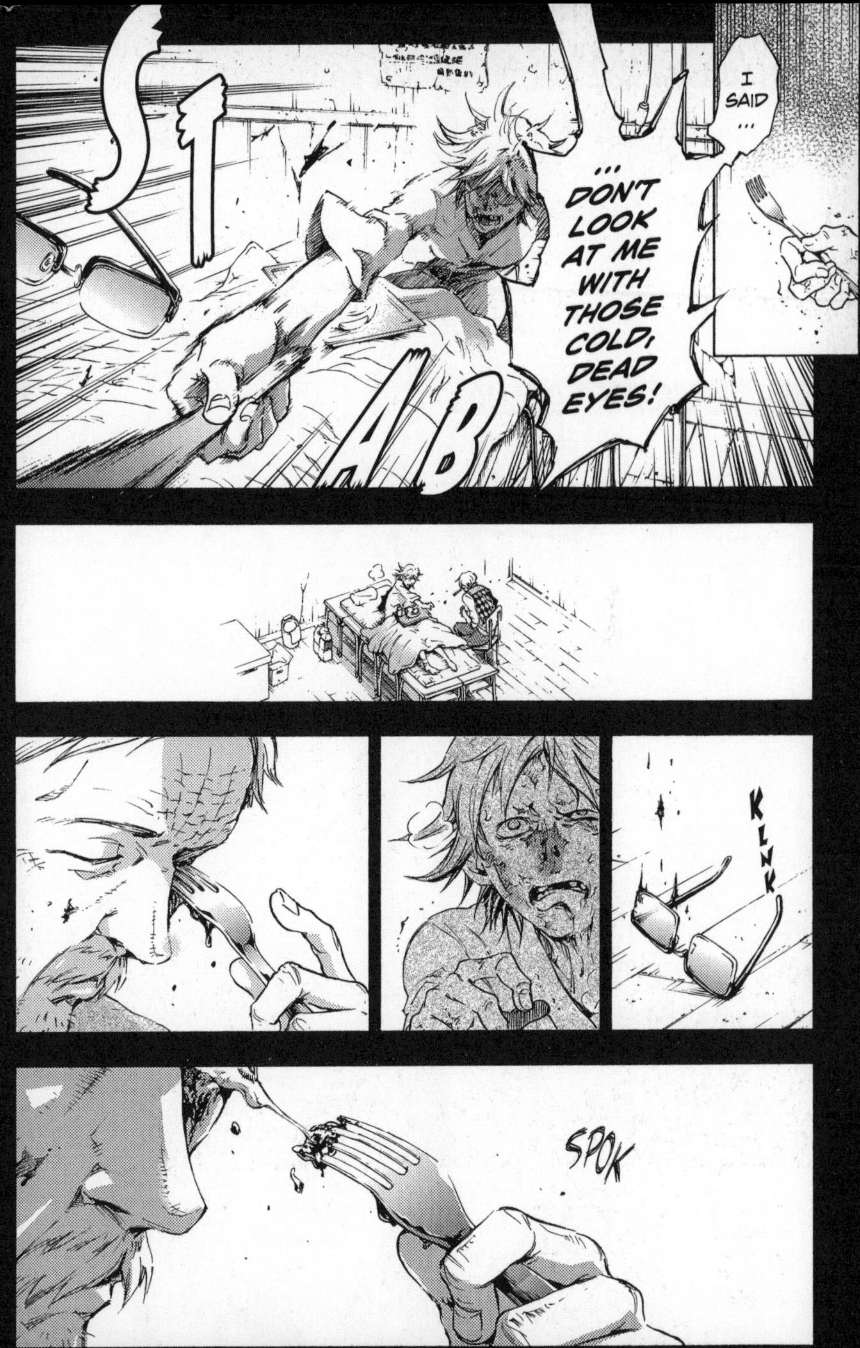
I SAID ...
... DON'T LOOK AT ME WITH THOSE COLD, DEAD EYES!
STAB
KLNK
SPOK

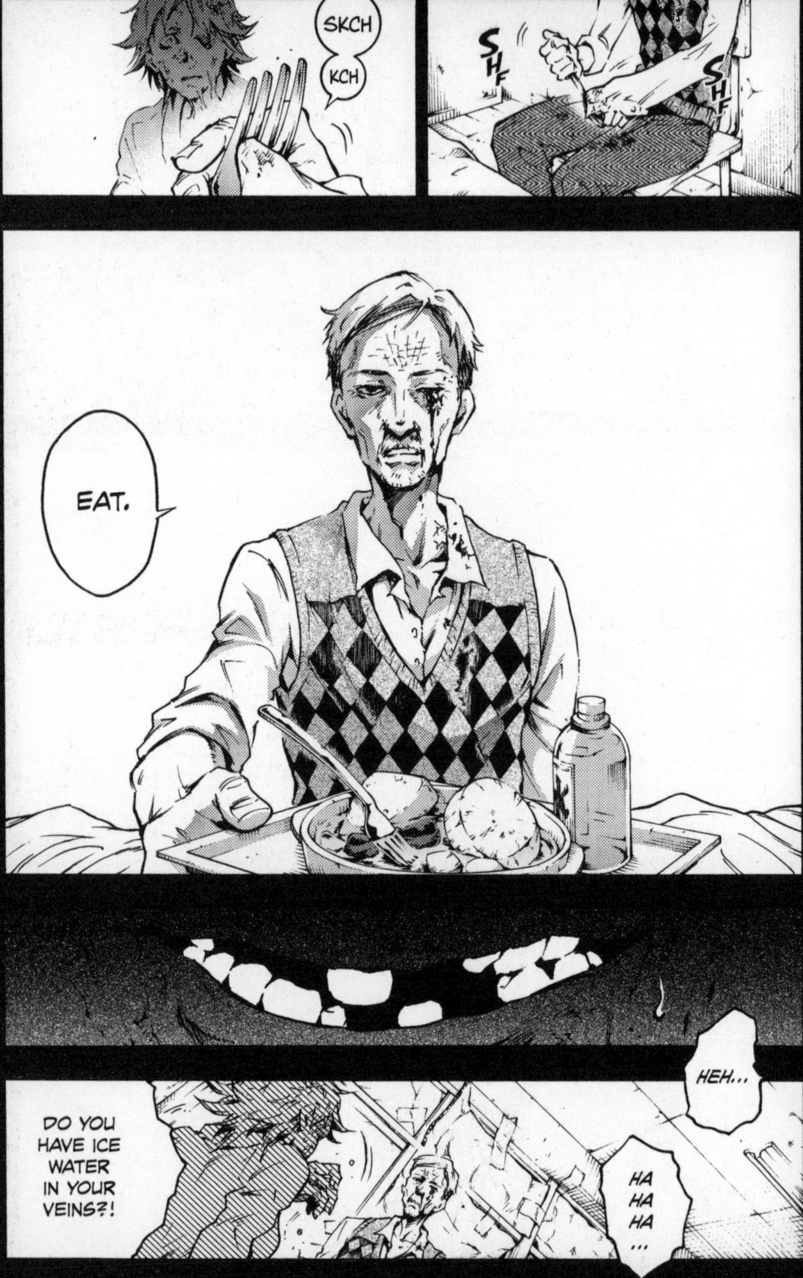
SHF
SHF
SKCH
KCH
EAT.
HEH...
HA HA HA ...
DO YOU HAVE ICE WATER IN YOUR VEINS?!

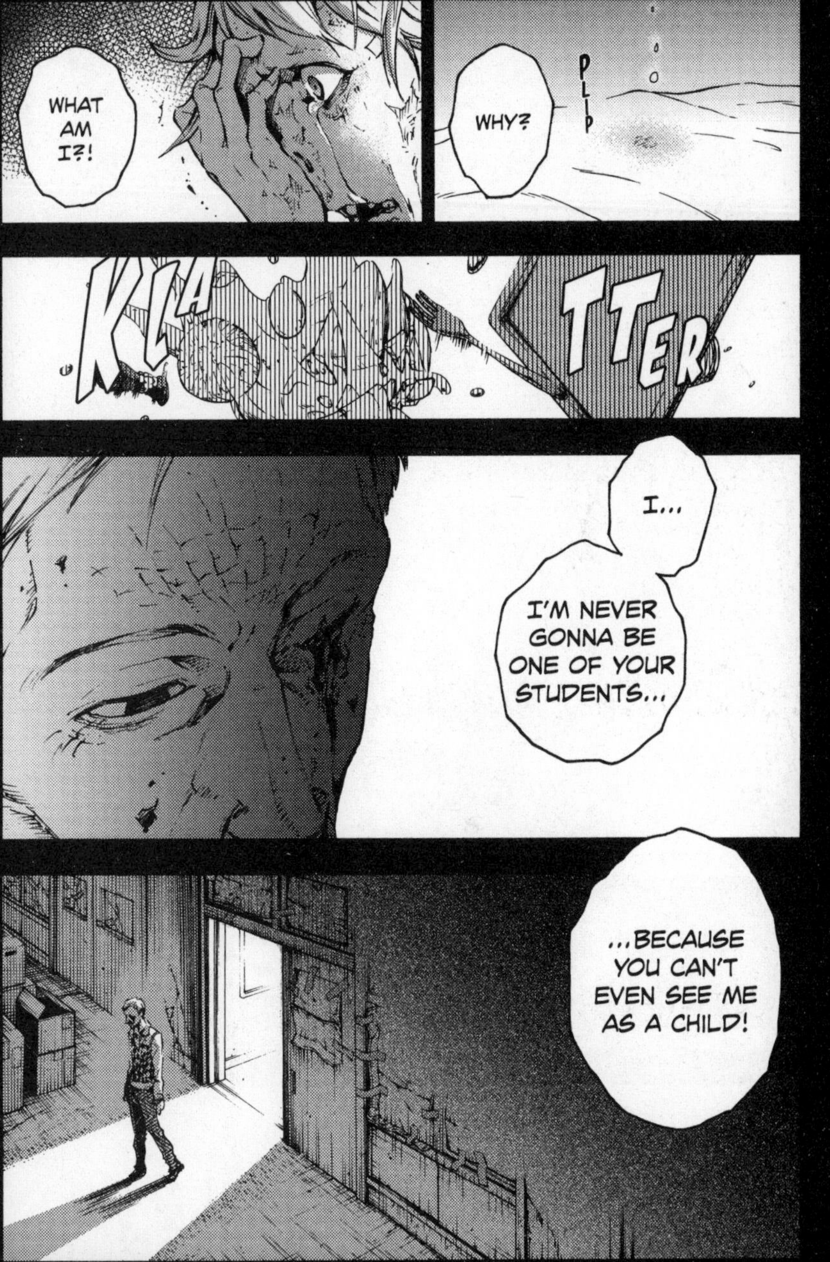
PLIP
WHY?
WHAT AM I?!
KLATTER
I...
I'M NEVER GONNA BE ONE OF YOUR STUDENTS...
...BECAUSE YOU CAN'T EVEN SEE ME AS A CHILD!

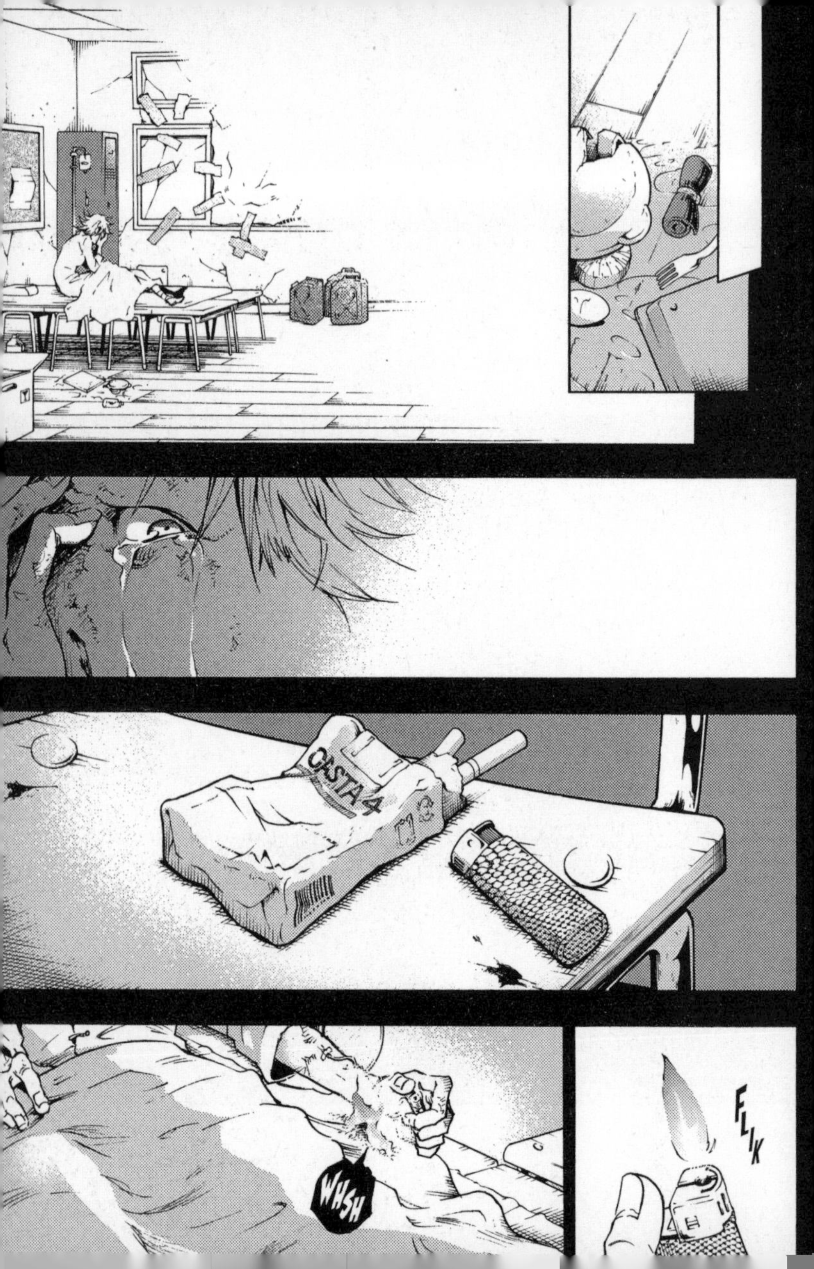
CASTA 4
FLIK
WHSH

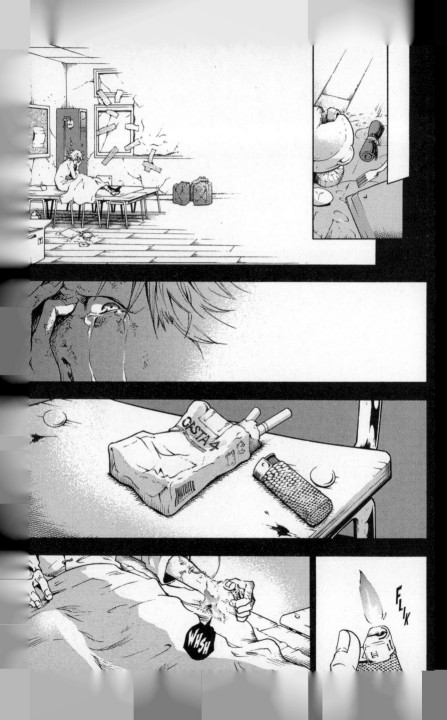

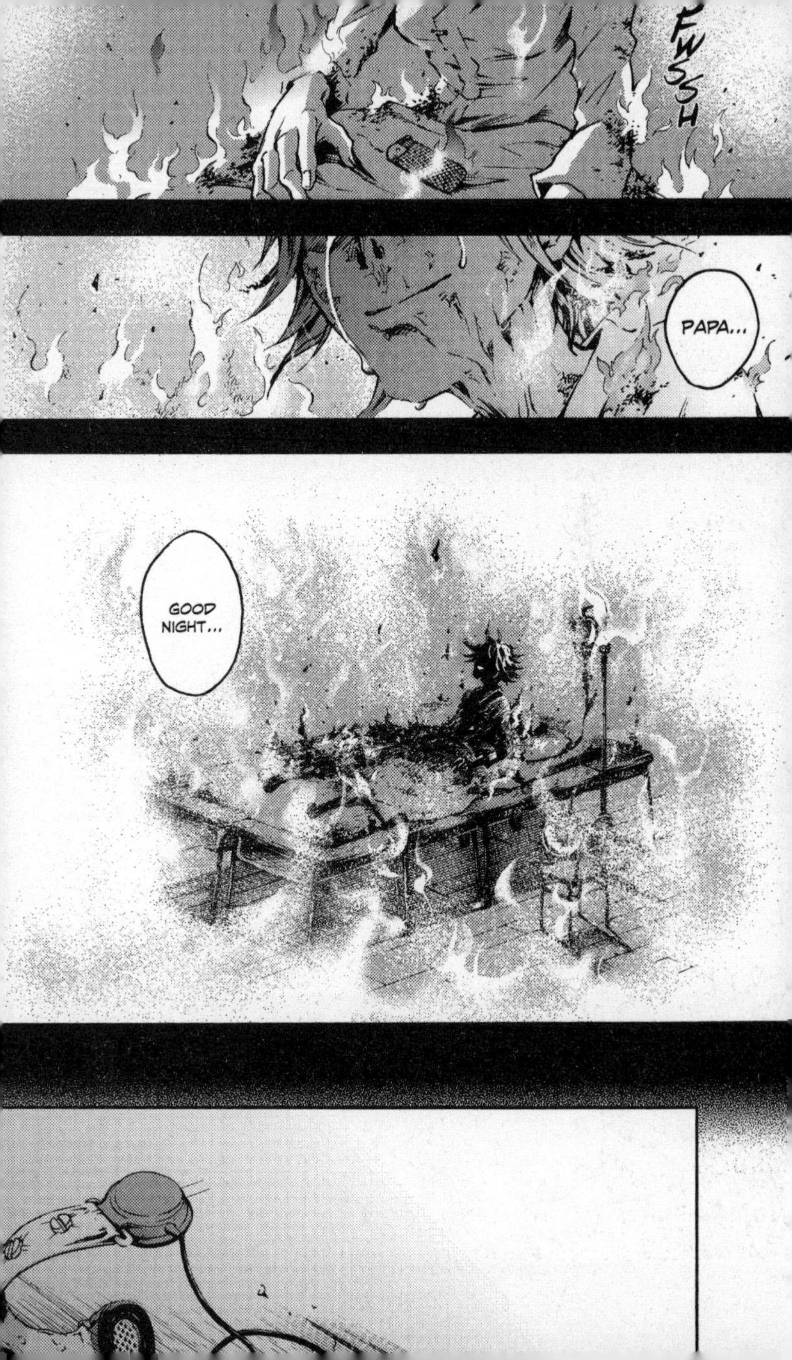
FWSSH
PAPA...
GOOD NIGHT...

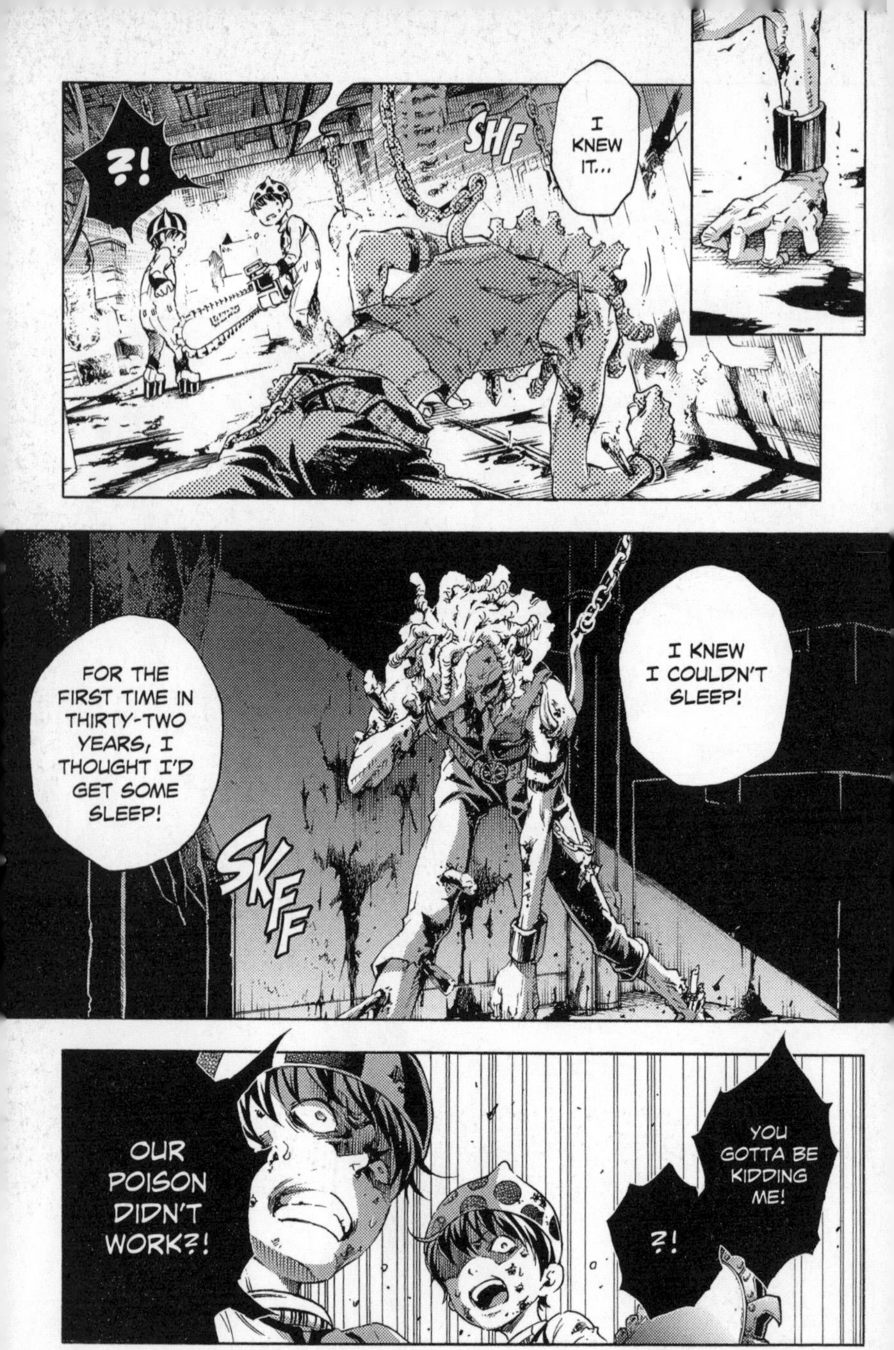
I KNEW IT...
SHF
?!
I KNEW I COULDN'T SLEEP!
FOR THE FIRST TIME IN THIRTY-TWO YEARS, I THOUGHT I'D GET SOME SLEEP!
SKFF
YOU GOTTA BE KIDDING ME!
?!
OUR POISON DIDN'T WORK?!

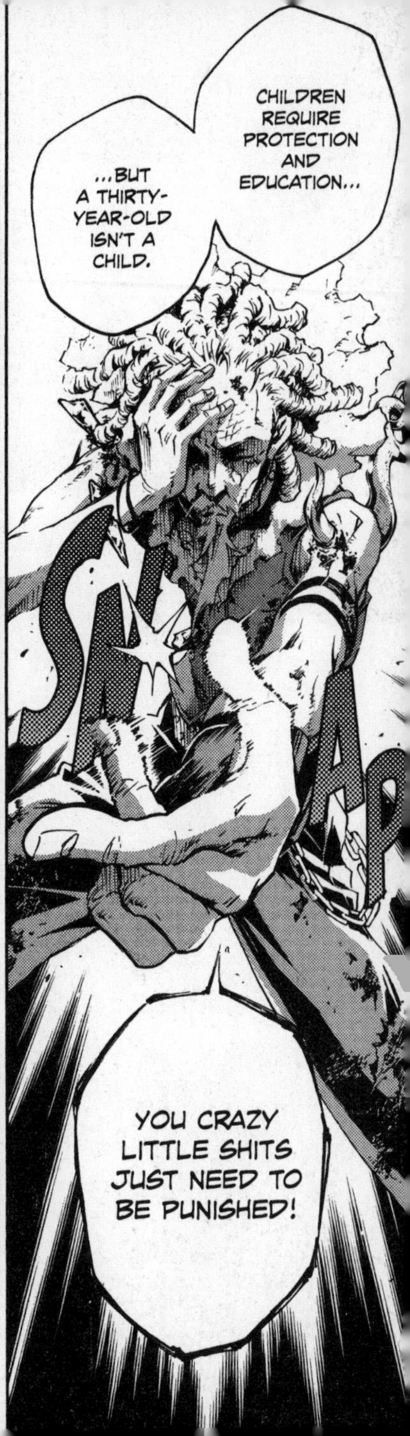
CHILDREN REQUIRE PROTECTION AND EDUCATION...
...BUT A THIRTY-YEAR-OLD ISN'T A CHILD.
YOU CRAZY LITTLE SHITS JUST NEED TO BE PUNISHED!

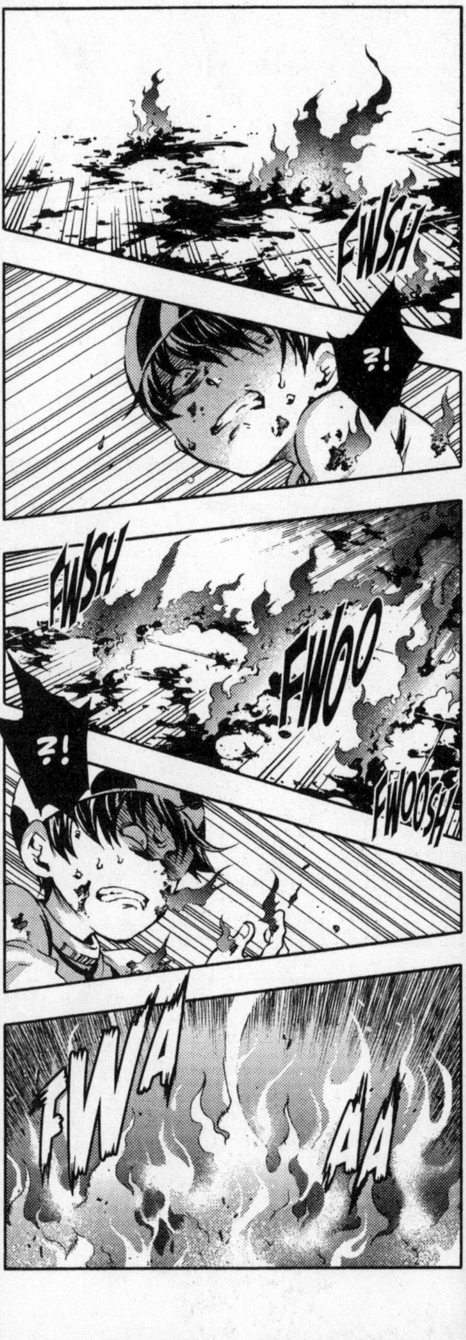
FWSH
?!
FWSH
FWOO
?!
FWOOSH
FWAAA

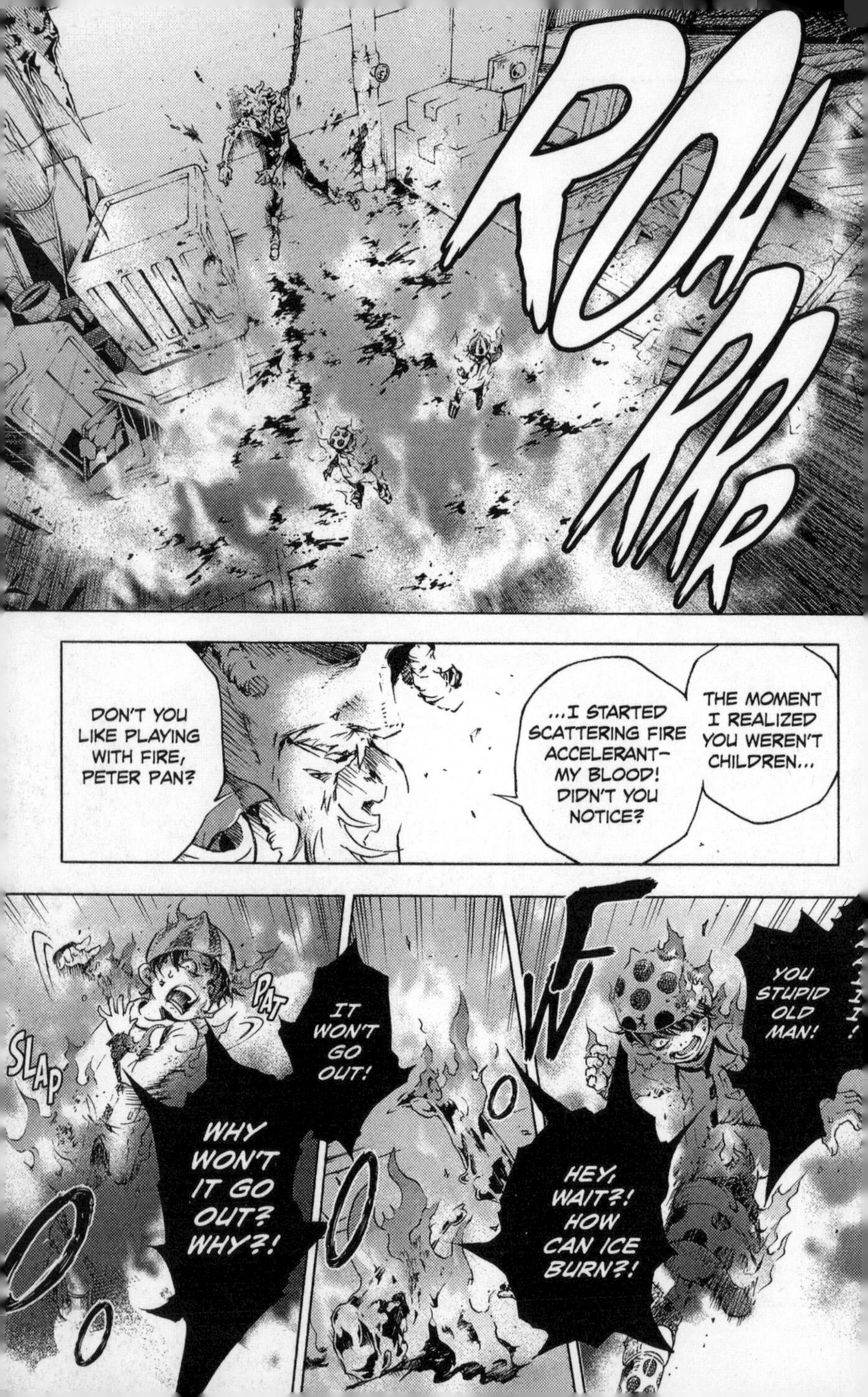
ROARRR
THE MOMENT I REALIZED YOU WEREN'T CHILDREN...
...I STARTED SCATTERING FIRE ACCELERANT— MY BLOOD! DIDN'T YOU NOTICE?
DON'T YOU LIKE PLAYING WITH FIRE, PETER PAN?
YOU STUPID OLD MAN!
HEY, WAIT?! HOW CAN ICE BURN?!
IT WON'T GO OUT!
WHY WON'T IT GO OUT? WHY?!
PAT
SLAP

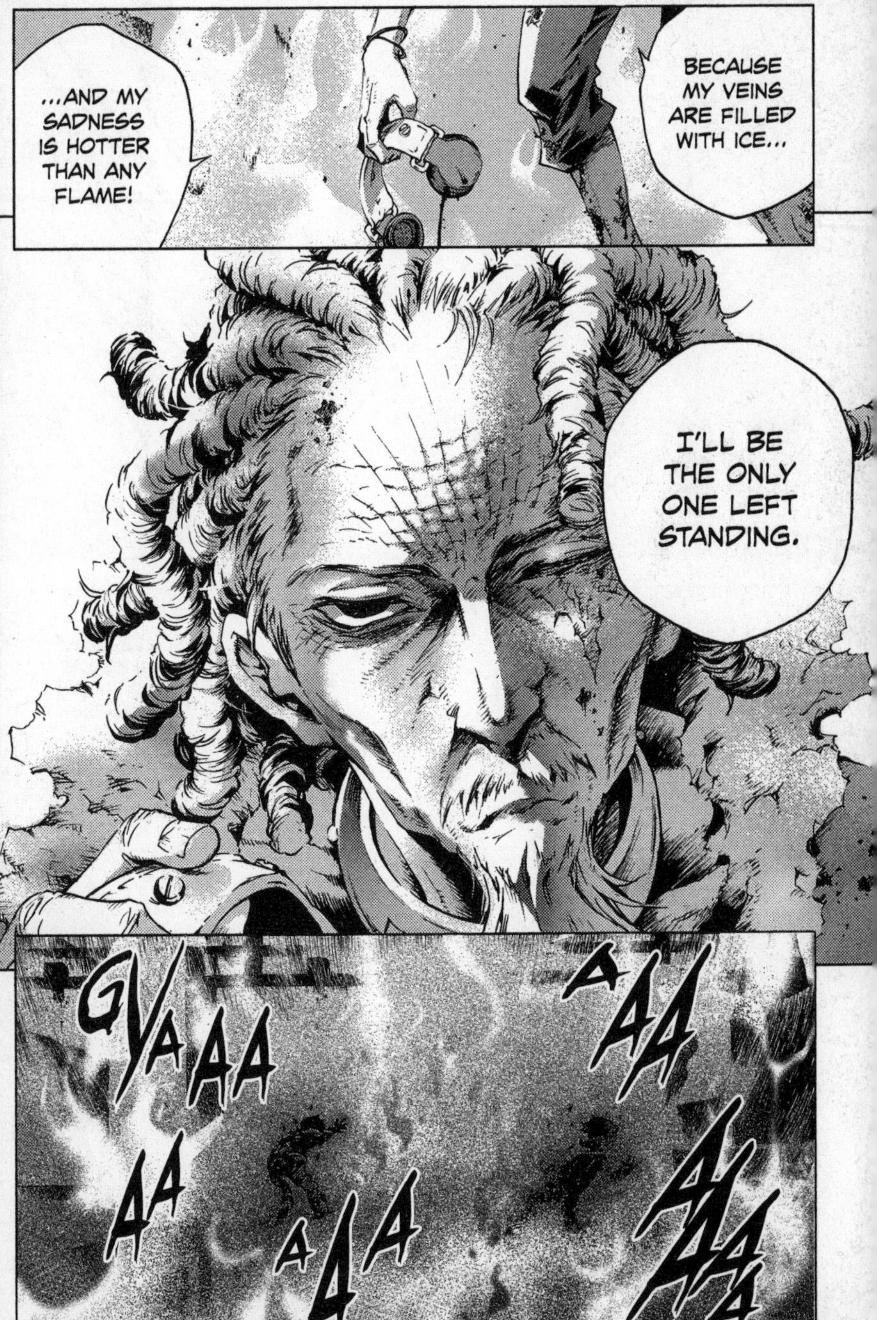
BECAUSE MY VEINS ARE FILLED WITH ICE...
...AND MY SADNESS IS HOTTER THAN ANY FLAME!
I'LL BE THE ONLY ONE LEFT STANDING.
AAA
AAAAA
AAAA
GYAAAAAA

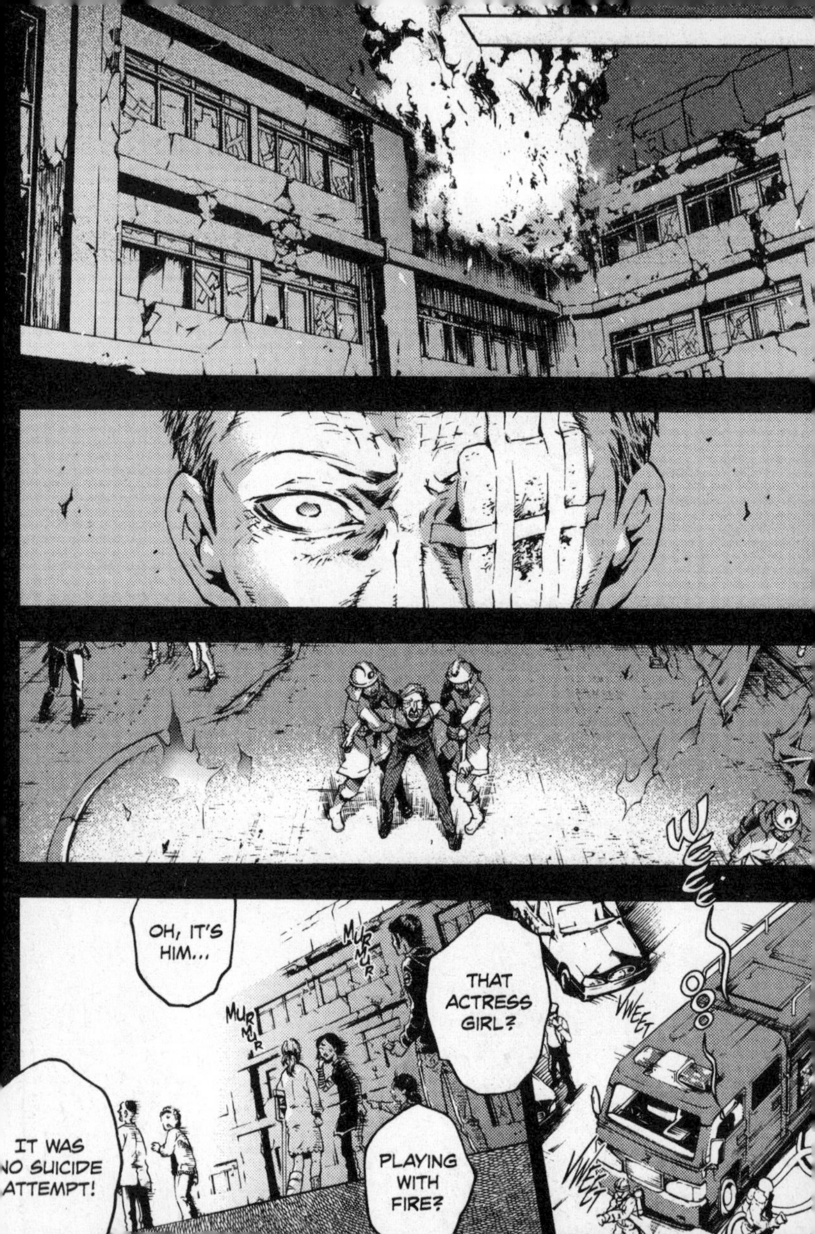
VWEET
THAT ACTRESS GIRL?
MURMUR
OH, IT'S HIM...
MURMUR
VWEET
PLAYING WITH FIRE?
IT WAS NO SUICIDE ATTEMPT!

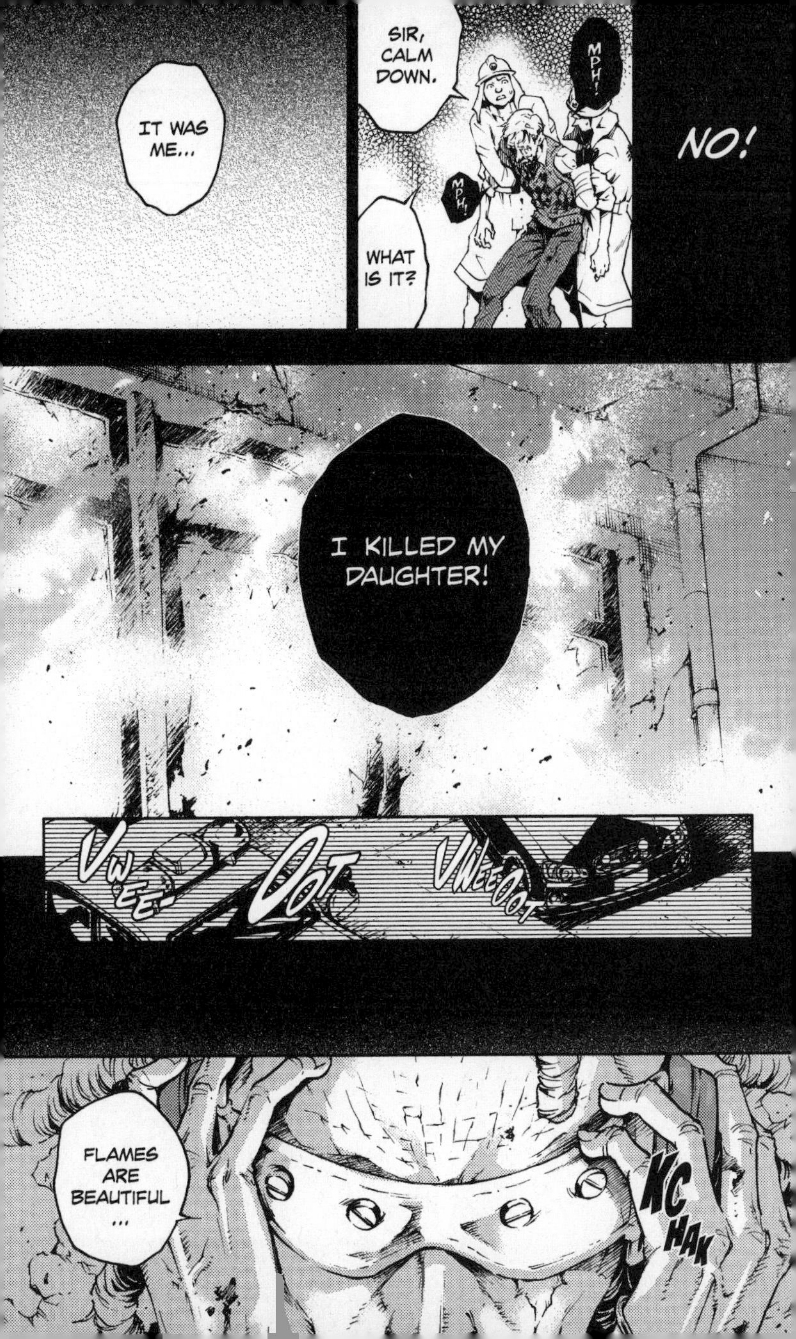
NO!
MPH!
SIR, CALM DOWN.
MPH!
WHAT IS IT?
IT WAS ME...
I KILLED MY DAUGHTER!
VWEEOOT
VWEE-OOT
KCHAK
FLAMES ARE BEAUTIFUL...

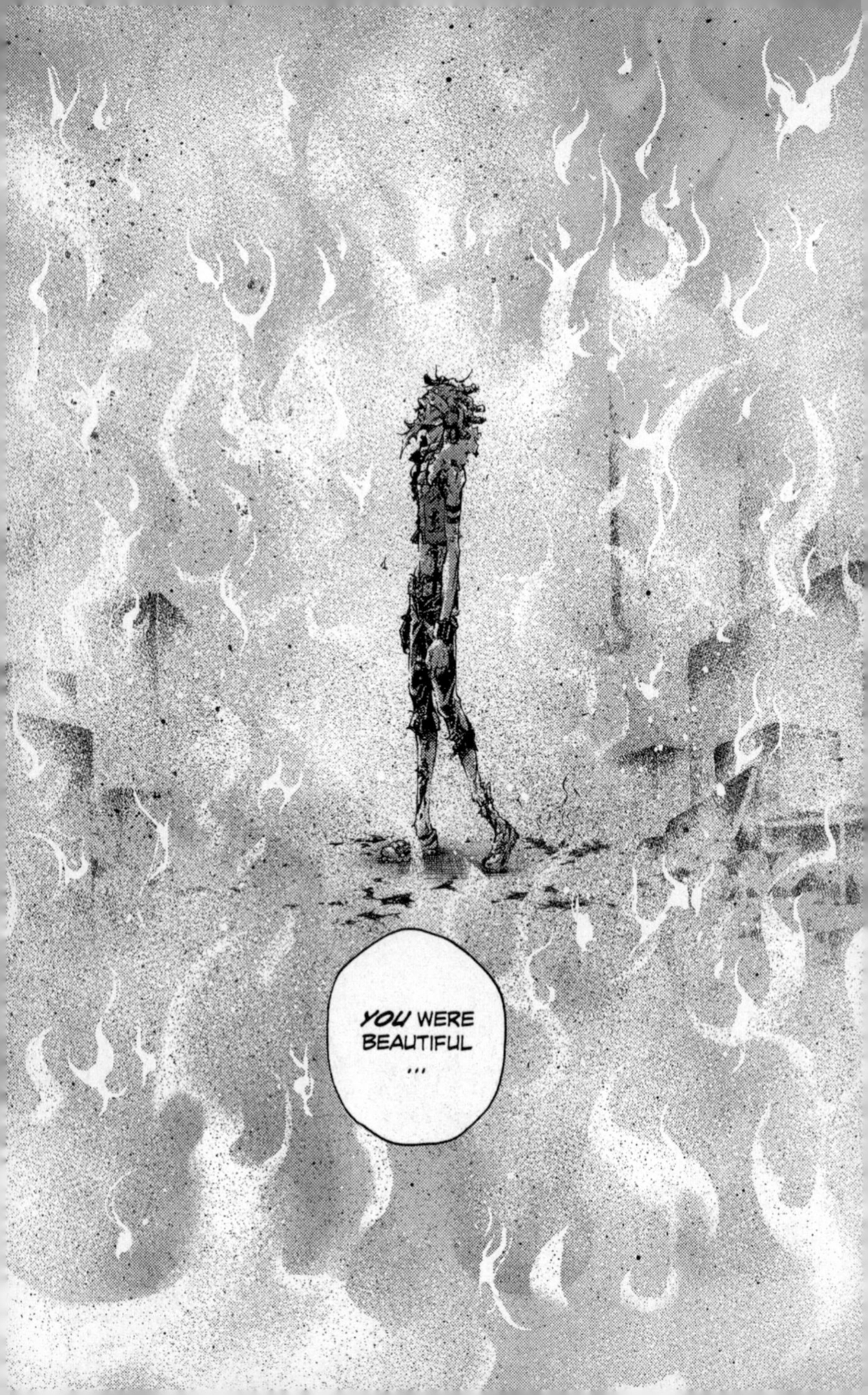
YOU WERE BEAUTIFUL ...

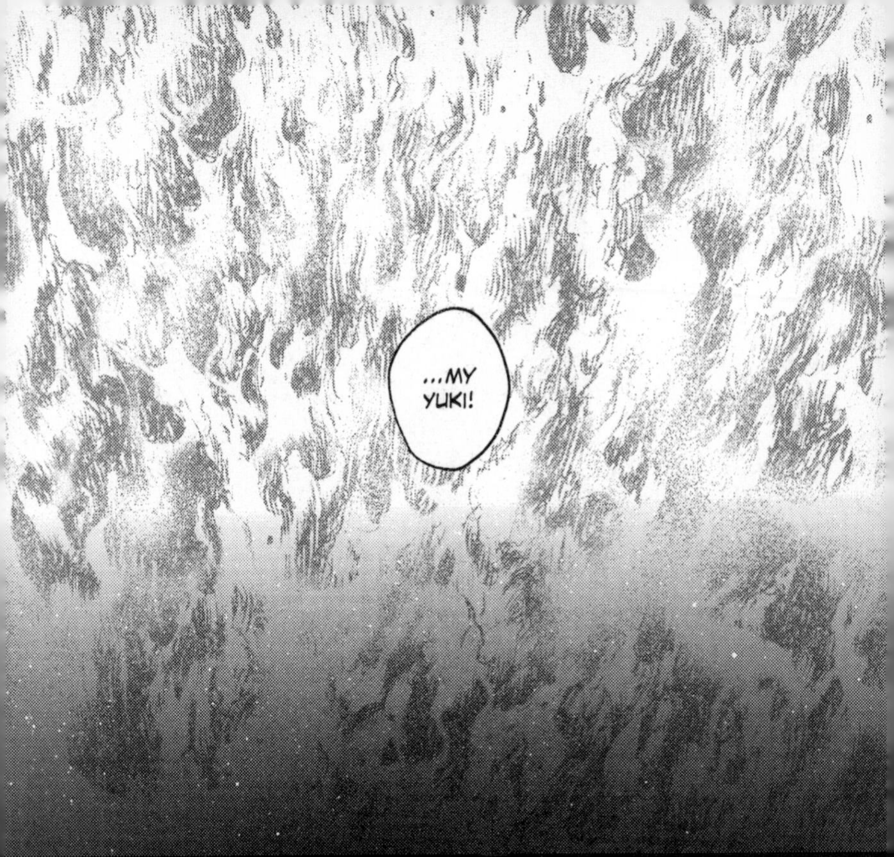
...MY YUKI!

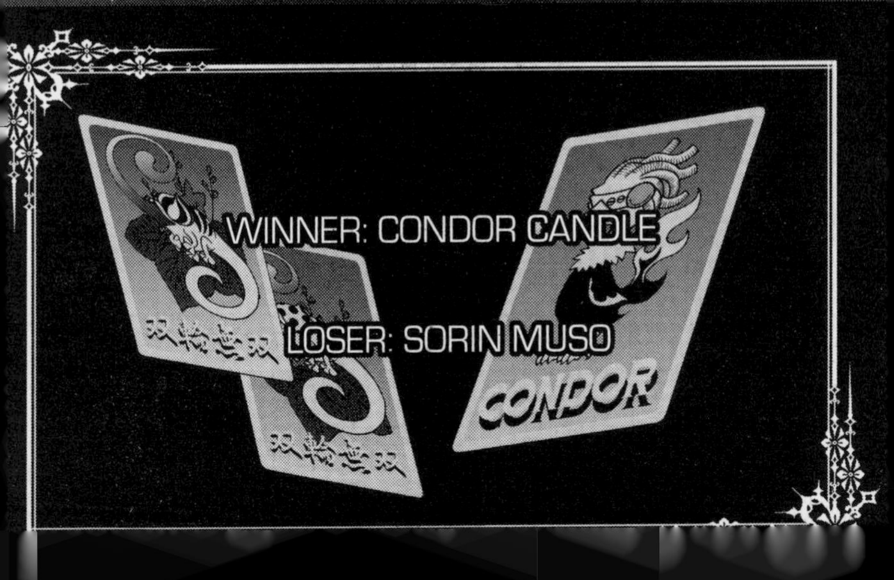
WINNER: CONDOR CANDLE
LOSER: SORIN MUSO
CONDOR

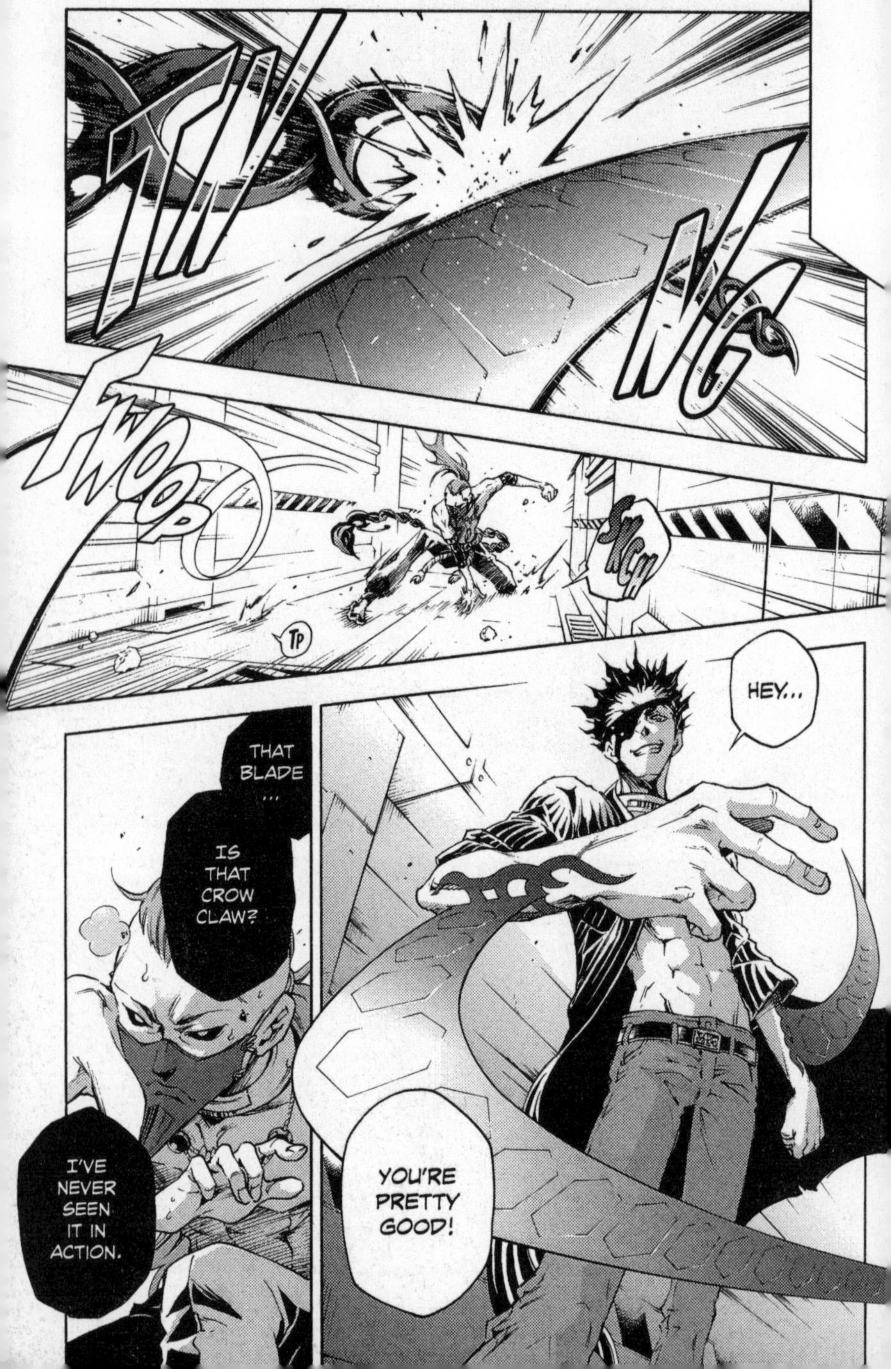
FWOOP
TP
HEY...
YOU'RE PRETTY GOOD!
THAT BLADE...
IS THAT CROW CLAW?
I'VE NEVER SEEN IT IN ACTION.

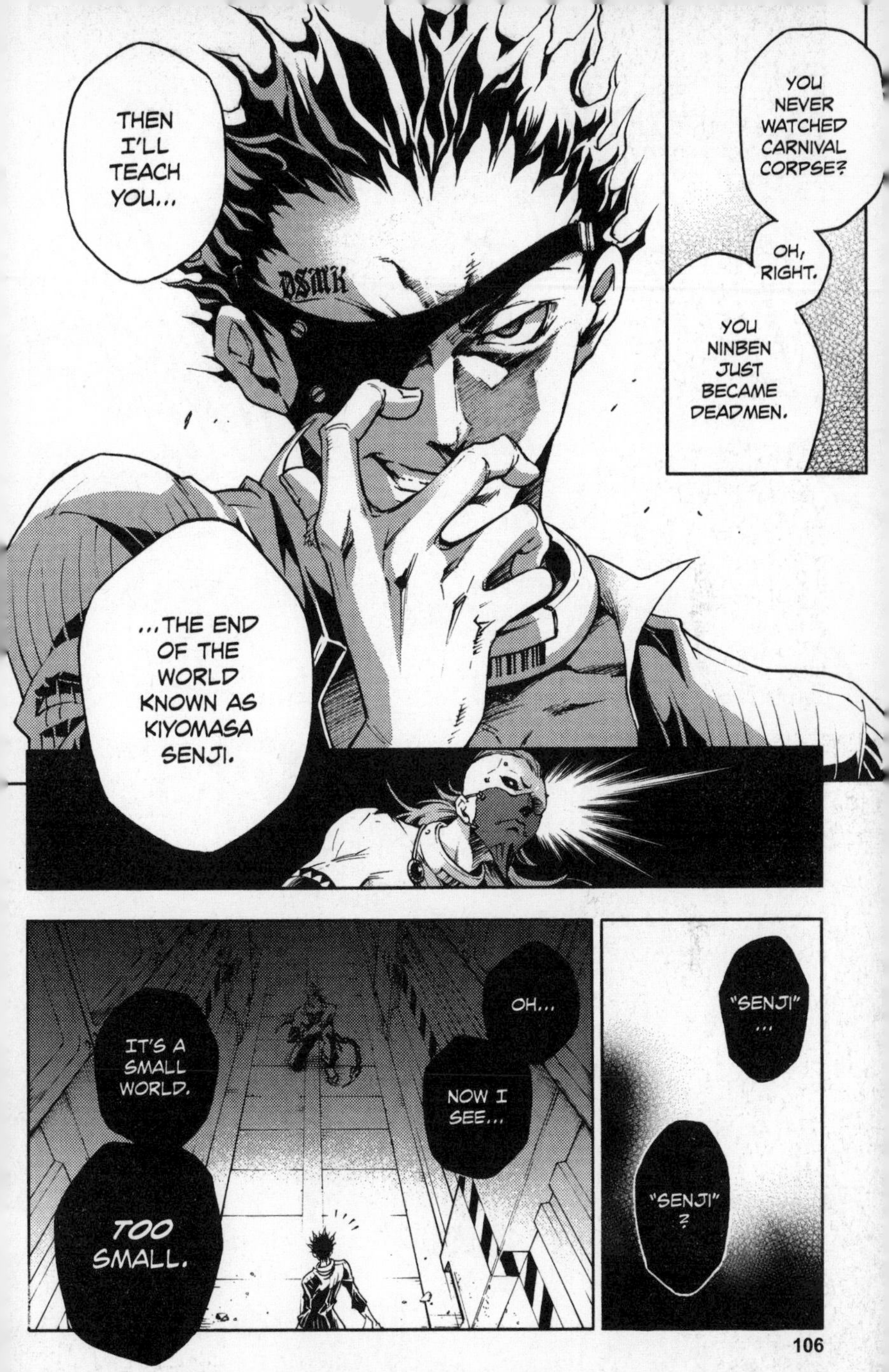
YOU NEVER WATCHED CARNIVAL CORPSE?
OH, RIGHT.
YOU NINBEN JUST BECAME DEADMEN.
THEN I'LL TEACH YOU...
...THE END OF THE WORLD KNOWN AS KIYOMASA SENJI.
"SENJI" ...
"SENJI" ?
OH...
NOW I SEE...
IT'S A SMALL WORLD.
TOO SMALL.

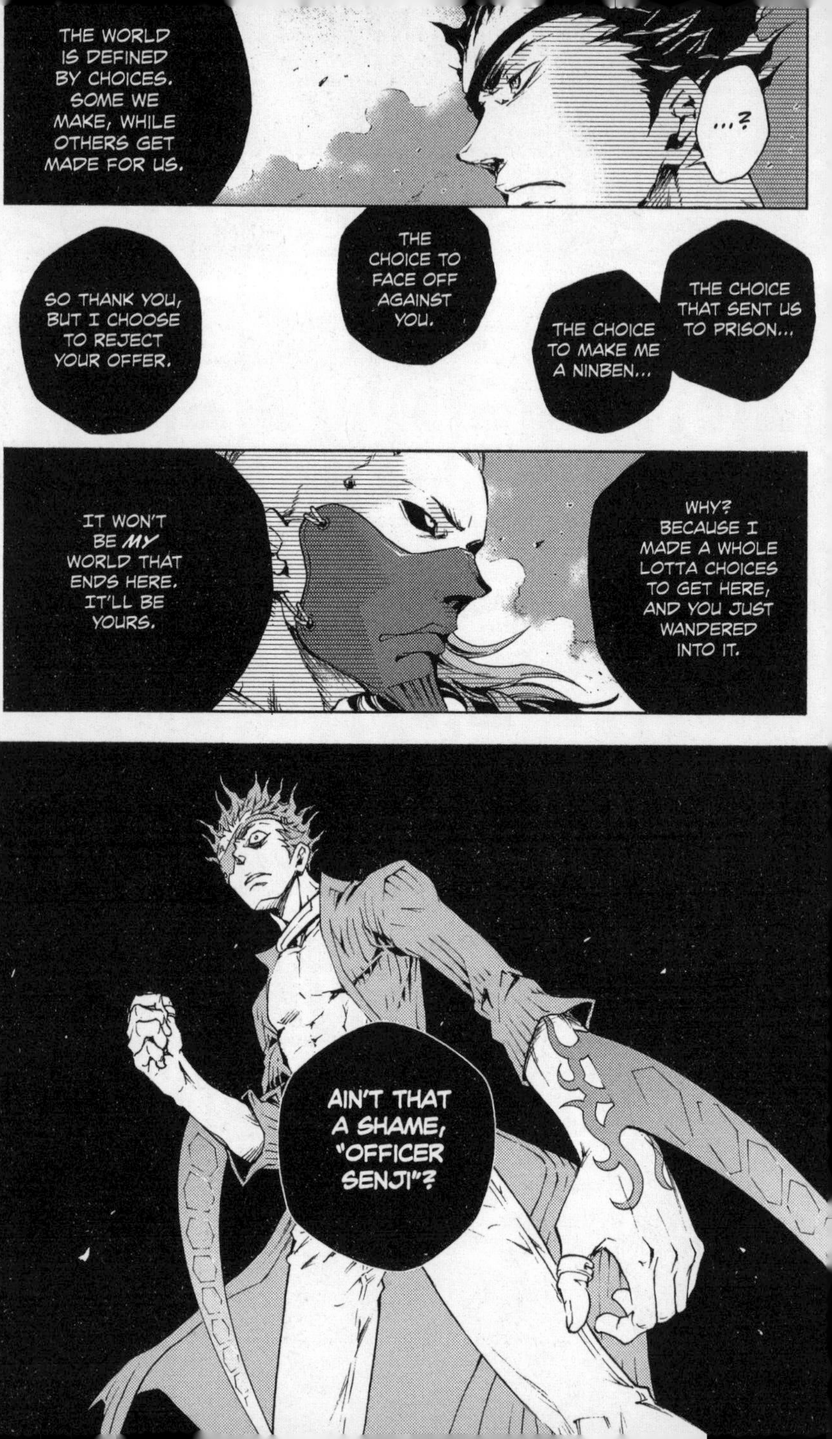
...?
THE WORLD IS DEFINED BY CHOICES. SOME WE MAKE, WHILE OTHERS GET MADE FOR US.
THE CHOICE THAT SENT US TO PRISON...
THE CHOICE TO MAKE ME A NINBEN...
THE CHOICE TO FACE OFF AGAINST YOU.
SO THANK YOU, BUT I CHOOSE TO REJECT YOUR OFFER.
WHY? BECAUSE I MADE A WHOLE LOTTA CHOICES TO GET HERE, AND YOU JUST WANDERED INTO IT.
IT WON'T BE *MY* WORLD THAT ENDS HERE. IT'LL BE YOURS.
AIN'T THAT A SHAME, "OFFICER SENJI"?

DEADMAN WONDER LAND

DDWL

DEADMAN WONDER LAND DEADMAN WONDER LAND
DDWL DDWL
DEADMAN WONDER LAND DEADMAN WONDER LAND DEADMAN WONDER LAND
DDWL DDWL DDWL
DEADMAN WONDER LAND DEADMAN WONDER LAND DEADMAN WONDER LAND
DDWL DDWL DDWL

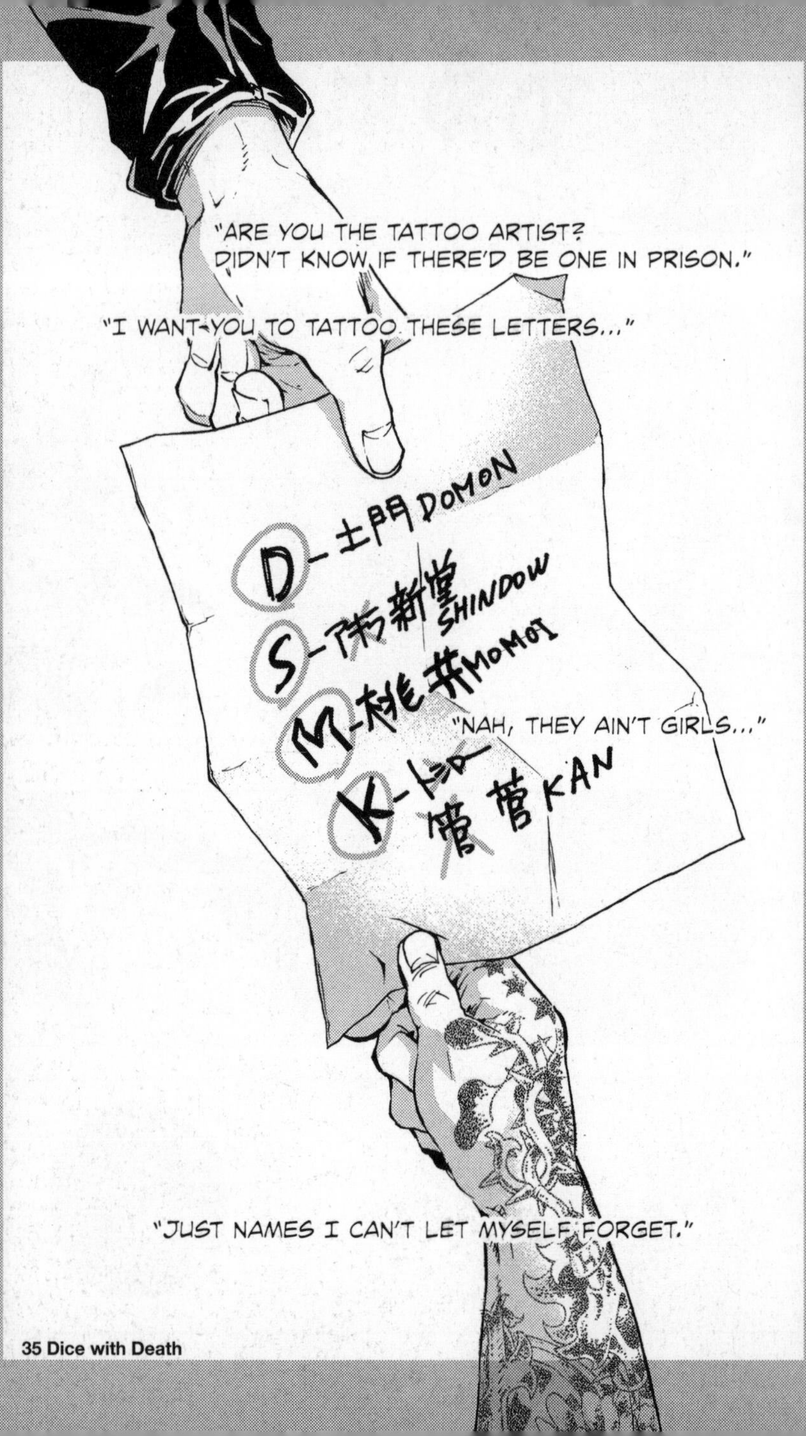
"ARE YOU THE TATTOO ARTIST? DIDN'T KNOW IF THERE'D BE ONE IN PRISON."
"I WANT YOU TO TATTOO THESE LETTERS..."
D-土門 DOMON
S-新堂 SHINDOW
M-桃井 MOMOI
K-菅 KAN
"NAH, THEY AIN'T GIRLS..."
"JUST NAMES I CAN'T LET MYSELF FORGET."

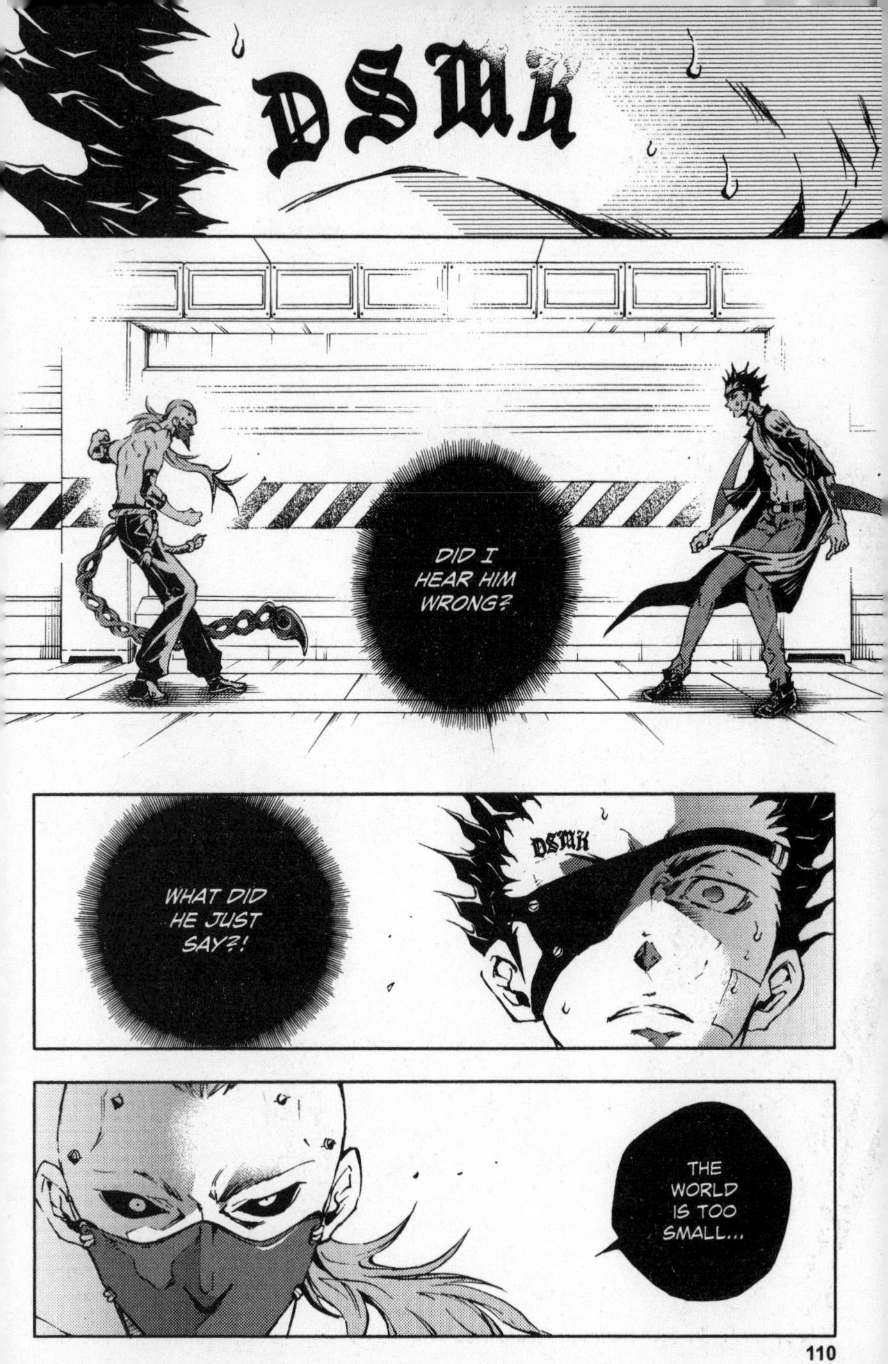
DSMK
DID I HEAR HIM WRONG?
WHAT DID HE JUST SAY?!
DSMK
THE WORLD IS TOO SMALL...

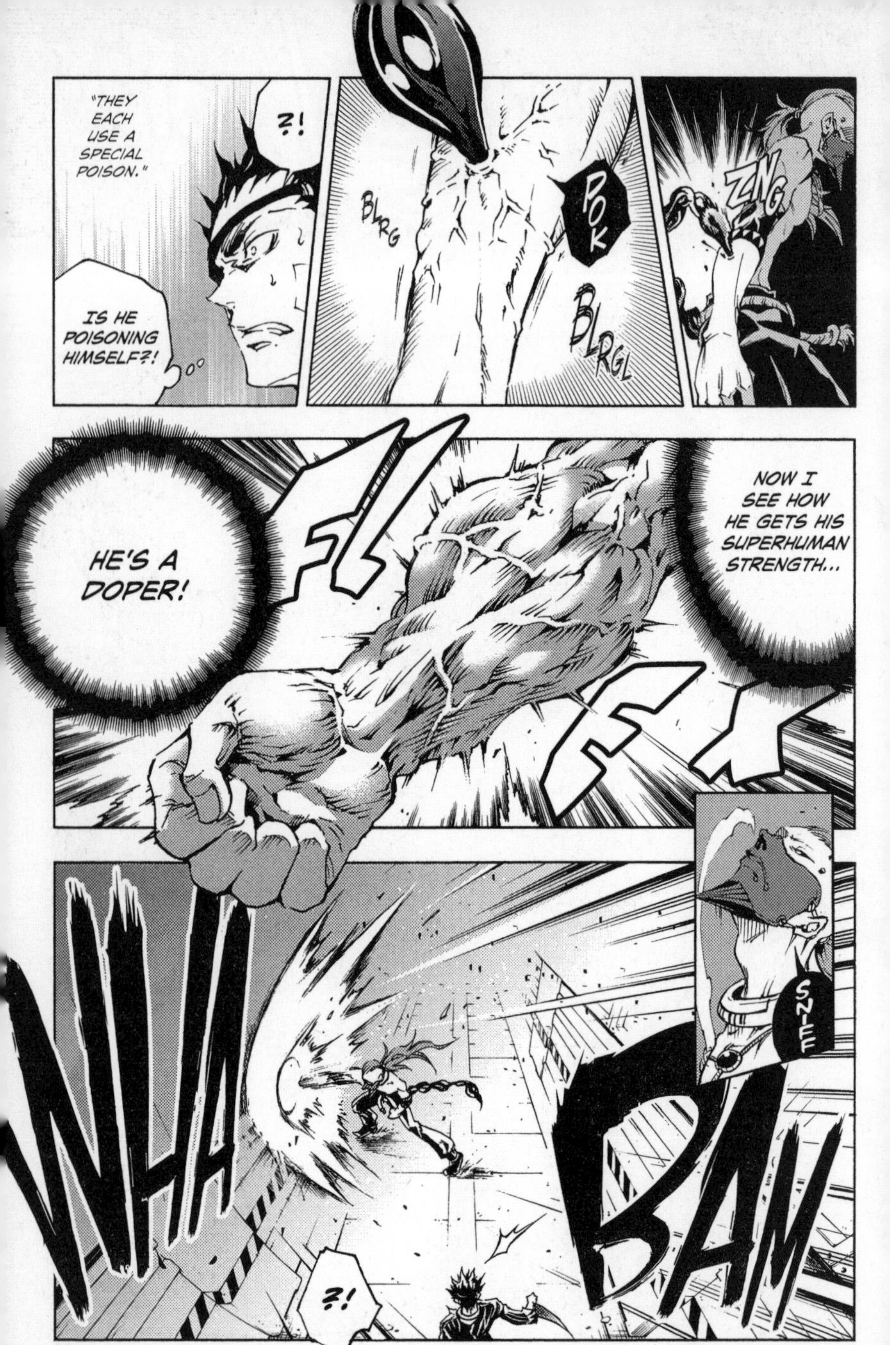
ZNG
POK
BLRG
BLRGL
"THEY EACH USE A SPECIAL POISON."
?!
IS HE POISONING HIMSELF?!
NOW I SEE HOW HE GETS HIS SUPERHUMAN STRENGTH...
HE'S A DOPER!
FL
FX
SNIFF
BAM
WHA
?!

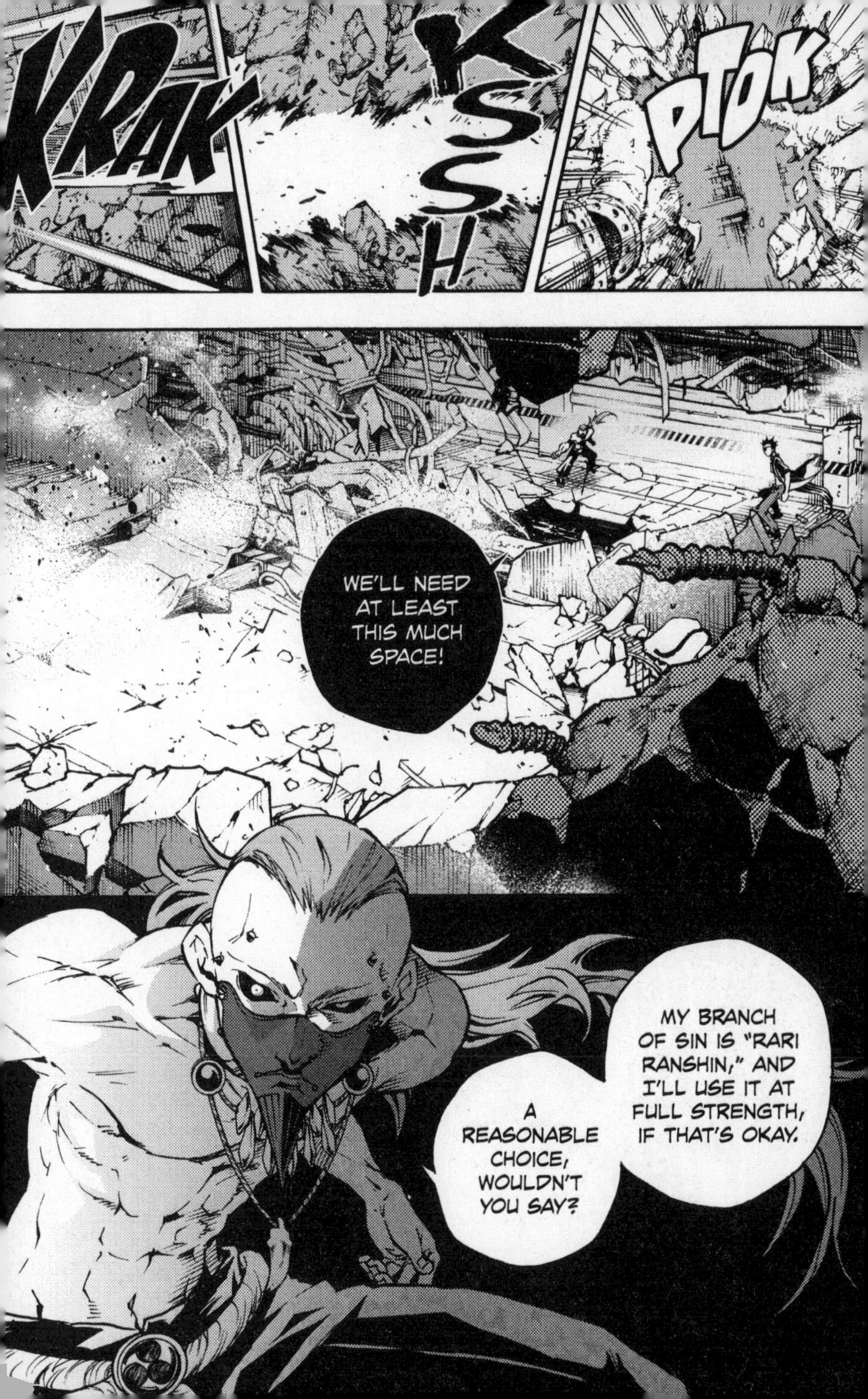
PTOK
KSSH
KRAK
WE'LL NEED AT LEAST THIS MUCH SPACE!
MY BRANCH OF SIN IS "RARI RANSHIN," AND I'LL USE IT AT FULL STRENGTH, IF THAT'S OKAY.
A REASONABLE CHOICE, WOULDN'T YOU SAY?

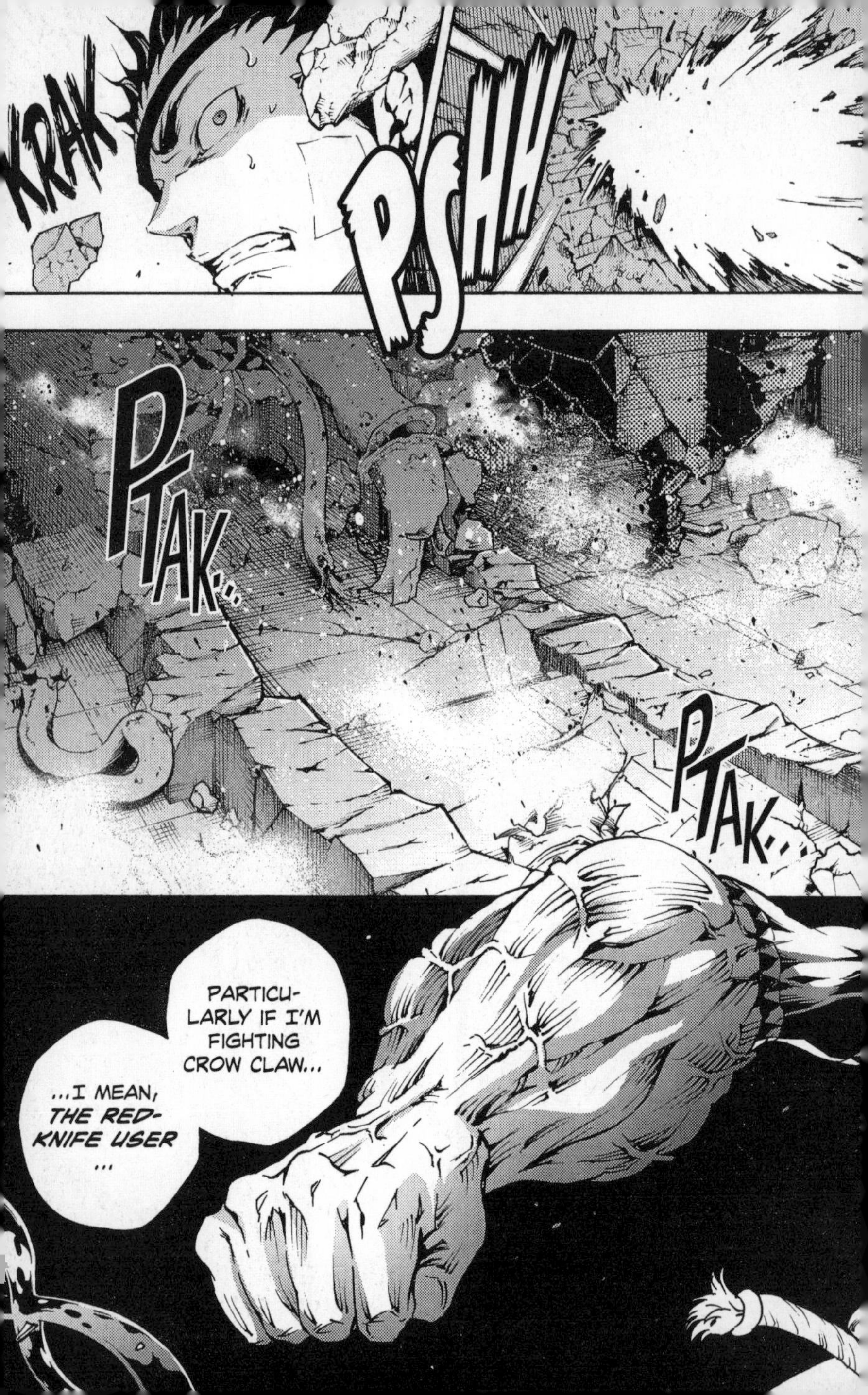
KRAK
PSHH
PTAK...
PTAK...
PARTICU-LARLY IF I'M FIGHTING CROW CLAW...
...I MEAN, *THE RED-KNIFE USER* ...

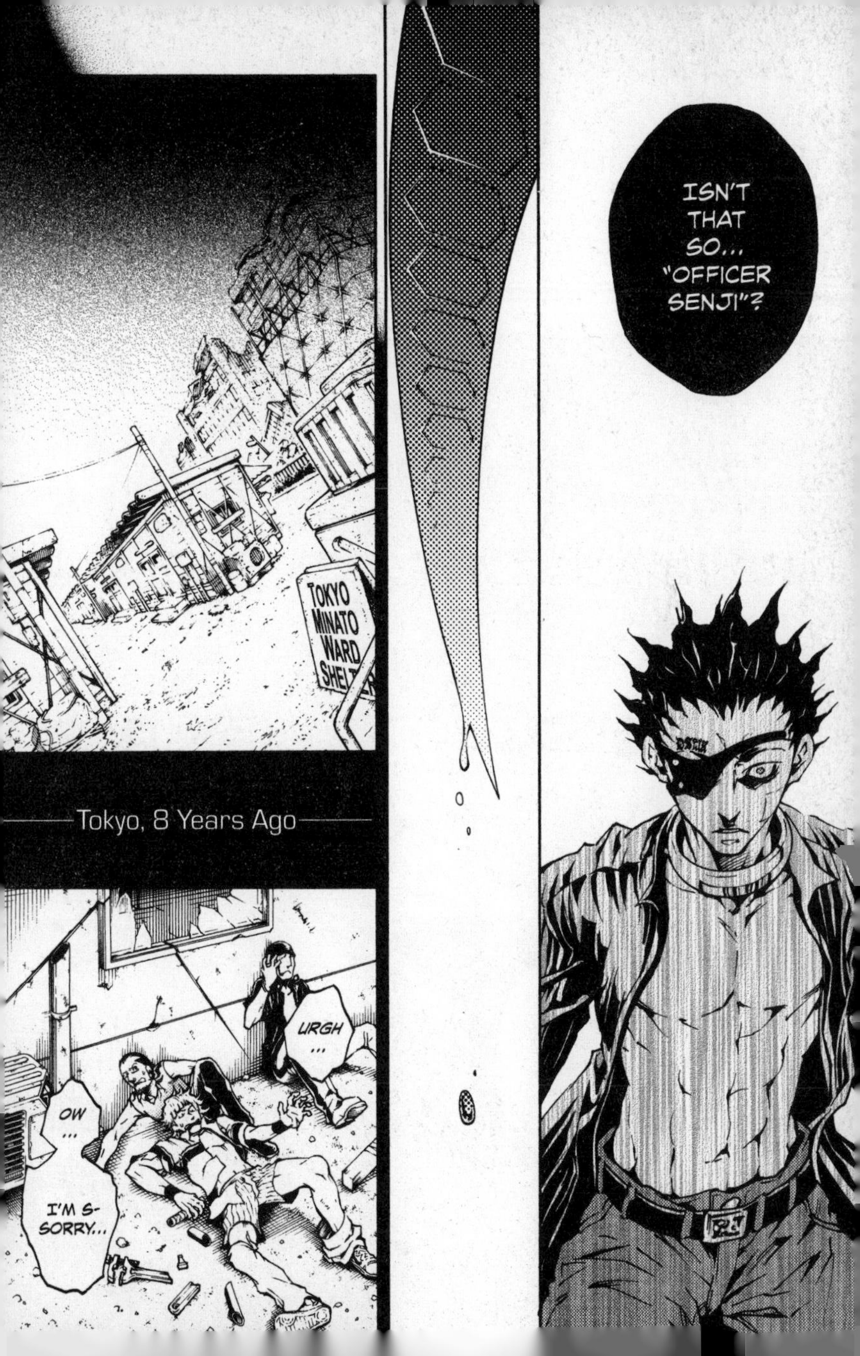
ISN'T THAT SO... "OFFICER SENJI"?
TOKYO MINATO WARD SHELTER
Tokyo, 8 Years Ago
URGH...
OW...
I'M S-SORRY...

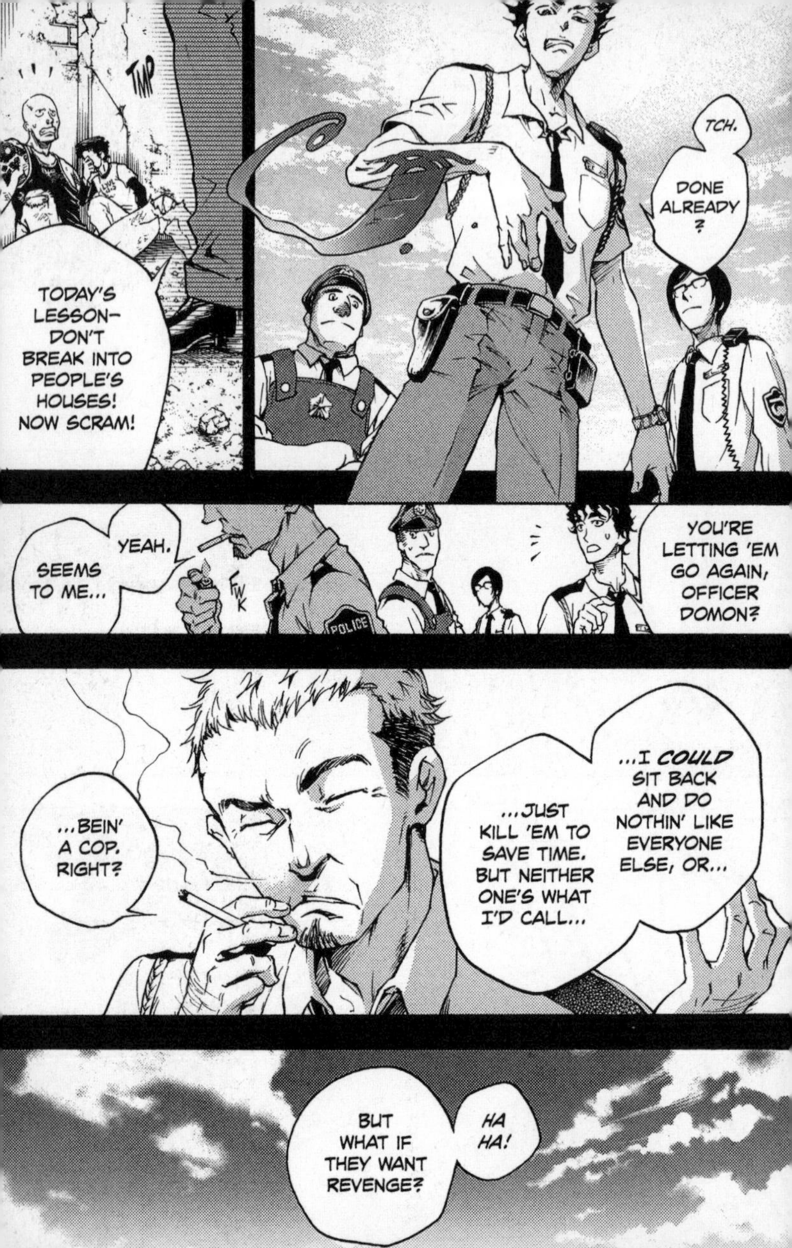
TCH.
DONE ALREADY?
TMP
TODAY'S LESSON— DON'T BREAK INTO PEOPLE'S HOUSES! NOW SCRAM!
YOU'RE LETTING 'EM GO AGAIN, OFFICER DOMON?
YEAH.
SEEMS TO ME...
FWK
...I *COULD* SIT BACK AND DO NOTHIN' LIKE EVERYONE ELSE, OR...
...JUST KILL 'EM TO SAVE TIME. BUT NEITHER ONE'S WHAT I'D CALL...
...BEIN' A COP. RIGHT?
HA HA!
BUT WHAT IF THEY WANT REVENGE?

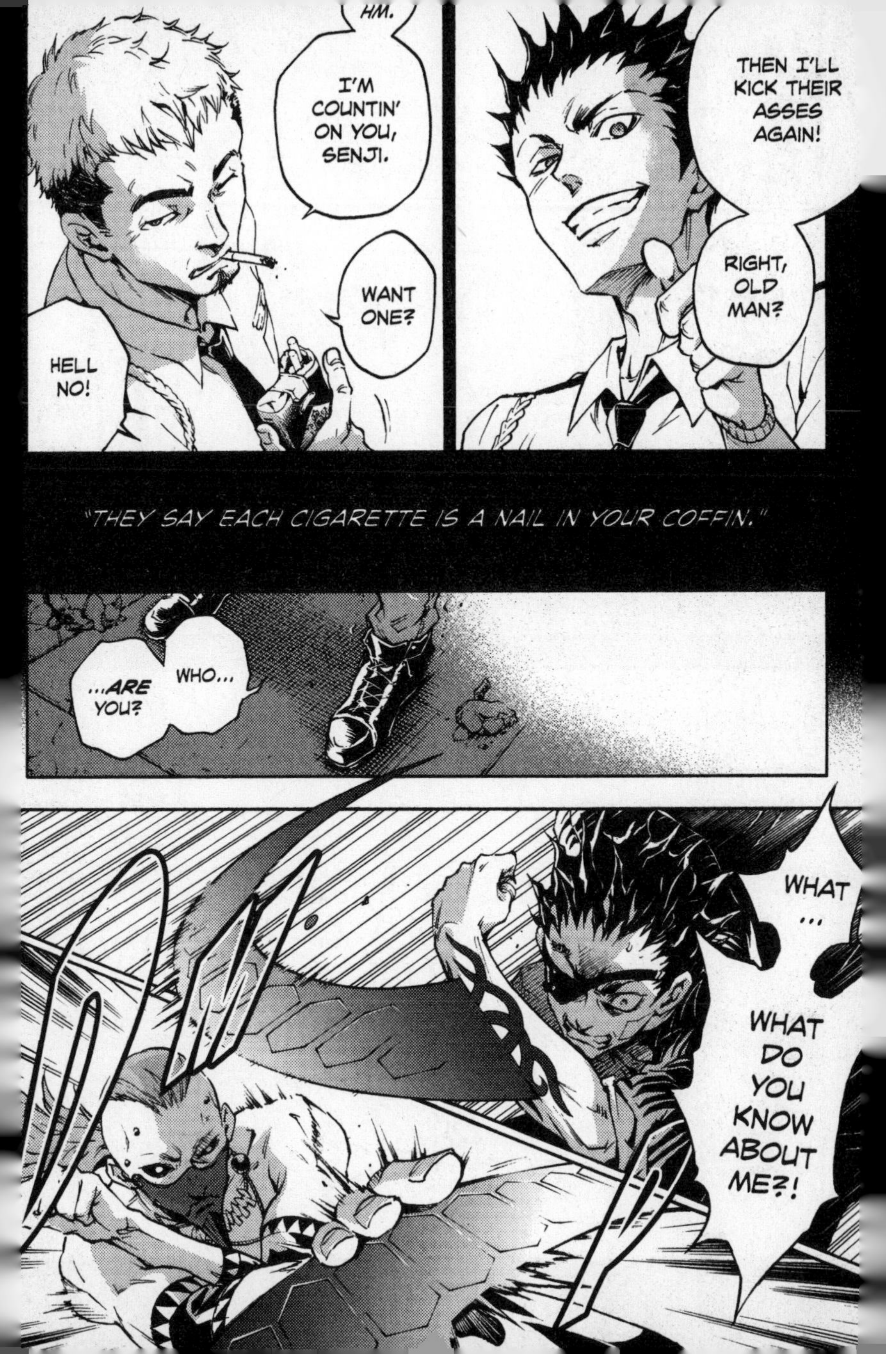
THEN I'LL KICK THEIR ASSES AGAIN!
RIGHT, OLD MAN?
HM.
I'M COUNTIN' ON YOU, SENJI.
WANT ONE?
HELL NO!
"THEY SAY EACH CIGARETTE IS A NAIL IN YOUR COFFIN."
WHO...
...ARE YOU?
WHAT...
WHAT DO YOU KNOW ABOUT ME?!

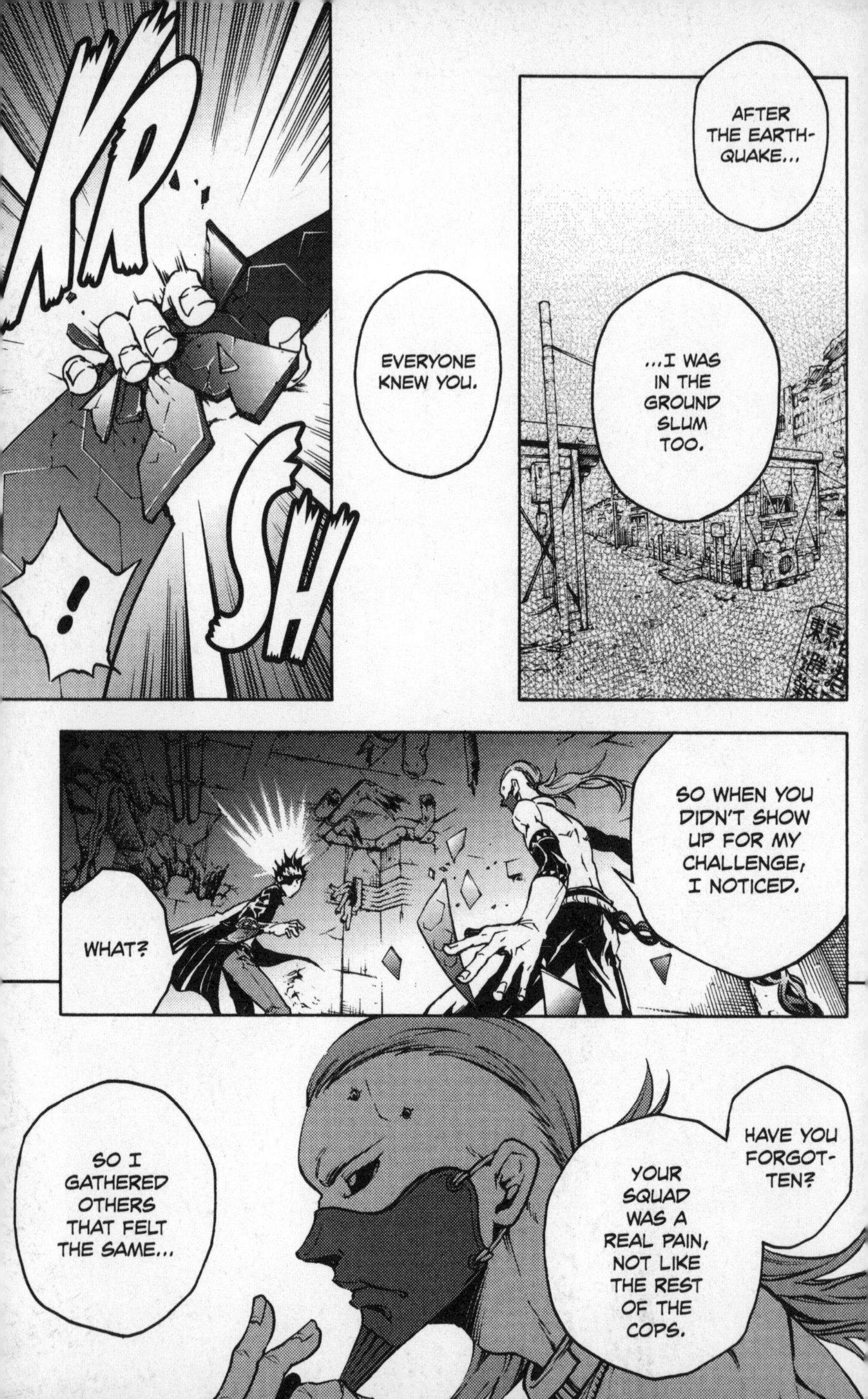

AFTER THE EARTH-QUAKE...
...I WAS IN THE GROUND SLUM TOO.
EVERYONE KNEW YOU.
KR
SH
!
SO WHEN YOU DIDN'T SHOW UP FOR MY CHALLENGE, I NOTICED.
WHAT?
HAVE YOU FORGOT-TEN?
YOUR SQUAD WAS A REAL PAIN, NOT LIKE THE REST OF THE COPS.
SO I GATHERED OTHERS THAT FELT THE SAME...

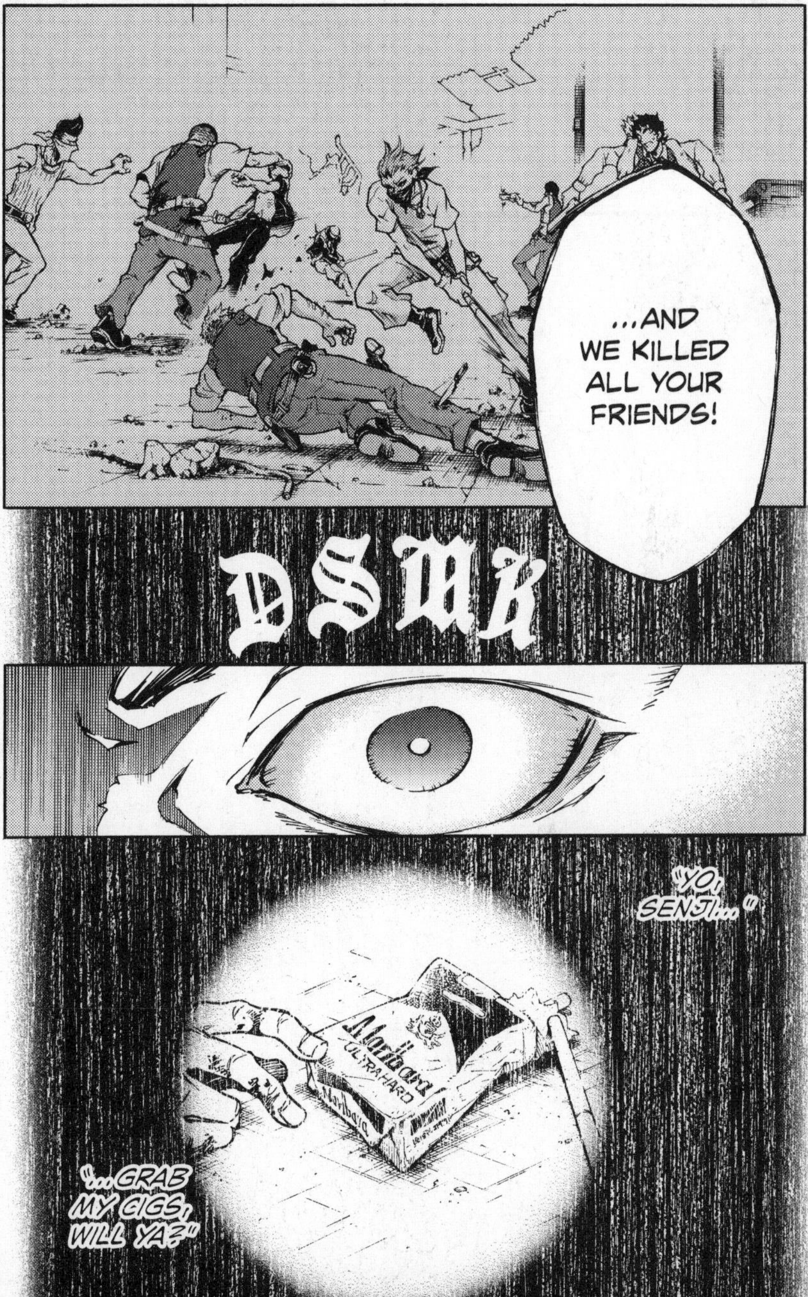
...AND WE KILLED ALL YOUR FRIENDS!
DSMK
"YO, SENJI..."
ULTRAHARD
"...GRAB MY CIGS, WILL YA?"

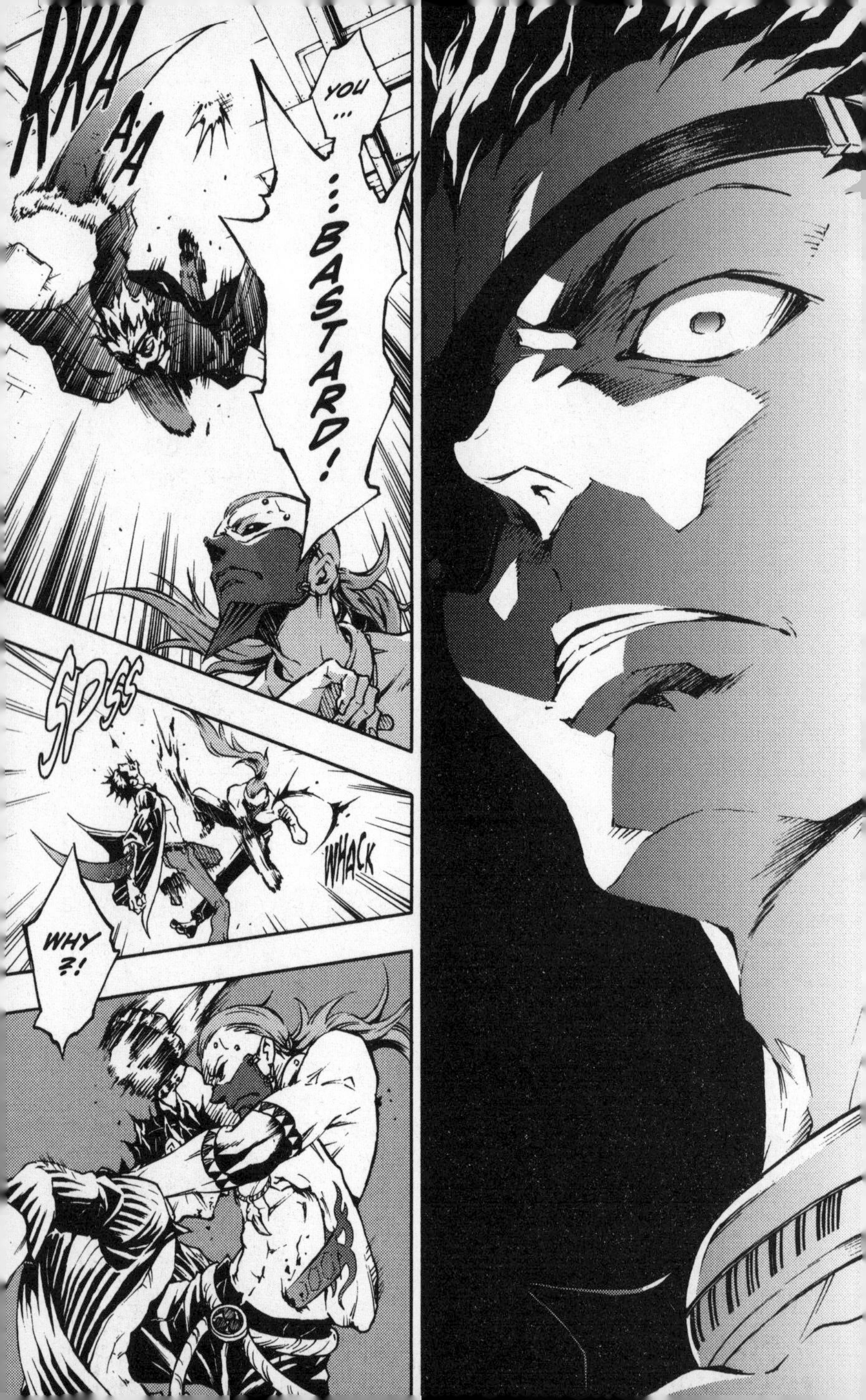
YOU ...
...BASTARD!
KRAAA
SPSS
WHACK
WHY?!

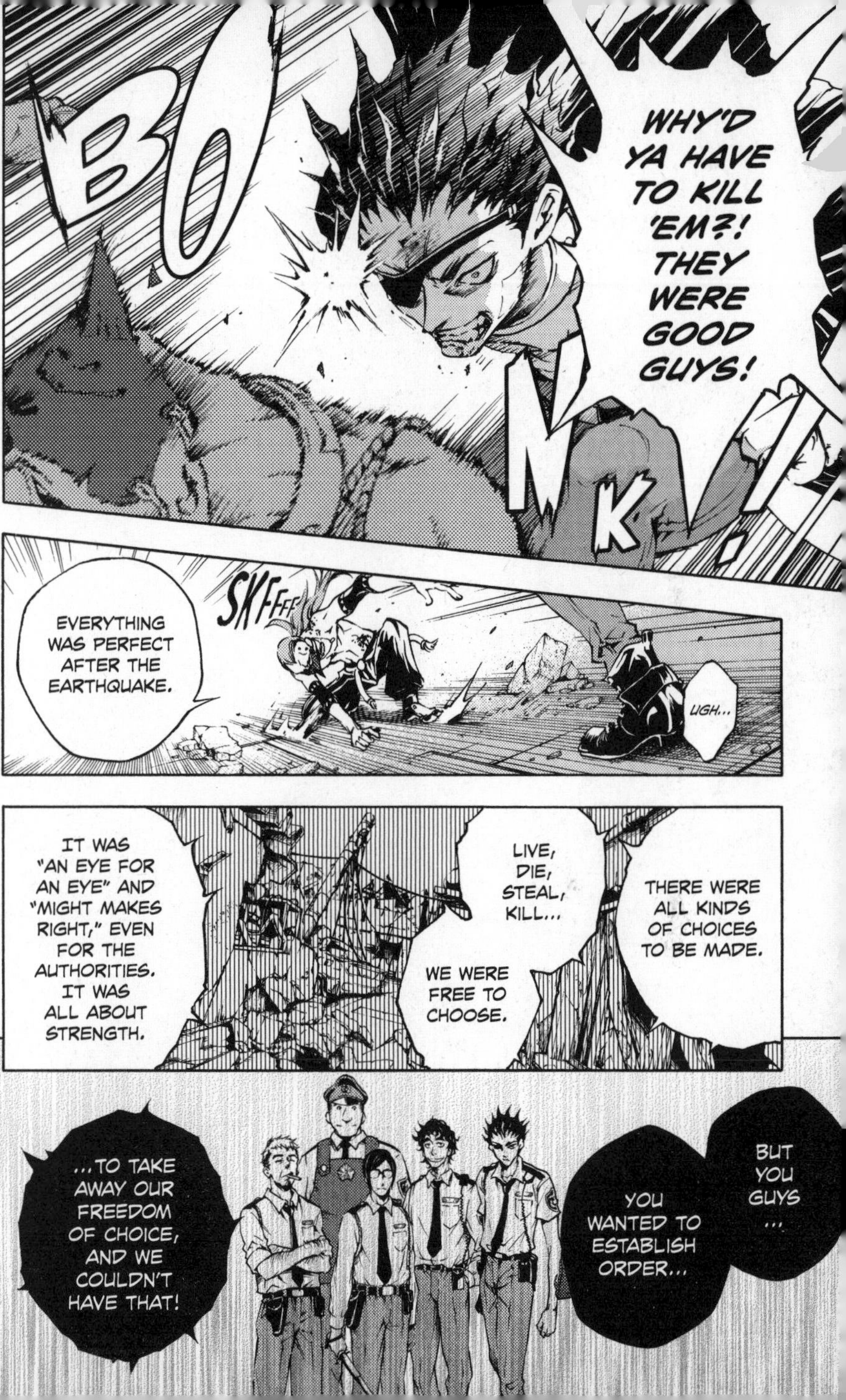
WHY'D YA HAVE TO KILL 'EM?! THEY WERE GOOD GUYS!
BONK
UGH...
SKFFFF
EVERYTHING WAS PERFECT AFTER THE EARTHQUAKE.
THERE WERE ALL KINDS OF CHOICES TO BE MADE.
LIVE, DIE, STEAL, KILL...
WE WERE FREE TO CHOOSE.
IT WAS "AN EYE FOR AN EYE" AND "MIGHT MAKES RIGHT," EVEN FOR THE AUTHORITIES. IT WAS ALL ABOUT STRENGTH.
BUT YOU GUYS...
YOU WANTED TO ESTABLISH ORDER...
...TO TAKE AWAY OUR FREEDOM OF CHOICE, AND WE COULDN'T HAVE THAT!

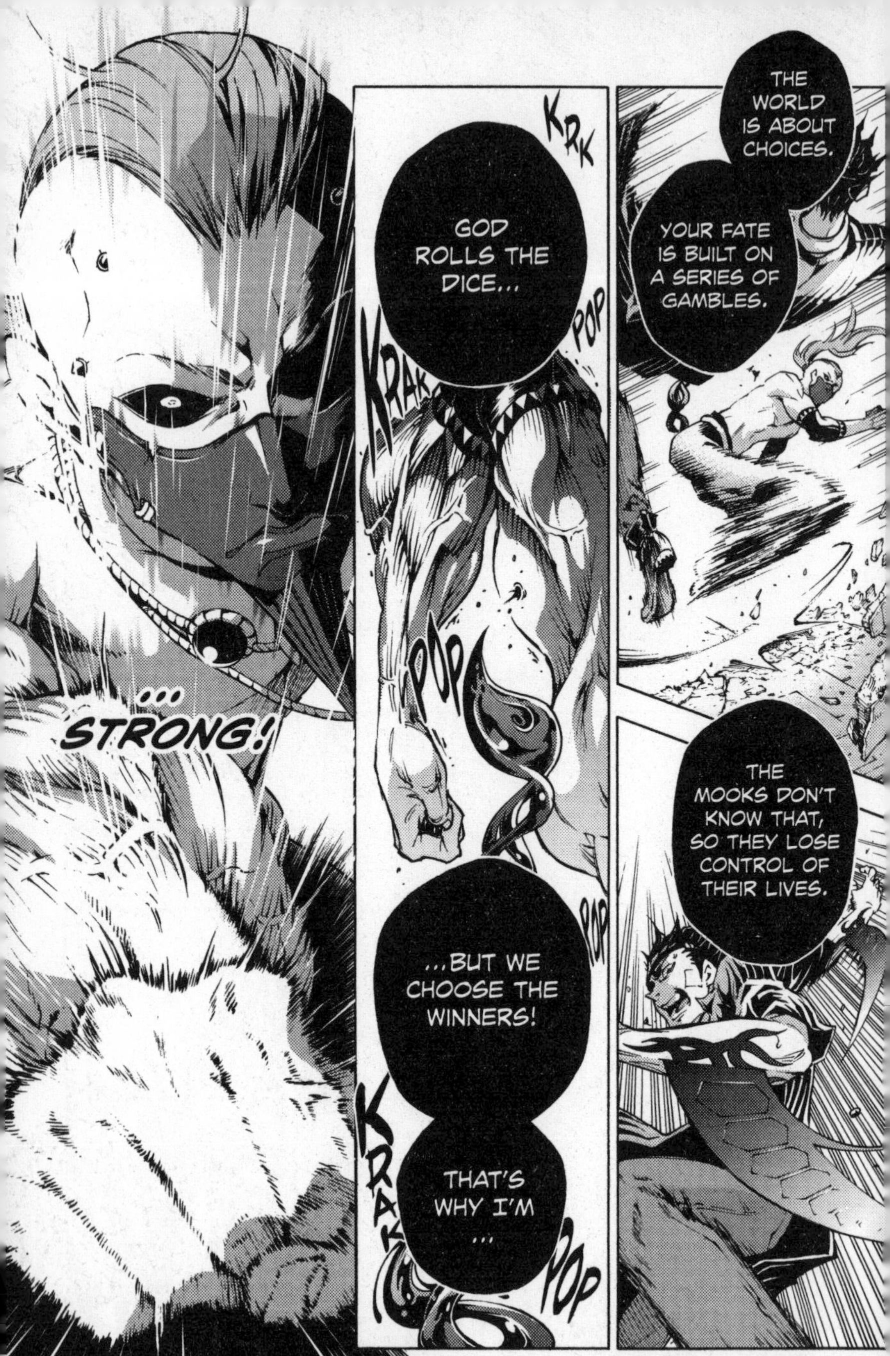
THE WORLD IS ABOUT CHOICES.
YOUR FATE IS BUILT ON A SERIES OF GAMBLES.
THE MOOKS DON'T KNOW THAT, SO THEY LOSE CONTROL OF THEIR LIVES.
KRK
GOD ROLLS THE DICE...
POP
KRAK
POP
POP
...BUT WE CHOOSE THE WINNERS!
KRAK
THAT'S WHY I'M ...
POP
... STRONG!

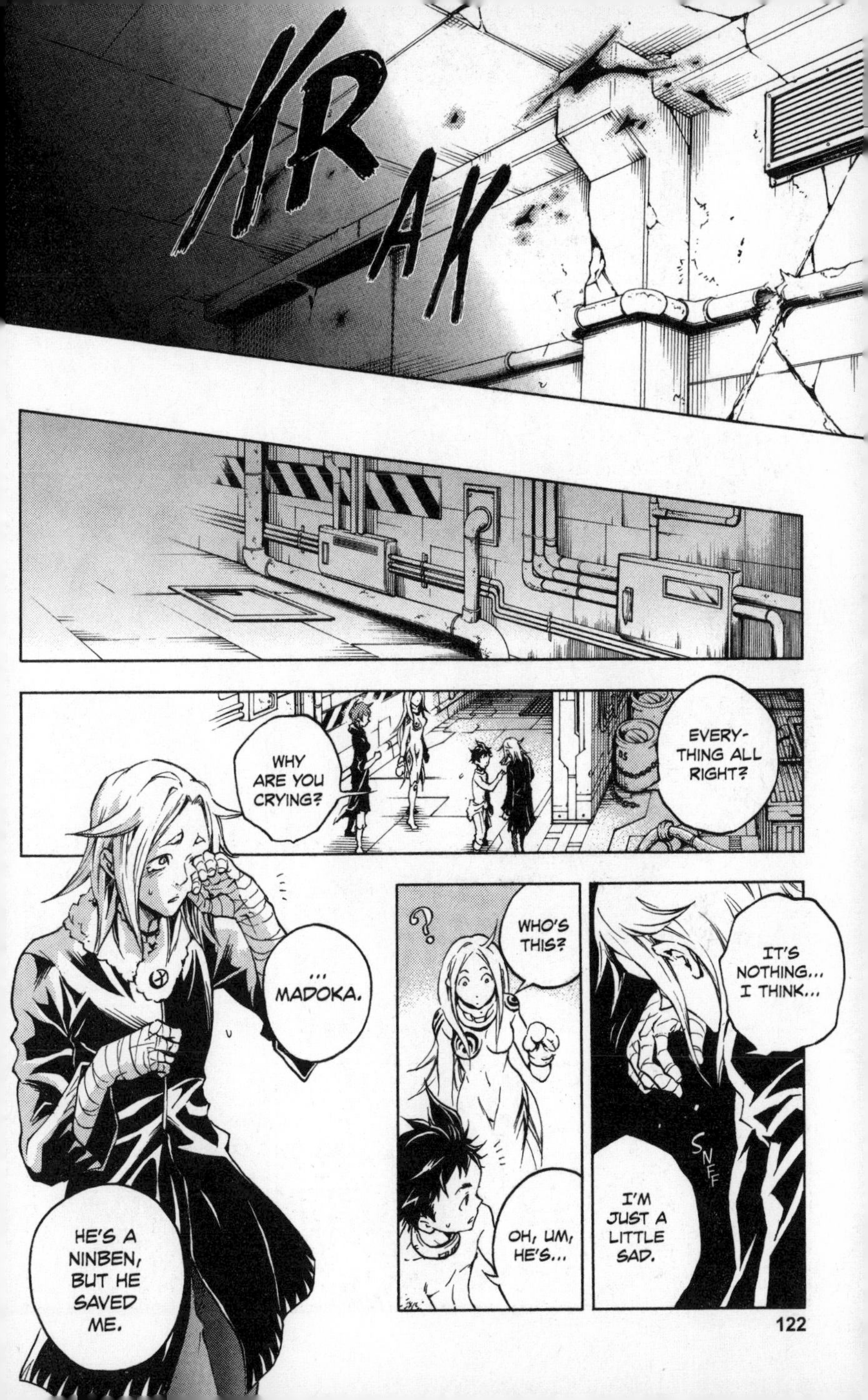
KRAK
EVERY-THING ALL RIGHT?
WHY ARE YOU CRYING?
IT'S NOTHING... I THINK...
SNFF
I'M JUST A LITTLE SAD.
WHO'S THIS?
OH, UM, HE'S...
...MADOKA.
HE'S A NINBEN, BUT HE SAVED ME.

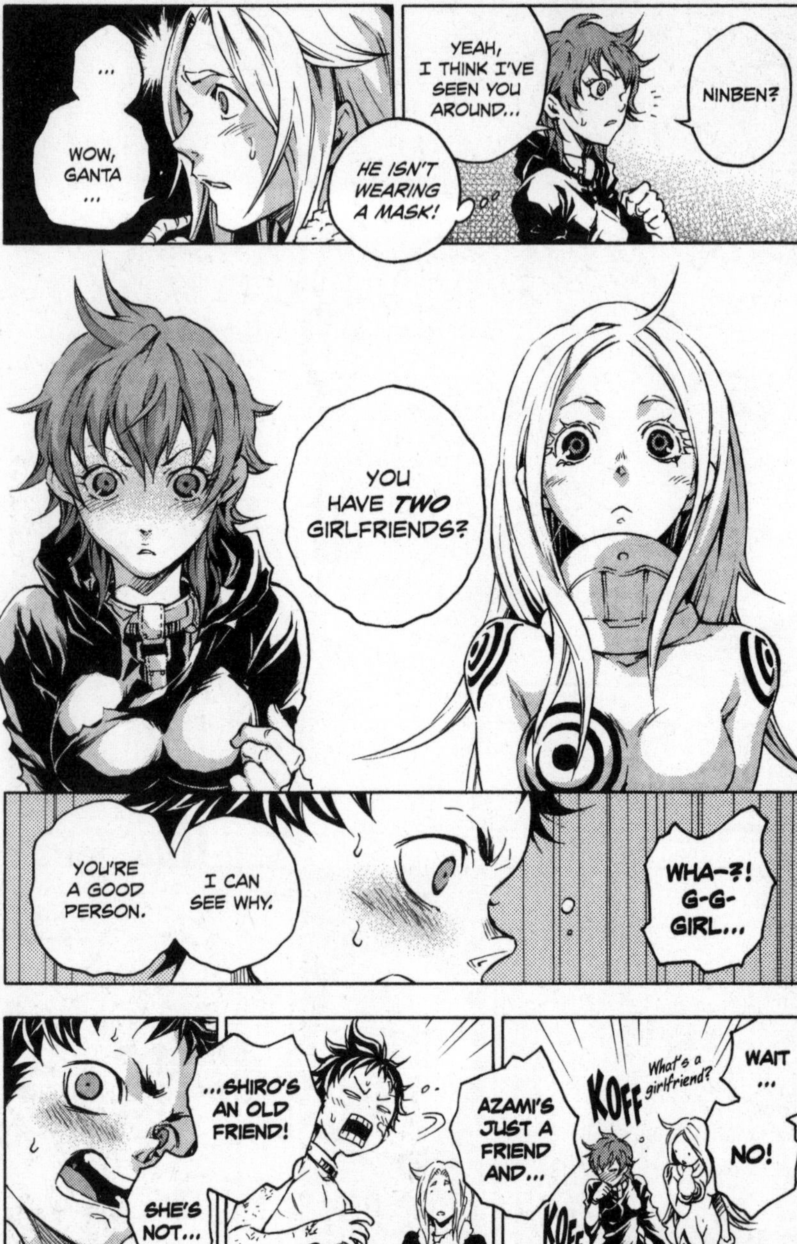
NINBEN?
YEAH, I THINK I'VE SEEN YOU AROUND...
HE ISN'T WEARING A MASK!
... WOW, GANTA ...
YOU HAVE TWO GIRLFRIENDS?
WHA-?! G-G-GIRL...
I CAN SEE WHY.
YOU'RE A GOOD PERSON.
WAIT ...
What's a girlfriend?
KOFF
NO!
KOFF
AZAMI'S JUST A FRIEND AND...
...SHIRO'S AN OLD FRIEND!
SHE'S NOT...

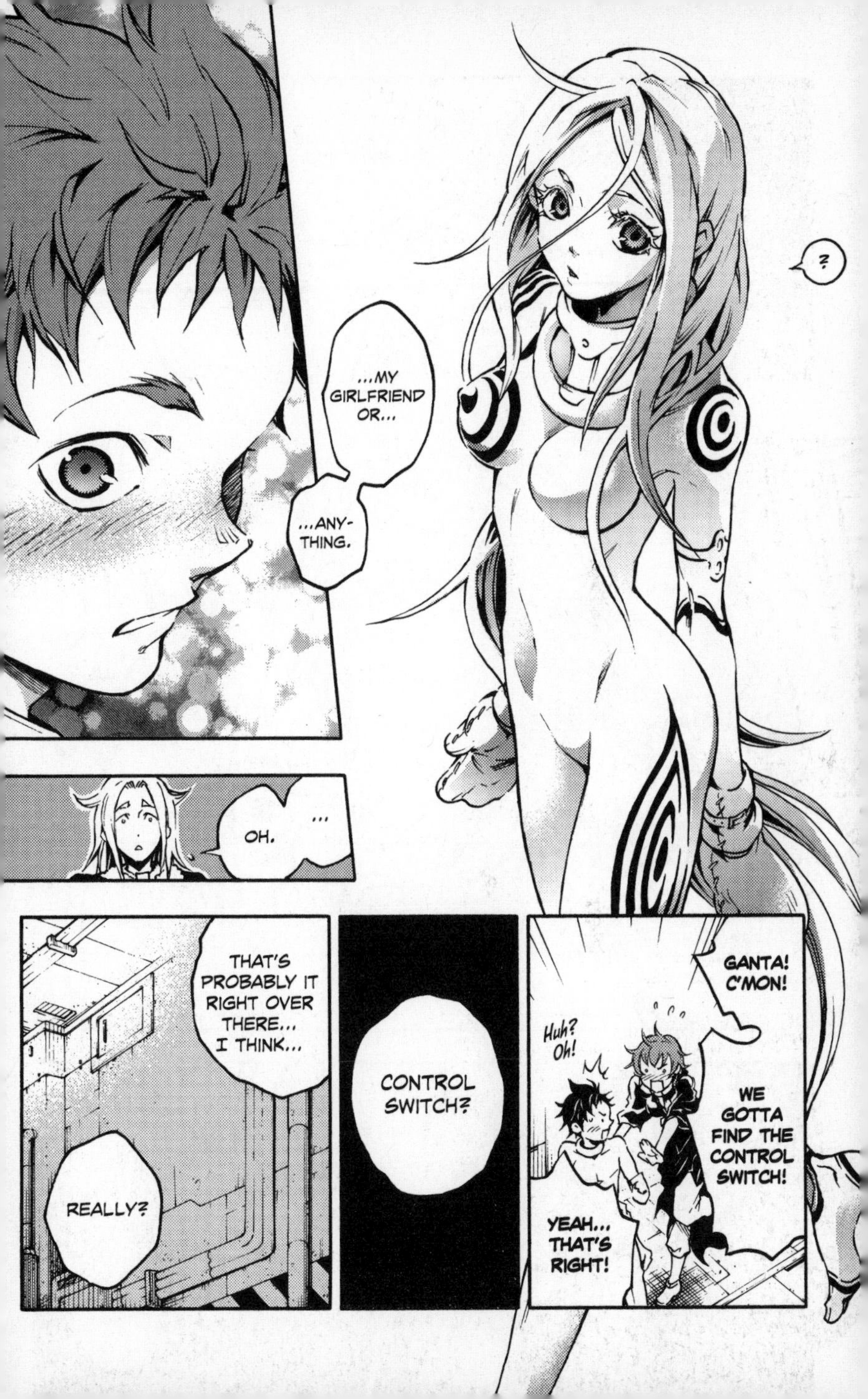
?
...MY GIRLFRIEND OR...
...ANY-THING.
...
OH.
GANTA! C'MON!
Huh? Oh!
WE GOTTA FIND THE CONTROL SWITCH!
YEAH... THAT'S RIGHT!
CONTROL SWITCH?
THAT'S PROBABLY IT RIGHT OVER THERE... I THINK...
REALLY?

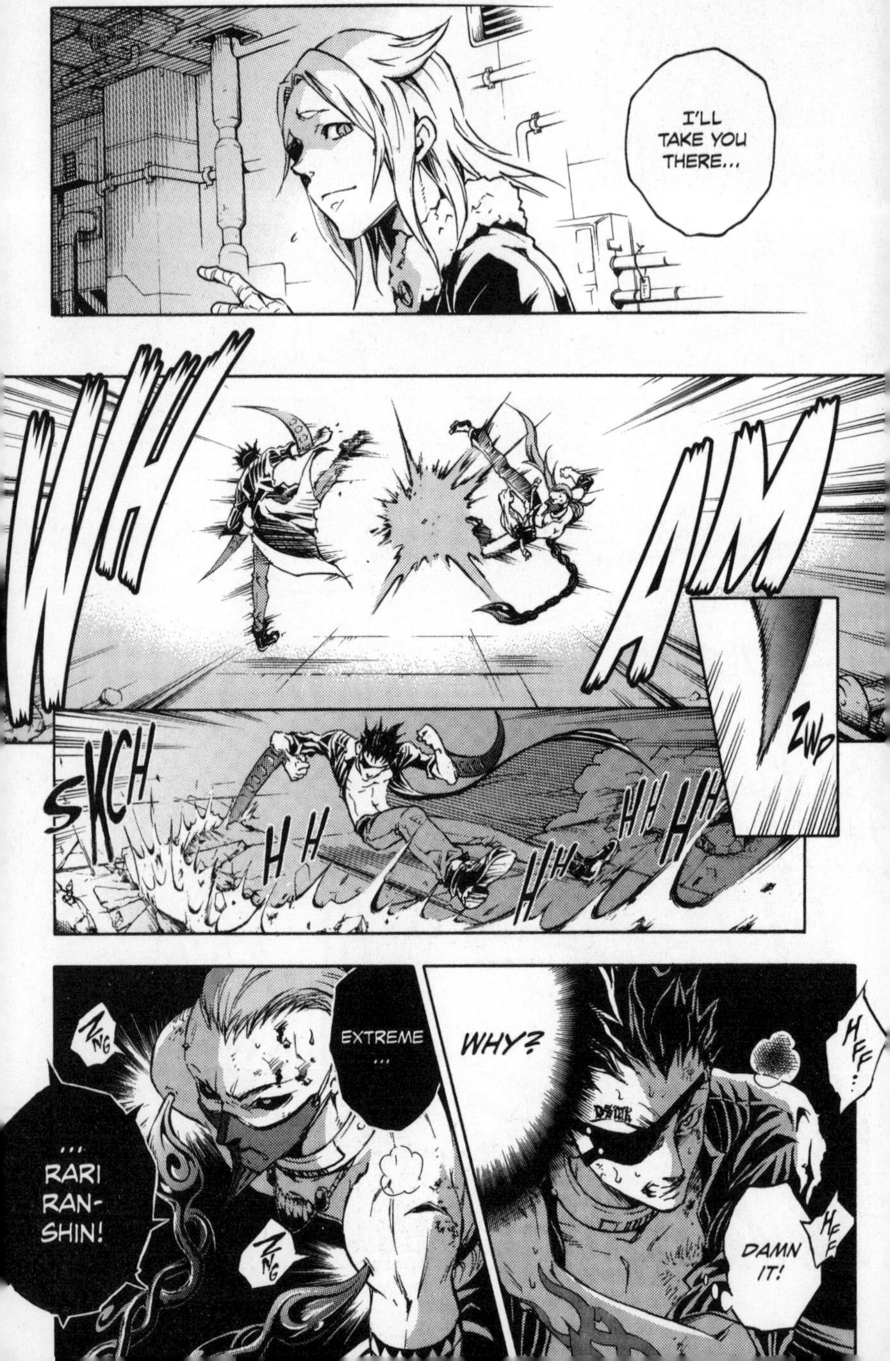
I'LL TAKE YOU THERE...
WHAM
ZWD
SKCH
HHHHH
HFF...
WHY?
HFF
DAMN IT!
EXTREME...
NNG
...RARI RAN-SHIN!
NNG

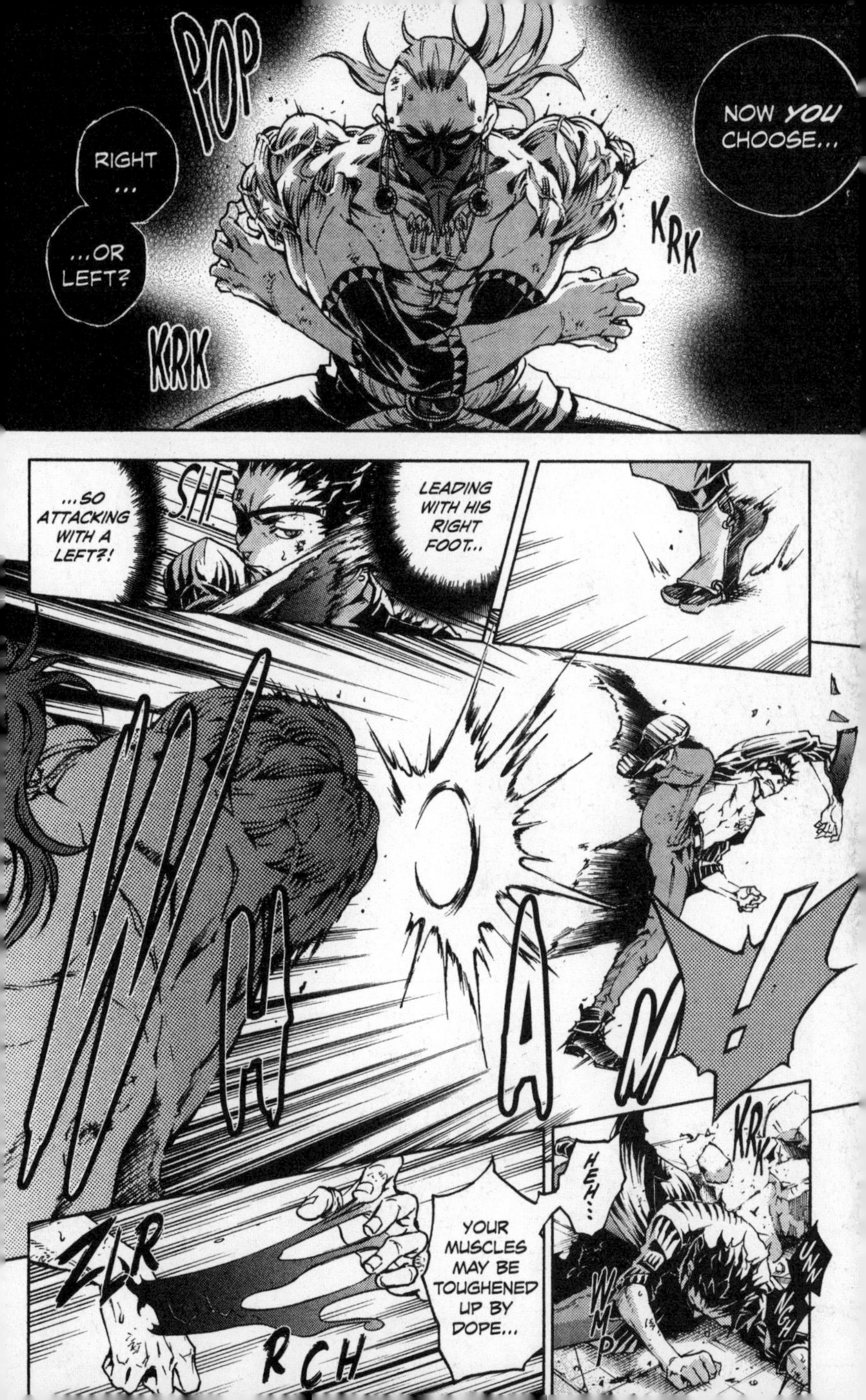
NOW *YOU* CHOOSE...
POP
RIGHT...
...OR LEFT?
KRK
KRK
LEADING WITH HIS RIGHT FOOT...
SHF
...SO ATTACKING WITH A LEFT?!
WHAM!
HEH...
KRK
UNNGH
WMP
YOUR MUSCLES MAY BE TOUGHENED UP BY DOPE...
ZLR
RCH

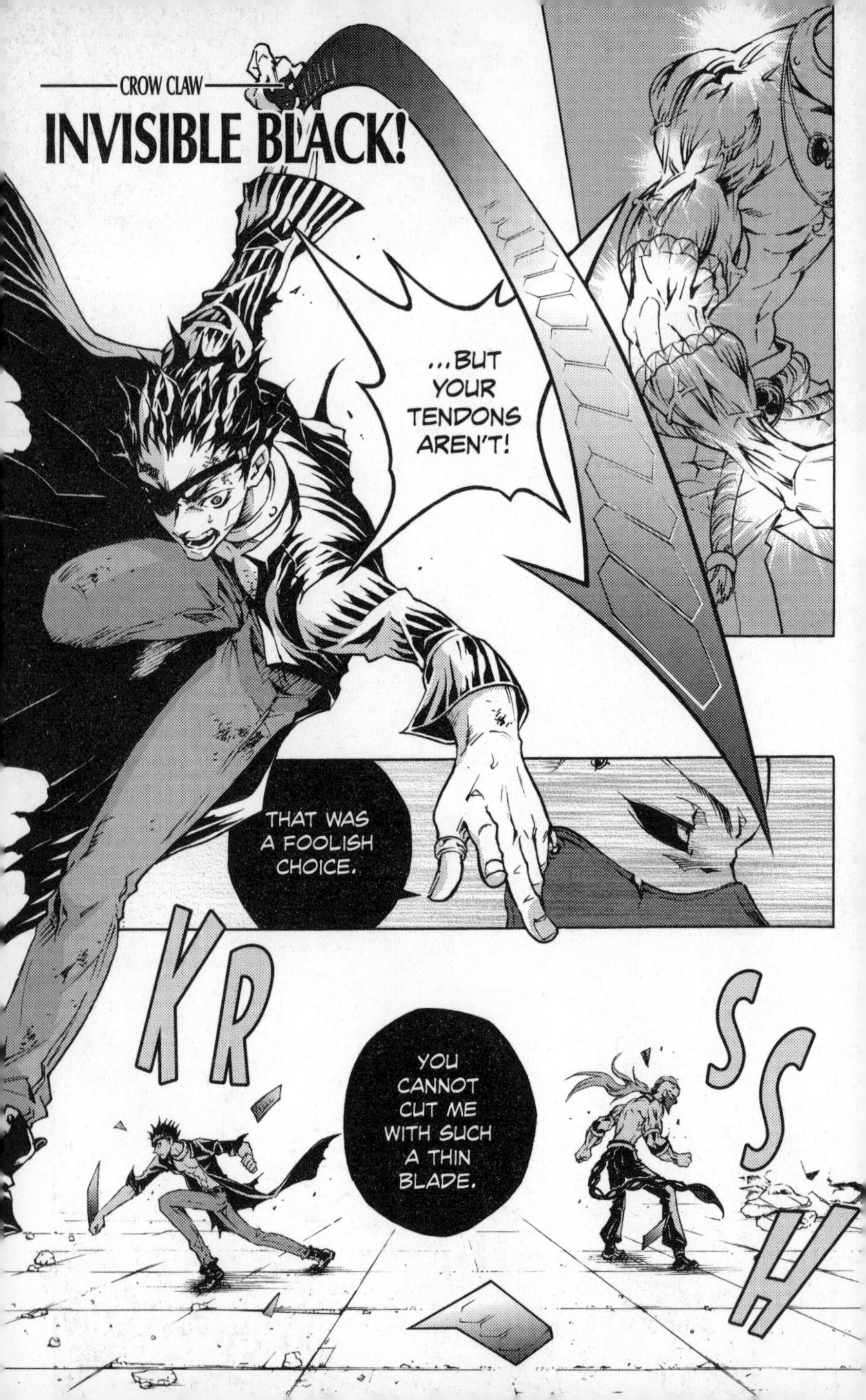
...BUT YOUR TENDONS AREN'T!
CROW CLAW
INVISIBLE BLACK!
THAT WAS A FOOLISH CHOICE.
KR
SSH
YOU CANNOT CUT ME WITH SUCH A THIN BLADE.

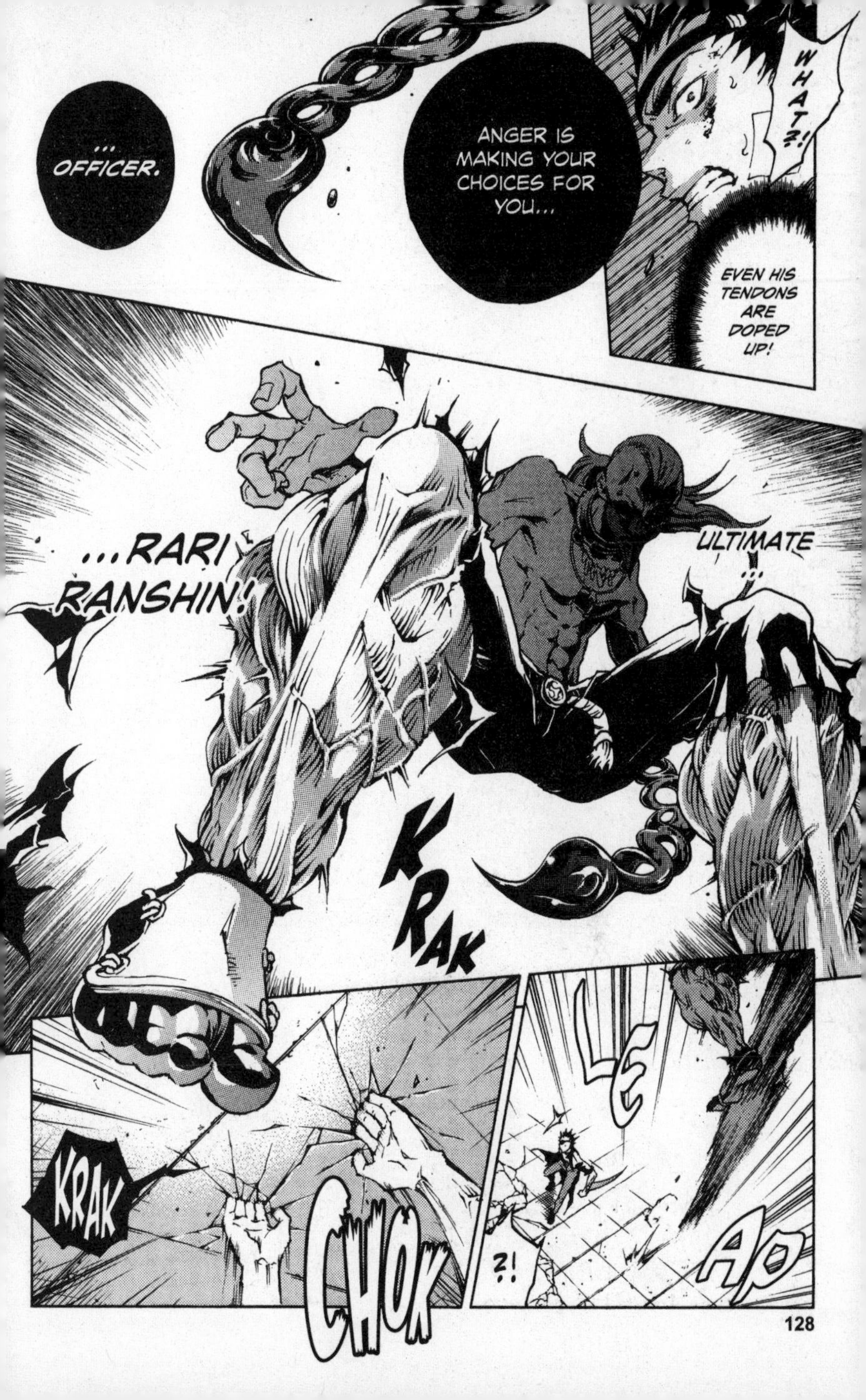
WHAT?!
EVEN HIS TENDONS ARE DOPED UP!
ANGER IS MAKING YOUR CHOICES FOR YOU...
...OFFICER.
ULTIMATE...
...RARI RANSHIN!
KRAK
LEAP
?!
KRAK
CHOK

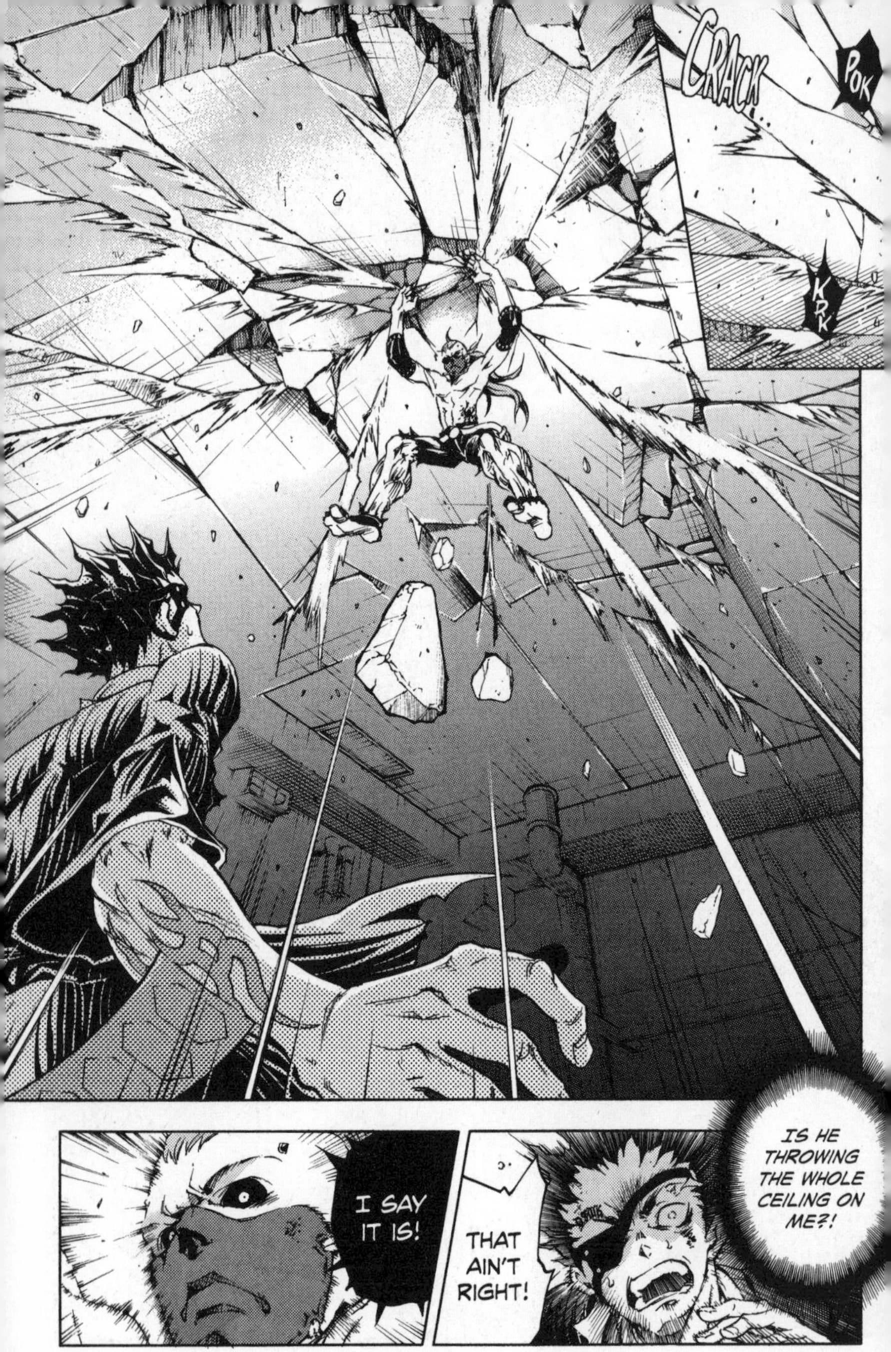
POK
CRACK...
KRK
IS HE THROWING THE WHOLE CEILING ON ME?!
THAT AIN'T RIGHT!
I SAY IT IS!

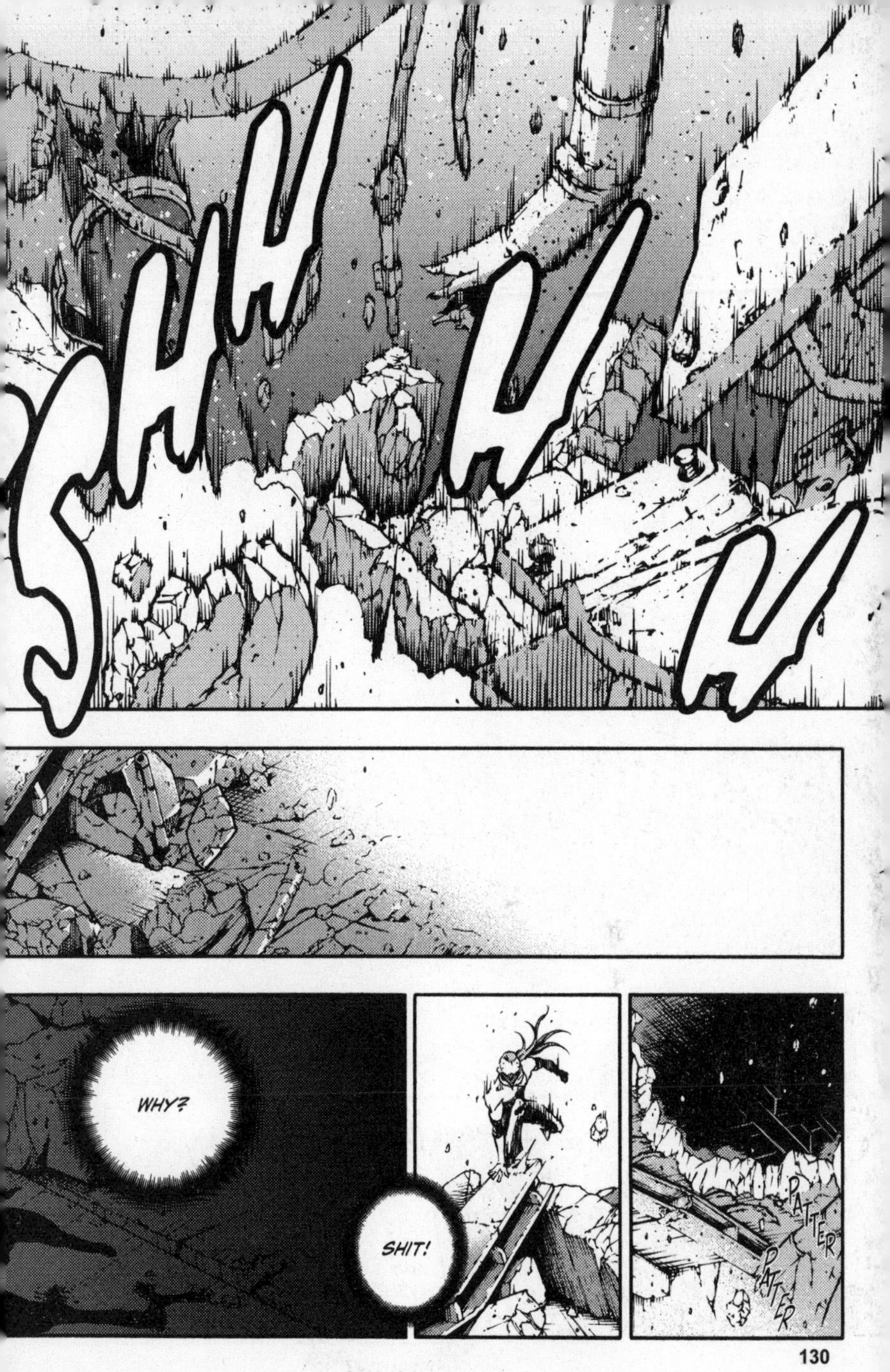
SHHHH
PATTER
PATTER
SHIT!
WHY?

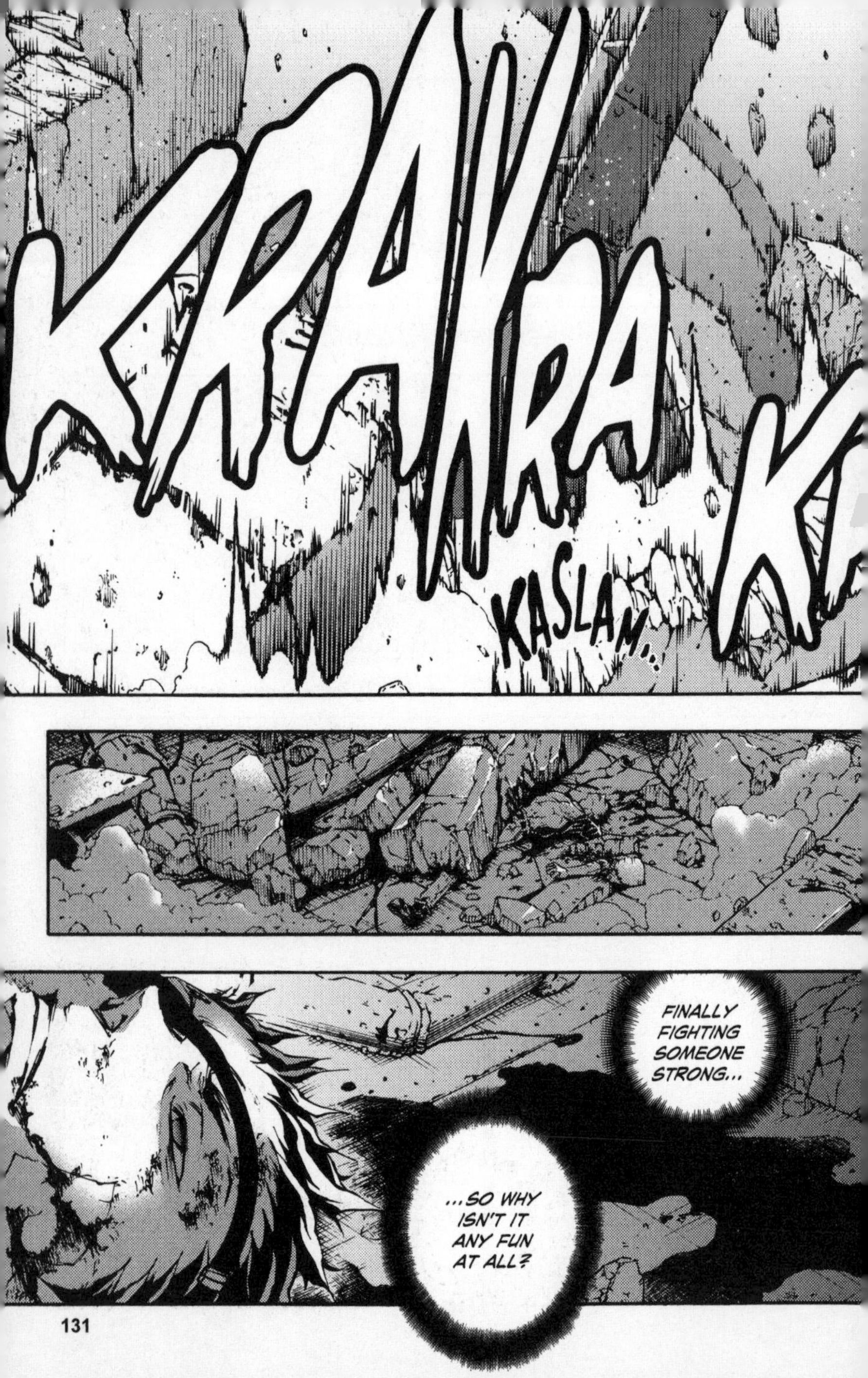
KASLAM..
FINALLY FIGHTING SOMEONE STRONG...
...SO WHY ISN'T IT ANY FUN AT ALL?

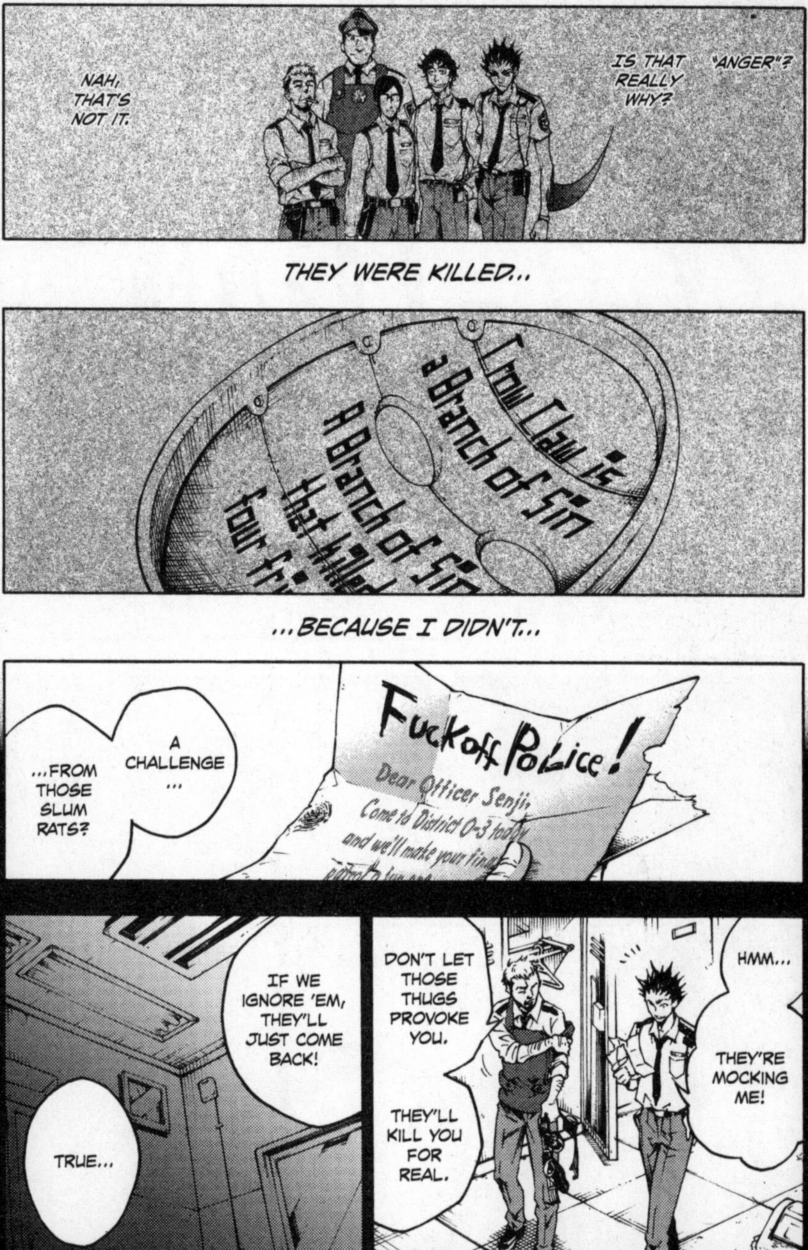
"ANGER"?
IS THAT REALLY WHY?
NAH, THAT'S NOT IT.
THEY WERE KILLED...
Crow Claw is
a Branch of Sin
A Branch of Sin
...BECAUSE I DIDN'T...
Fuckoff Police!
Dear Officer Senji,
A CHALLENGE...
...FROM THOSE SLUM RATS?
HMM...
THEY'RE MOCKING ME!
DON'T LET THOSE THUGS PROVOKE YOU.
THEY'LL KILL YOU FOR REAL.
IF WE IGNORE 'EM, THEY'LL JUST COME BACK!
TRUE...

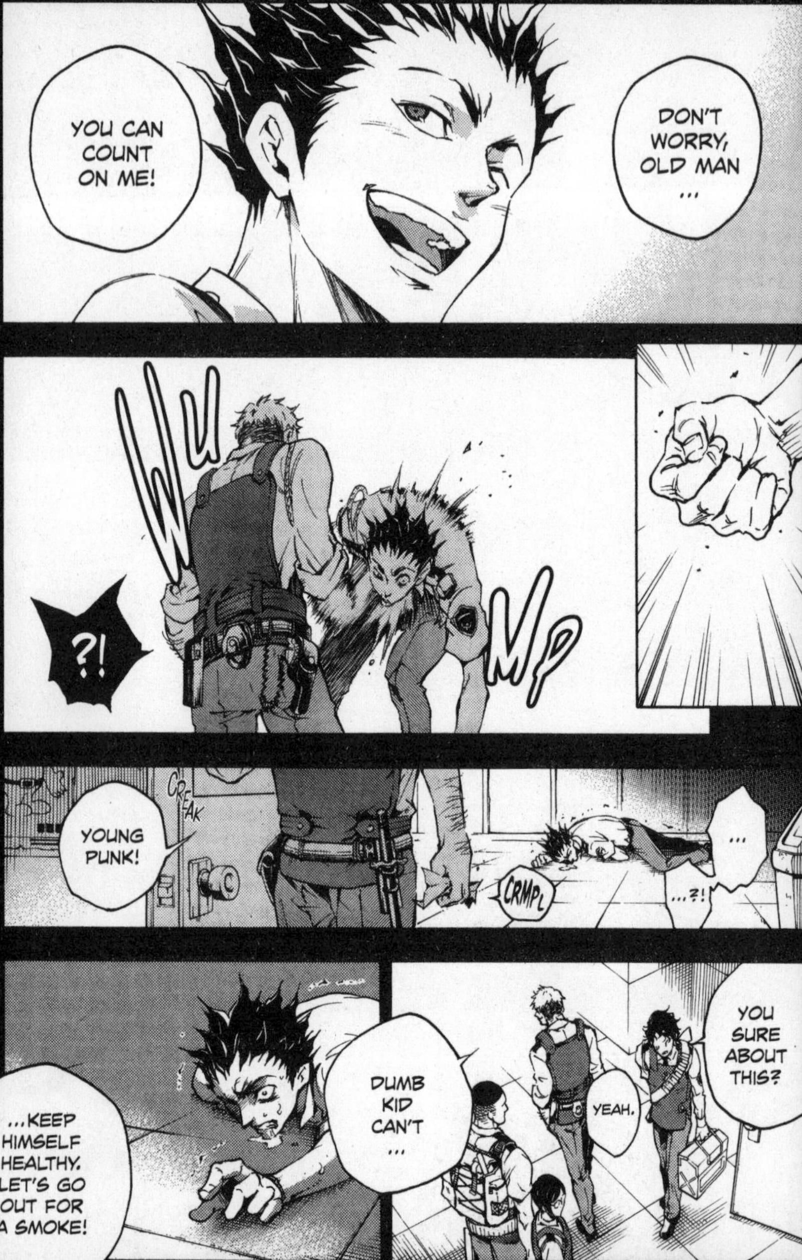
DON'T WORRY, OLD MAN ...
YOU CAN COUNT ON ME!
WUMP
?!
...
...?!
CRMPL
CREAK
YOUNG PUNK!
YOU SURE ABOUT THIS?
YEAH.
DUMB KID CAN'T ...
...KEEP HIMSELF HEALTHY. LET'S GO OUT FOR A SMOKE!

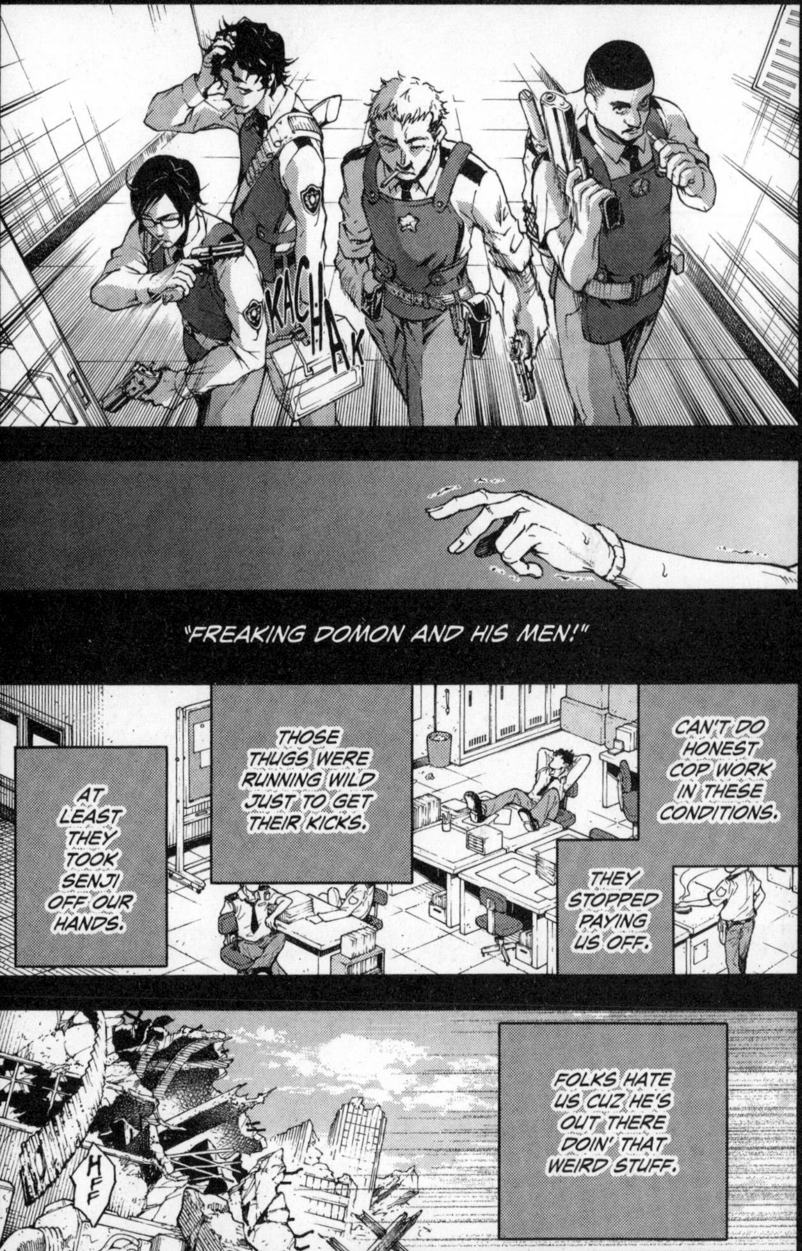
KACHAK
"FREAKING DOMON AND HIS MEN!"
CAN'T DO HONEST COP WORK IN THESE CONDITIONS.
THEY STOPPED PAYING US OFF.
THOSE THUGS WERE RUNNING WILD JUST TO GET THEIR KICKS.
AT LEAST THEY TOOK SENJI OFF OUR HANDS.
FOLKS HATE US CUZ HE'S OUT THERE DOIN' THAT WEIRD STUFF.
HFF

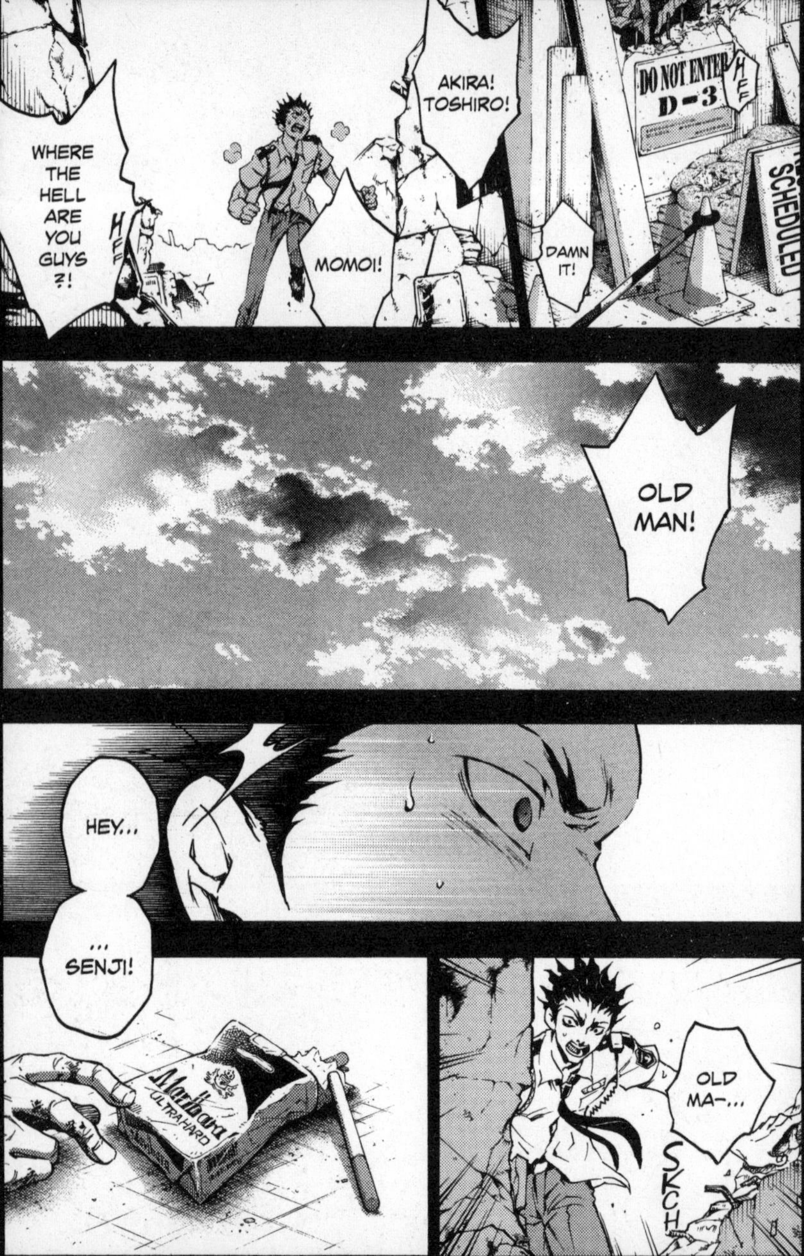
DO NOT ENTER
D-3
HFF
AKIRA! TOSHIRO!
SCHEDULED
DAMN IT!
MOMOI!
WHERE THE HELL ARE YOU GUYS?!
HFF
OLD MAN!
HEY...
...SENJI!
OLD MA-...
SKCH
ULTRA HARD

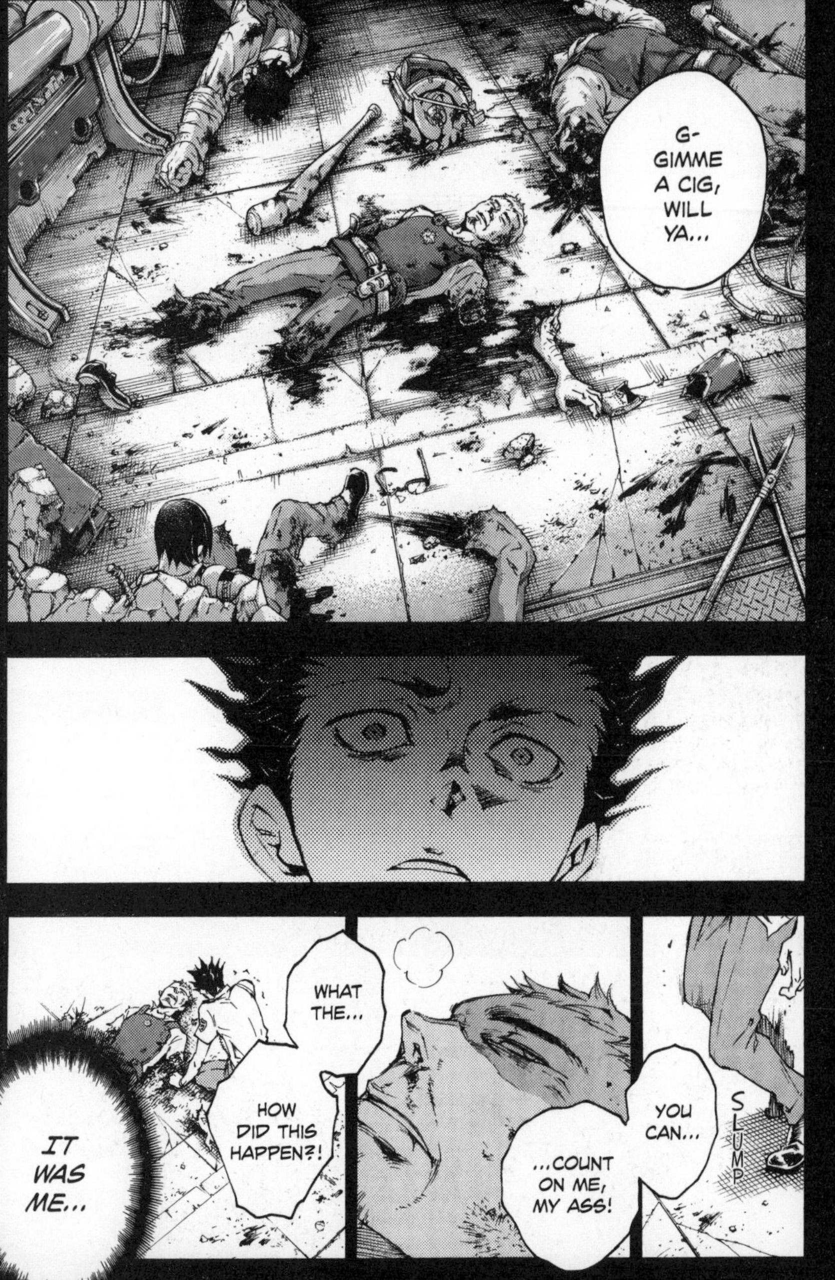
G- GIMME A CIG, WILL YA...
SLUMP
YOU CAN...
...COUNT ON ME, MY ASS!
WHAT THE...
HOW DID THIS HAPPEN?!
IT WAS ME...

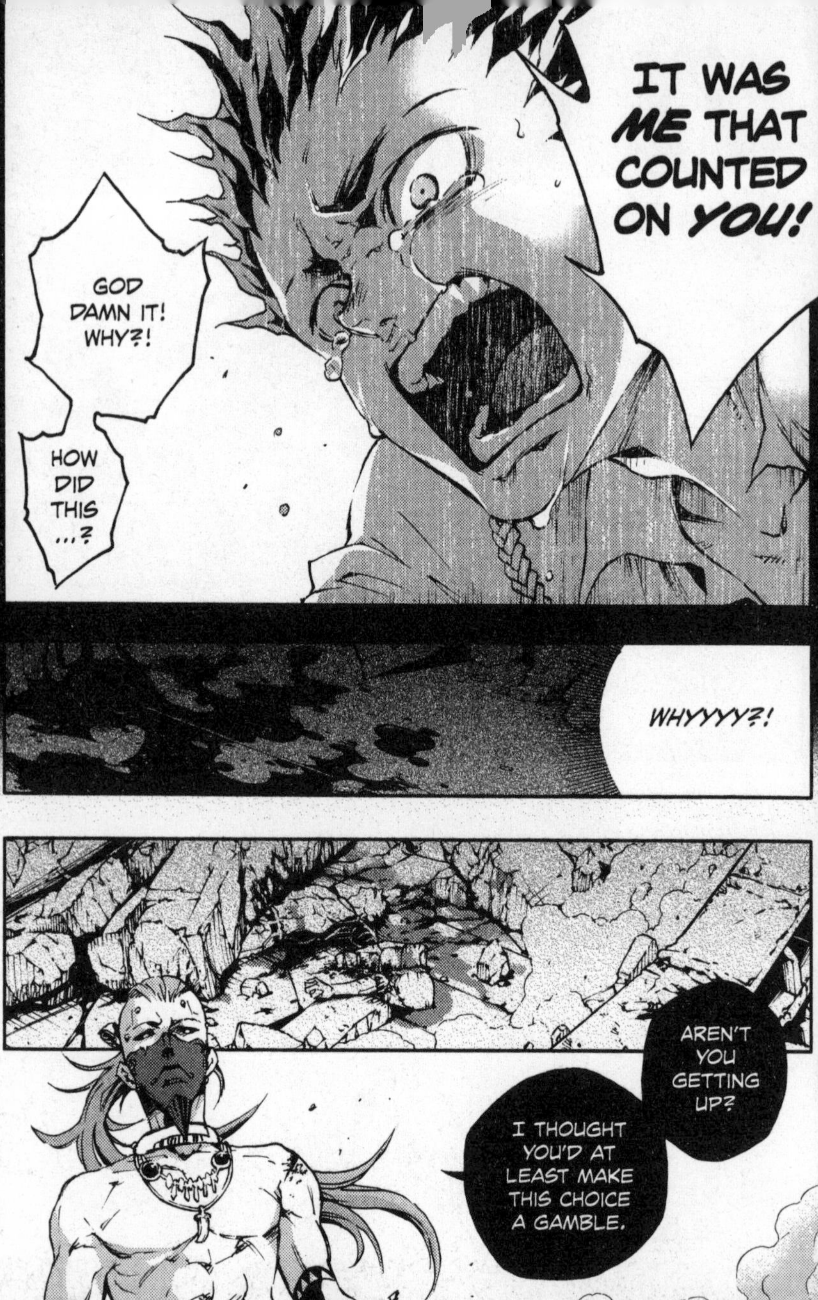
IT WAS *ME* THAT COUNTED ON *YOU!*
GOD DAMN IT! WHY?!
HOW DID THIS ...?
WHYYYY?!
AREN'T YOU GETTING UP?
I THOUGHT YOU'D AT LEAST MAKE THIS CHOICE A GAMBLE.

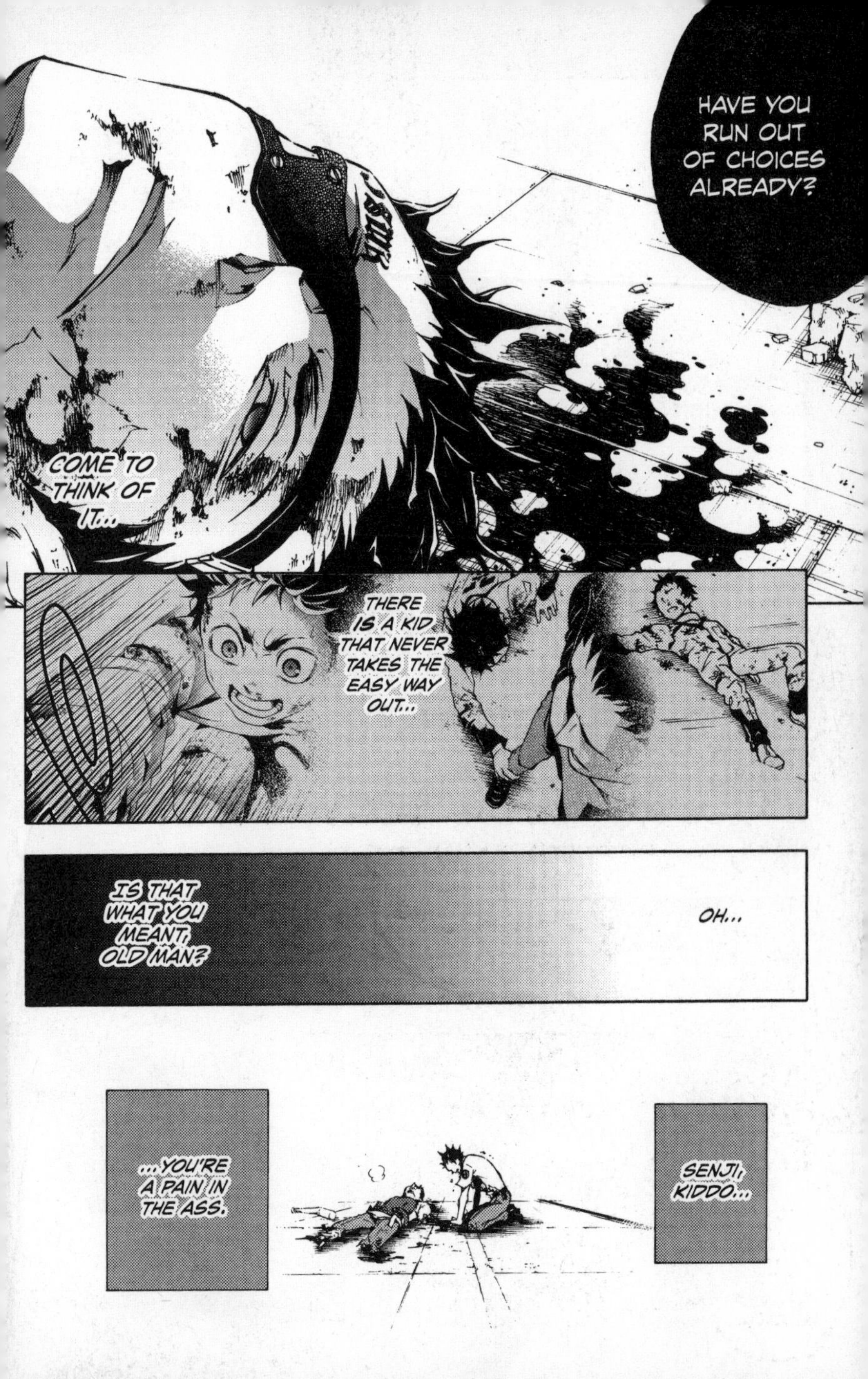
HAVE YOU RUN OUT OF CHOICES ALREADY?
COME TO THINK OF IT...
THERE IS A KID THAT NEVER TAKES THE EASY WAY OUT...
OH...
IS THAT WHAT YOU MEANT, OLD MAN?
SENJI, KIDDO...
...YOU'RE A PAIN IN THE ASS.

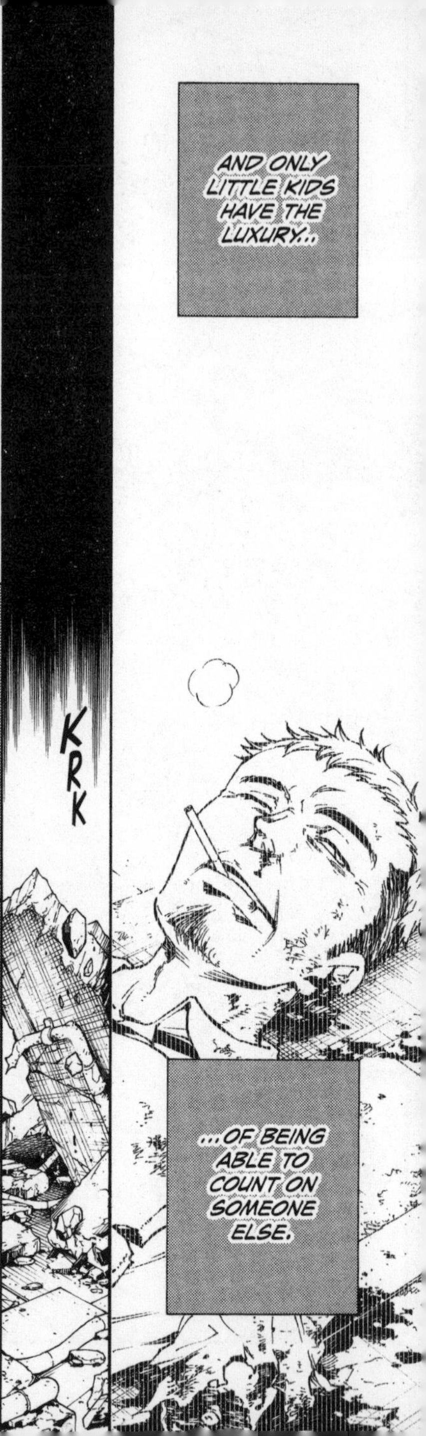
AND ONLY LITTLE KIDS HAVE THE LUXURY...
KRK
...OF BEING ABLE TO COUNT ON SOMEONE ELSE.

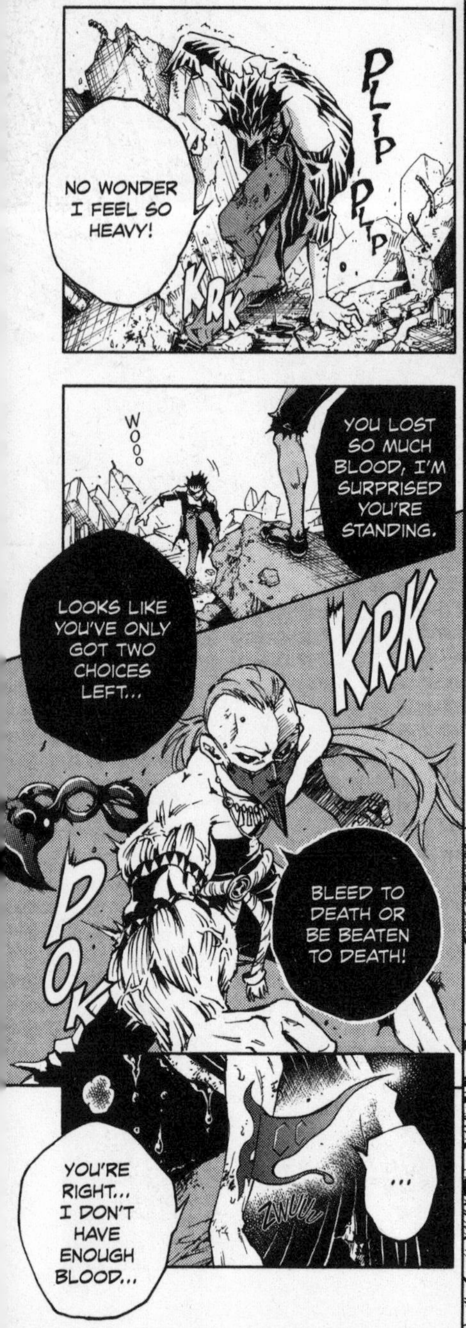
PLIP
PLIP
NO WONDER I FEEL SO HEAVY!
KRK
YOU LOST SO MUCH BLOOD, I'M SURPRISED YOU'RE STANDING.
WOOO
KRK
LOOKS LIKE YOU'VE ONLY GOT TWO CHOICES LEFT...
BLEED TO DEATH OR BE BEATEN TO DEATH!
POK
...
YOU'RE RIGHT... I DON'T HAVE ENOUGH BLOOD...

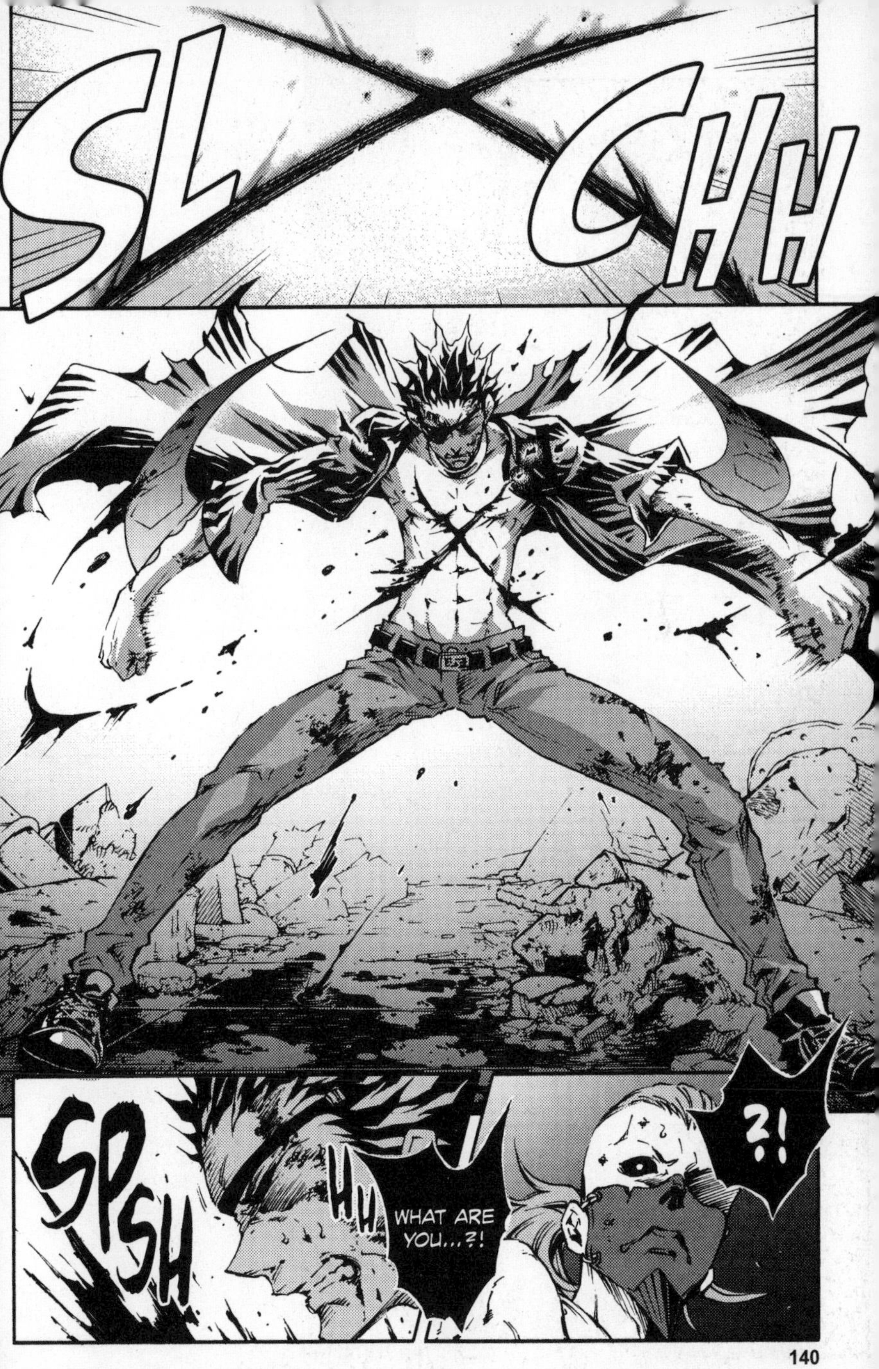
SL CHH
?!
WHAT ARE YOU...?!
HH
SPSH

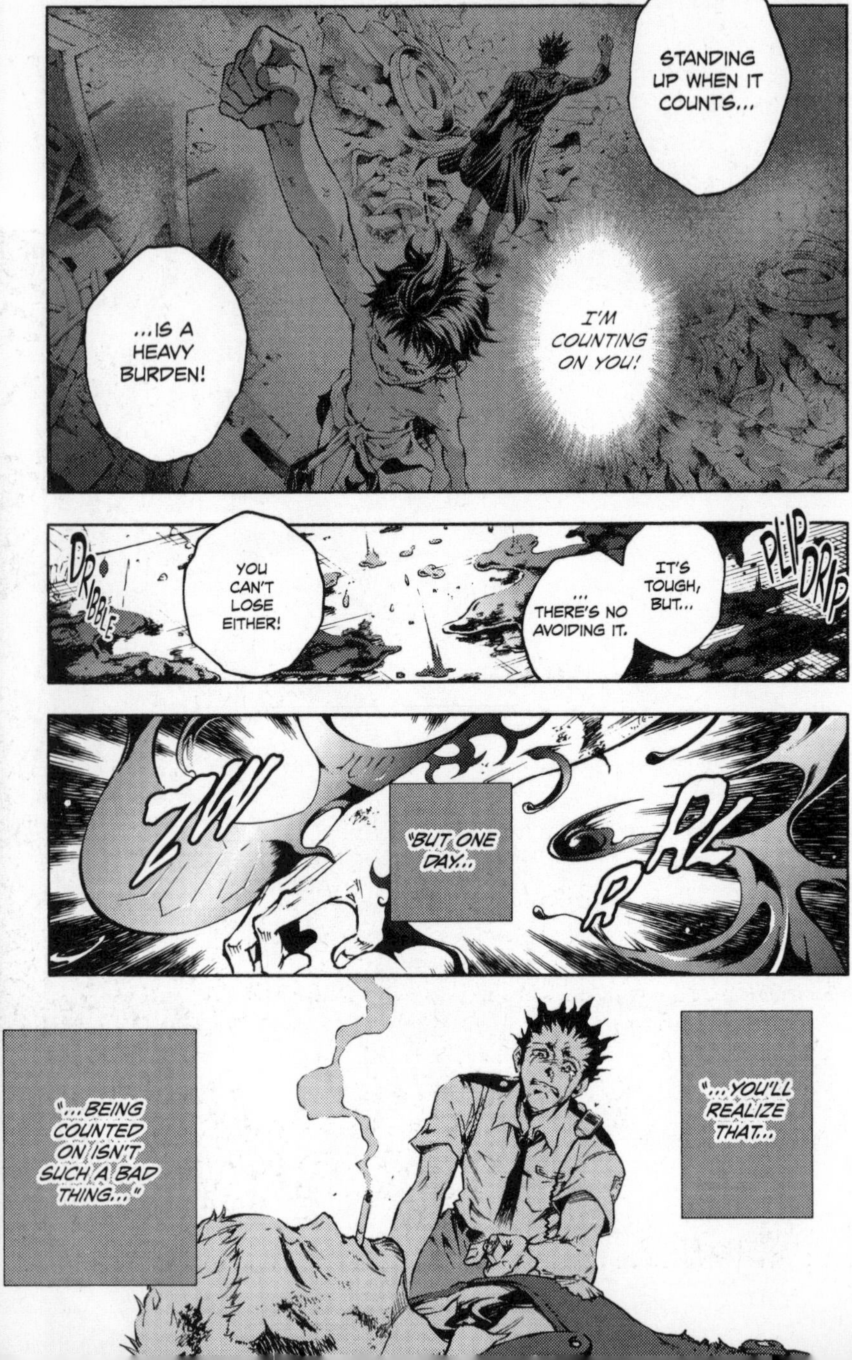
STANDING UP WHEN IT COUNTS...
I'M COUNTING ON YOU!
...IS A HEAVY BURDEN!
PLIP DRIP
IT'S TOUGH, BUT...
... THERE'S NO AVOIDING IT.
YOU CAN'T LOSE EITHER!
DRIBBLE
RRL
"BUT ONE DAY...
ZW
"...YOU'LL REALIZE THAT...
"...BEING COUNTED ON ISN'T SUCH A BAD THING..."

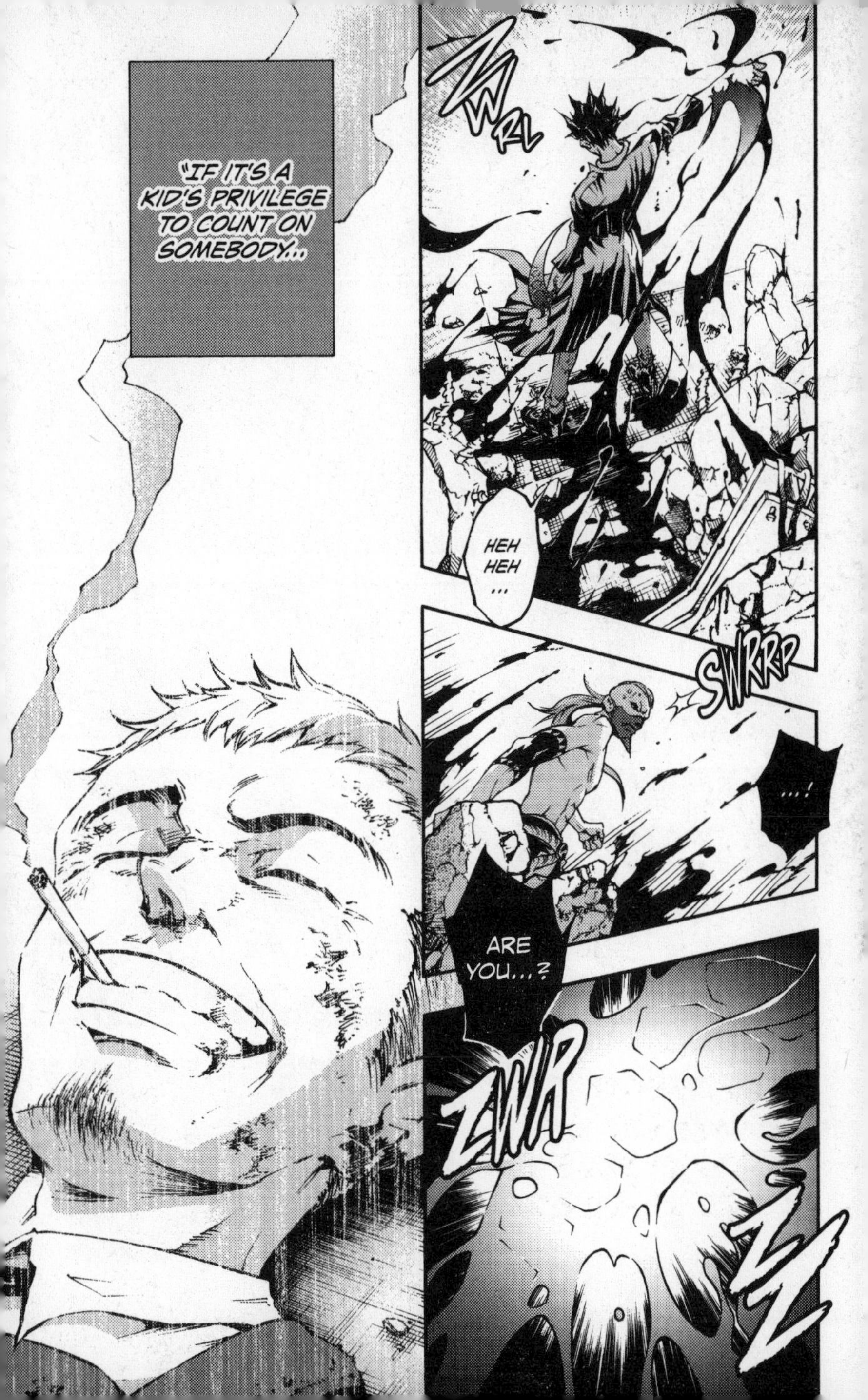
ZWRL
HEH HEH ...
SWRRP
...!
ARE YOU...?
ZWAP
"IF IT'S A KID'S PRIVILEGE TO COUNT ON SOMEBODY...

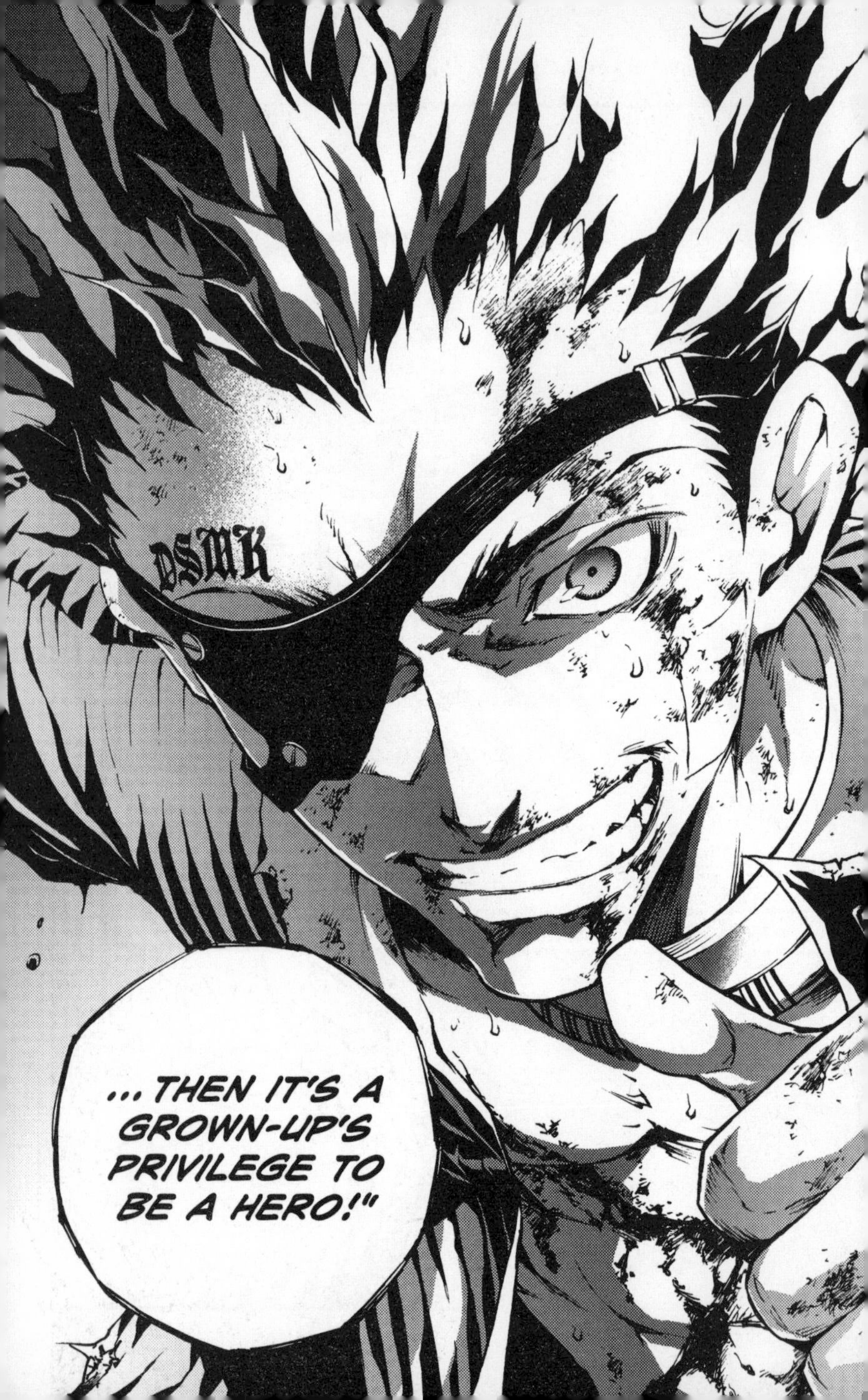
DSMK
...THEN IT'S A GROWN-UP'S PRIVILEGE TO BE A HERO!"

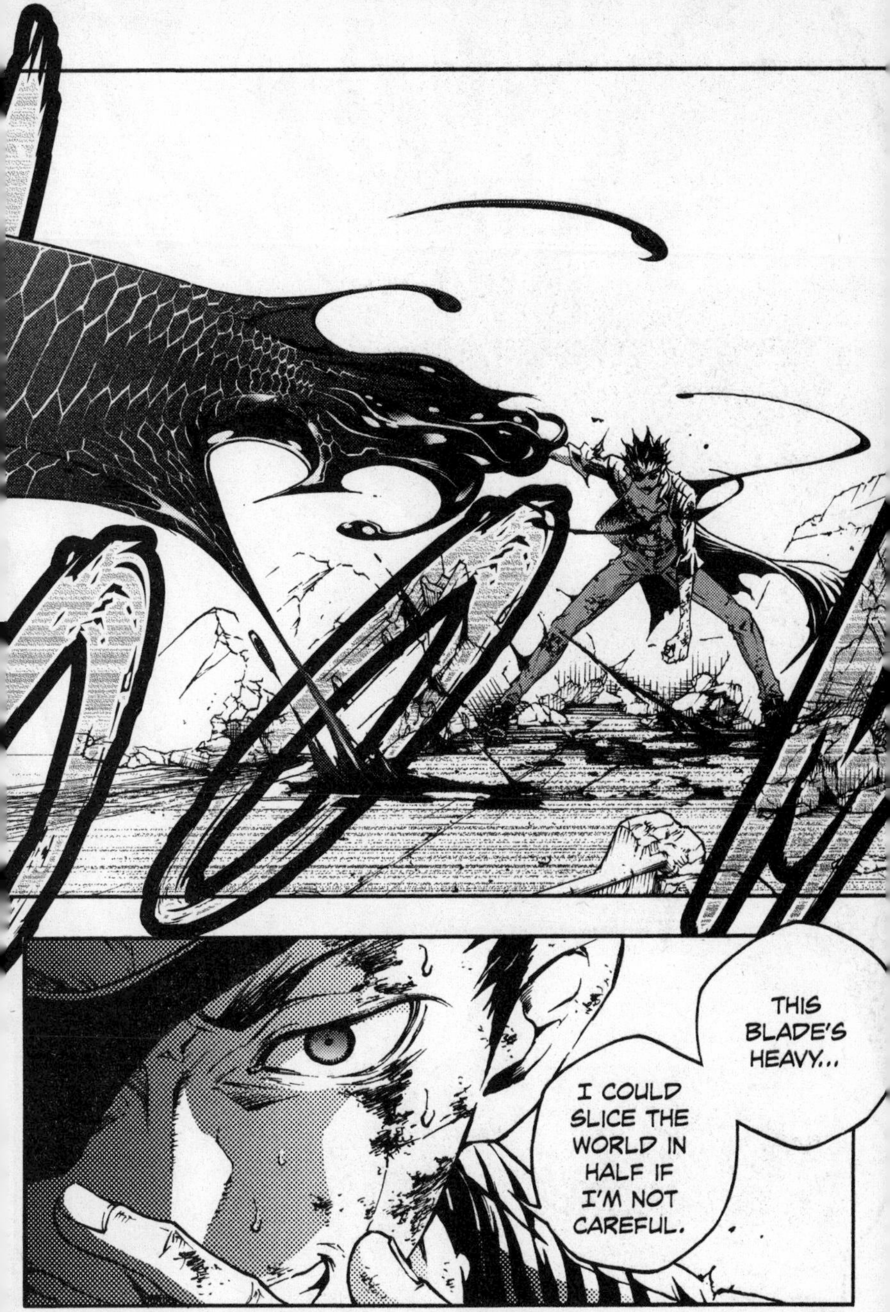
THIS BLADE'S HEAVY...
I COULD SLICE THE WORLD IN HALF IF I'M NOT CAREFUL.

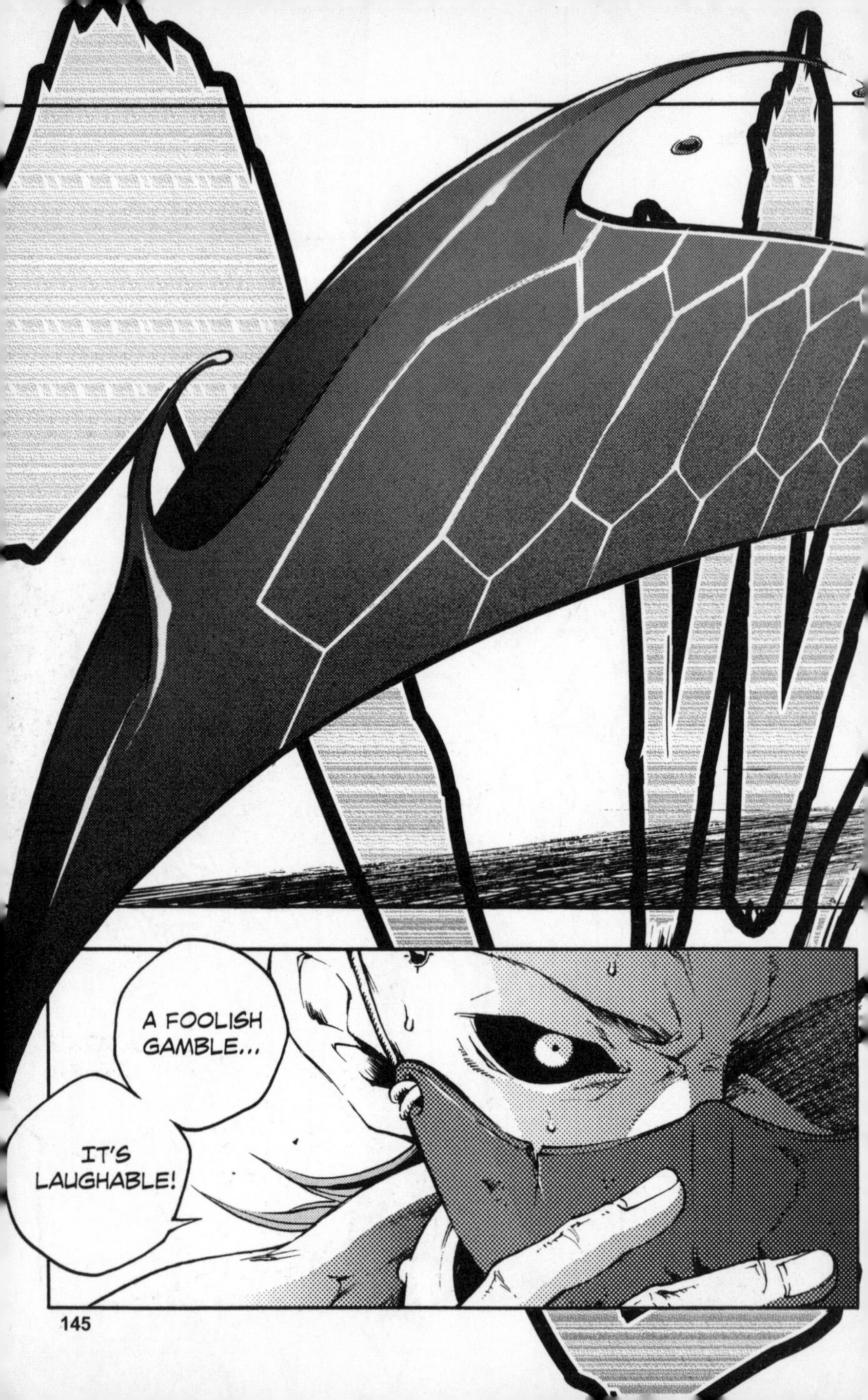
A FOOLISH GAMBLE...
IT'S LAUGHABLE!

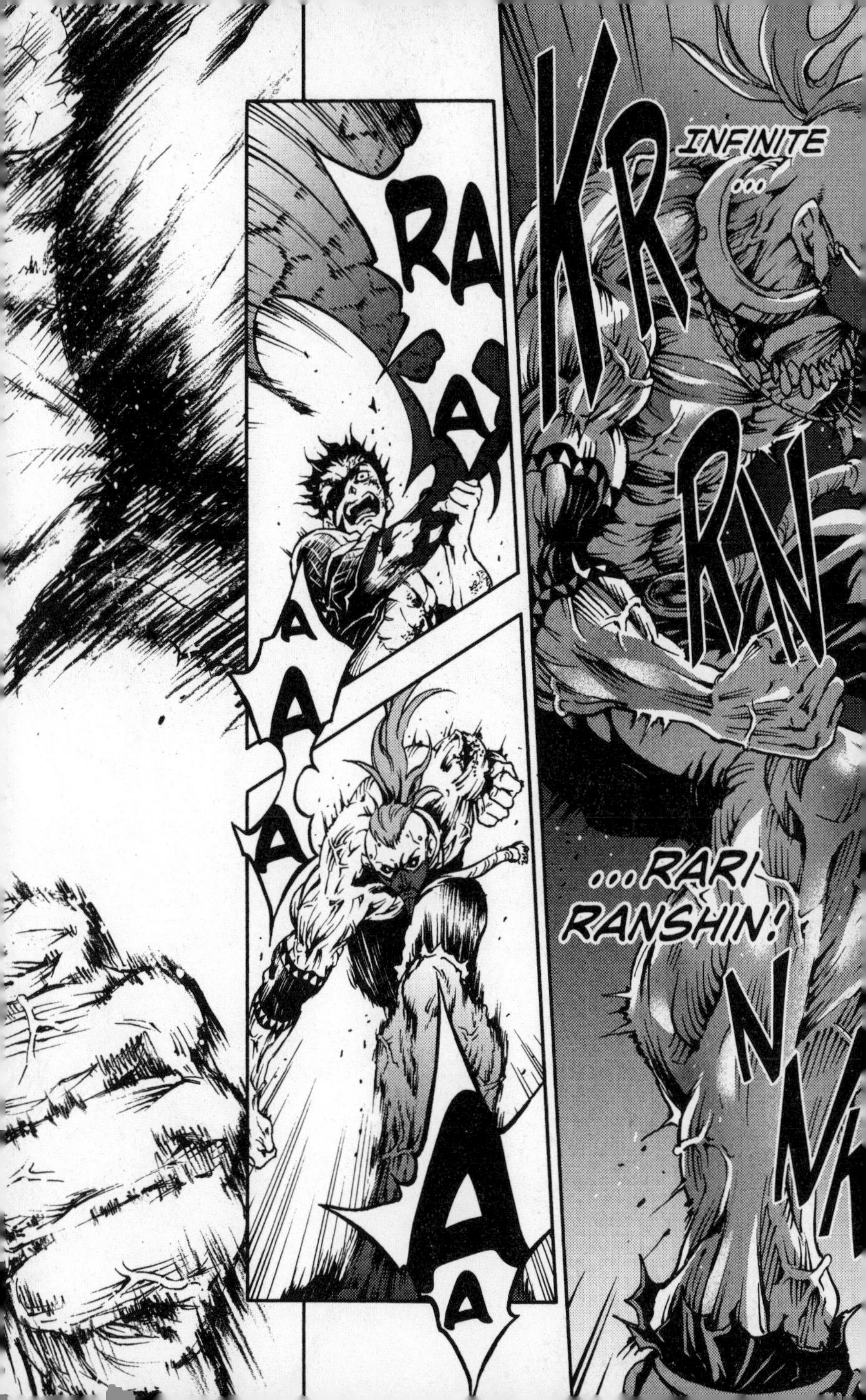
KR
INFINITE...
RN
...RARI RANSHIN!
N
N
RA
A
A
A
A
A
A

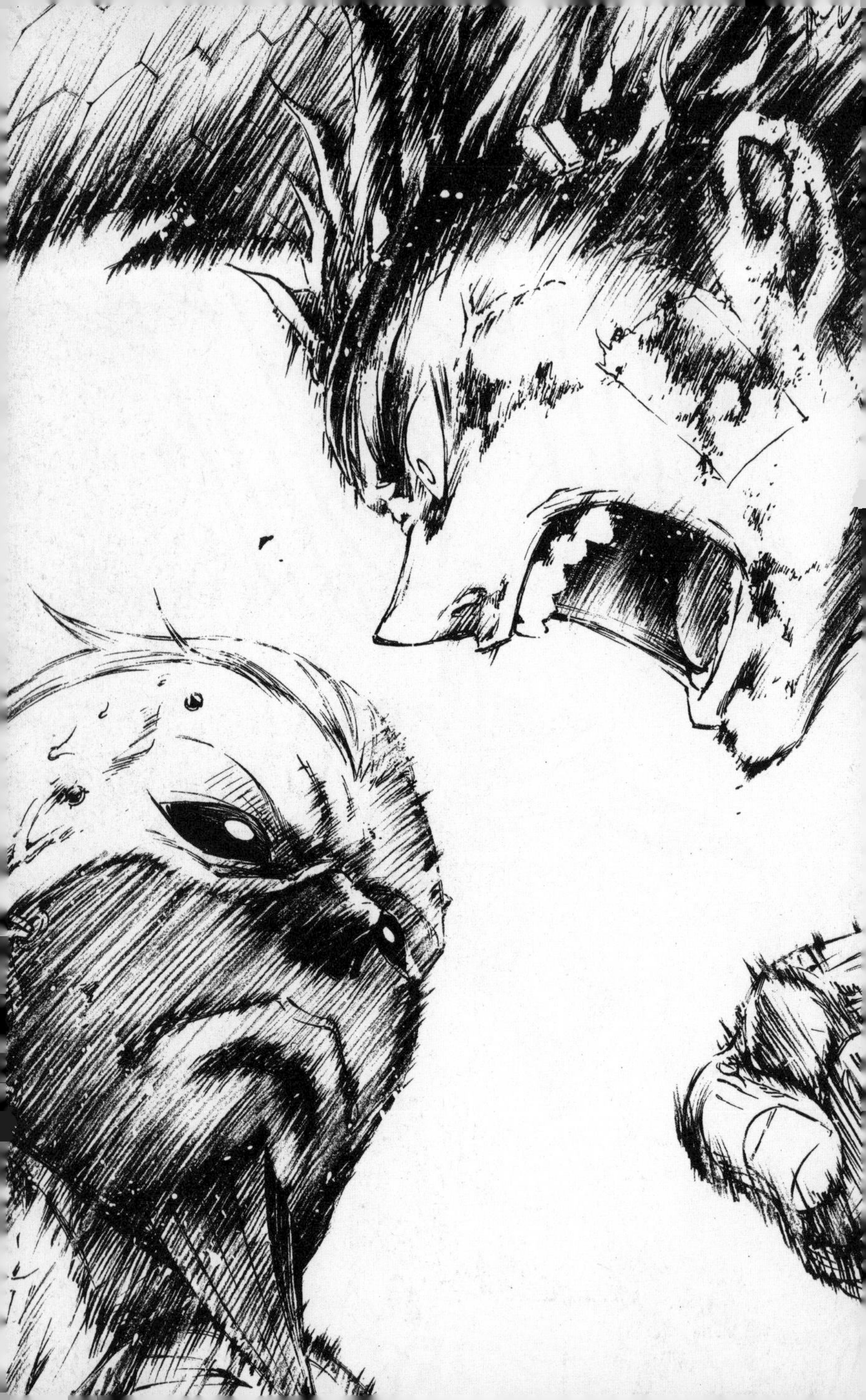

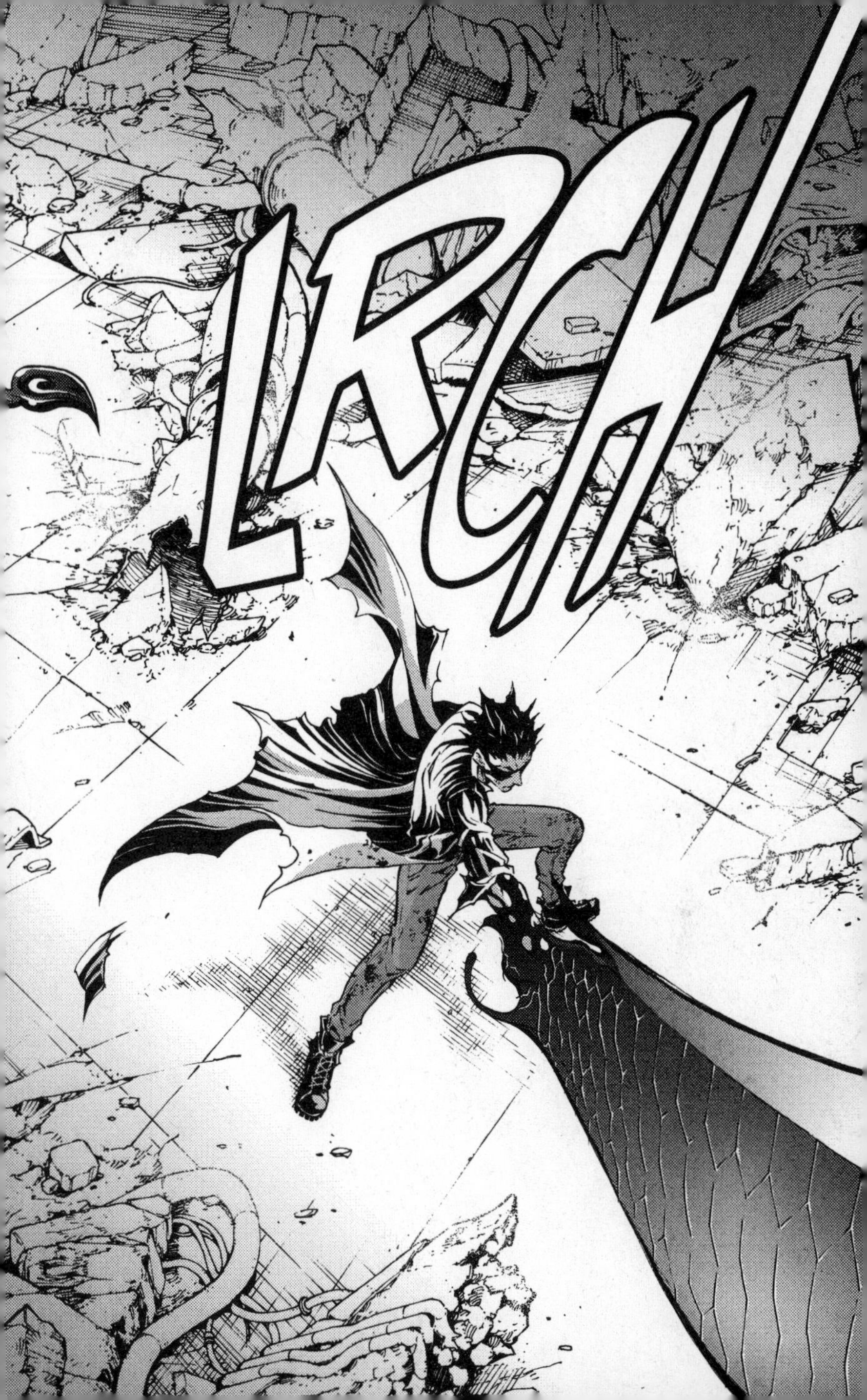
LRCH

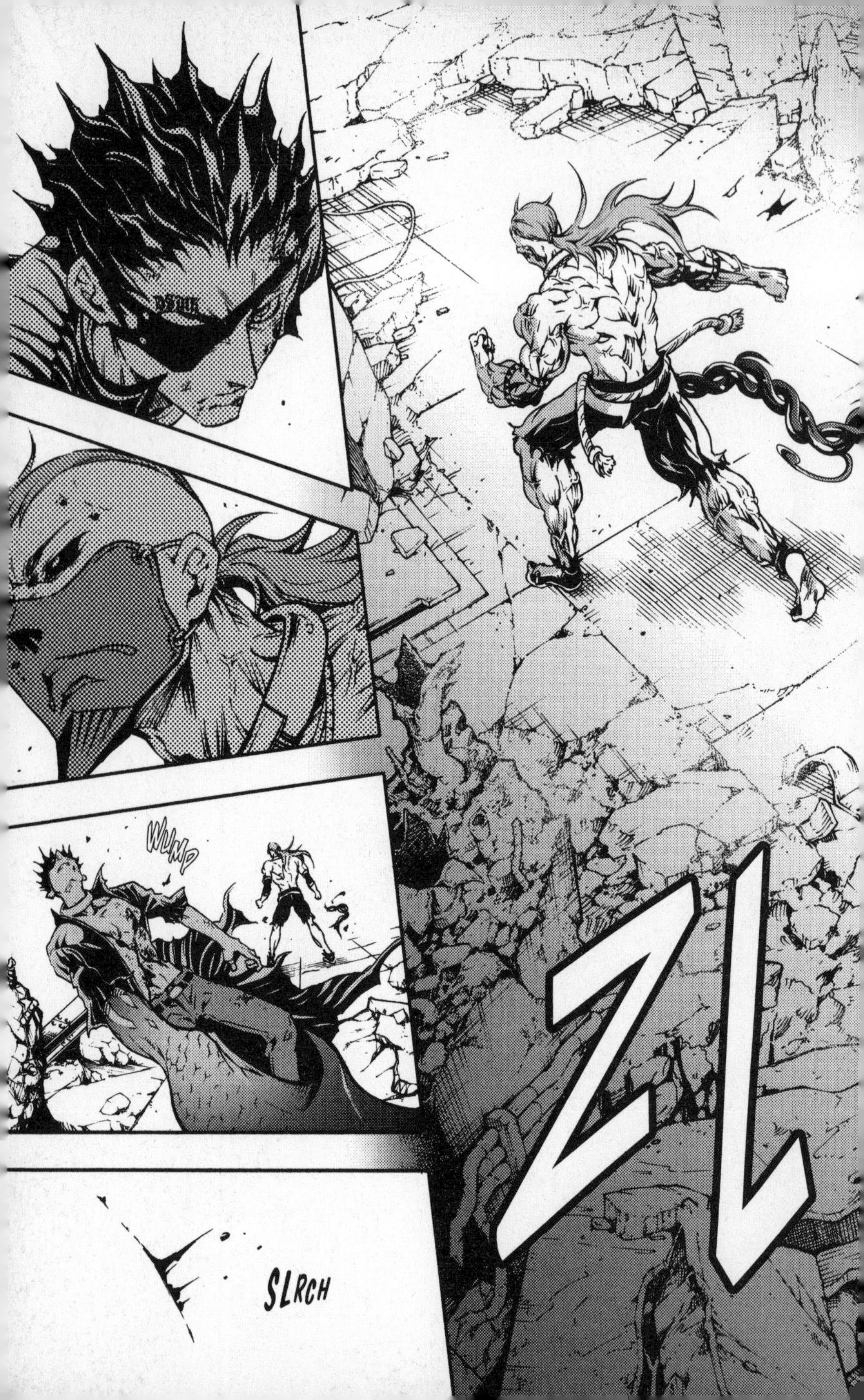
ZL
WUMP
SLRCH

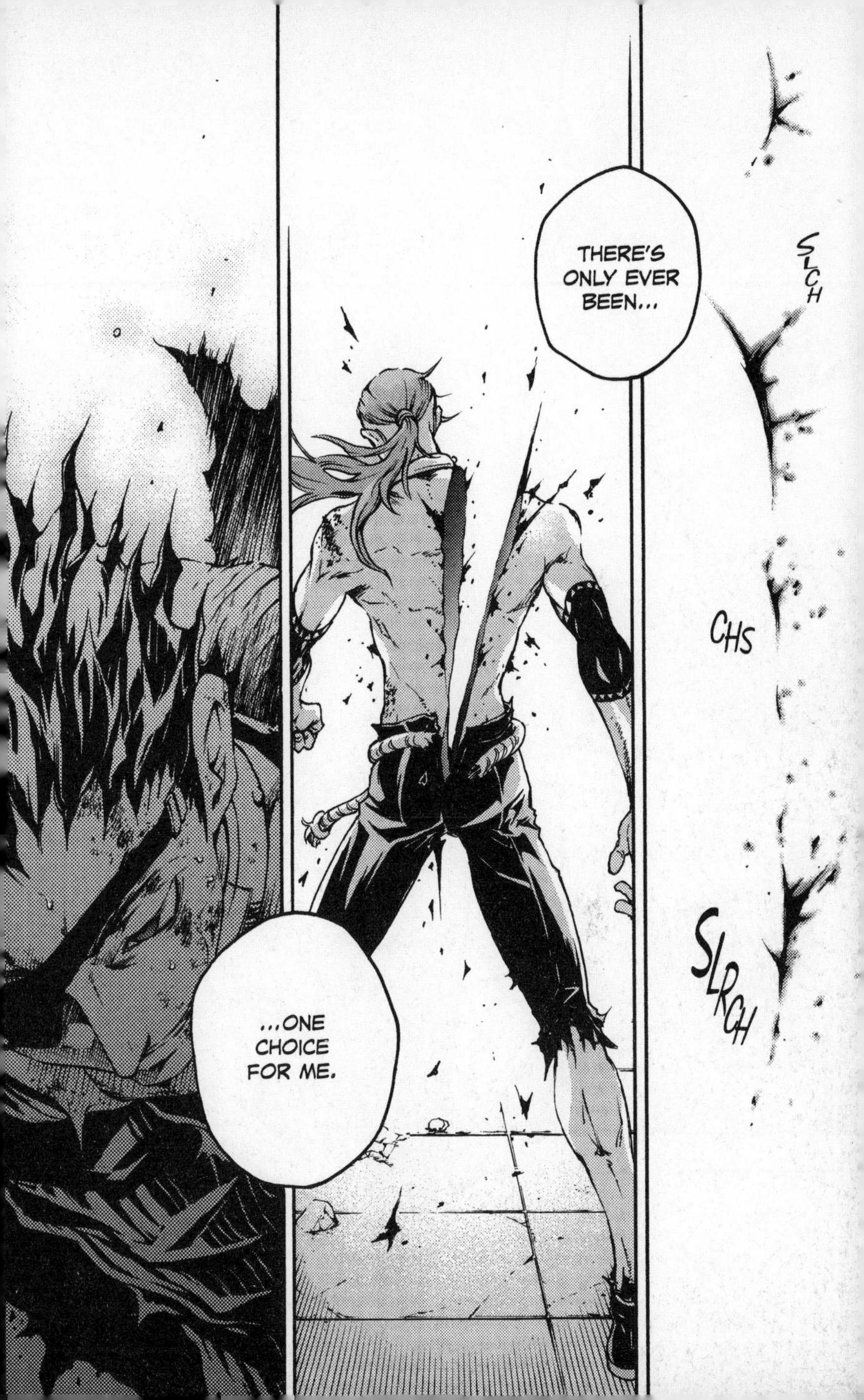
SLCH
CHS
SLRCH
THERE'S ONLY EVER BEEN...
...ONE CHOICE FOR ME.

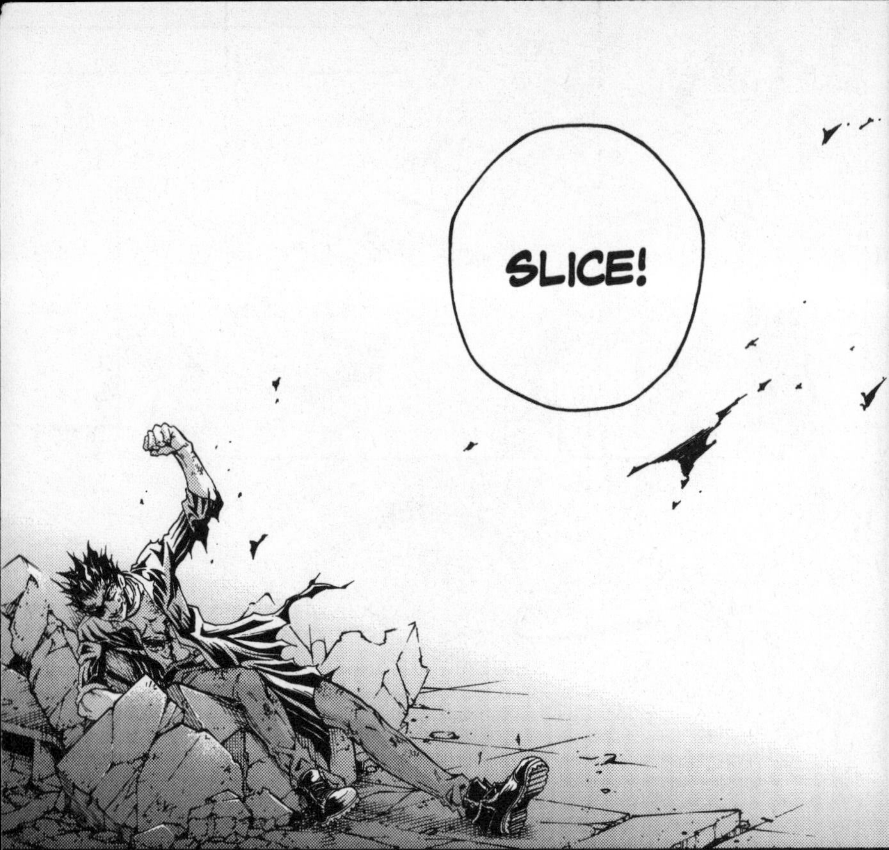
SLICE!
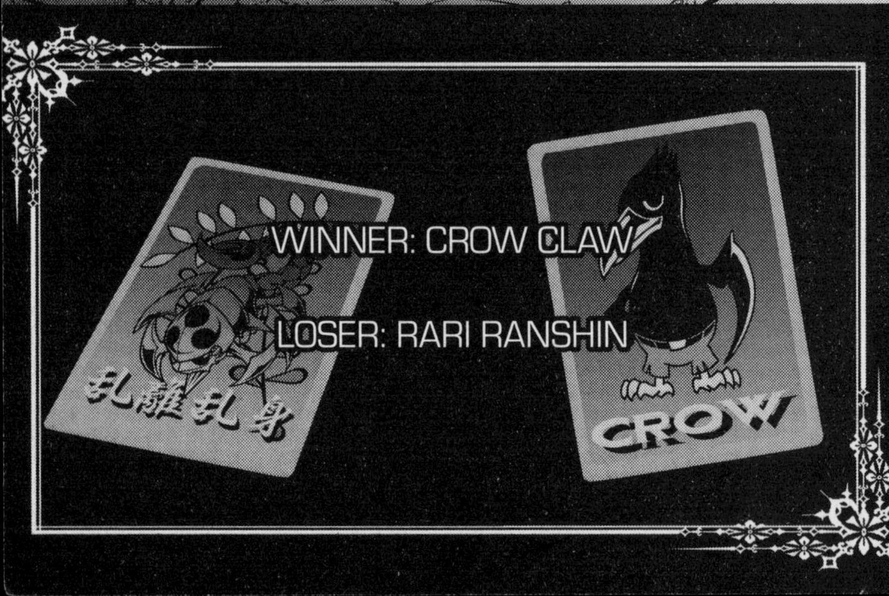
WINNER: CROW CLAW
LOSER: RARI RANSHIN
乱離乱身
CROW

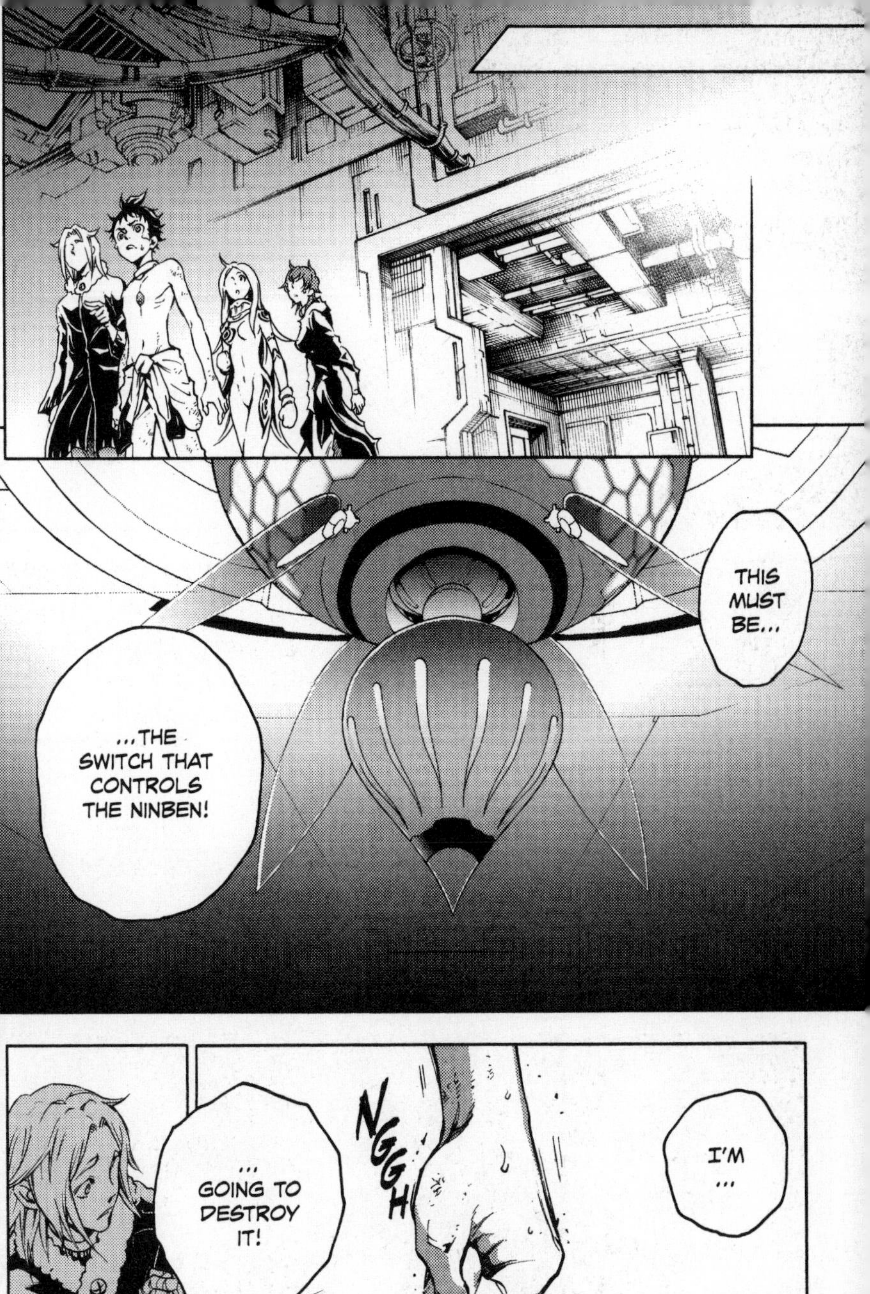
THIS MUST BE...
...THE SWITCH THAT CONTROLS THE NINBEN!
I'M ...
NGGH
... GOING TO DESTROY IT!

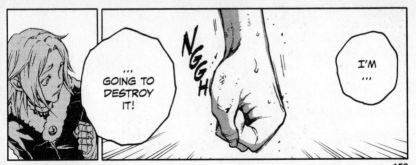

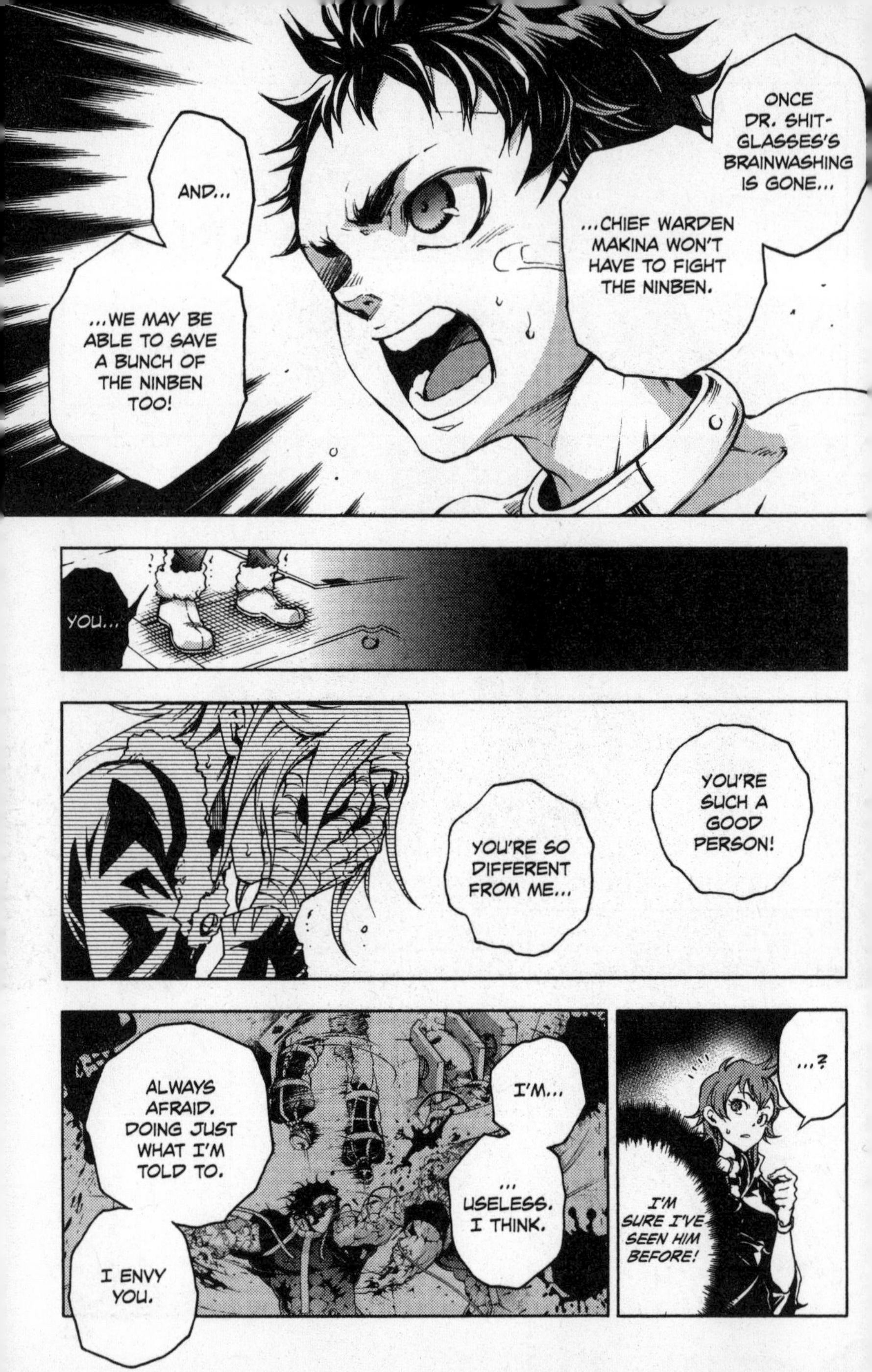
ONCE DR. SHIT-GLASSES'S BRAINWASHING IS GONE...
...CHIEF WARDEN MAKINA WON'T HAVE TO FIGHT THE NINBEN.
AND...
...WE MAY BE ABLE TO SAVE A BUNCH OF THE NINBEN TOO!
YOU...
YOU'RE SUCH A GOOD PERSON!
YOU'RE SO DIFFERENT FROM ME...
...?
I'M SURE I'VE SEEN HIM BEFORE!
I'M...
... USELESS. I THINK.
ALWAYS AFRAID. DOING JUST WHAT I'M TOLD TO.
I ENVY YOU.

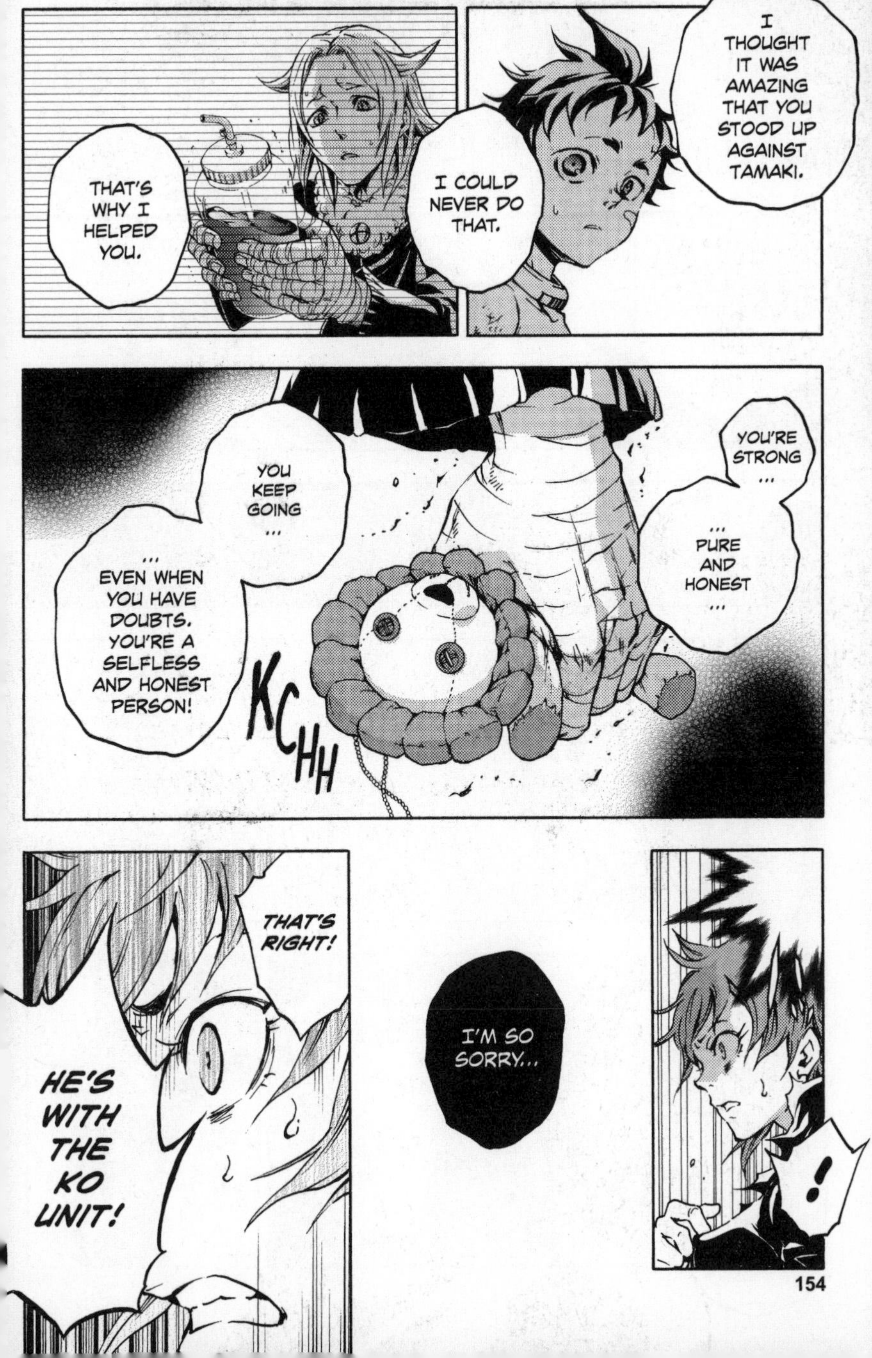
I THOUGHT IT WAS AMAZING THAT YOU STOOD UP AGAINST TAMAKI.
I COULD NEVER DO THAT.
THAT'S WHY I HELPED YOU.
YOU'RE STRONG ...
... PURE AND HONEST ...
YOU KEEP GOING ...
... EVEN WHEN YOU HAVE DOUBTS. YOU'RE A SELFLESS AND HONEST PERSON!
KCHH
!
I'M SO SORRY...
THAT'S RIGHT!
HE'S WITH THE KO UNIT!

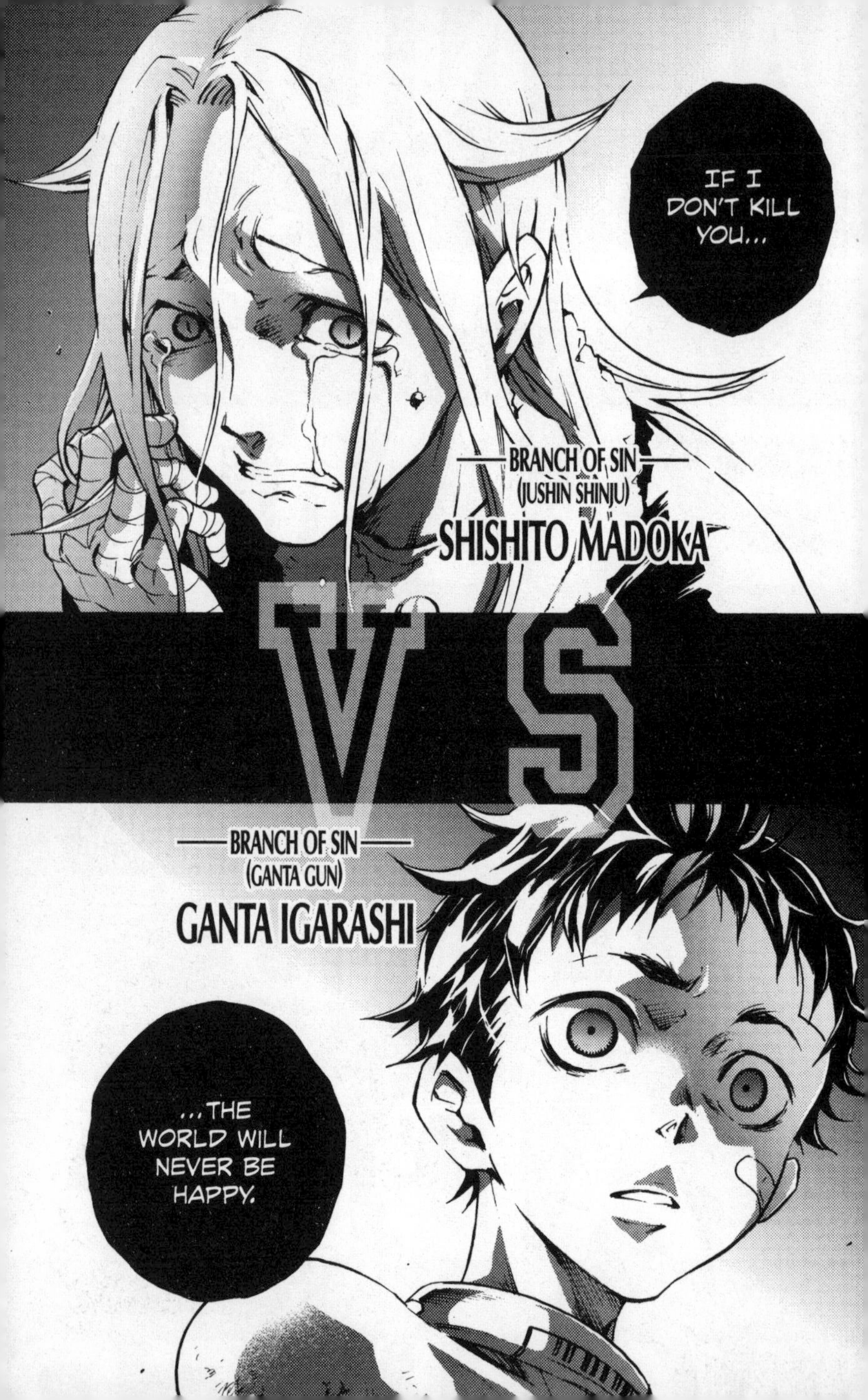
IF I DON'T KILL YOU...
—BRANCH OF SIN— (JUSHIN SHINJU)
SHISHITO MADOKA
VS
—BRANCH OF SIN— (GANTA GUN)
GANTA IGARASHI
...THE WORLD WILL NEVER BE HAPPY.

WONDER

LAND

EADMA

WONDER

LAND

EADMA

WONDER

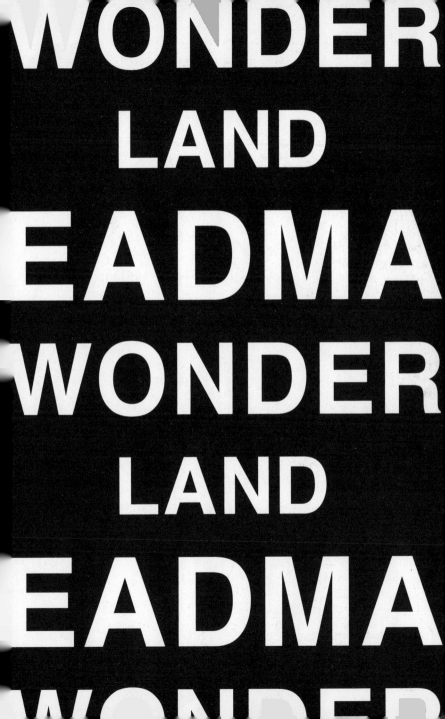

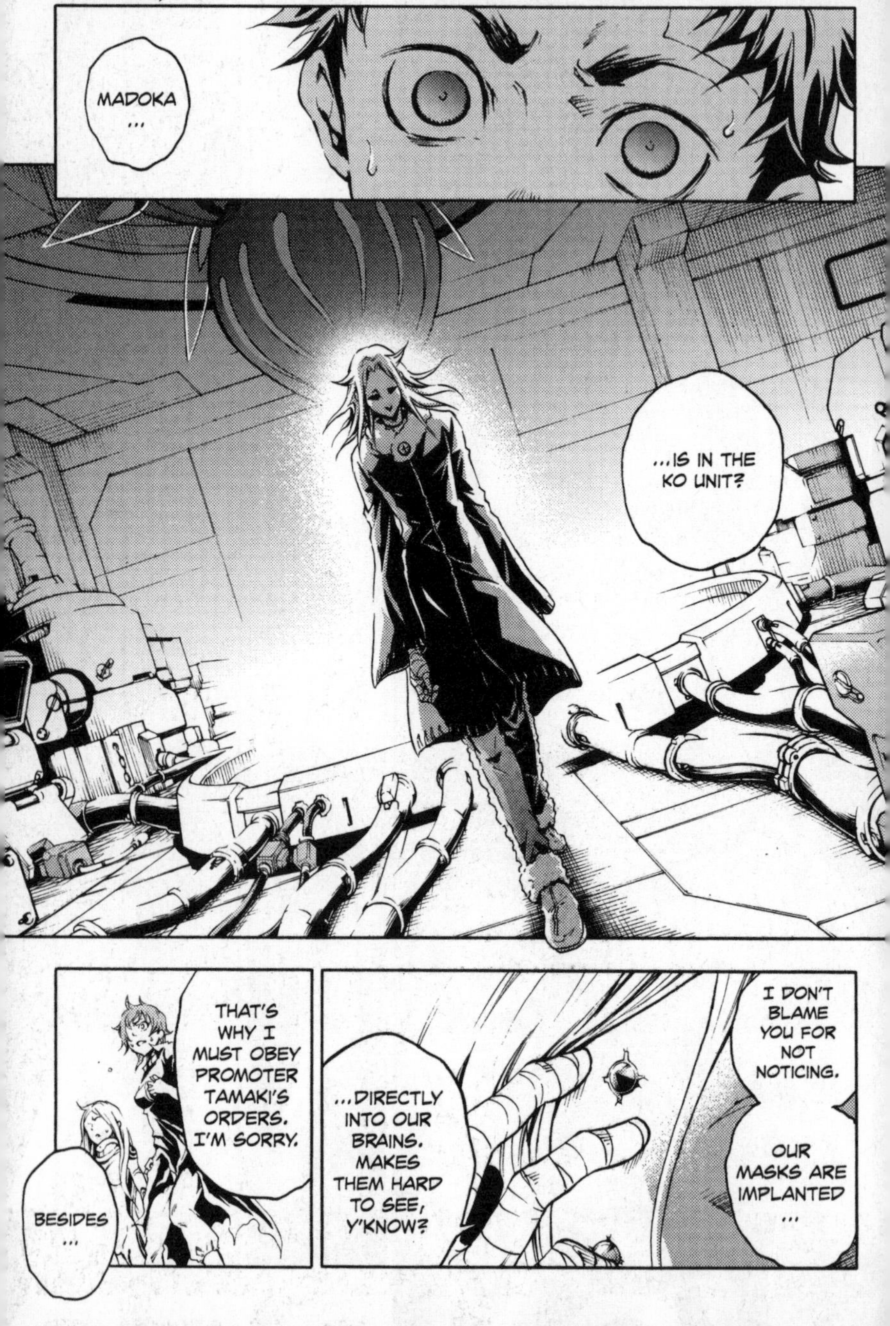
MADOKA ...
...IS IN THE KO UNIT?
I DON'T BLAME YOU FOR NOT NOTICING.
OUR MASKS ARE IMPLANTED ...
...DIRECTLY INTO OUR BRAINS. MAKES THEM HARD TO SEE, Y'KNOW?
THAT'S WHY I MUST OBEY PROMOTER TAMAKI'S ORDERS. I'M SORRY.
BESIDES ...

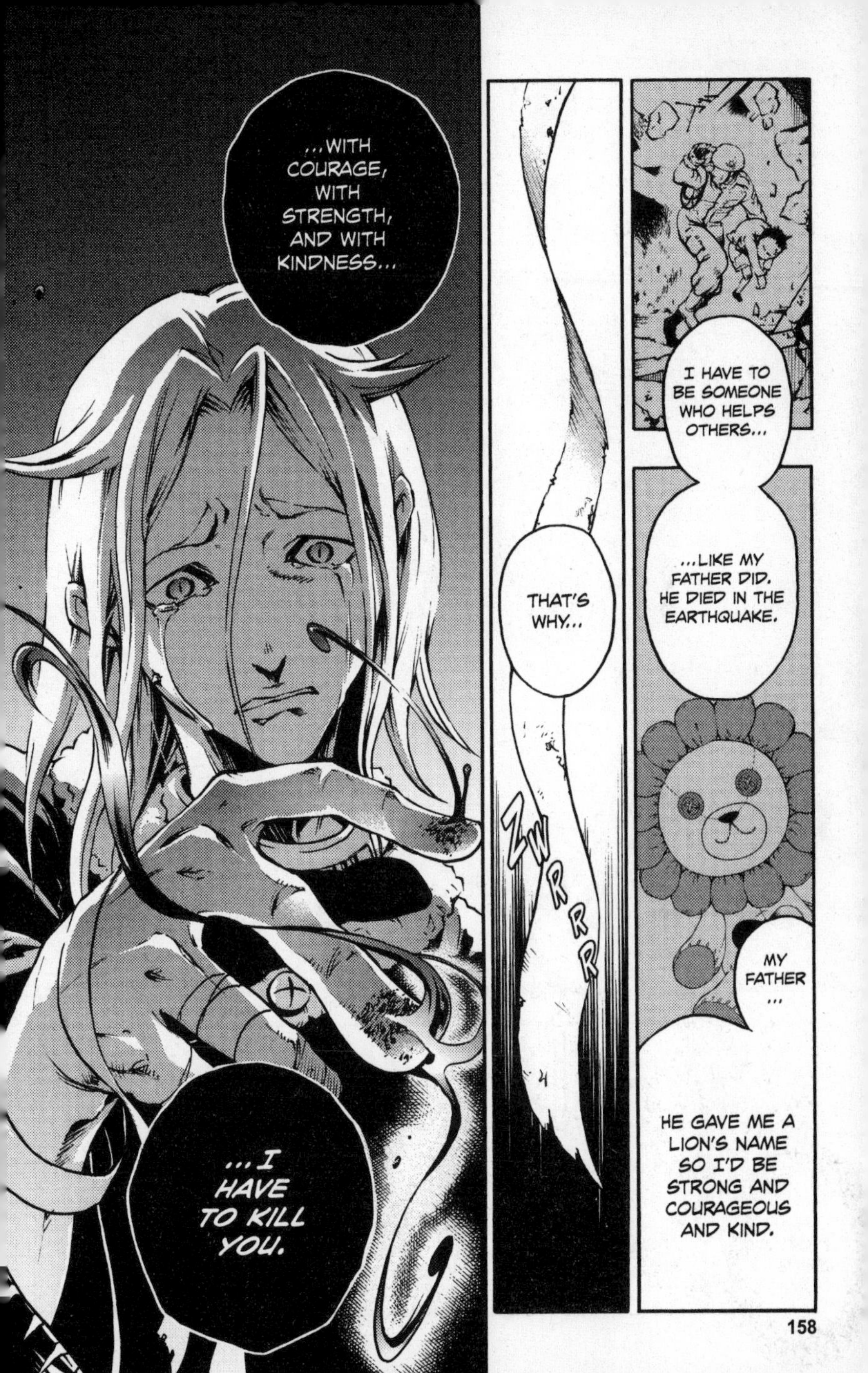
I HAVE TO BE SOMEONE WHO HELPS OTHERS...
...LIKE MY FATHER DID. HE DIED IN THE EARTHQUAKE.
MY FATHER...
HE GAVE ME A LION'S NAME SO I'D BE STRONG AND COURAGEOUS AND KIND.
THAT'S WHY...
ZWRRRR
...WITH COURAGE, WITH STRENGTH, AND WITH KINDNESS...
...I HAVE TO KILL YOU.

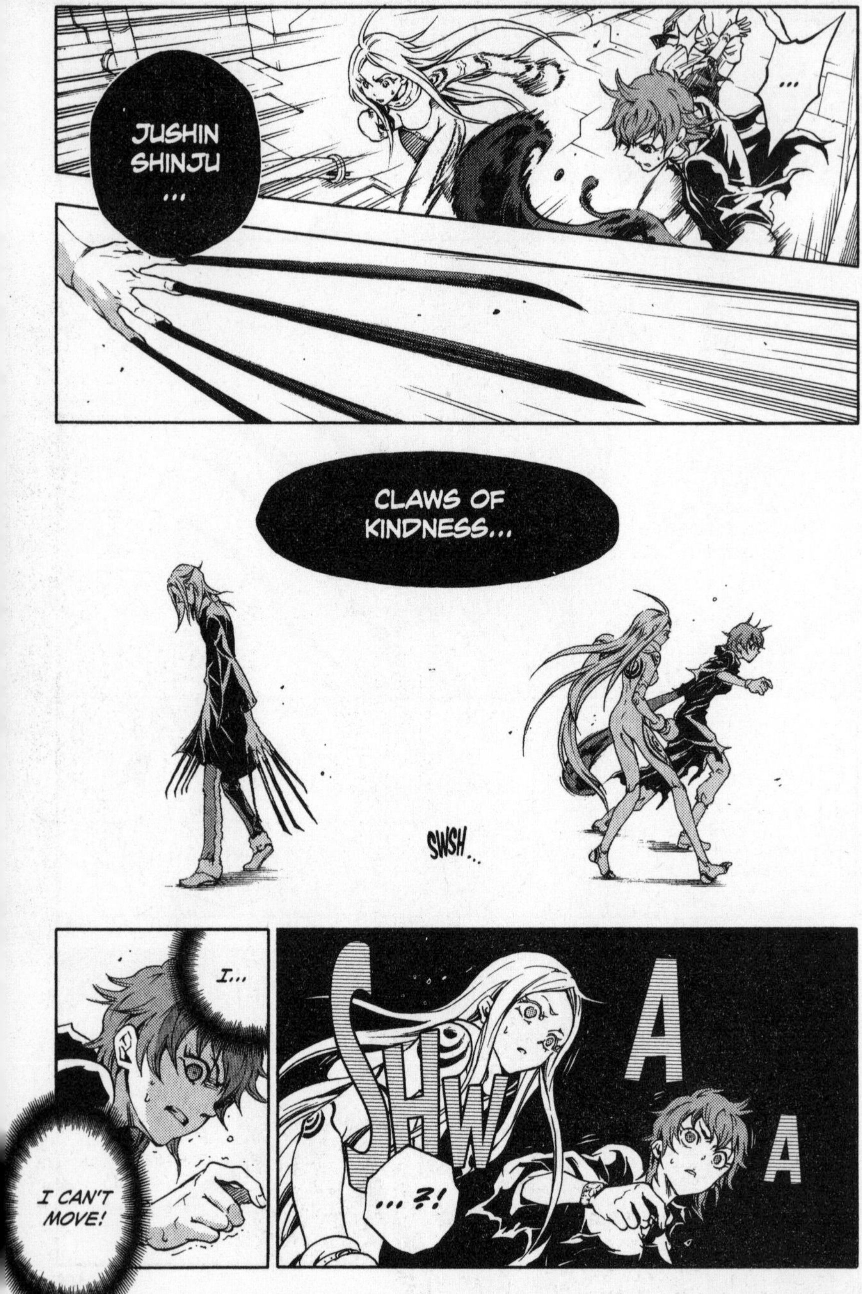
...
JUSHIN SHINJU ...
CLAWS OF KINDNESS...
SWSH...
SHWAAA
...?!
I...
I CAN'T MOVE!

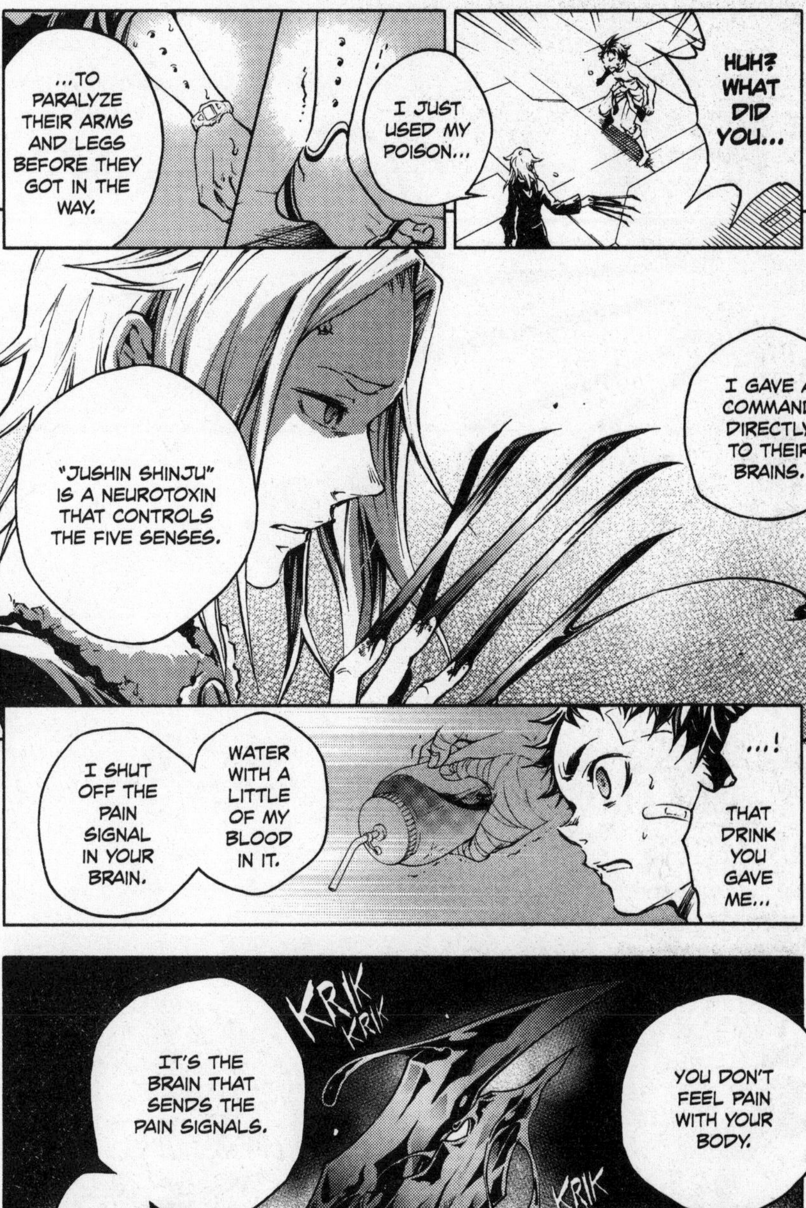
HUH? WHAT DID YOU...
I JUST USED MY POISON...
...TO PARALYZE THEIR ARMS AND LEGS BEFORE THEY GOT IN THE WAY.
I GAVE A COMMAND DIRECTLY TO THEIR BRAINS.
"JUSHIN SHINJU" IS A NEUROTOXIN THAT CONTROLS THE FIVE SENSES.
...!
THAT DRINK YOU GAVE ME...
WATER WITH A LITTLE OF MY BLOOD IN IT.
I SHUT OFF THE PAIN SIGNAL IN YOUR BRAIN.
YOU DON'T FEEL PAIN WITH YOUR BODY.
KRIK KRIK
IT'S THE BRAIN THAT SENDS THE PAIN SIGNALS.
KRIK
IT'S TRUE.

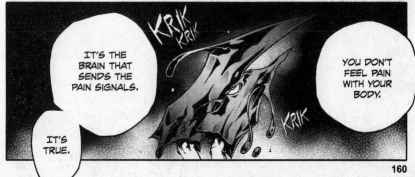

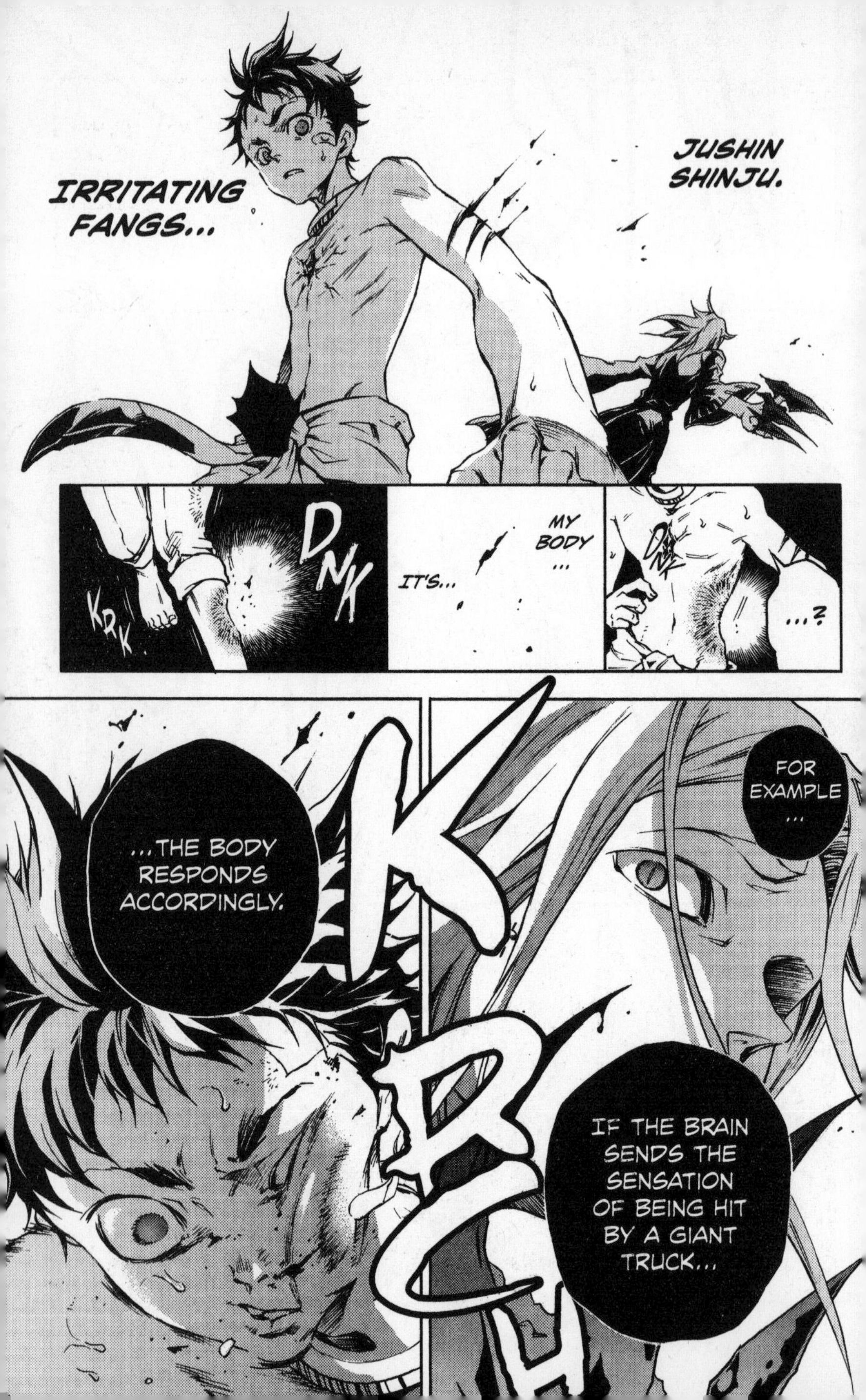
JUSHIN SHINJU.
IRRITATING FANGS...
...?
DNK
MY BODY ...
IT'S...
DNK
KRK
FOR EXAMPLE ...
IF THE BRAIN SENDS THE SENSATION OF BEING HIT BY A GIANT TRUCK...
...THE BODY RESPONDS ACCORDINGLY.

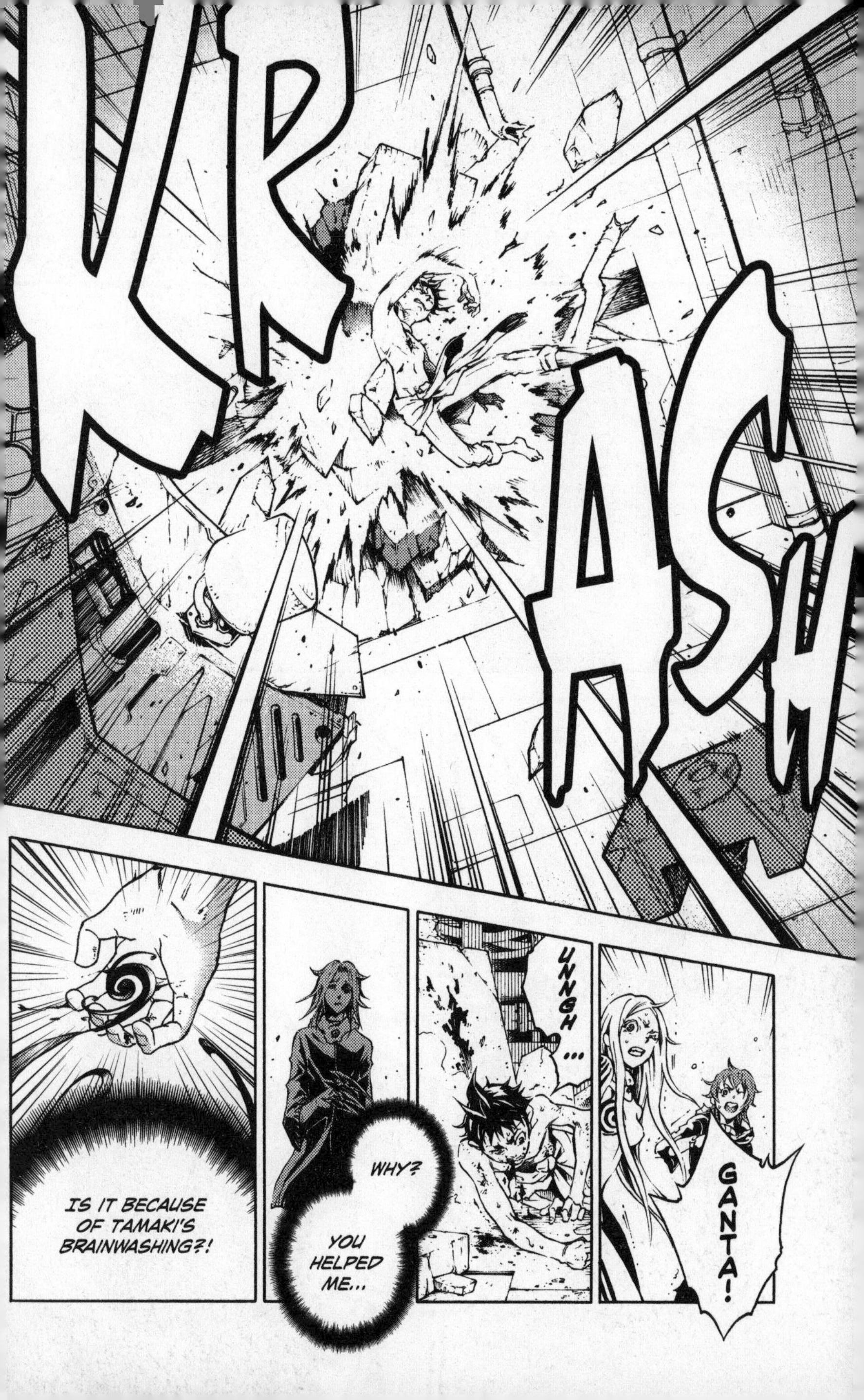
KRASH
GANTA!
UNNGH...
WHY?
YOU HELPED ME...
IS IT BECAUSE OF TAMAKI'S BRAINWASHING?!

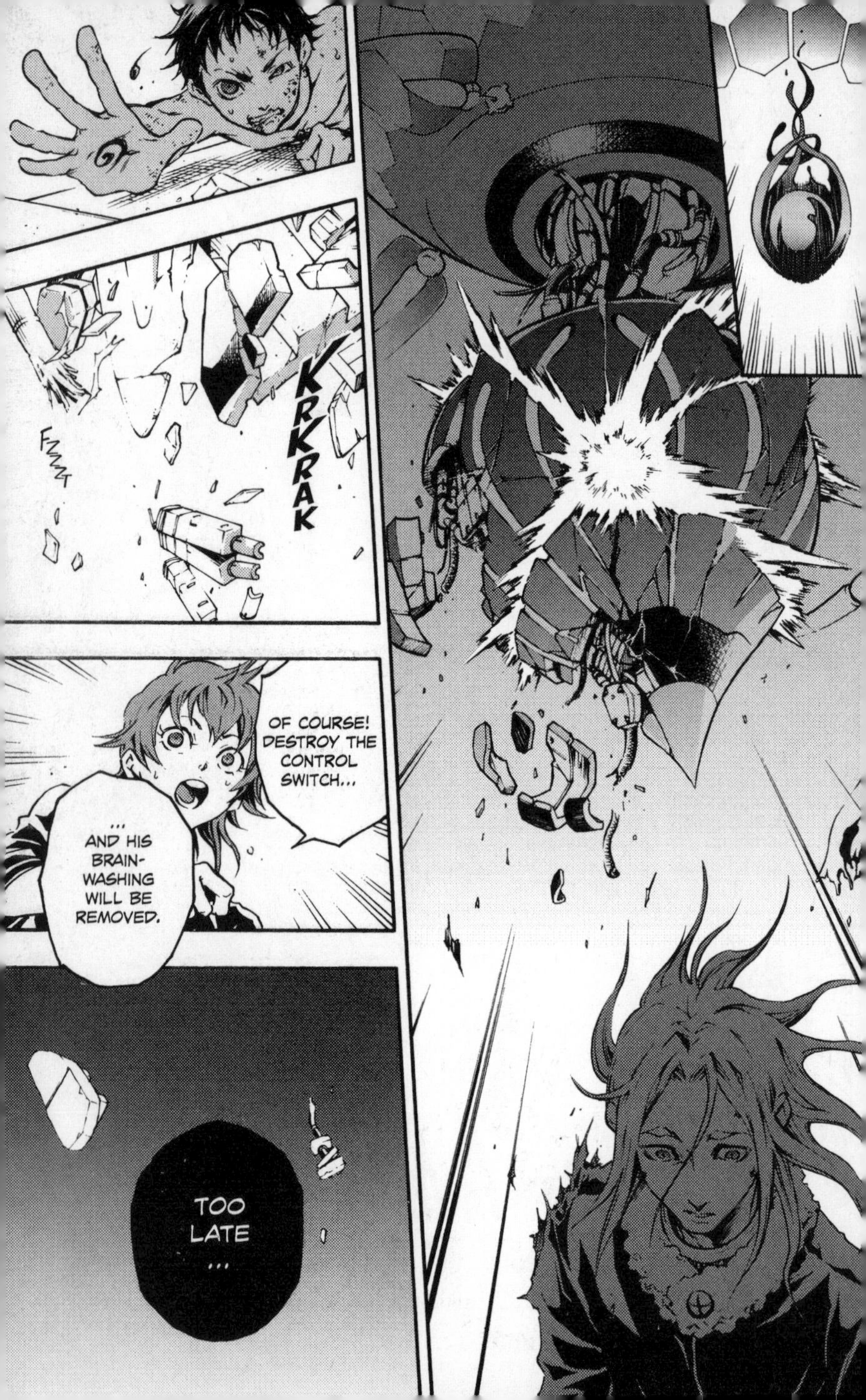
KRKRAK
FZZZT
OF COURSE! DESTROY THE CONTROL SWITCH...
... AND HIS BRAIN-WASHING WILL BE REMOVED.
TOO LATE ...

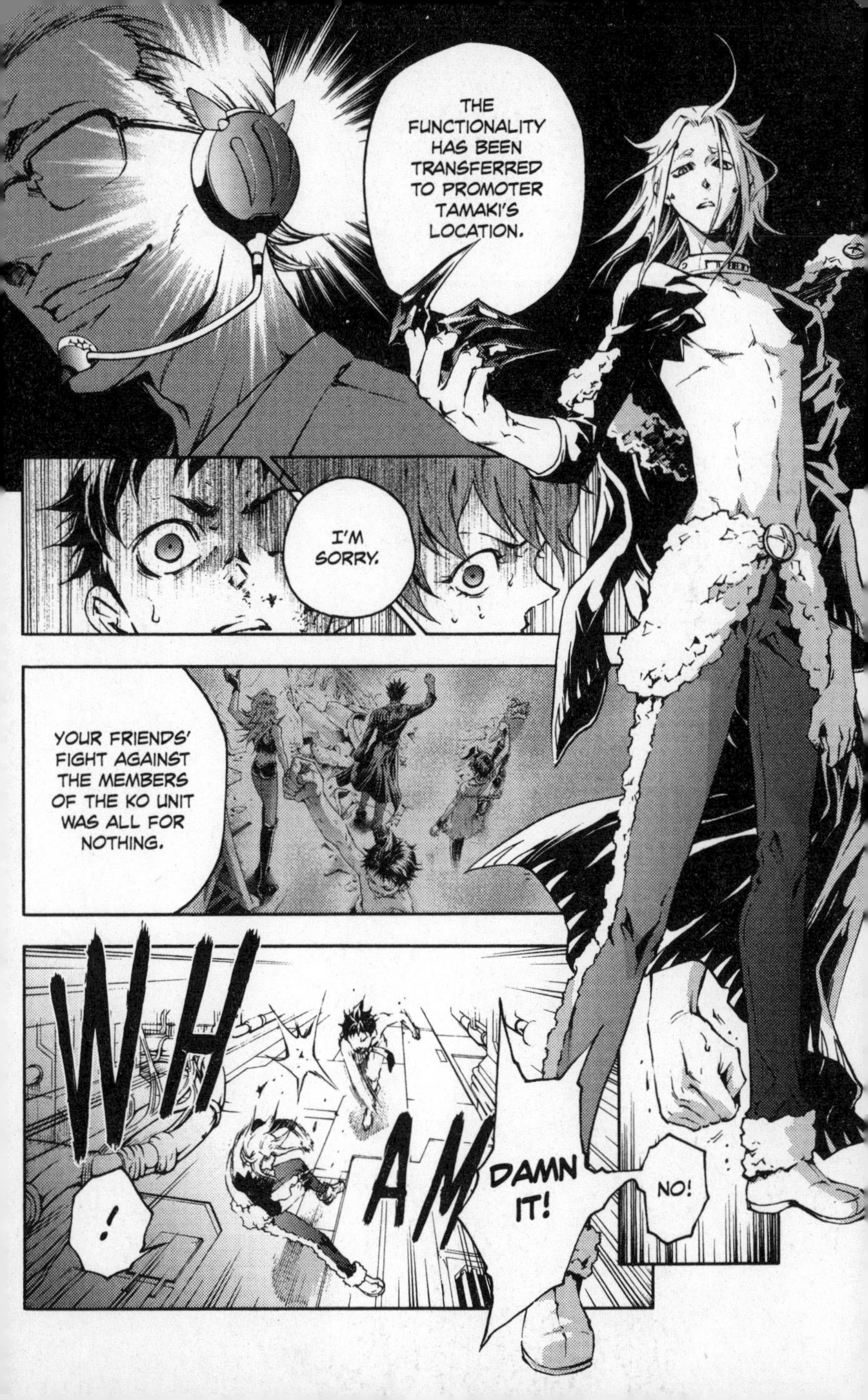
THE FUNCTIONALITY HAS BEEN TRANSFERRED TO PROMOTER TAMAKI'S LOCATION.
I'M SORRY.
YOUR FRIENDS' FIGHT AGAINST THE MEMBERS OF THE KO UNIT WAS ALL FOR NOTHING.
NO!
DAMN IT!
WHAM
!

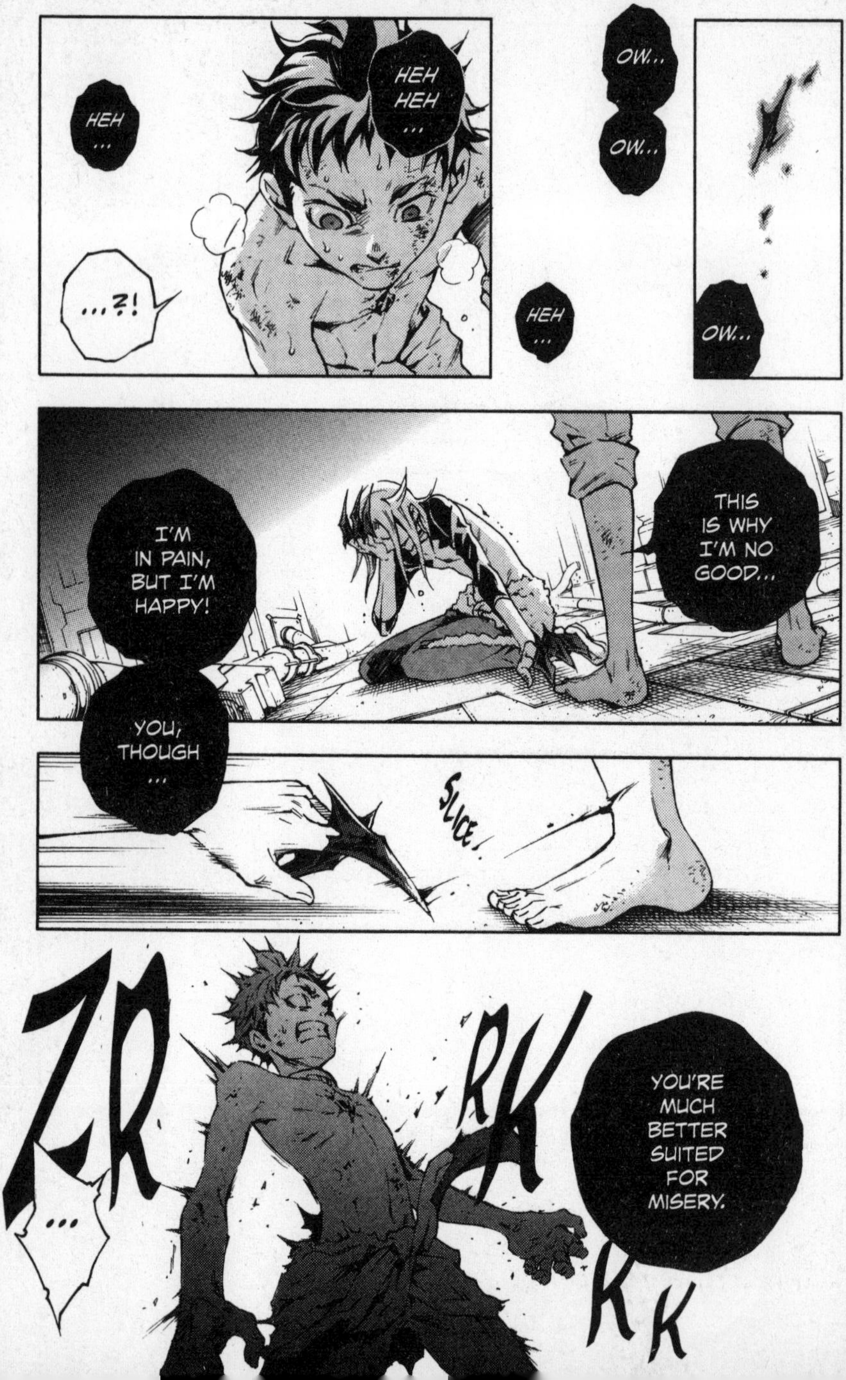
OW...
OW...
OW...
HEH ...
HEH HEH ...
HEH ...
...?!
THIS IS WHY I'M NO GOOD...
I'M IN PAIN, BUT I'M HAPPY!
YOU, THOUGH ...
SLICE
YOU'RE MUCH BETTER SUITED FOR MISERY.
ZRRKKK
...

ONE PERSON'S JOY IS ANOTHER PERSON'S PAIN.
IT'S LIKE EMOTIONAL "CONSERVATION OF MASS."
THAT'S WHY I TRIED TO BECOME A HUMAN TRASH CAN.
THEY USED BLACK AND WHITE TACKS TO PLAY OTHELLO ON MY BACK.
THEY GOT A KICK OUT OF MY CRYING AND SCREAMING
SOMEHOW IT GAVE THEM LAUGHTER.

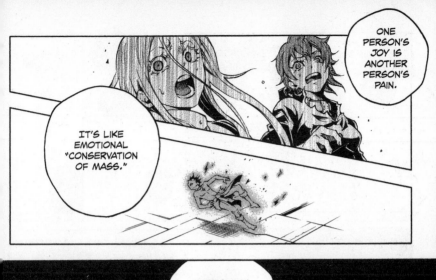

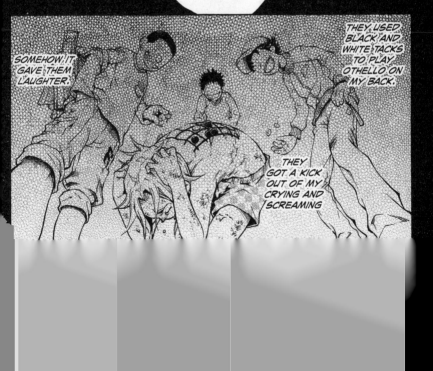

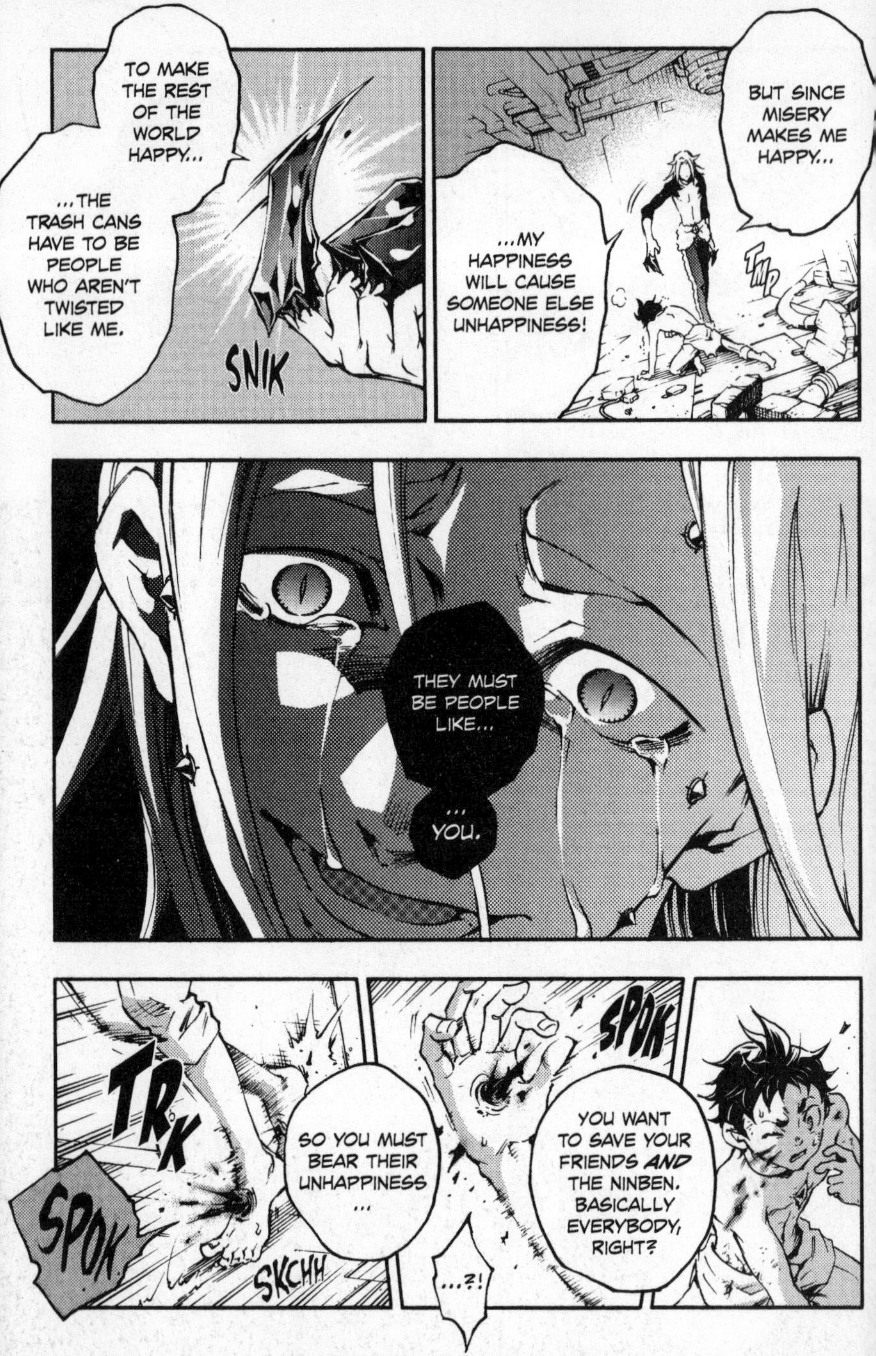
BUT SINCE MISERY MAKES ME HAPPY...
...MY HAPPINESS WILL CAUSE SOMEONE ELSE UNHAPPINESS!
TMP
TO MAKE THE REST OF THE WORLD HAPPY...
...THE TRASH CANS HAVE TO BE PEOPLE WHO AREN'T TWISTED LIKE ME.
SNIK
THEY MUST BE PEOPLE LIKE...
... YOU.
SPOK
YOU WANT TO SAVE YOUR FRIENDS AND THE NINBEN. BASICALLY EVERYBODY, RIGHT?
...?!
SO YOU MUST BEAR THEIR UNHAPPINESS ...
TRK
SPOK
SKCHH

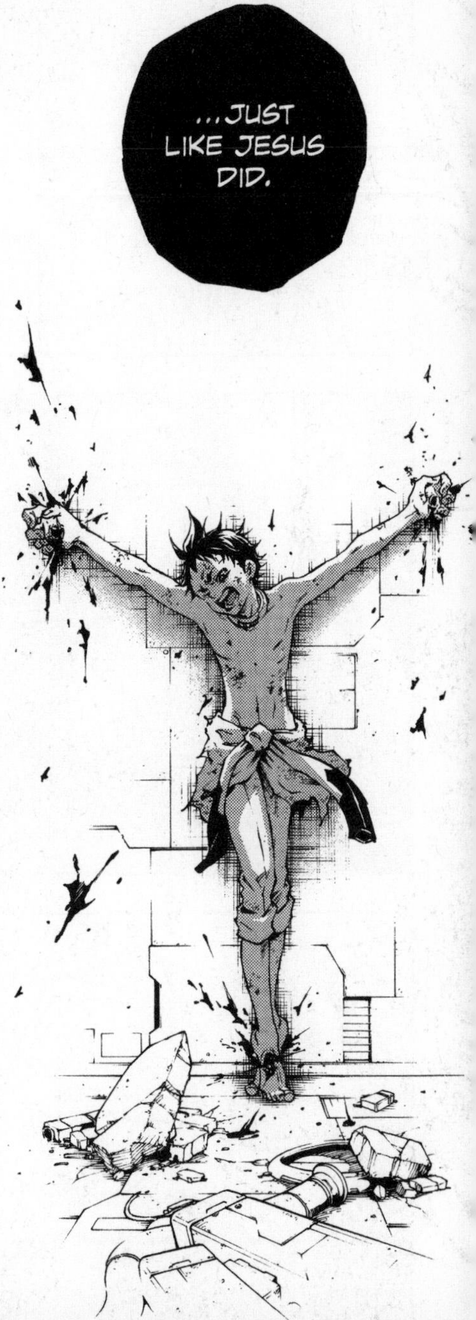
...JUST LIKE JESUS DID.

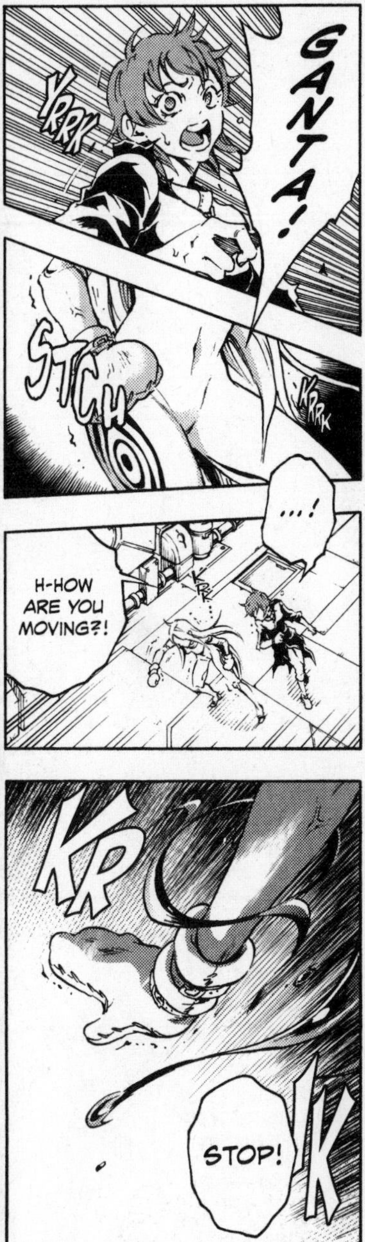
GANTA!
YRRK
STCH
KRRK
...!
H-HOW ARE YOU MOVING?!
KR
STOP!
IK

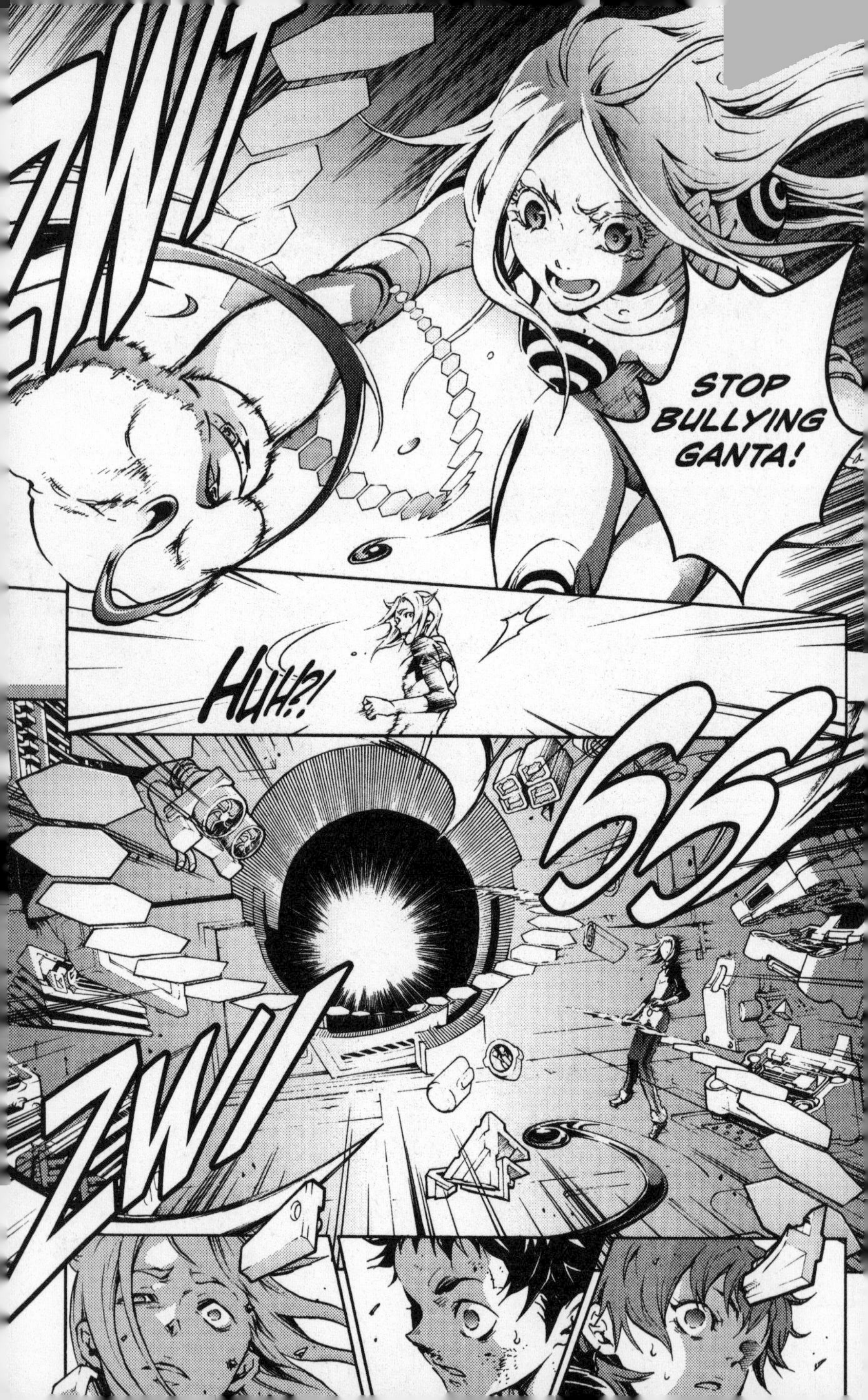
STOP BULLYING GANTA!
HUH?!

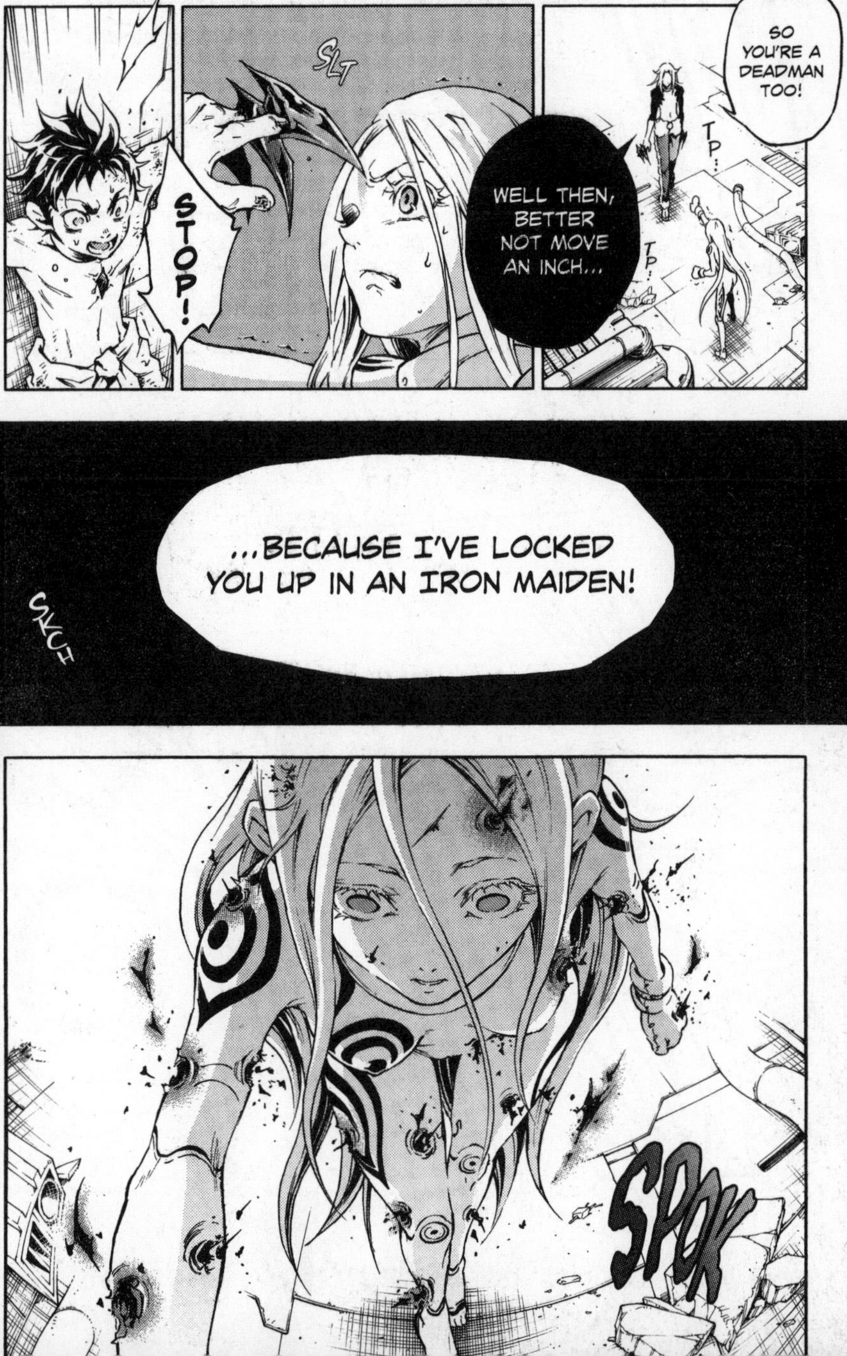
SO YOU'RE A DEADMAN TOO!
TP...
TP...
SLT
WELL THEN, BETTER NOT MOVE AN INCH...
STOP!
...BECAUSE I'VE LOCKED YOU UP IN AN IRON MAIDEN!
SKCH
SPOK

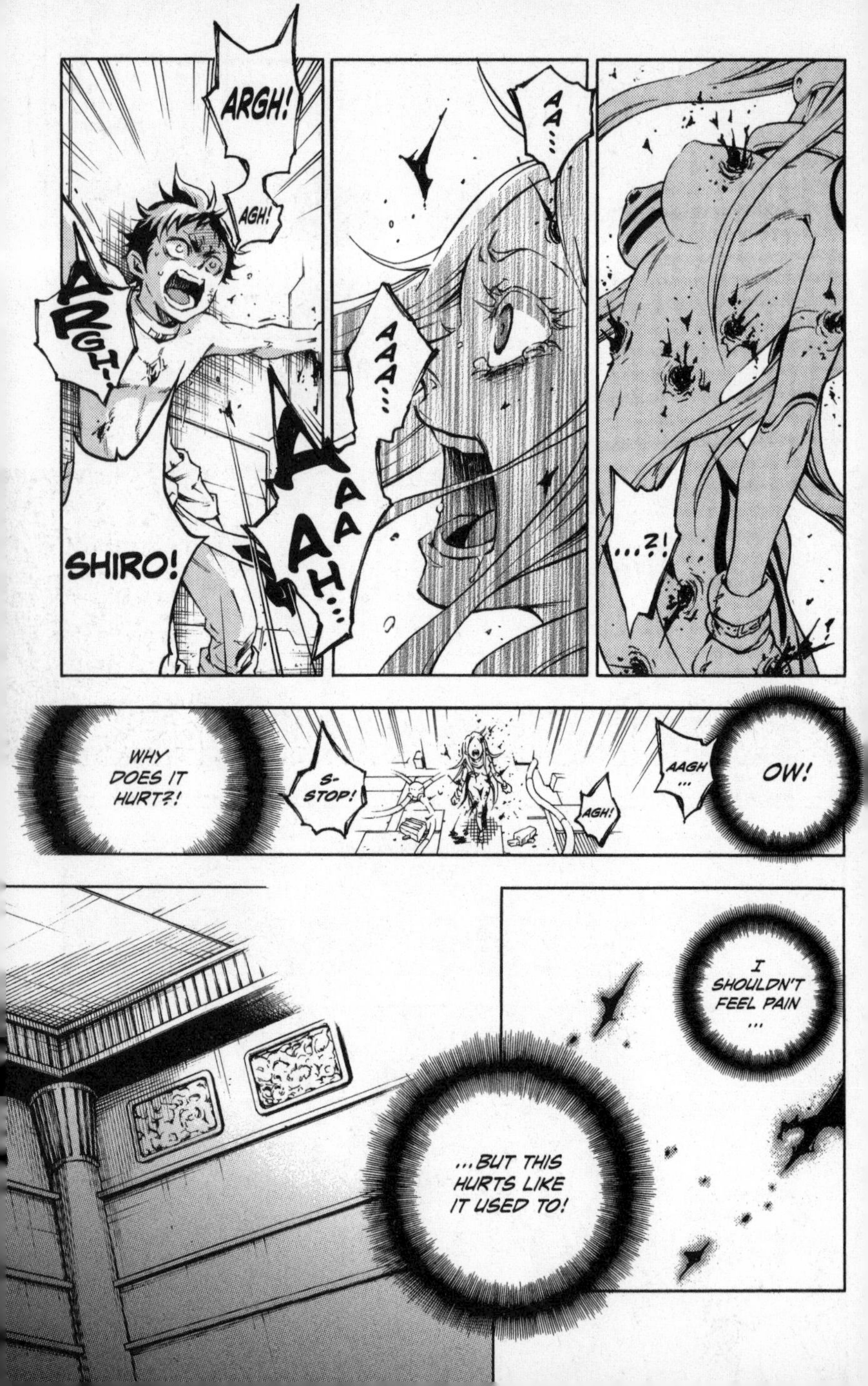
...?!
AA...
AAA...
AAAH...
ARGH!
AGH!
ARGH!
SHIRO!
OW!
AAGH ...
AGH!
S-STOP!
WHY DOES IT HURT?!
I SHOULDN'T FEEL PAIN ...
...BUT THIS HURTS LIKE IT USED TO!

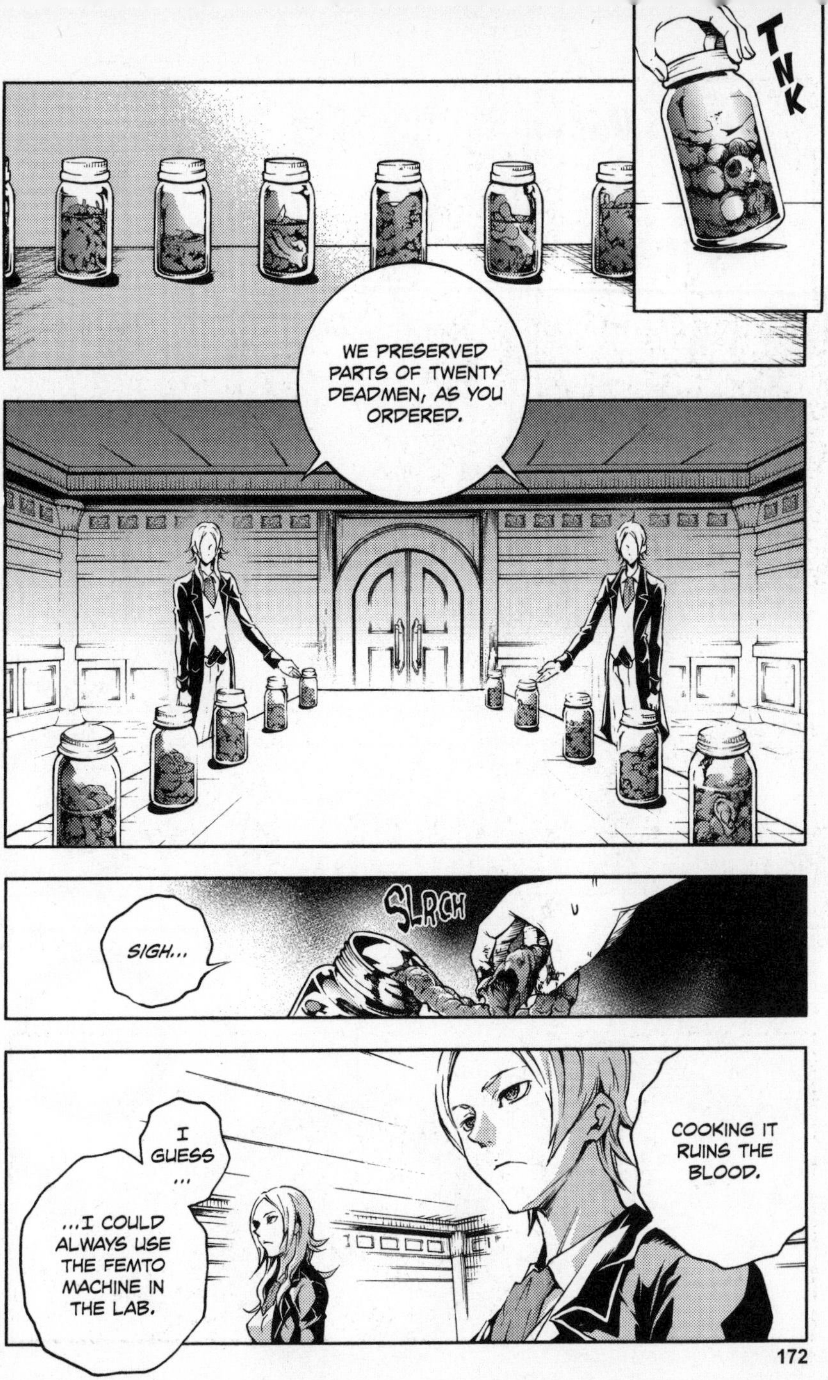
TNK
WE PRESERVED PARTS OF TWENTY DEADMEN, AS YOU ORDERED.
SLRCH
SIGH...
COOKING IT RUINS THE BLOOD.
I GUESS...
...I COULD ALWAYS USE THE FEMTO MACHINE IN THE LAB.

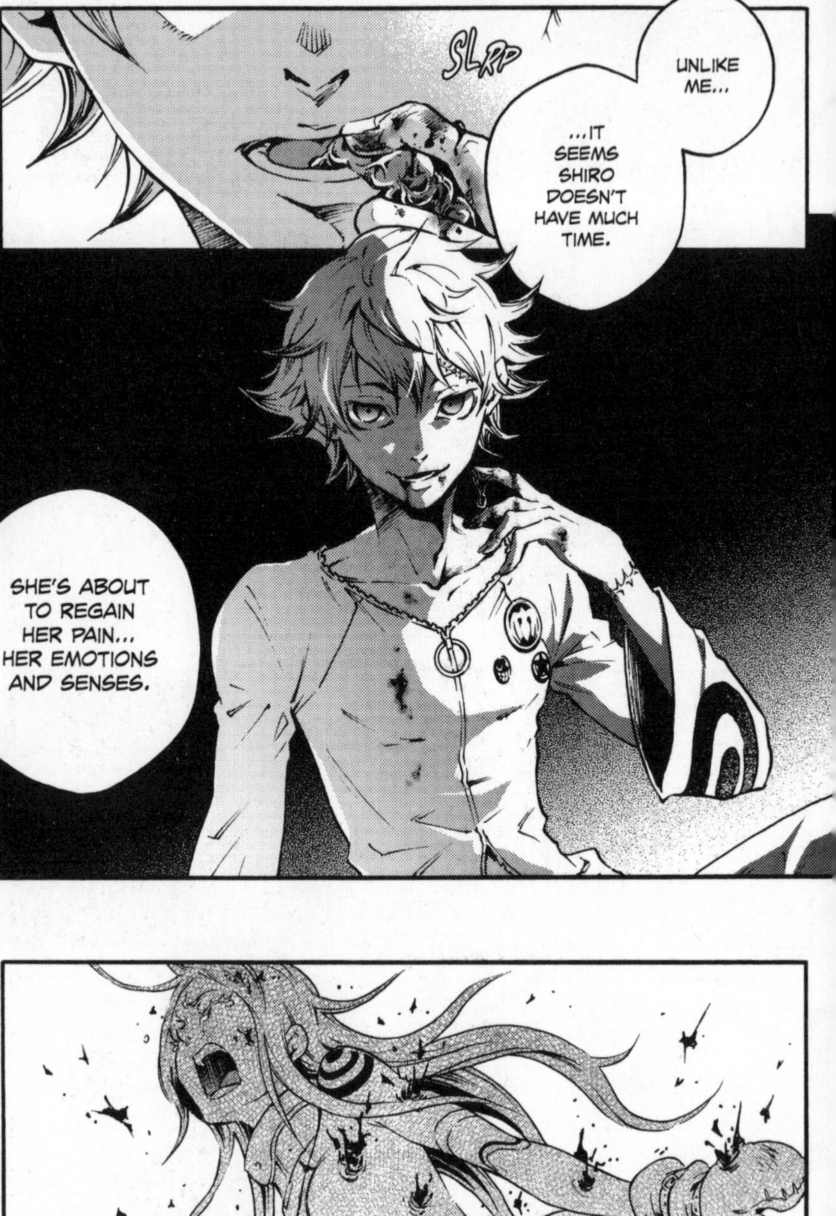
UNLIKE ME...
...IT SEEMS SHIRO DOESN'T HAVE MUCH TIME.
SLRP
SHE'S ABOUT TO REGAIN HER PAIN... HER EMOTIONS AND SENSES.

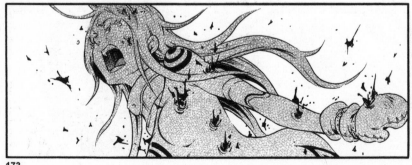

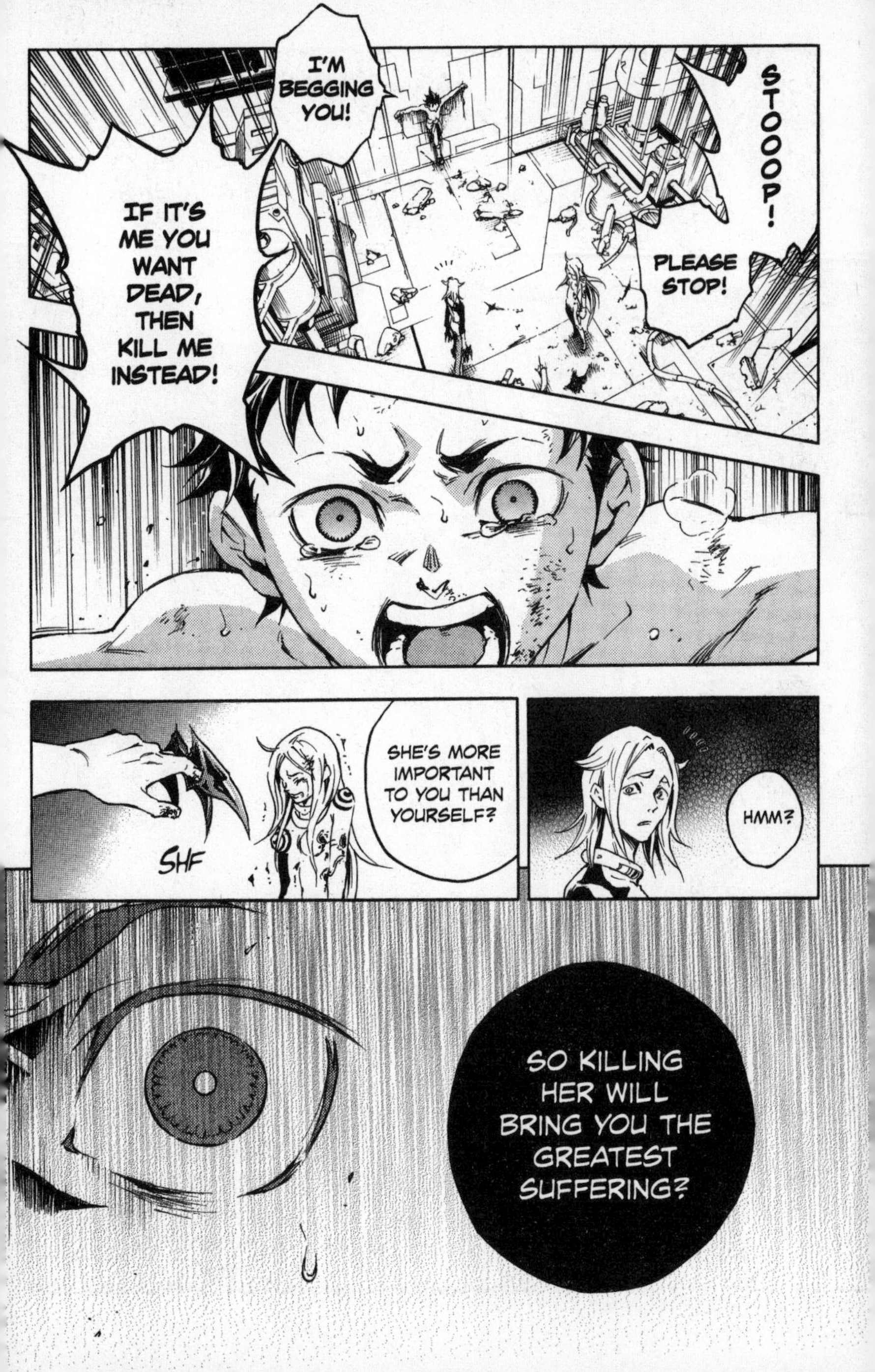
STOOOP!
PLEASE STOP!
I'M BEGGING YOU!
IF IT'S ME YOU WANT DEAD, THEN KILL ME INSTEAD!
HMM?
SHE'S MORE IMPORTANT TO YOU THAN YOURSELF?
SHF
SO KILLING HER WILL BRING YOU THE GREATEST SUFFERING?

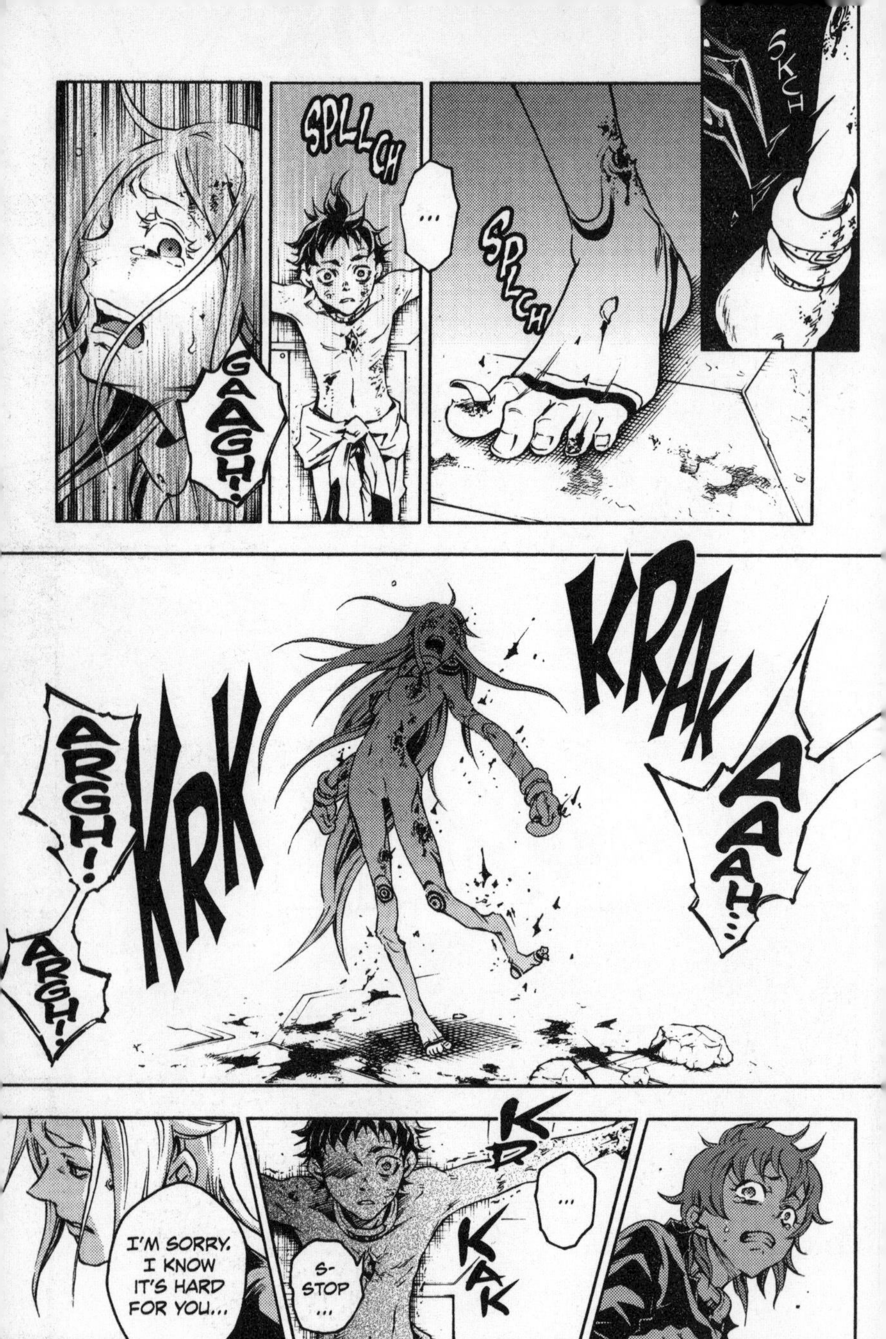

SKCH
SPLCH
SPLLCH
...
GAAGH!
KRAK
AAAAH...
KRK
ARGH!
ARGH!
...
KD
KAK
S-STOP...
I'M SORRY. I KNOW IT'S HARD FOR YOU...

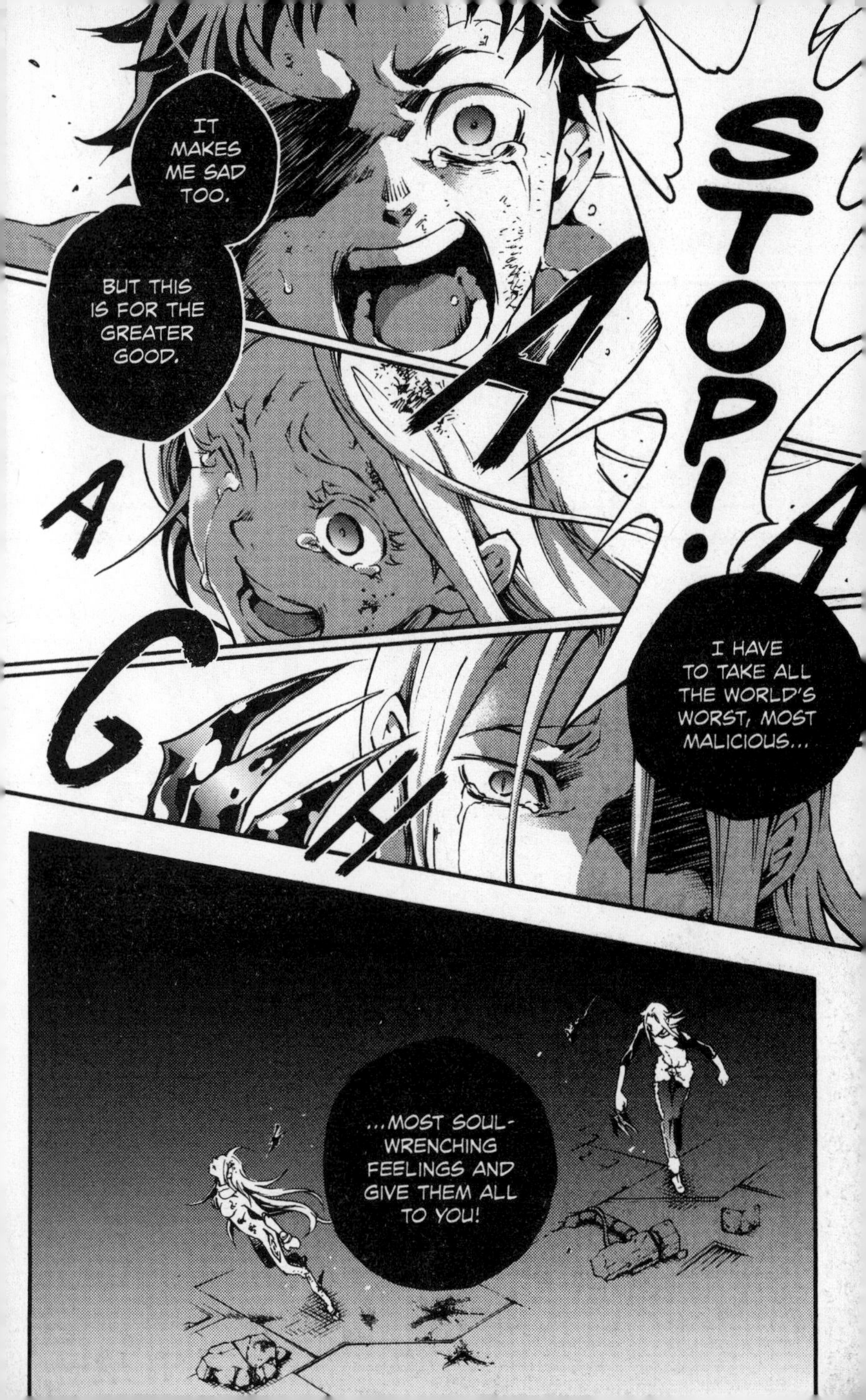
STOP!
AAAGH
IT MAKES ME SAD TOO.
BUT THIS IS FOR THE GREATER GOOD.
I HAVE TO TAKE ALL THE WORLD'S WORST, MOST MALICIOUS...
...MOST SOUL-WRENCHING FEELINGS AND GIVE THEM ALL TO YOU!

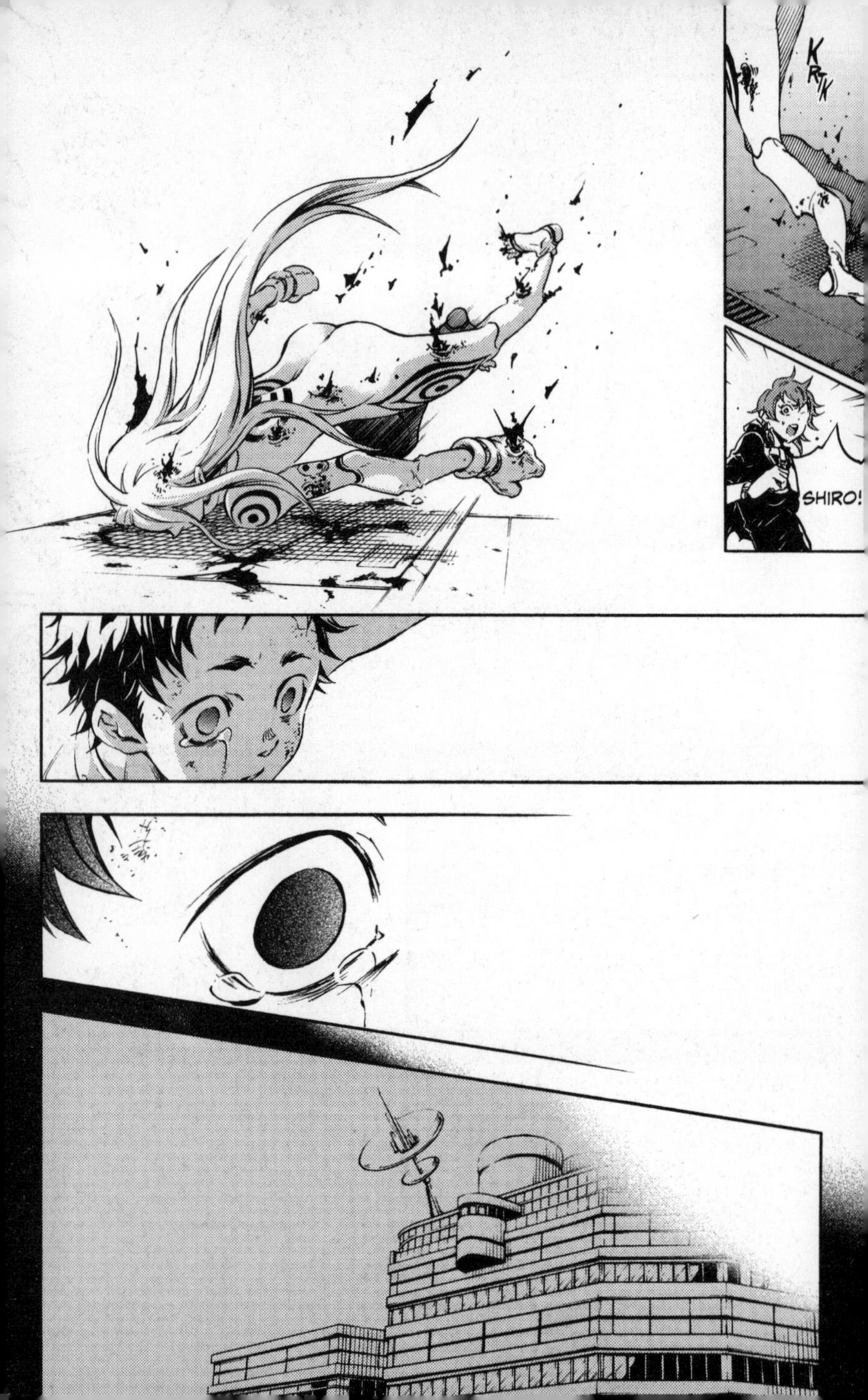
KRTIK
SHIRO!

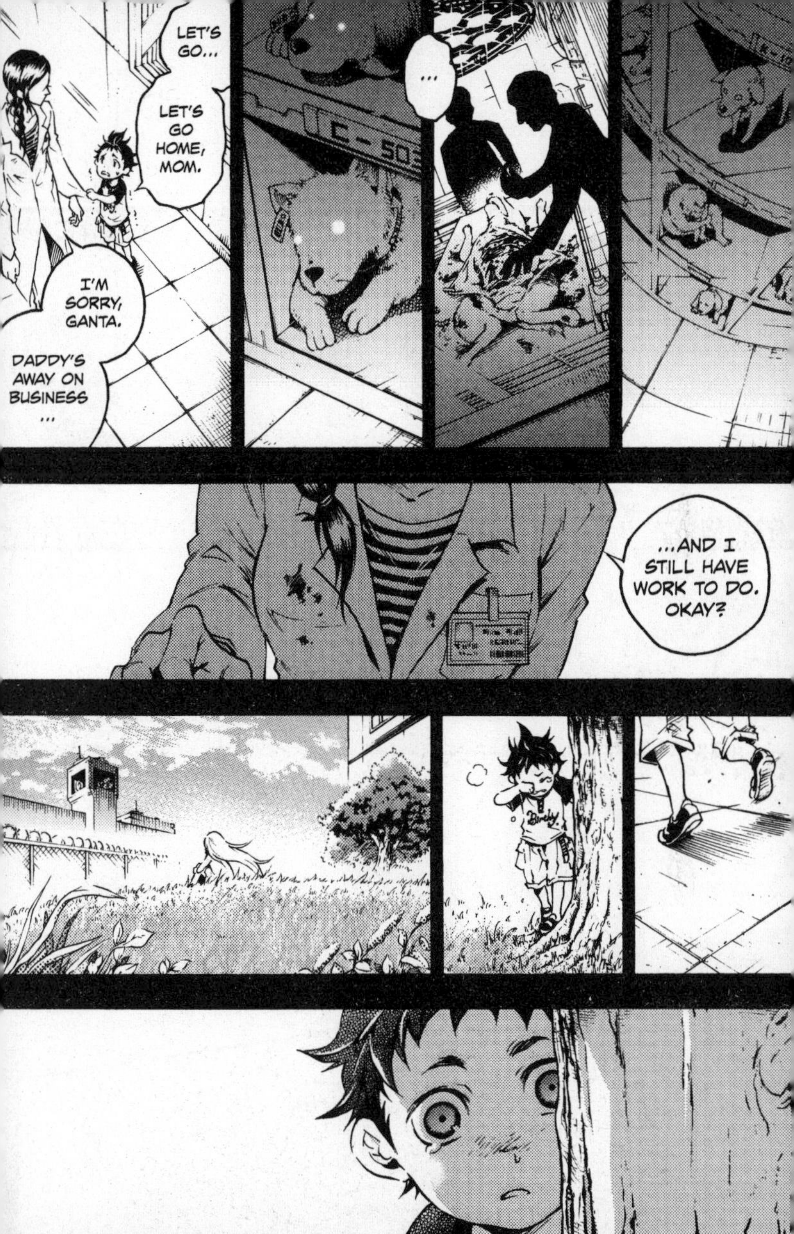
...
LET'S GO...
LET'S GO HOME, MOM.
I'M SORRY, GANTA.
DADDY'S AWAY ON BUSINESS ...
...AND I STILL HAVE WORK TO DO. OKAY?

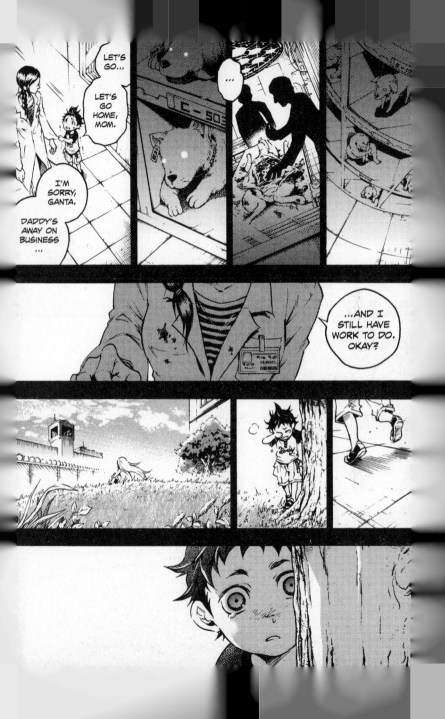

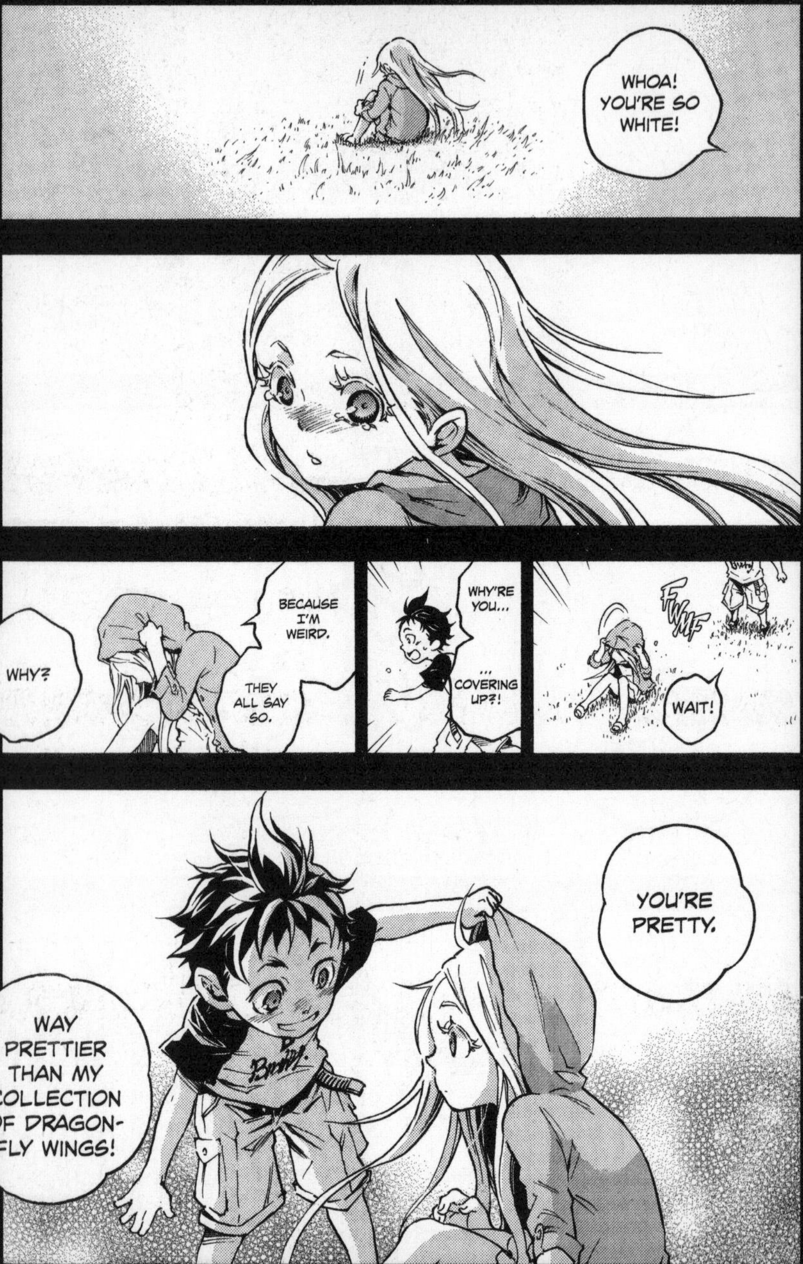
WHOA! YOU'RE SO WHITE!
FWMF
WAIT!
WHY'RE YOU...
...COVERING UP?!
BECAUSE I'M WEIRD.
WHY?
THEY ALL SAY SO.
YOU'RE PRETTY.
WAY PRETTIER THAN MY COLLECTION OF DRAGON-FLY WINGS!

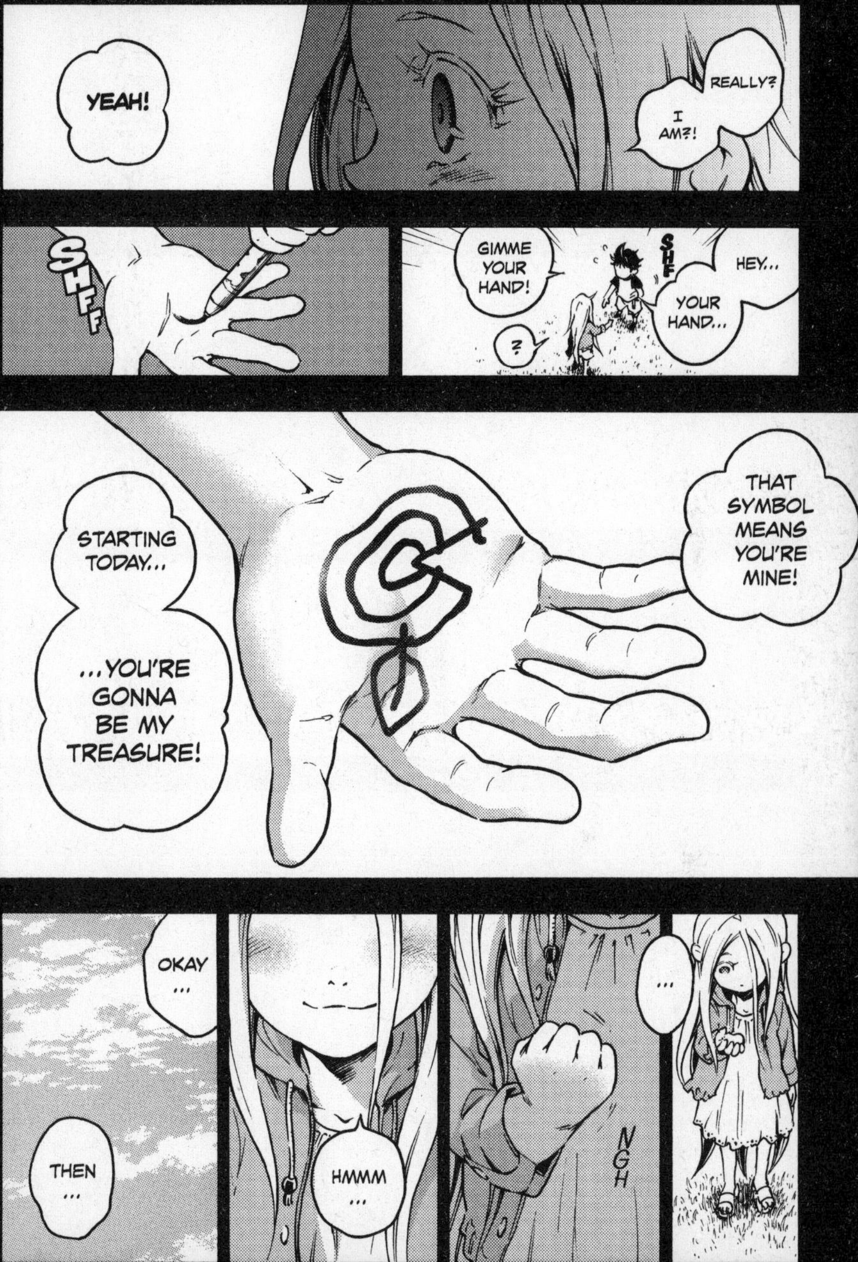

REALLY?
I AM?!
YEAH!
HEY...
YOUR HAND...
SHF
GIMME YOUR HAND!
?
SHFF
THAT SYMBOL MEANS YOU'RE MINE!
STARTING TODAY...
...YOU'RE GONNA BE MY TREASURE!
...
NGH
HMMM ...
OKAY ...
THEN ...

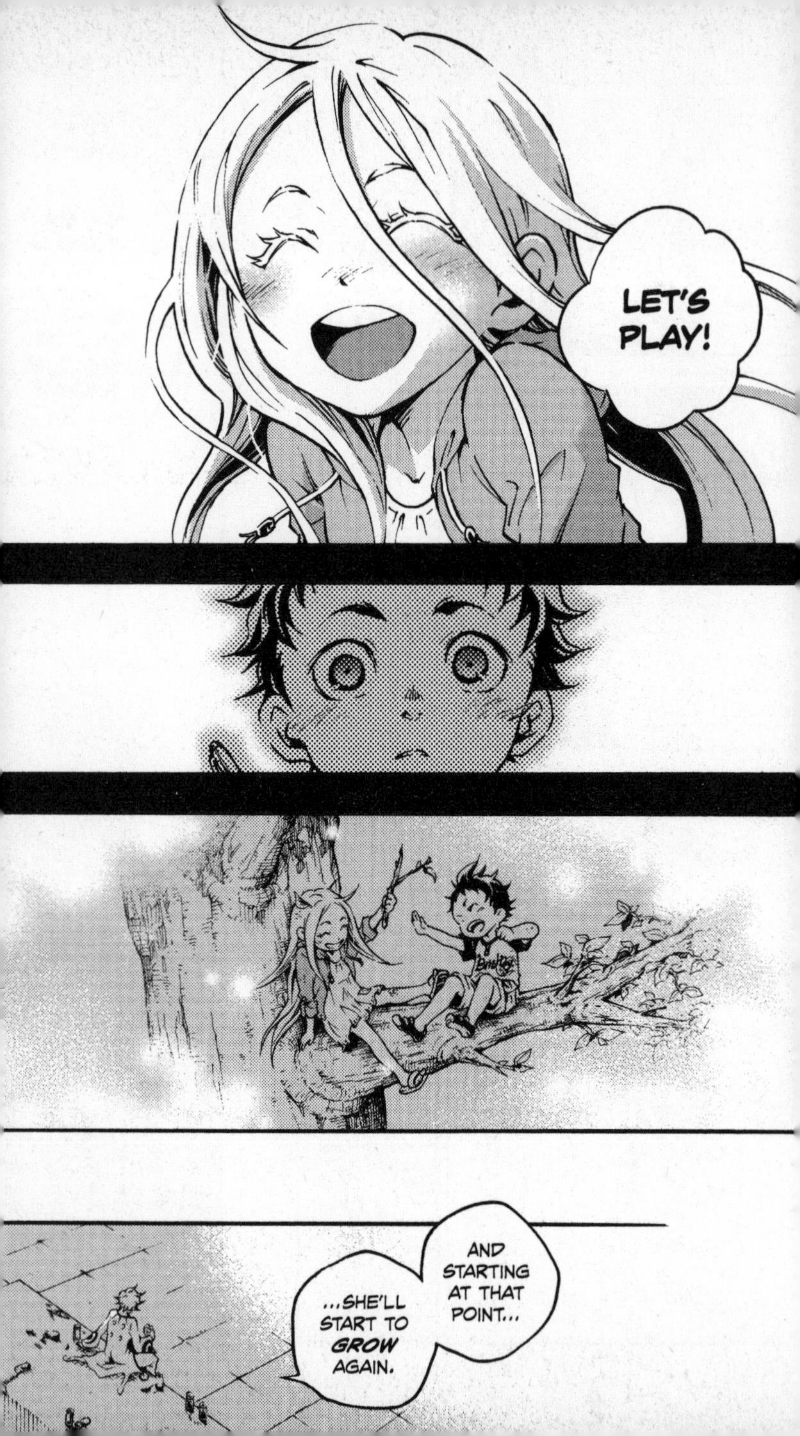
LET'S PLAY!
AND STARTING AT THAT POINT...
...SHE'LL START TO ***GROW*** AGAIN.

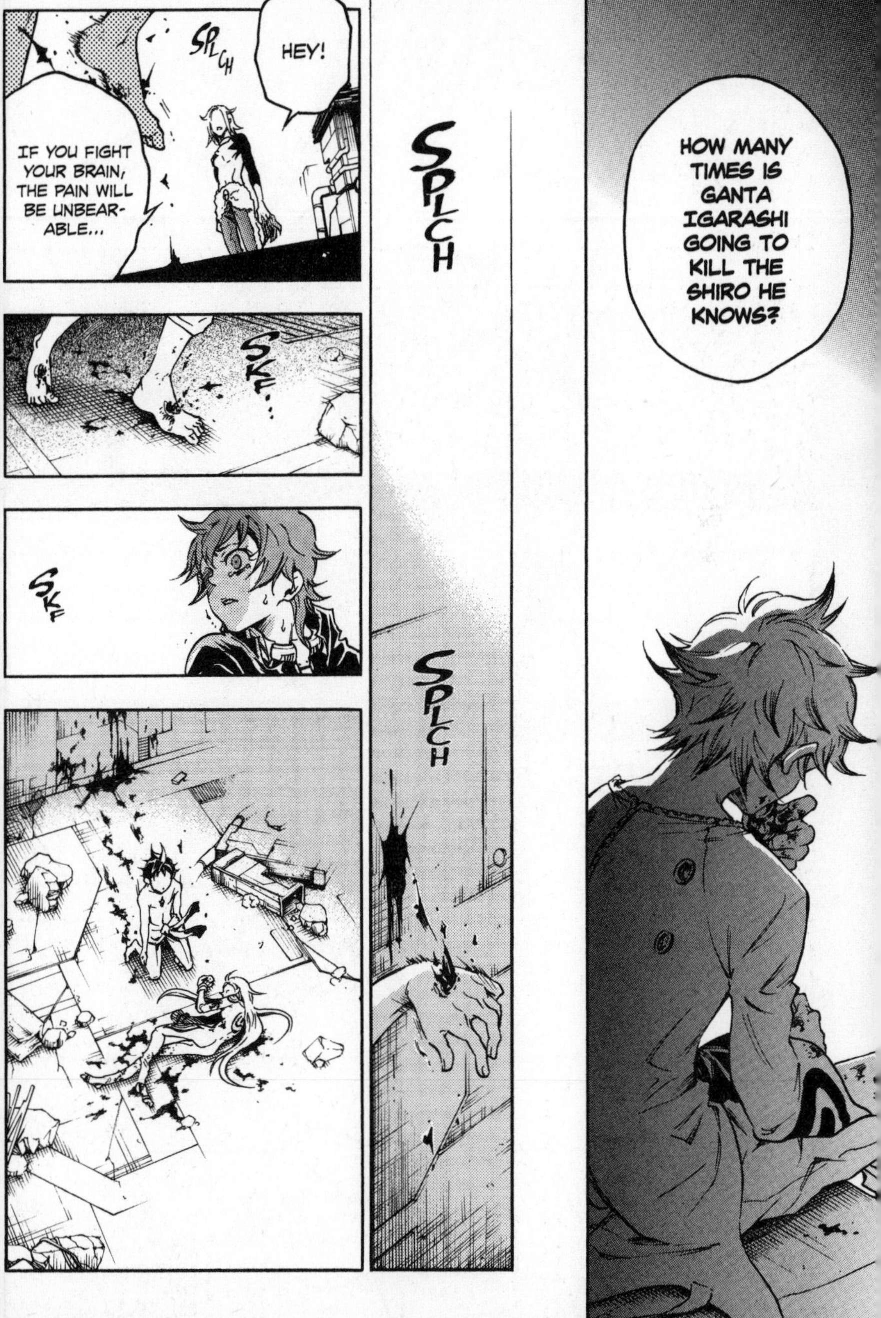
HOW MANY TIMES IS GANTA IGARASHI GOING TO KILL THE SHIRO HE KNOWS?
SPLCH
SPLCH
HEY!
SPLCH
IF YOU FIGHT YOUR BRAIN, THE PAIN WILL BE UNBEARABLE...
SKF...
SKF

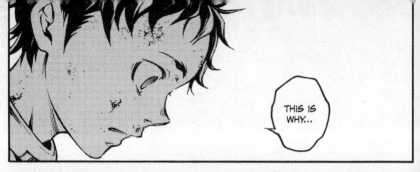

THIS IS WHY...
...YOU'RE SO FRUSTRATING.
I'M ON YOUR SIDE!
WHY DO YOU ALWAYS COME?
WHY ARE YOU SO STUPID?
WHY ARE YOU...?
PLIP

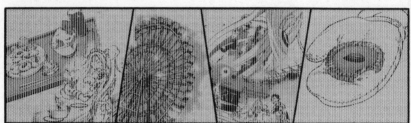

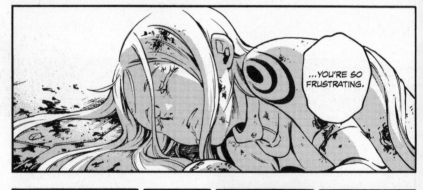

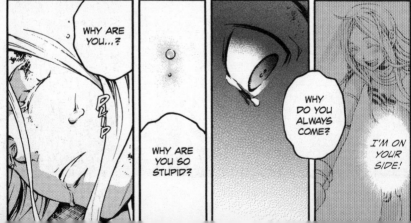

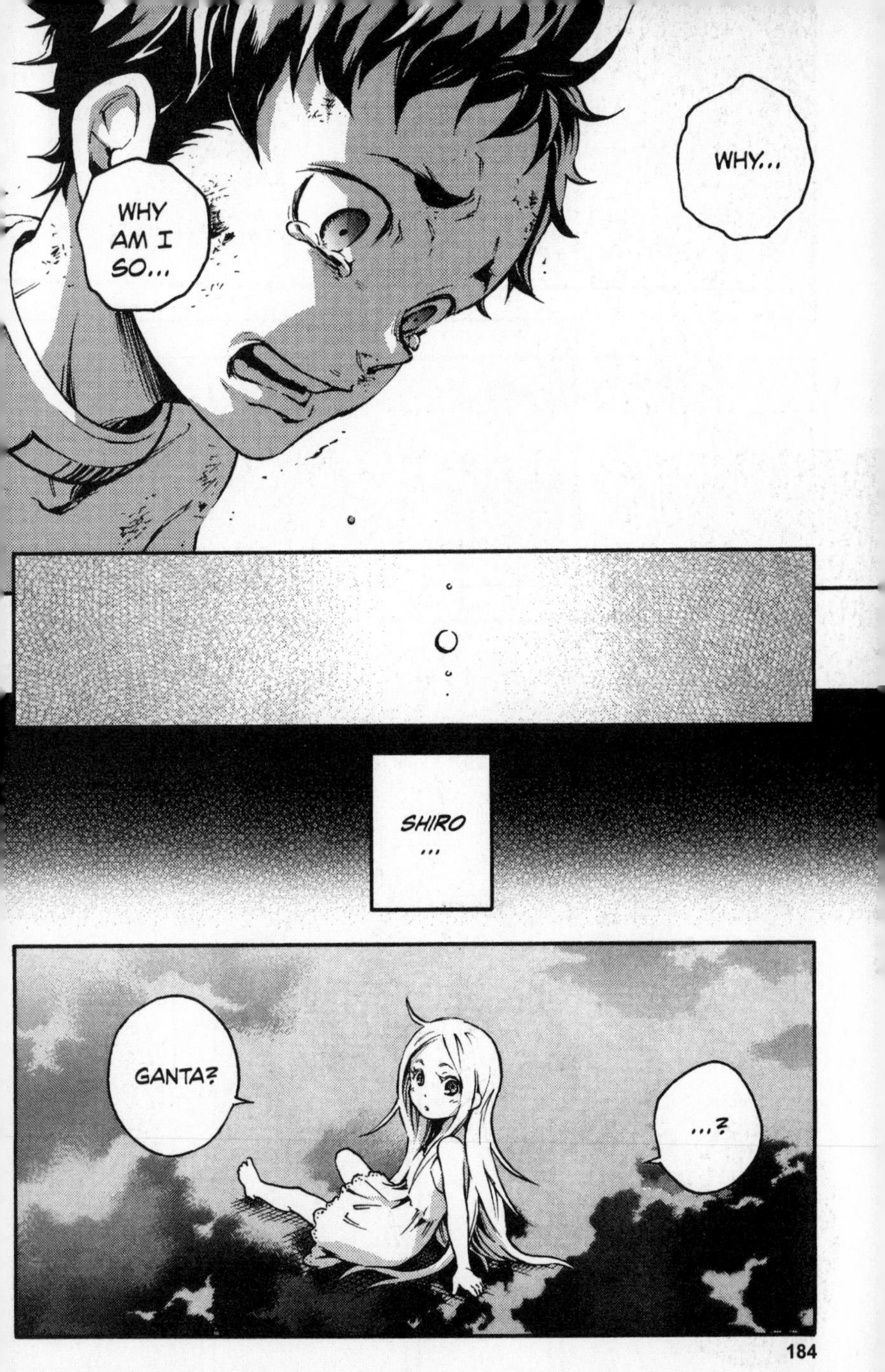
WHY...
WHY AM I SO...
SHIRO ...
...?
GANTA?

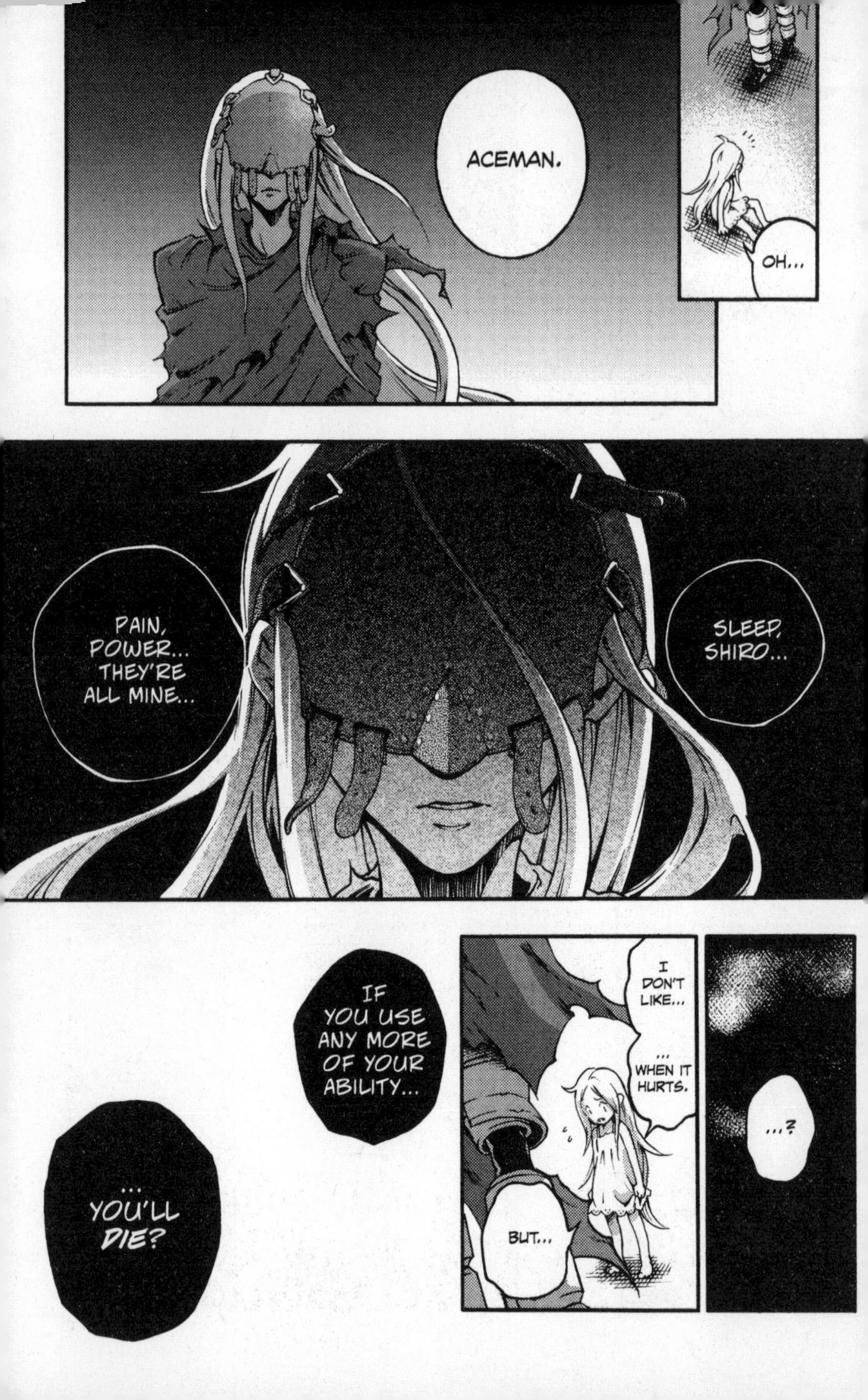
OH...
ACEMAN.
SLEEP, SHIRO...
PAIN, POWER... THEY'RE ALL MINE...
...?
I DON'T LIKE...
... WHEN IT HURTS.
BUT...
IF YOU USE ANY MORE OF YOUR ABILITY...
... YOU'LL *DIE*?

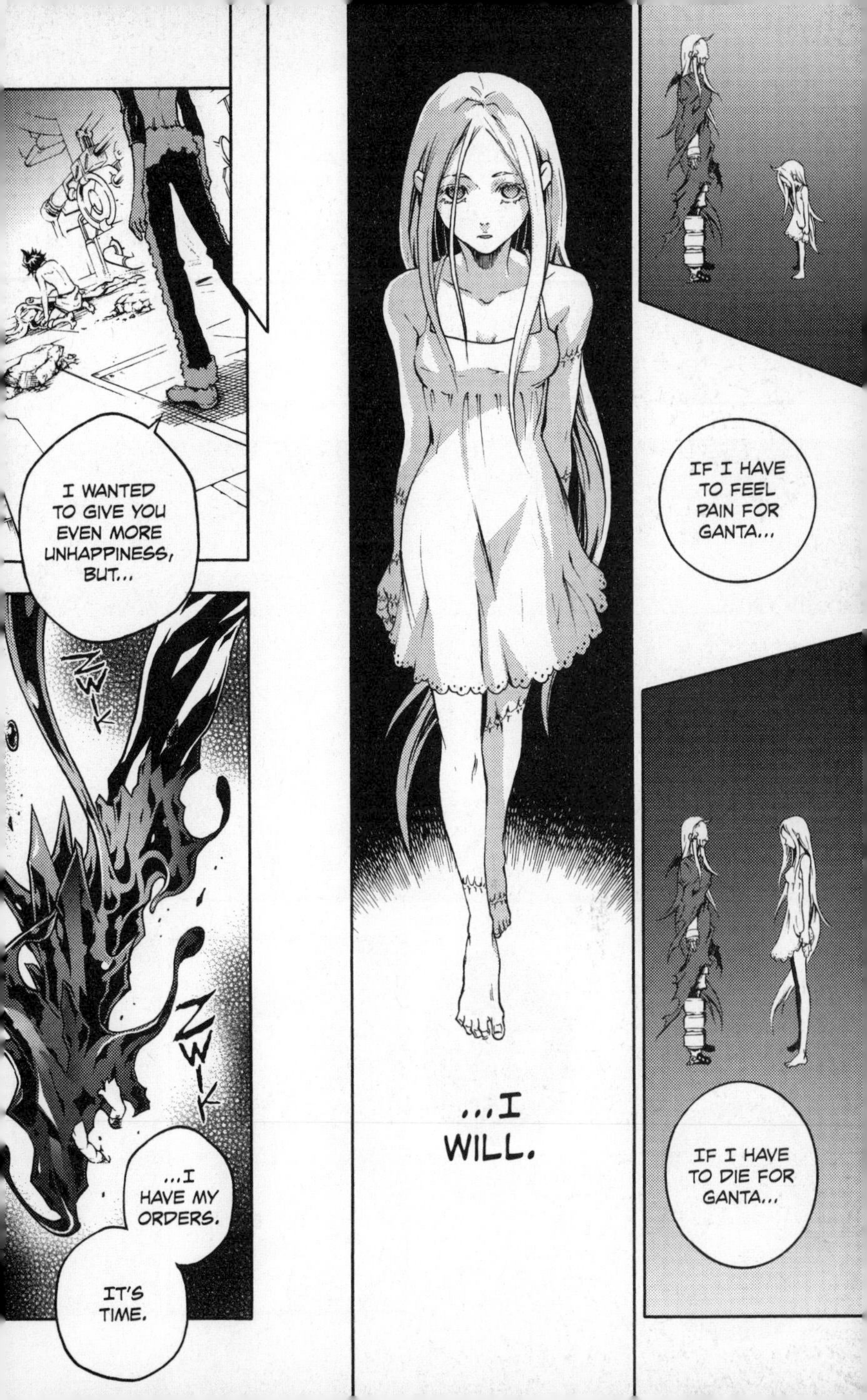
IF I HAVE TO FEEL PAIN FOR GANTA...
IF I HAVE TO DIE FOR GANTA...
...I WILL.
I WANTED TO GIVE YOU EVEN MORE UNHAPPINESS, BUT...
NWIK
NWIK
...I HAVE MY ORDERS.
IT'S TIME.

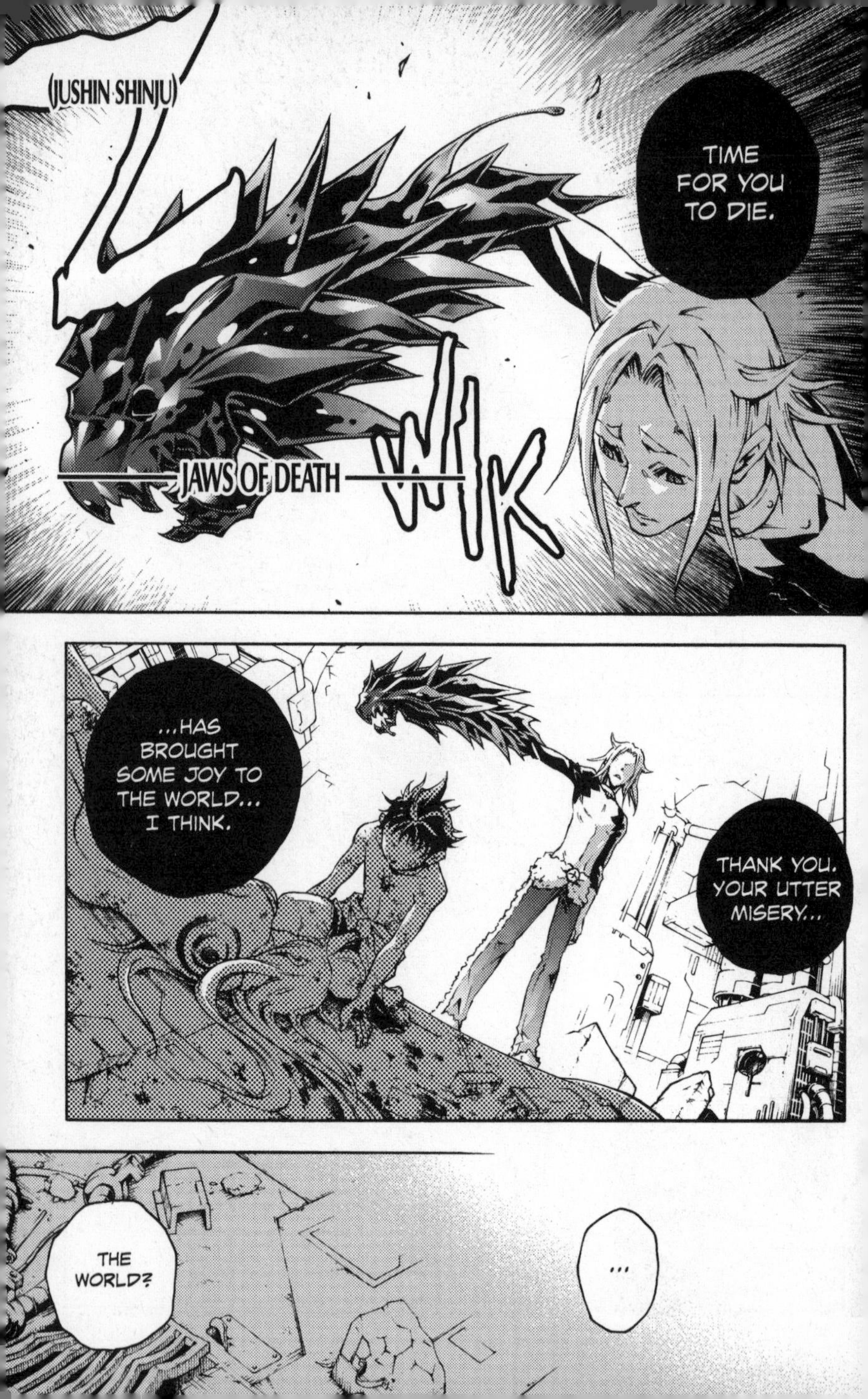
TIME FOR YOU TO DIE.
(JUSHIN SHINJU)
JAWS OF DEATH
THANK YOU. YOUR UTTER MISERY...
...HAS BROUGHT SOME JOY TO THE WORLD... I THINK.
...
THE WORLD?

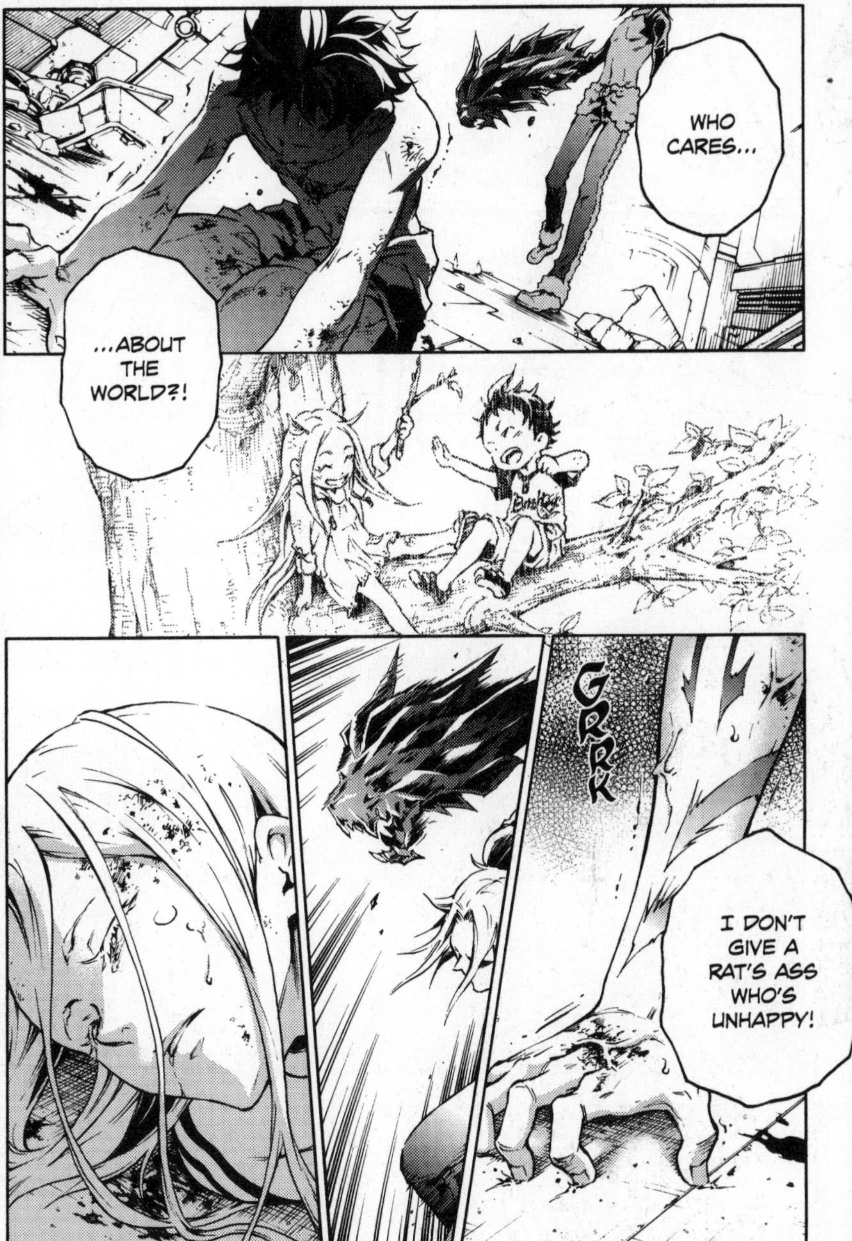
WHO CARES...
...ABOUT THE WORLD?!
GRRK
I DON'T GIVE A RAT'S ASS WHO'S UNHAPPY!

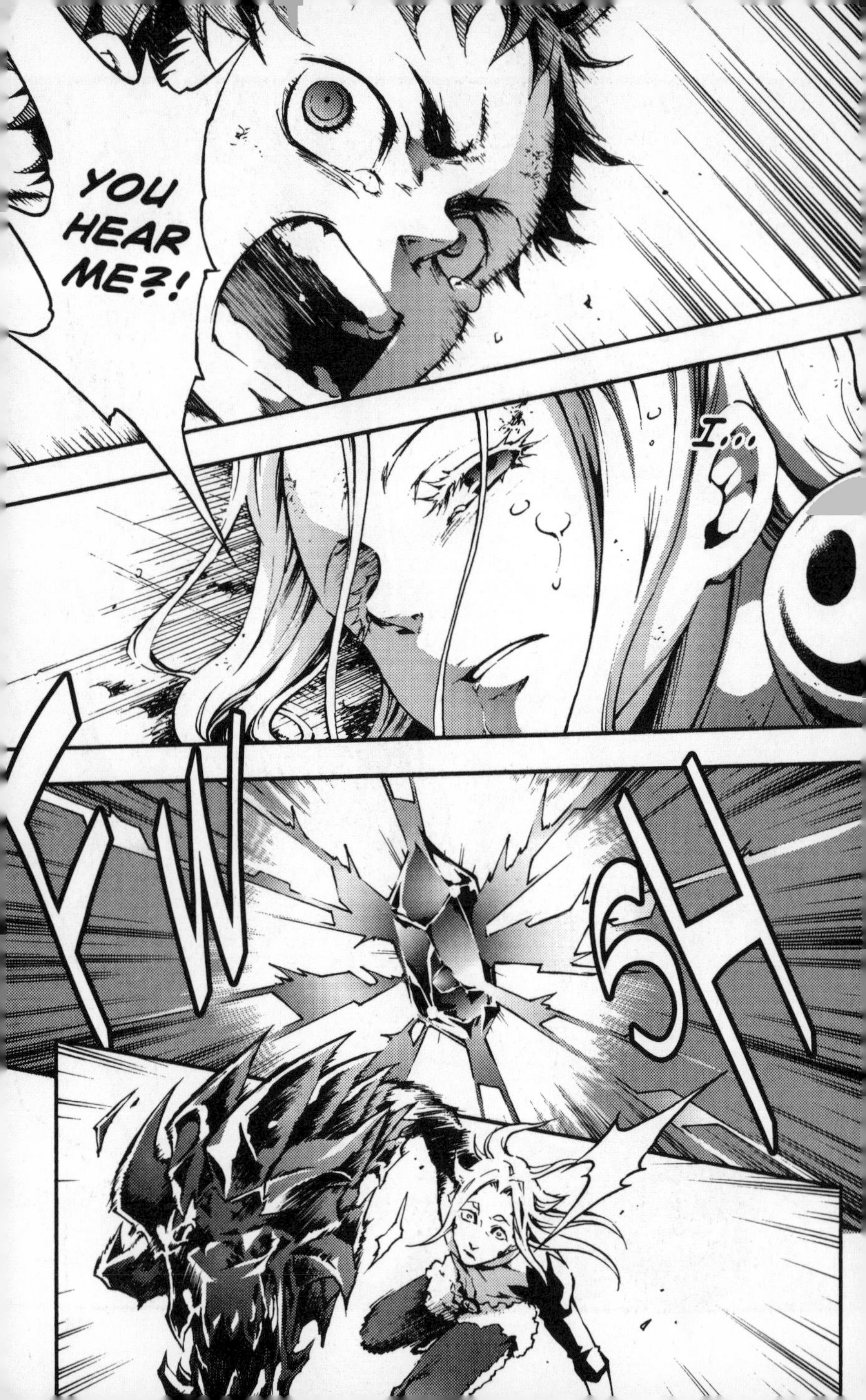
YOU HEAR ME?!
I...

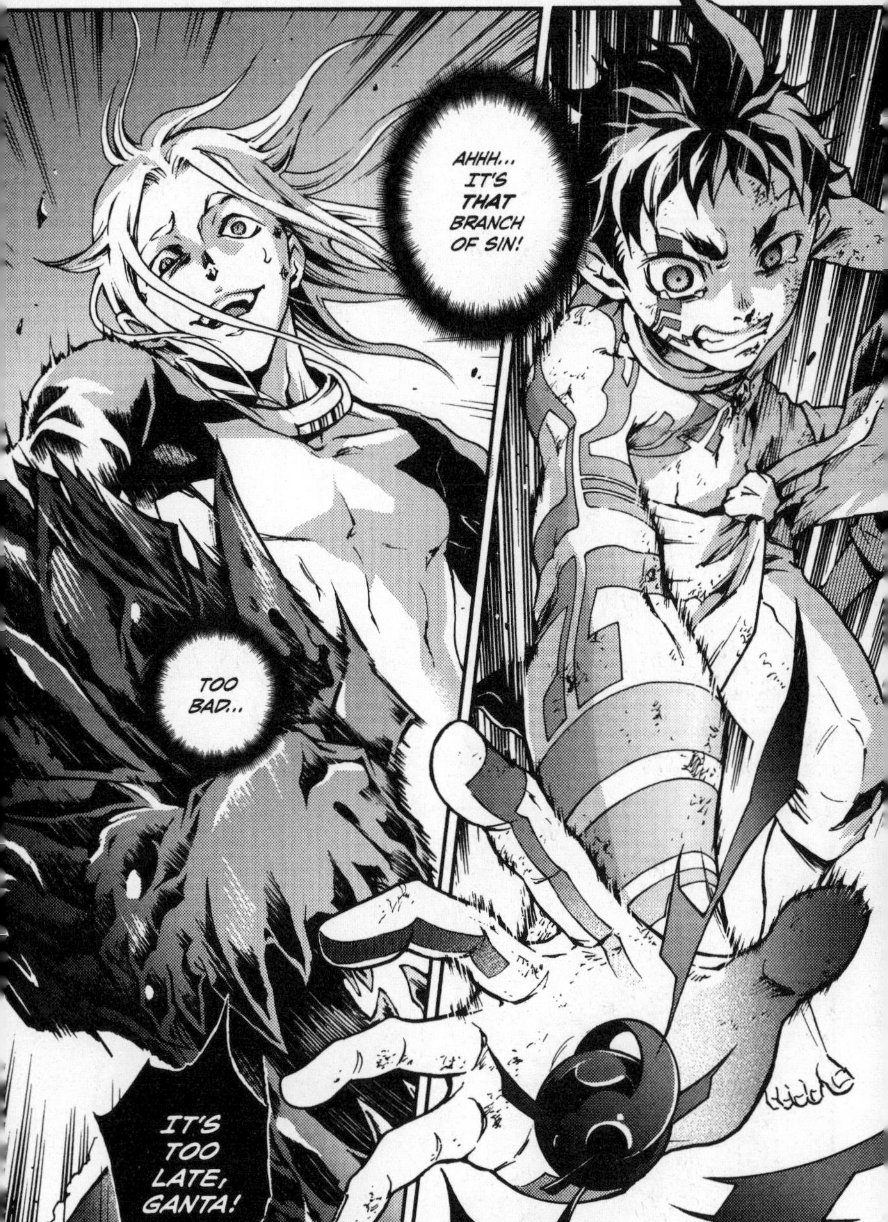
AHHH... IT'S THAT BRANCH OF SIN!
TOO BAD...
IT'S TOO LATE, GANTA!

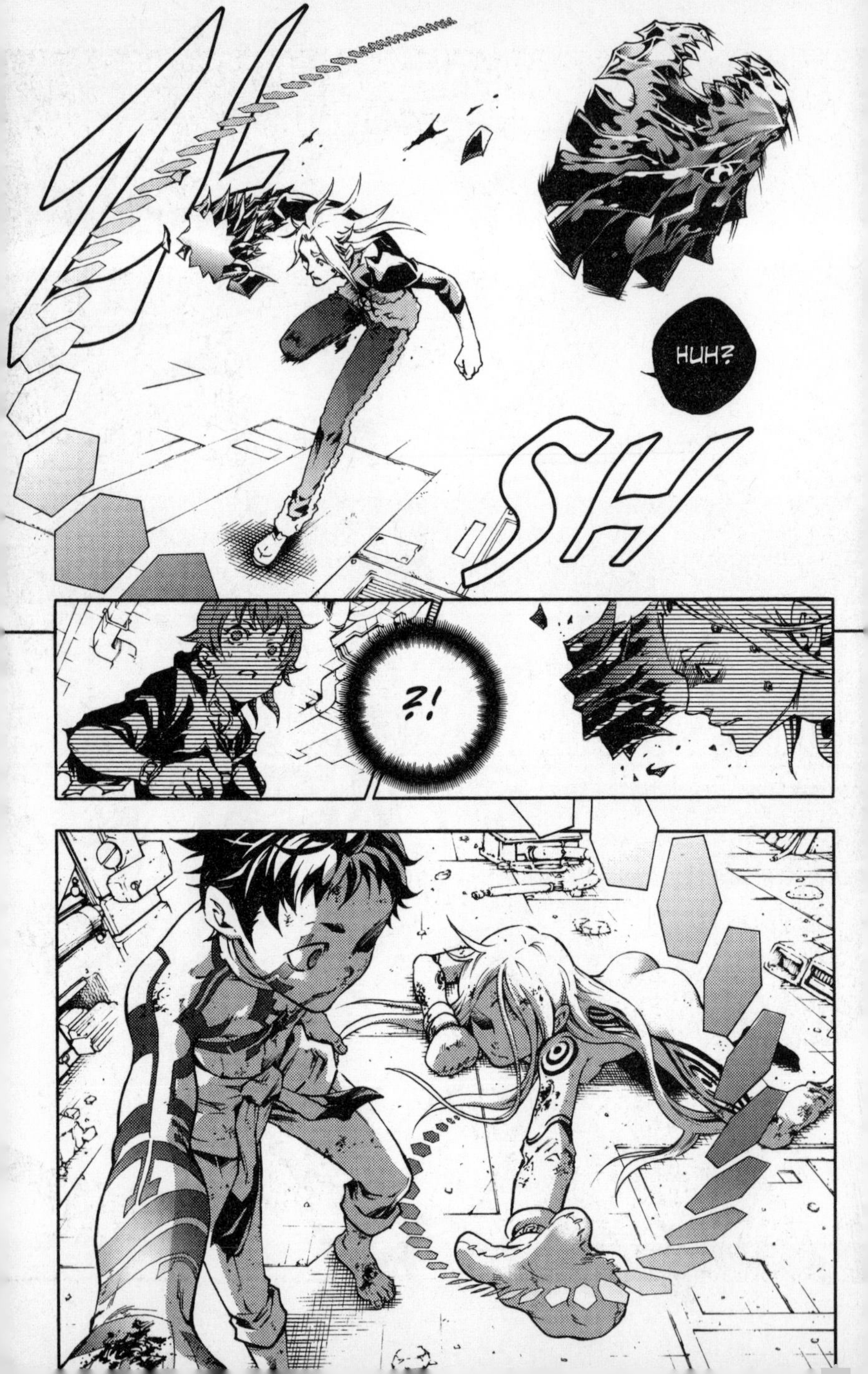
HUH?
SH
?!

AS LONG AS I...

...HAVE GANTA...

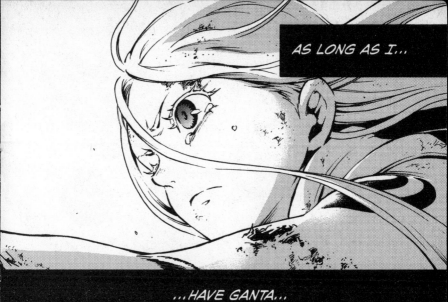

IF...

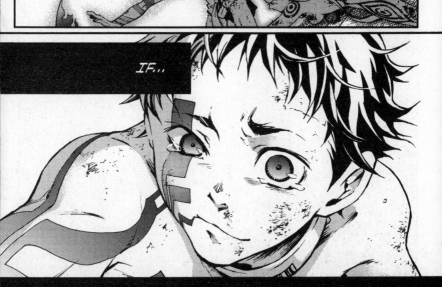

...I HAVE SHIRO...

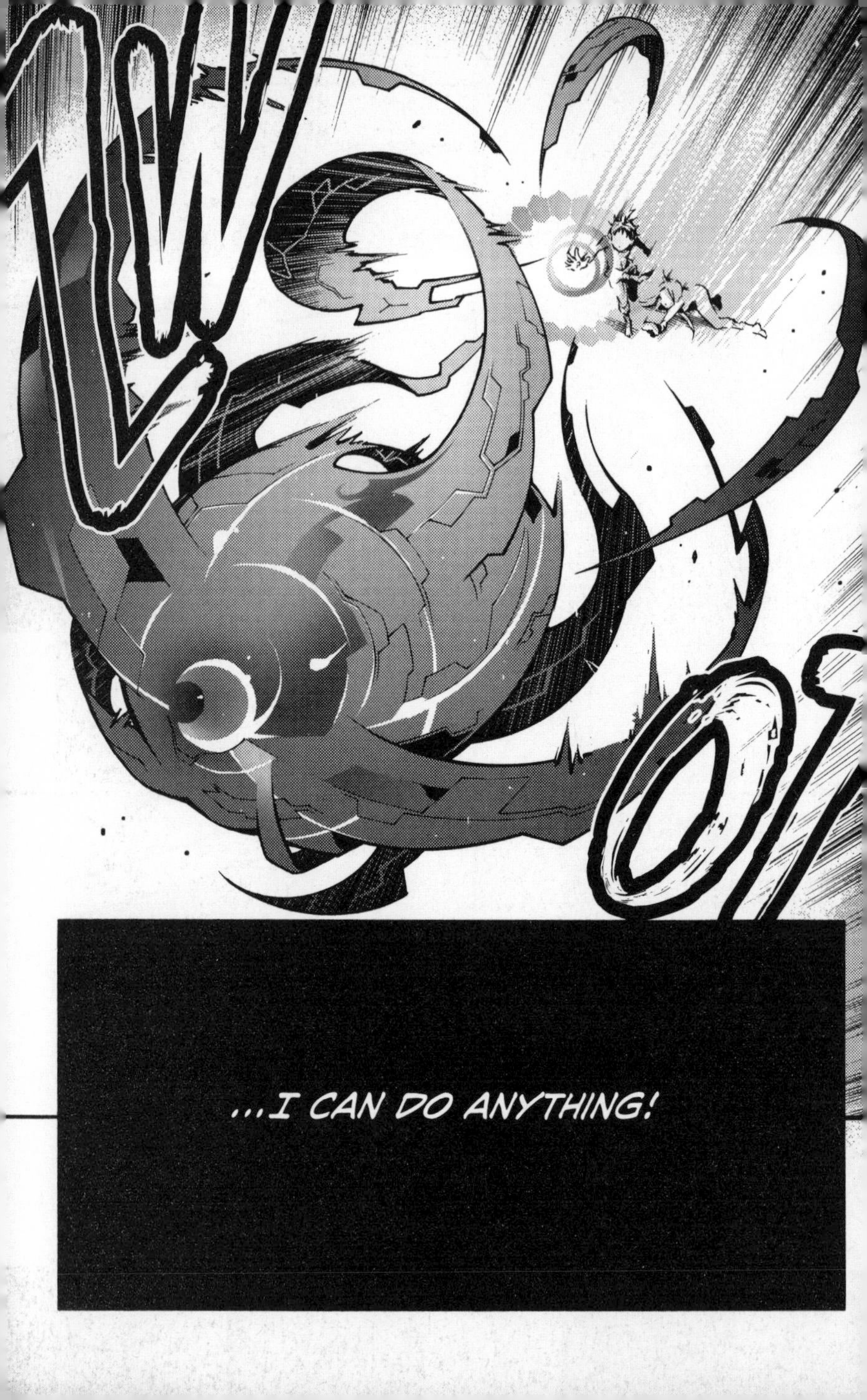
...I CAN DO ANYTHING!

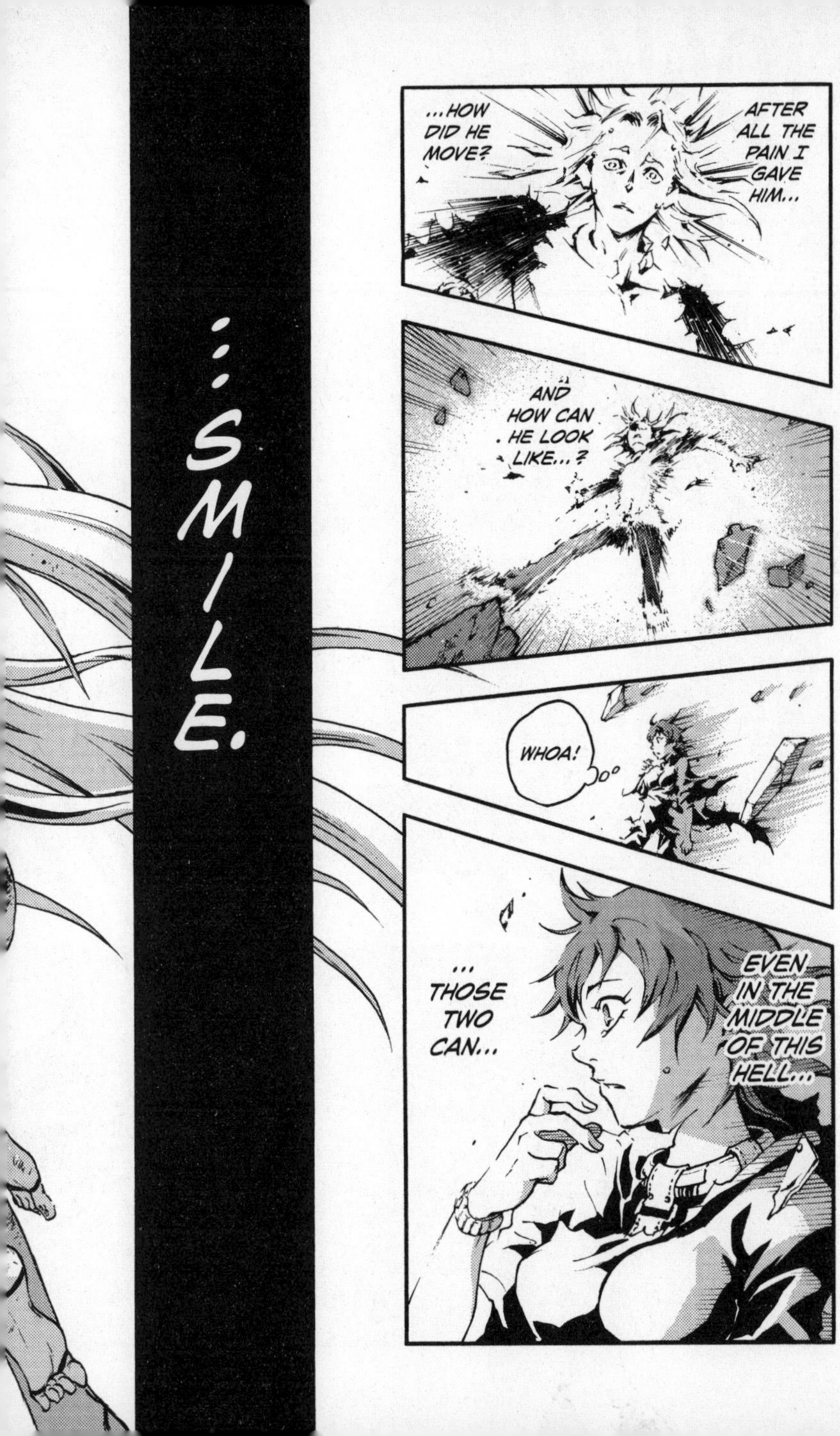
AFTER ALL THE PAIN I GAVE HIM...
...HOW DID HE MOVE?
AND HOW CAN HE LOOK LIKE...?
WHOA!
EVEN IN THE MIDDLE OF THIS HELL...
...THOSE TWO CAN...
...SMILE.

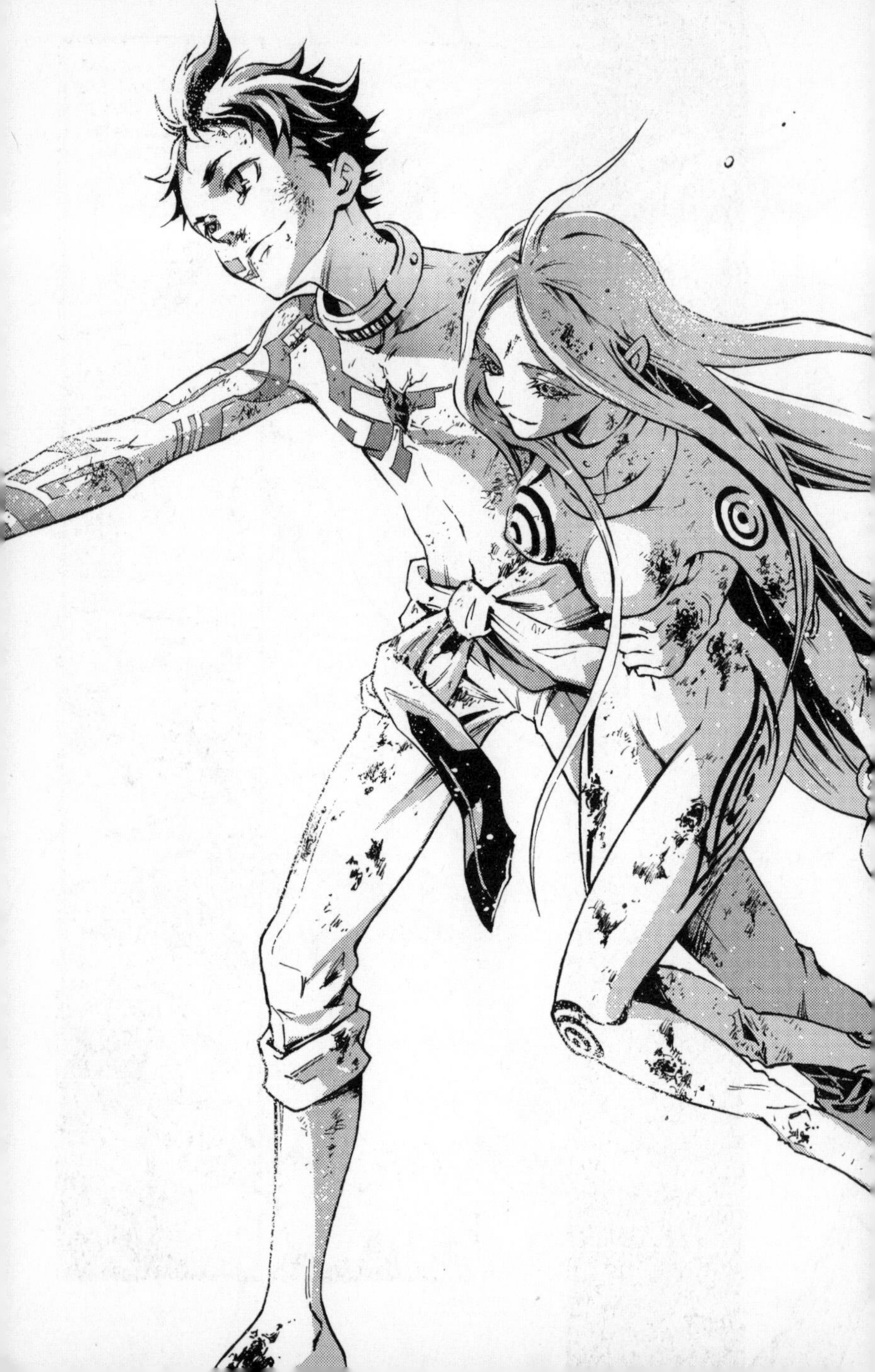

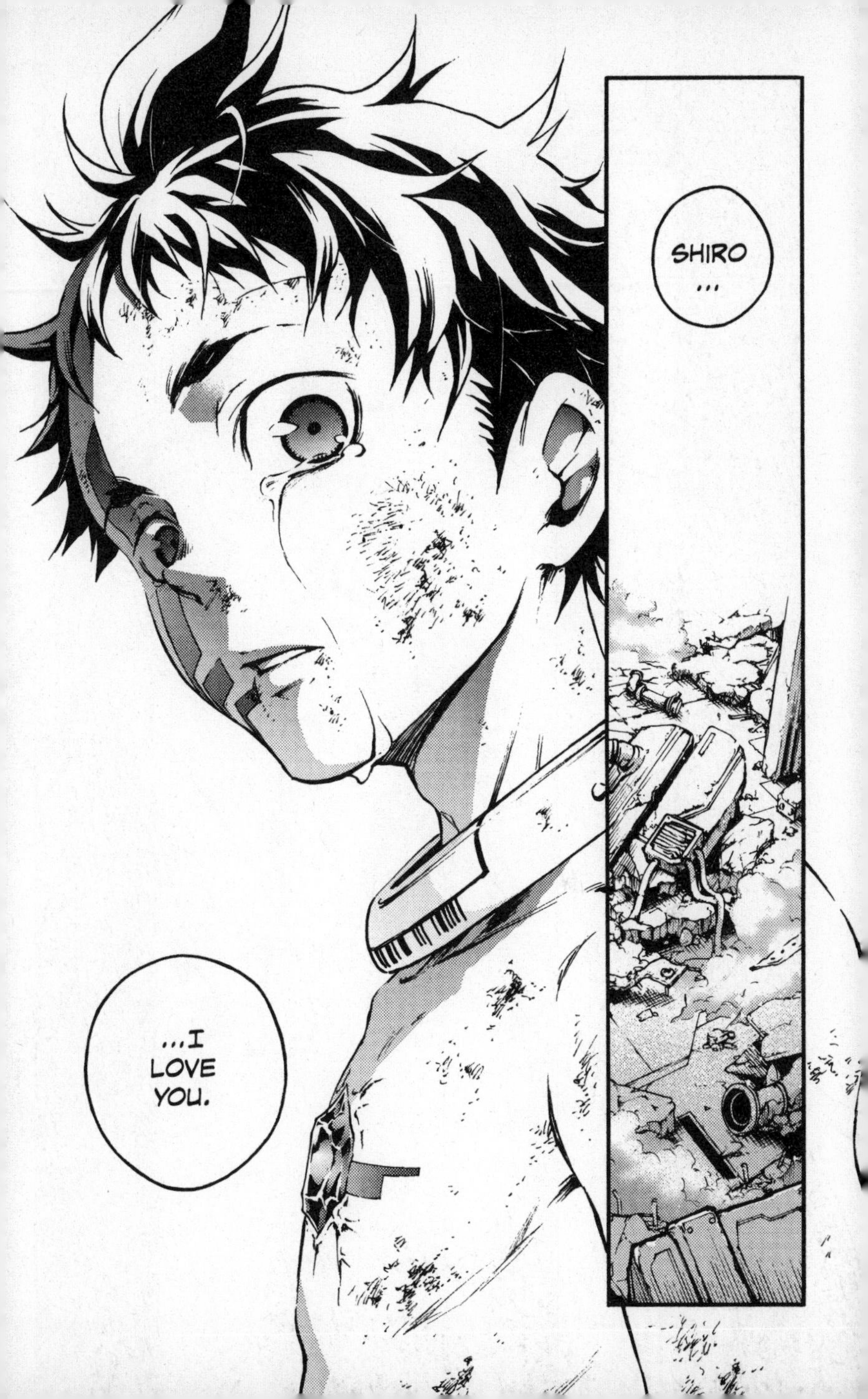
SHIRO ...
...I LOVE YOU.

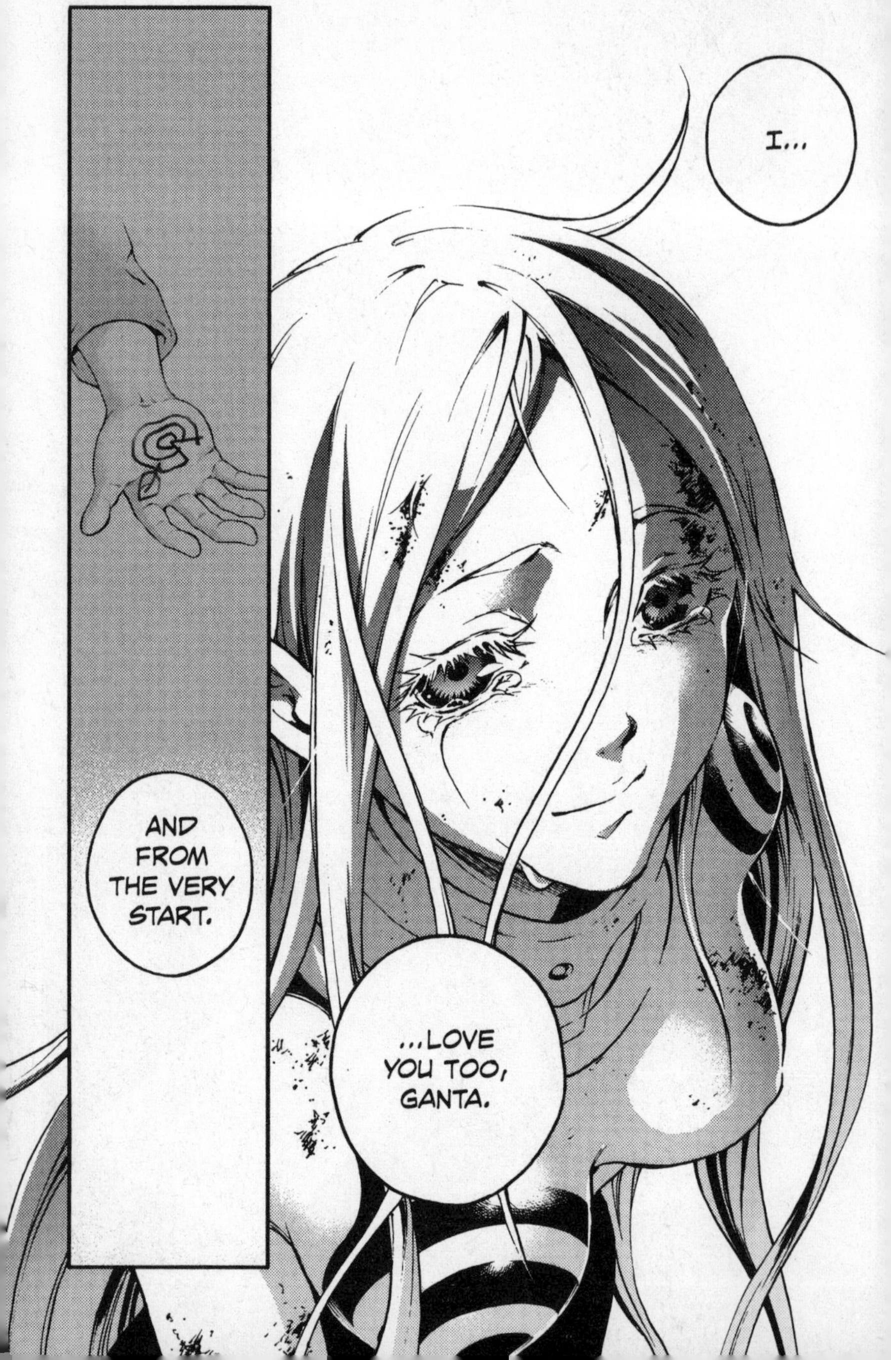
I...
...LOVE YOU TOO, GANTA.
AND FROM THE VERY START.

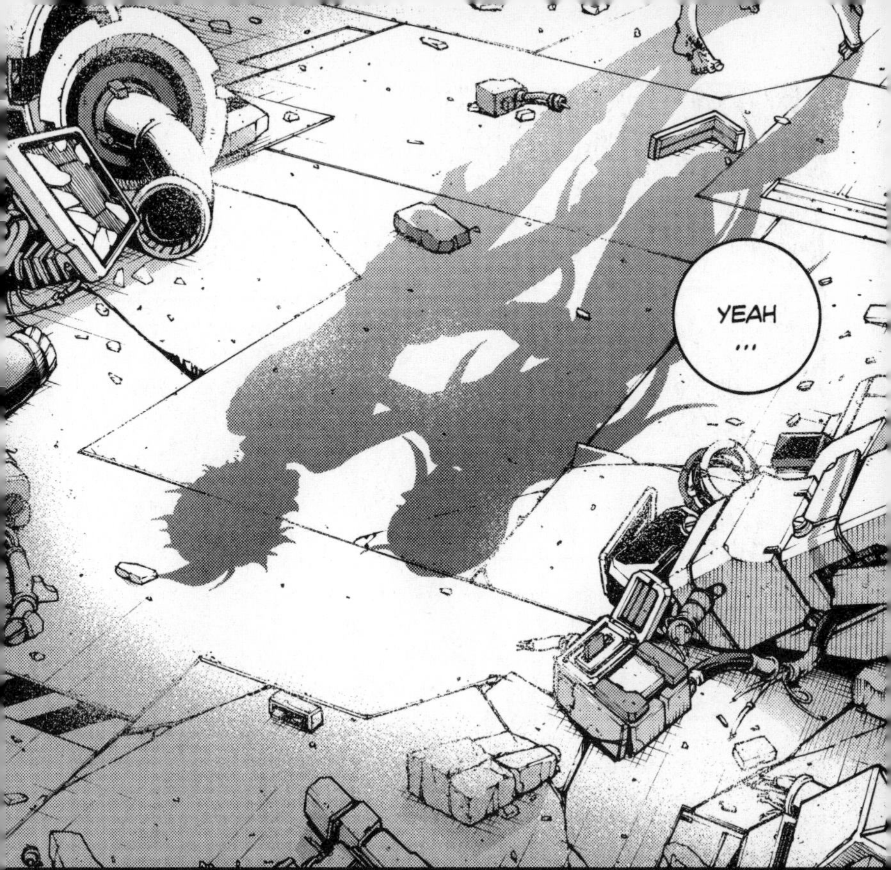
YEAH
...
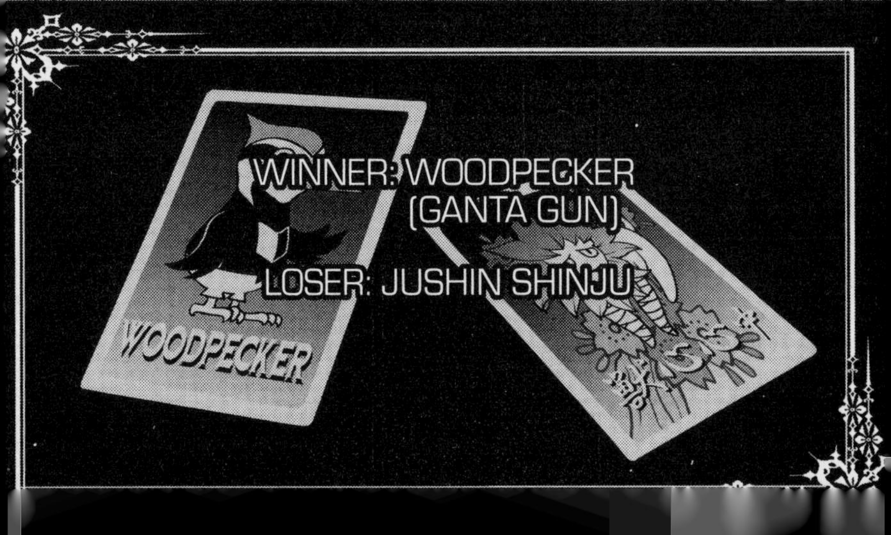
WINNER: WOODPECKER
(GANTA GUN)
LOSER: JUSHIN SHINJU
WOODPECKER

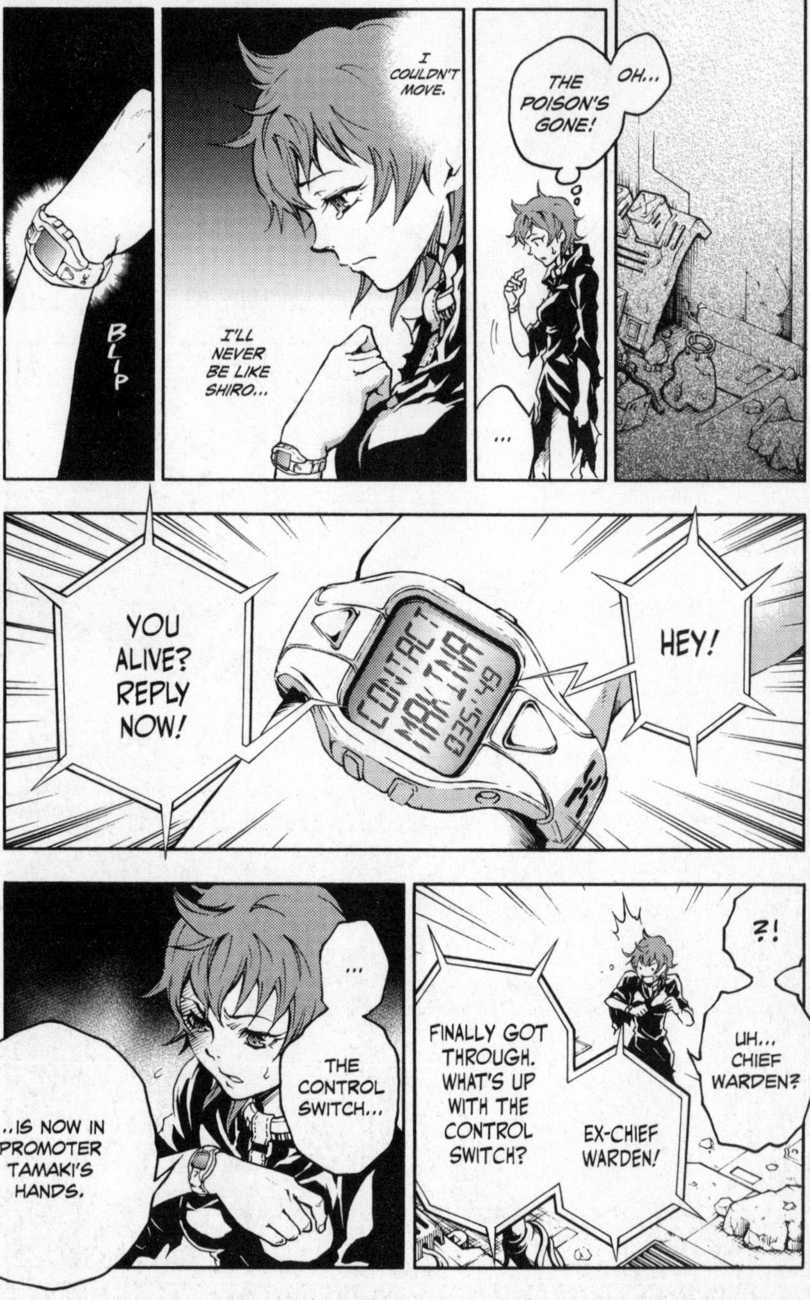
OH...
THE POISON'S GONE!
...
I COULDN'T MOVE.
I'LL NEVER BE LIKE SHIRO...
BLIP
HEY!
YOU ALIVE? REPLY NOW!
?!
UH... CHIEF WARDEN?
EX-CHIEF WARDEN!
FINALLY GOT THROUGH. WHAT'S UP WITH THE CONTROL SWITCH?
...
THE CONTROL SWITCH...
...IS NOW IN PROMOTER TAMAKI'S HANDS.

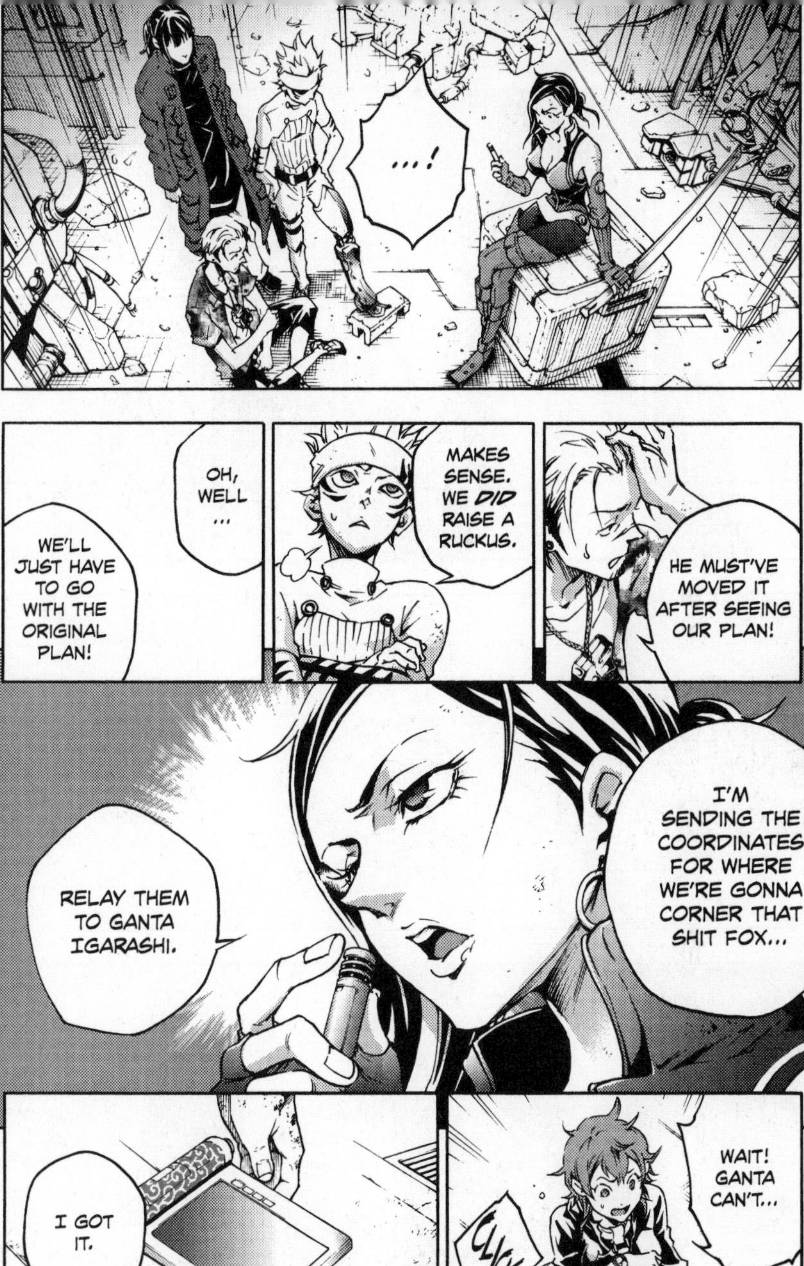
...!
HE MUST'VE MOVED IT AFTER SEEING OUR PLAN!
MAKES SENSE. WE *DID* RAISE A RUCKUS.
OH, WELL ...
WE'LL JUST HAVE TO GO WITH THE ORIGINAL PLAN!
BEEP
I'M SENDING THE COORDINATES FOR WHERE WE'RE GONNA CORNER THAT SHIT FOX...
RELAY THEM TO GANTA IGARASHI.
WAIT! GANTA CAN'T...
CLICK
I GOT IT.

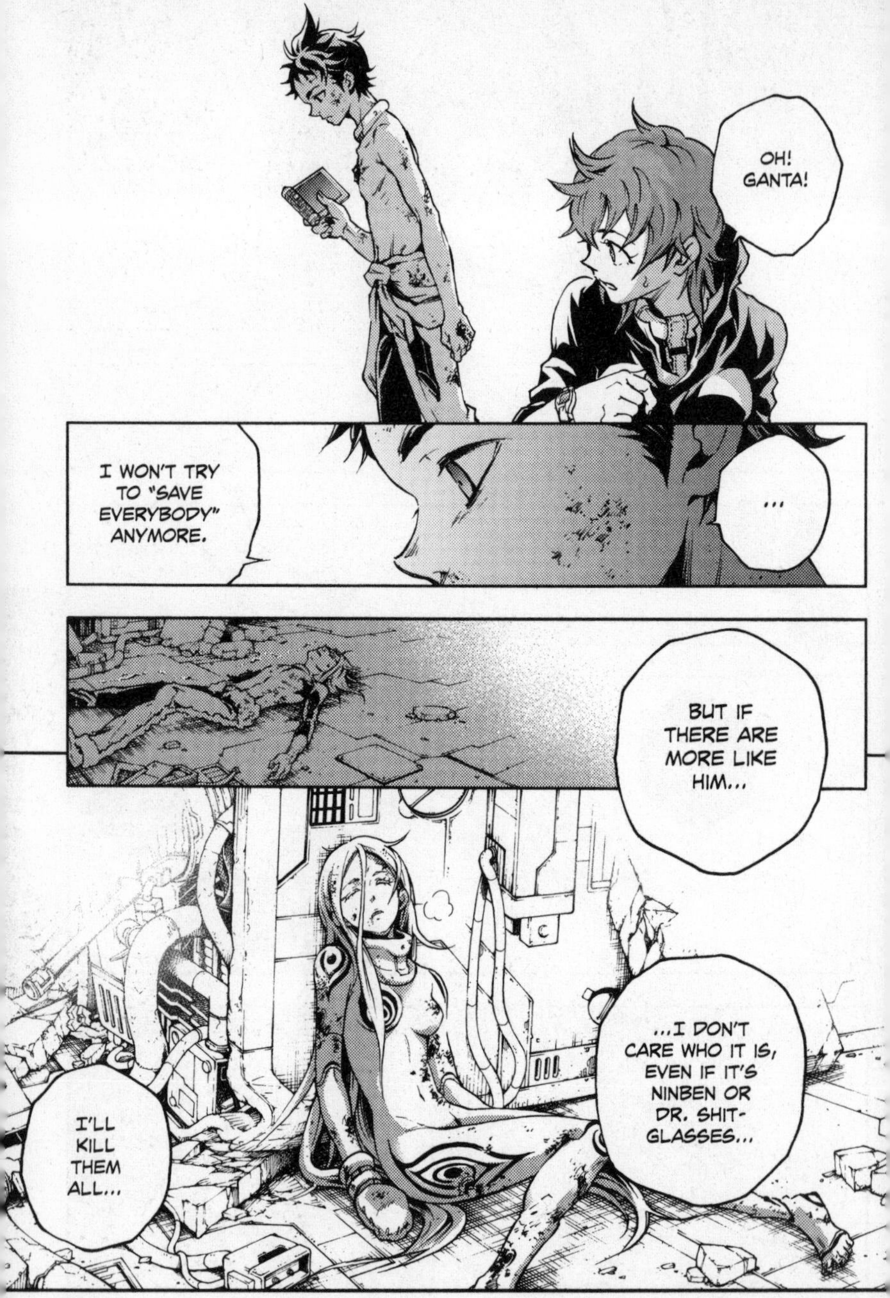
OH! GANTA!
...
I WON'T TRY TO "SAVE EVERYBODY" ANYMORE.
BUT IF THERE ARE MORE LIKE HIM...
...I DON'T CARE WHO IT IS, EVEN IF IT'S NINBEN OR DR. SHIT-GLASSES...
I'LL KILL THEM ALL...

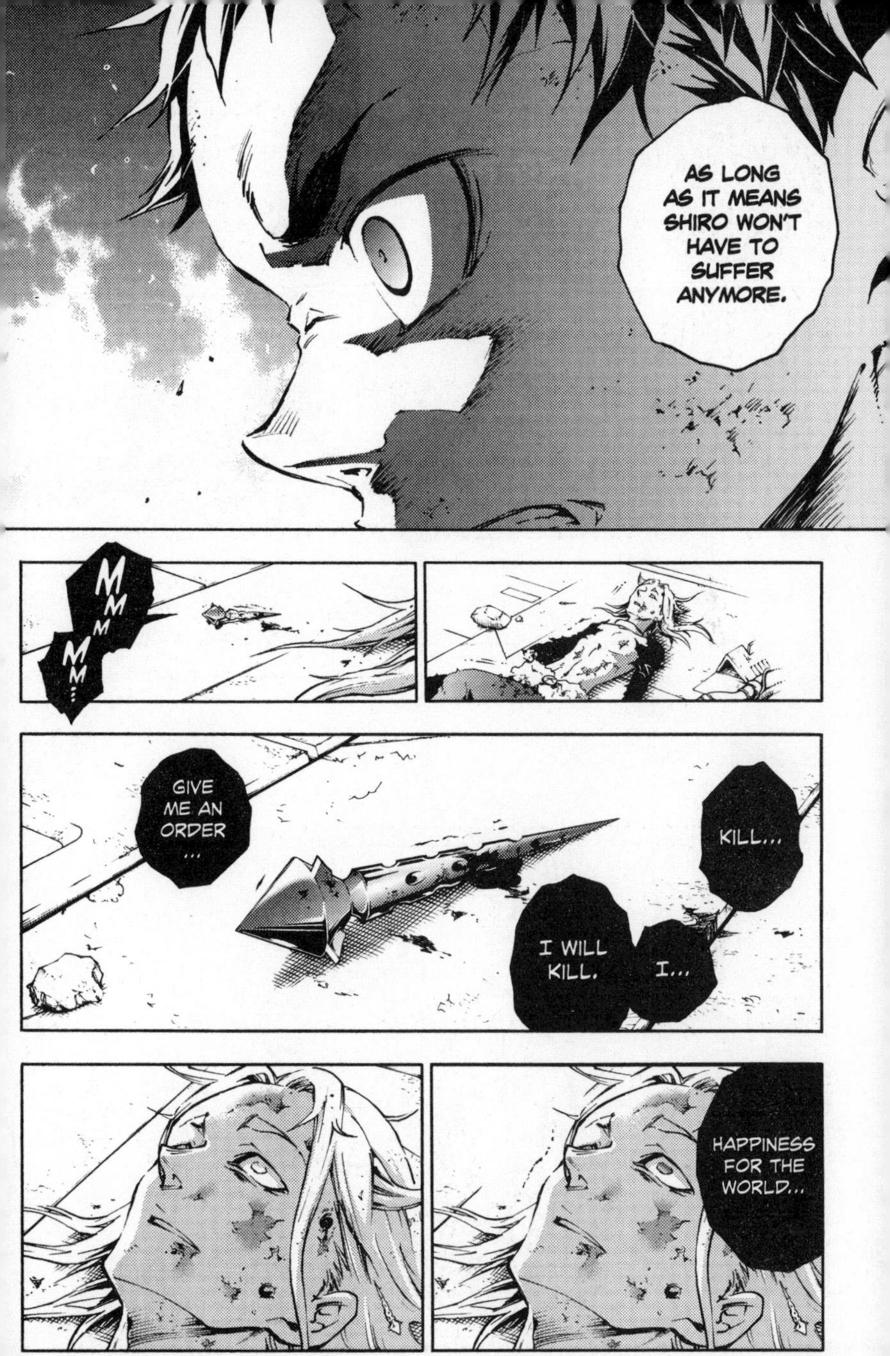
AS LONG AS IT MEANS SHIRO WON'T HAVE TO SUFFER ANYMORE.
MMMMM...
KILL...
I...
I WILL KILL.
GIVE ME AN ORDER ...
HAPPINESS FOR THE WORLD...

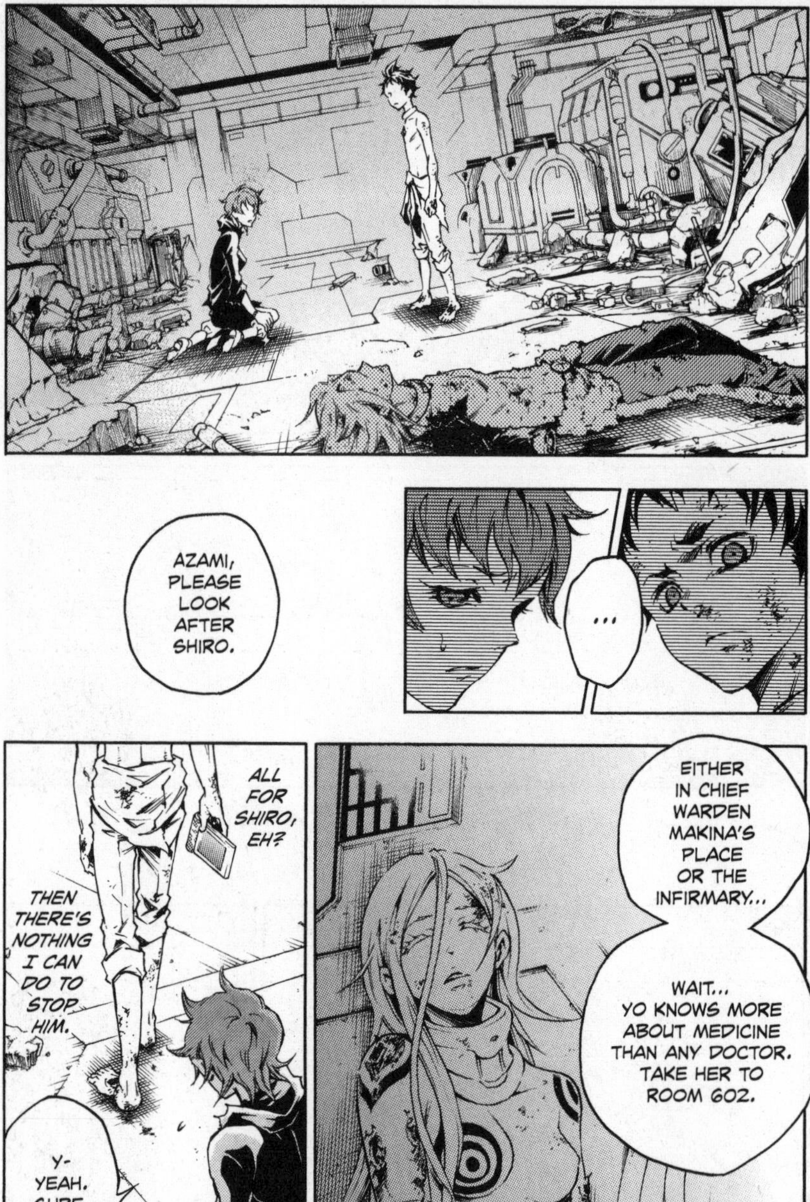
...
AZAMI, PLEASE LOOK AFTER SHIRO.
EITHER IN CHIEF WARDEN MAKINA'S PLACE OR THE INFIRMARY...
WAIT... YO KNOWS MORE ABOUT MEDICINE THAN ANY DOCTOR. TAKE HER TO ROOM 602.
ALL FOR SHIRO, EH?
THEN THERE'S NOTHING I CAN DO TO STOP HIM.
Y-YEAH. SURE.

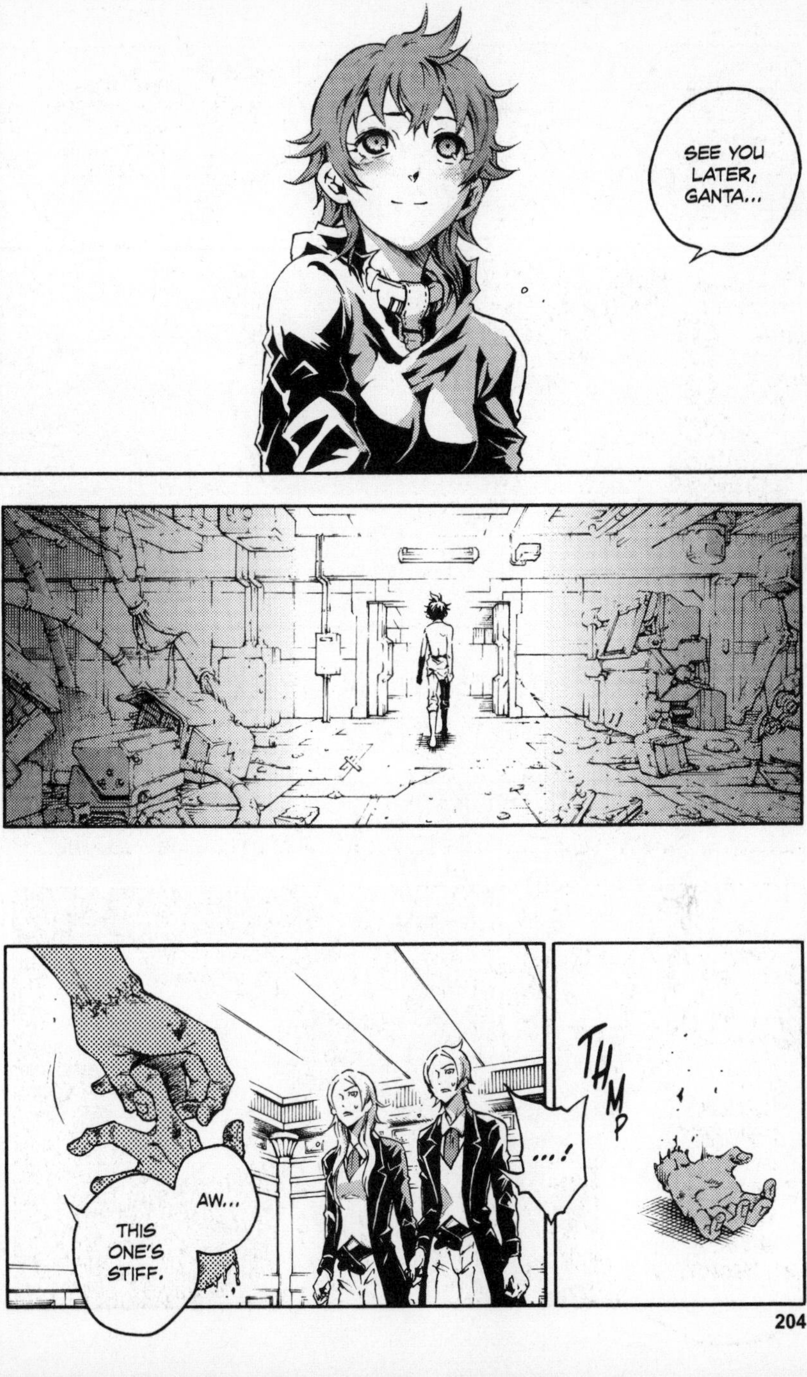
SEE YOU LATER, GANTA...
THMP
...!
AW... THIS ONE'S STIFF.

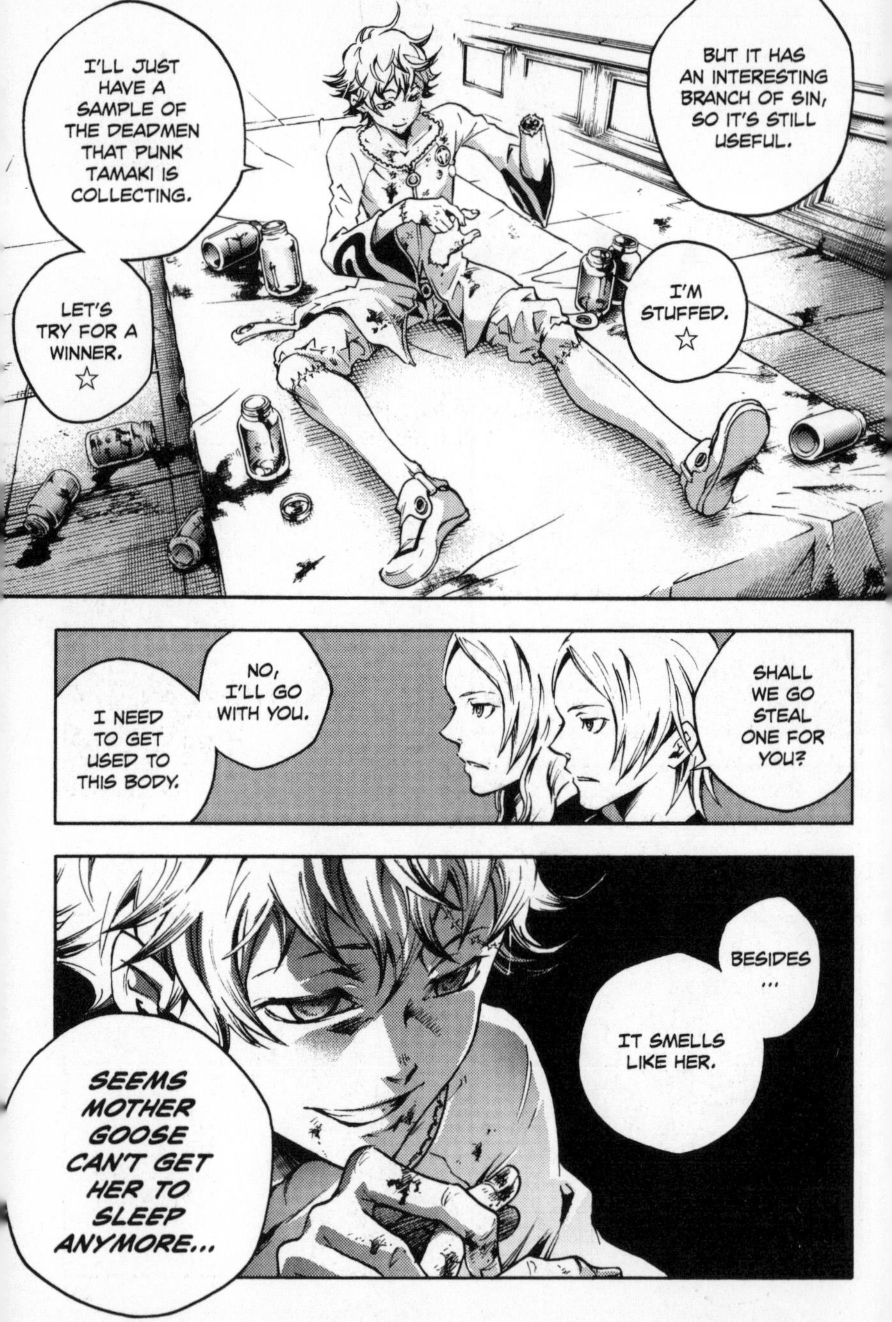
BUT IT HAS AN INTERESTING BRANCH OF SIN, SO IT'S STILL USEFUL.
I'LL JUST HAVE A SAMPLE OF THE DEADMEN THAT PUNK TAMAKI IS COLLECTING.
I'M STUFFED. ☆
LET'S TRY FOR A WINNER. ☆
SHALL WE GO STEAL ONE FOR YOU?
NO, I'LL GO WITH YOU.
I NEED TO GET USED TO THIS BODY.
BESIDES ...
IT SMELLS LIKE HER.
SEEMS MOTHER GOOSE CAN'T GET HER TO SLEEP ANYMORE...

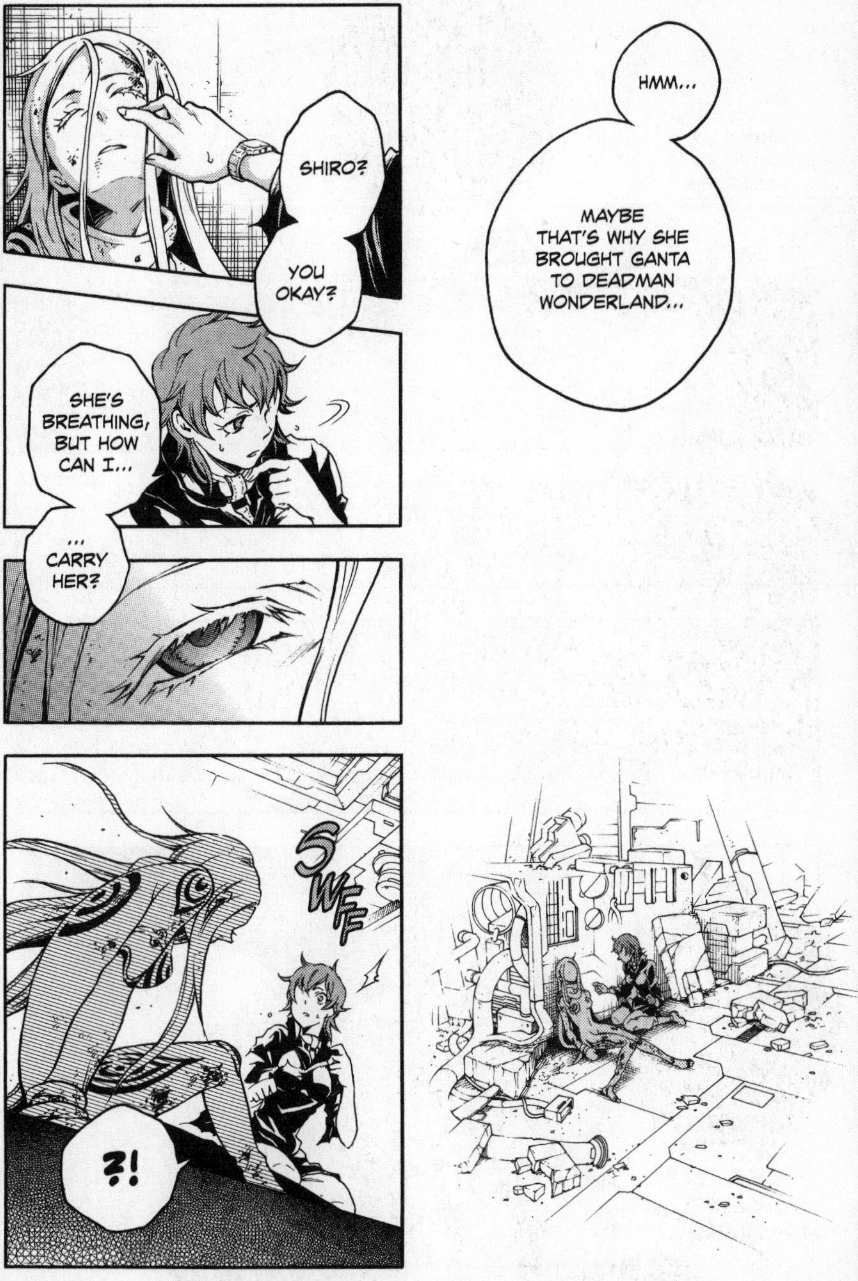
HMM...
MAYBE THAT'S WHY SHE BROUGHT GANTA TO DEADMAN WONDERLAND...
SHIRO?
YOU OKAY?
SHE'S BREATHING, BUT HOW CAN I...
... CARRY HER?
SWFF
?!

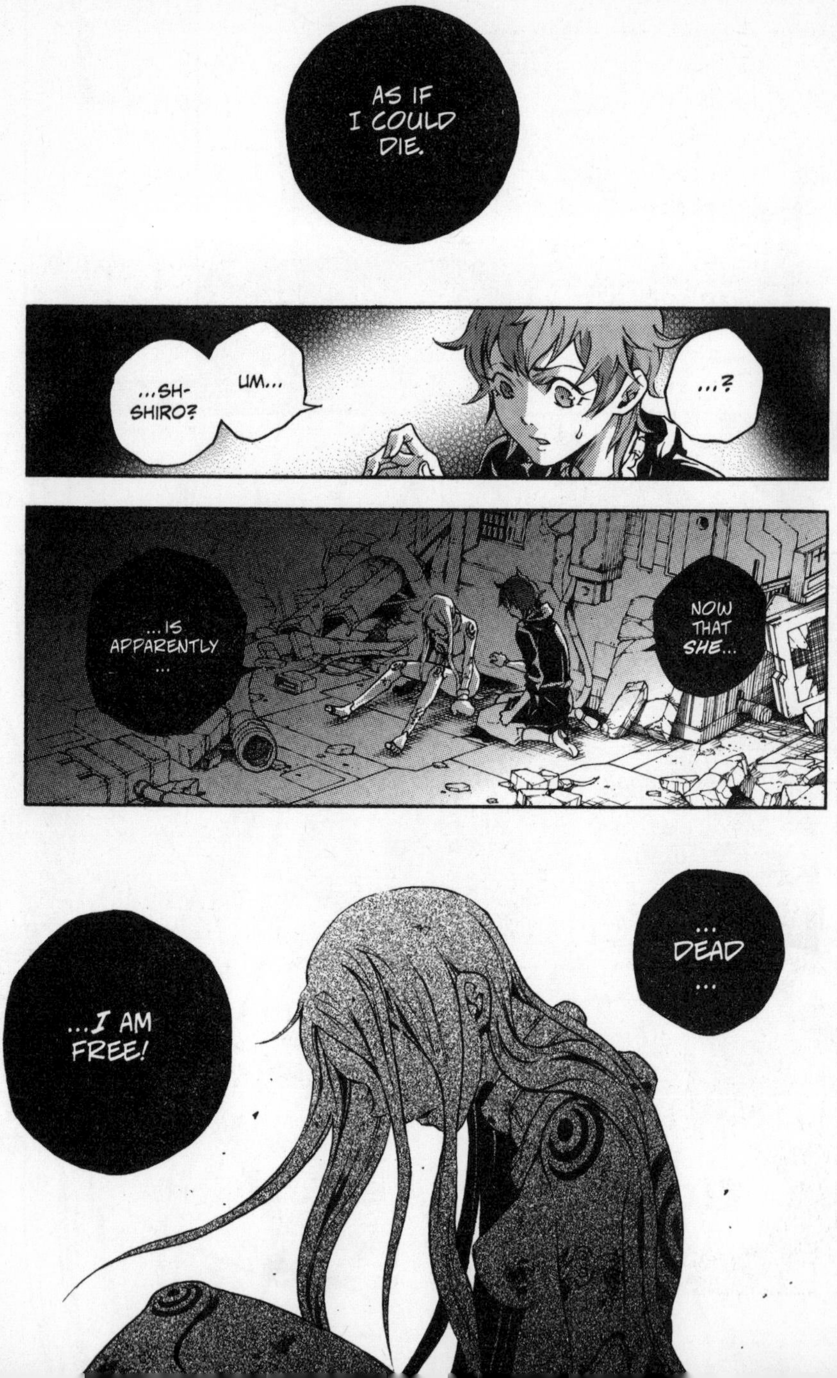
AS IF I COULD DIE.
...?
UM...
...SH-SHIRO?
NOW THAT SHE...
...IS APPARENTLY ...
... DEAD ...
...I AM FREE!

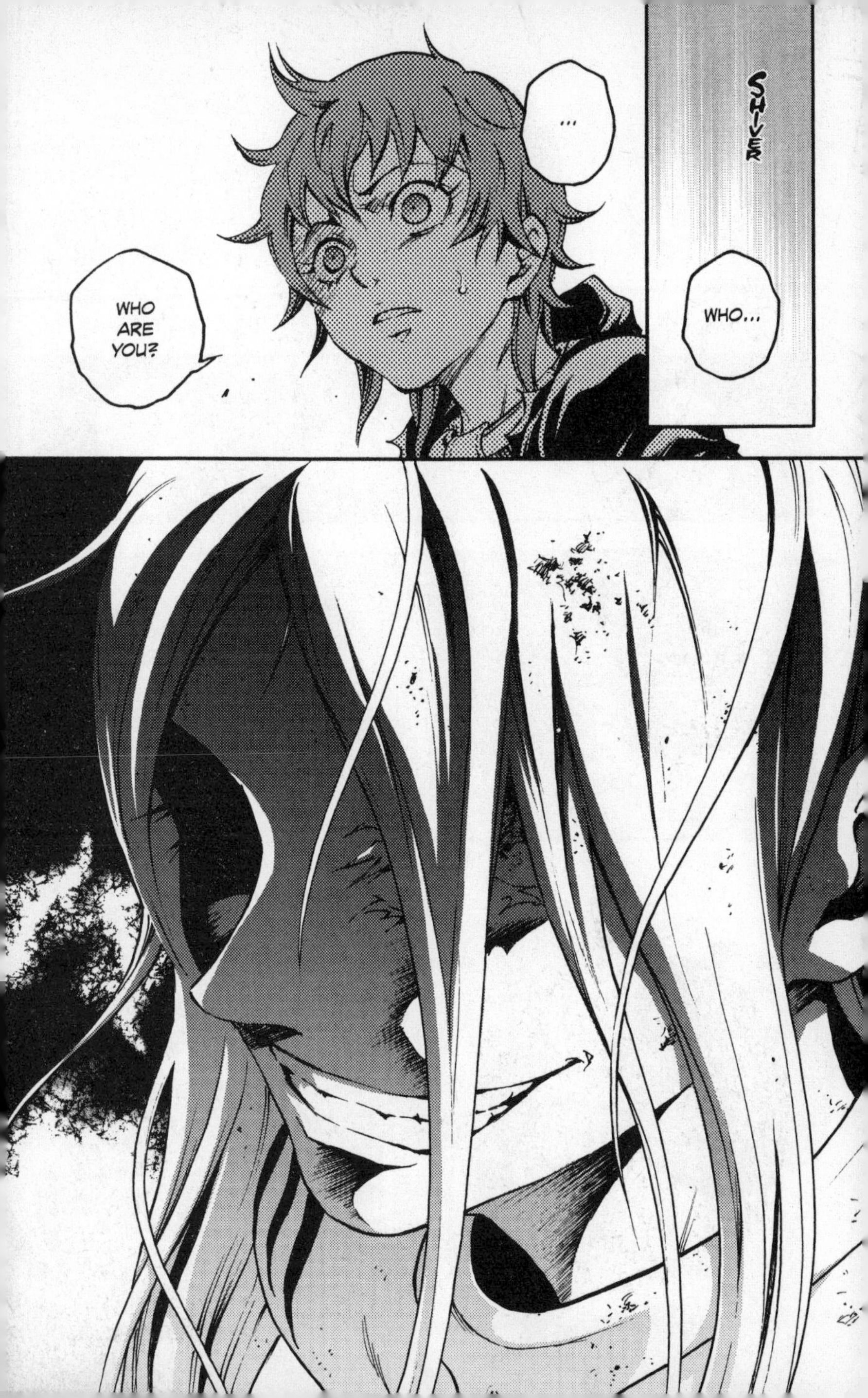
SHIVER
WHO...
...
WHO ARE YOU?

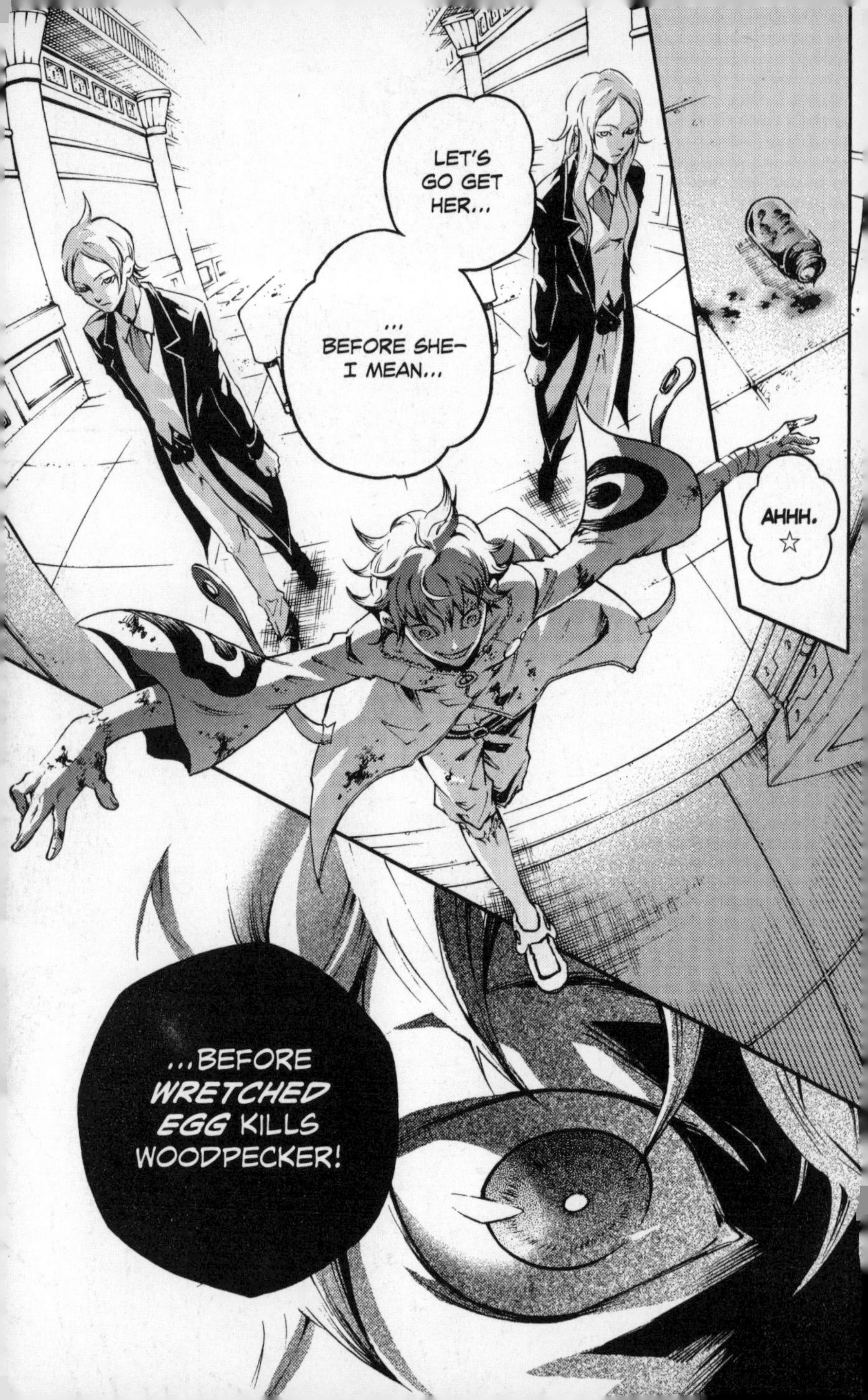
LET'S GO GET HER...
... BEFORE SHE— I MEAN...
AHHH. ☆
...BEFORE *WRETCHED EGG* KILLS WOODPECKER!

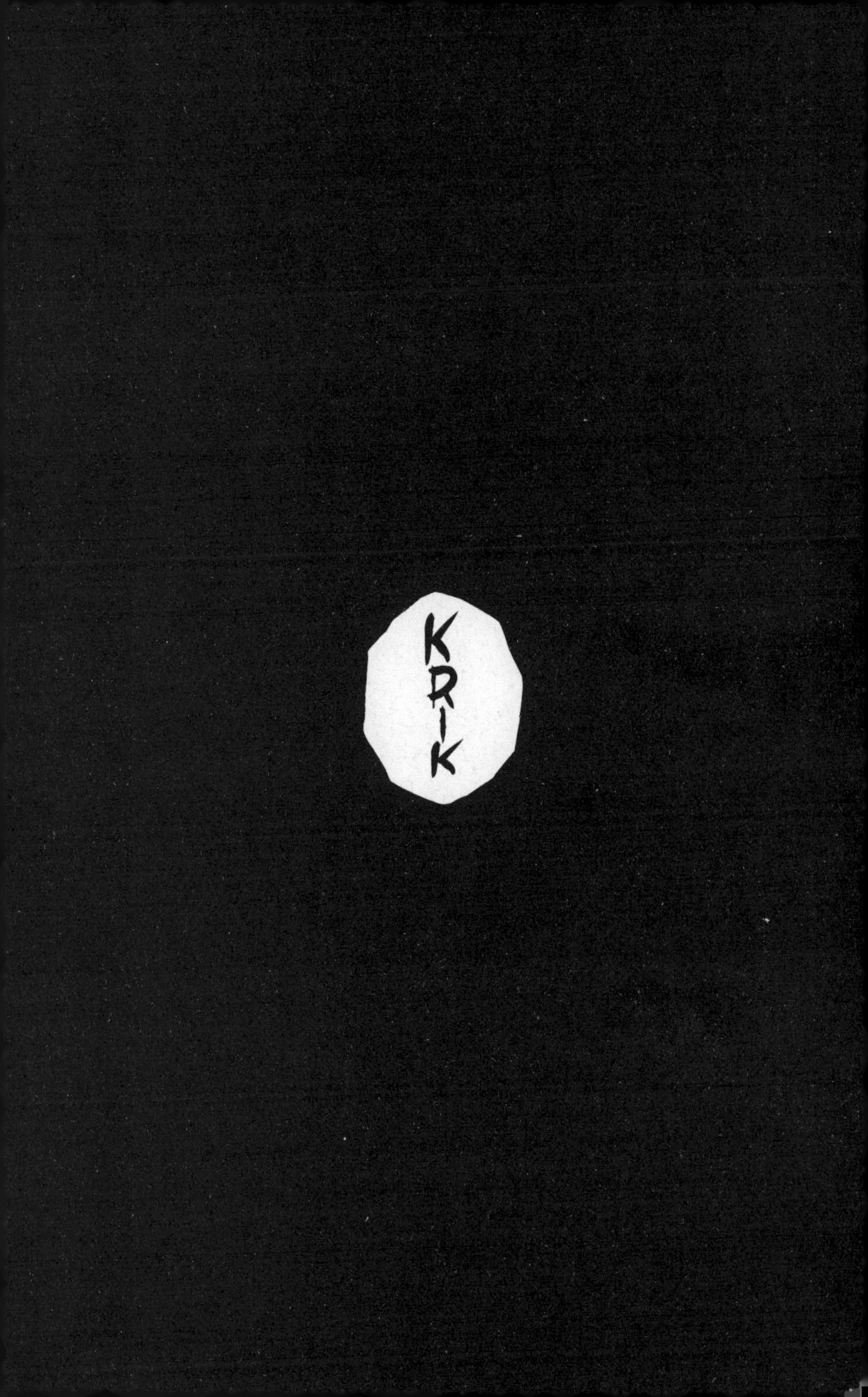
KRIK

DEADMAN WONDERLAND 8

Jinsei Kataoka
Kazuma Kondou

STAFF

Yukitsune Amakusa

Karaiko

Shinji Sato

Ryuichi Saitaniya

Taro Tsuchiya

Taku Nakamura

Toshihiro Noguchi

CONTINUED IN VOLUME 9

DEADMAN WONDERLAND

DEADMAN WONDERLAND
VOLUME 8
VIZ MEDIA EDITION

STORY & ART BY
JINSEI KATAOKA, KAZUMA KONDOU

DEADMAN WONDERLAND VOLUME 8
©JINSEI KATAOKA 2010 ©KAZUMA KONDOU 2010
EDITED BY KADOKAWA SHOTEN
FIRST PUBLISHED IN JAPAN IN 2010 BY KADOKAWA CORPORATION, TOKYO.
ENGLISH TRANSLATION RIGHTS ARRANGED WITH KADOKAWA CORPORATION, TOKYO.

TRANSLATION/JOE YAMAZAKI
ENGLISH ADAPTATION/STAN!
TOUCH-UP ART & LETTERING/JAMES GAUBATZ
DESIGN/SAM ELZWAY
EDITOR/JENNIFER LEBLANC

THE STORIES, CHARACTERS AND INCIDENTS MENTIONED
IN THIS PUBLICATION ARE ENTIRELY FICTIONAL.

NO PORTION OF THIS BOOK MAY BE REPRODUCED
OR TRANSMITTED IN ANY FORM OR BY ANY MEANS WITHOUT
WRITTEN PERMISSION FROM THE COPYRIGHT HOLDERS.

PRINTED IN THE U.S.A.

PUBLISHED BY VIZ MEDIA, LLC
P.O. BOX 77010
SAN FRANCISCO, CA 94107

10 9 8 7 6 5 4 3 2 1
FIRST PRINTING, APRIL 2015

www.viz.com

PARENTAL ADVISORY
DEADMAN WONDERLAND is rated T+ and is
recommended for older teens. This volume
contains scenes of supernatural horror and
violence, and suggestive themes.
ratings.viz.com

RATED
T+
FOR OLDER TEEN